OLIVER POSTGATE

Seeing Things

an autobiography

Illustrations by Peter Firmin

PAN BOOKS

First published 2000 by Sidgwick & Jackson

This edition published 2001 by Pan Books
an imprint of Macmillan Publishers Ltd
25 Eccleston Place, London SW1W 9NF
Basingstoke and Oxford
Associated companies throughout the world
www.macmillan.com

ISBN 0 330 39000 7

1 3 5 7 9 8 6 4 2

A CIP catalogue record for this book is available from
the British Library.

Typeset by SetSystems Ltd, Saffron Walden, Essex
Printed and bound in Great Britain by
Mackays of Chatham plc, Chatham, Kent

Seeing Things

DISCLAIMER

This is not a story, this is a life.

Having spent much of my life writing stories, I am used to being in control of the material I have thought up. I can alter it, mould it to my fancy and fit it tidily into a plot with a beginning, a proper middle and an end.

I tried to do the same with this and of course it didn't work. My life was already there, already fully inconsistent, irrevocably tangled, ill-timed and beset with incongruous events.

I suppose if I had been a dedicated person, one like my grandfather, who had a single guiding purpose throughout his life, there might have been a significant narrative on which to thread the events. But, although I have committed myself fairly passionately to various causes and purposes, these have come and gone as randomly as the circumstances that gave rise to them.

Even the main work of my life, making films for children's television – *Noggin the Nog, Ivor the Engine, The Clangers, Bagpuss* and the others – was not something I deliberately trained for and set out to do. It was something I slipped into almost by accident, because of some trouble with magnets.

So, in the end, I simply looked through my memory for the pieces that have, for reasons of their own, stayed with me, perhaps because they once made sense, illuminated some perception, caused grief or joy, or were just fun. I have assembled the incidents in more or less chronological order and have put together what seems to be a sort of travel book.

The engine wasn't reliable, the track was badly laid, it led through dark tunnels and into weedy sidings, and as to where it was heading ... your guess is as good as mine!

But I hope you will enjoy the scenery.

Oliver Postgate
December 1999

CONTENTS

1

STROKING BEES

I. Going back.

On a dull day in the early 1990s, I took the number 13 bus to Hendon, got off at the corner of Shirehall Lane and walked along it towards the house where I was born.

Shirehall Lane, a quiet suburban street, was definitely familiar. The big elm trees had gone but the same houses were there, though they seemed smaller and closer together than I remembered. But as well as that, something was different, something was missing. Then I saw what it was: people. Nobody was coming or going, nothing was happening. The street was deserted.

As I walked I tried to conjure up the people who used to be about. For a start there were two sorts of ice-cream man, Wall's and Eldorado. They would be coming along on their box-tricycles, pinging their bells. Errand boys on their heavy bikes would whistle as they passed. The dustman's cart had two big horses. The rag-and-bone man had one very small horse which pulled a small cart loaded with strange articles. The ice-man had a noisy black lorry which dripped. He carried a huge gleaming block of ice on a sacking pad on his shoulder, holding it with a pair of fearsome black tongs – I was afraid of him. Hopeful people with suitcases were going from door to door selling things – brushes, laces, insurance, salvation – to the housewives in the houses.

I turned the corner into the cul-de-sac and saw a line of small, shabby, semi-detached houses. In 1925, in one of these, number four, I was born and had spent the first ten years of my life. I walked up to number four and stood in front of it. No wave of recognition came over me, no golden memories flooded back into my heart. The only feeling I had about that poky pebble-dashed house was that it was quite extraordinarily small.

Then, gradually, I began to realize what was wrong. In those days I had been much nearer the ground. So, rather creakily, I lowered myself on to all fours, leaned forwards, nudged open the garden gate with my head and peered in at child, or perhaps large dog, level.

That did the trick. The first thing I saw, just inside the gate, was a piece of thick metal pipe sticking up out of the ground. On top of it was a small metal box with a curved top and a grille in its side. I don't know what it was – a drain-ventilator perhaps – but sixty-five years before I had known it well and had enjoyed its company. I now looked at it with great affection, recalling very clearly the feel of its sun-warmed metal under my hand.

Beyond the pipe-thing, under the skinny privet hedge, I could feel again the black beetly earth between the roots and, behind that, at the foot of the house, I saw with a shudder the violent texture of the edge of the rendering. There the bottom of the thick stony skin of the house had curled up and broken off, leaving a jagged edge of powdery cement to moulder away and suppurate shiny brown pebbles. The mixture had fallen as a loose gritty scree against the side of the house. It was still there.

Feeling slightly foolish, I hauled myself to my feet and dusted off my knees. So, yes, that was the house. I now recognized the raised brick path which wended its way from the gate to the front doorstep. But it was only three paces from end to end, and where was the wide lawn where the tall horn-poppies grew? I had roamed the flower-beds lifting off their pointed hats so that the bright yellow-gold flowers could spread out in the sun, and when a bee landed on a flower I would stroke its back with my finger.

My mother had been quite alarmed when I told her about stroking the bees. She seemed to think it was the wrong thing to do, but I was very close to them and I was sure they didn't mind. I think she may have told me not to do it any more but I don't remember whether or not I obeyed her. I wore a pale blue sort of blouse and padded pants, and in the sunshine the front garden was my kingdom.

I could remember stroking the bees quite clearly but equally clearly I could see that the garden in my memory had absolutely no connection with the garden in front of me. So, rather dispirited, I turned away. Going back hadn't really been a lot of help. I realised that if I wanted to see how things were all those years ago I would have to rely on the pictures that were already in my head – if I could find them.

As I walked away I tried to look at the inside of the house as it had been when I was young. The first thing I saw, on my mother's dressing-table, was a jar shaped like a small casserole. That was magical. Except for the knob on the top which was a clear mauve-coloured marble, it was made of pale purple translucent glass. When I lifted the lid, very carefully as it was crisp and fragile, it would ring like a bell. The jar was completely filled by an ephemeral ball of swan's down which, if I lifted it by its ribbon-tag, would spring softly out and release a cloud of marvellously smelling pink powder, so fine that it floated in the air. Sometimes the cloud would float into a shaft of sunlight where it would light up like a flame.

Most of my parents' bedroom was occupied by an immensely tall four-poster bed. This had fluted pillars of shiny dark wood. The flutes bulged slightly but were held together by a tight concave band of the same wood, amazingly smooth and delicate of form. I would wrap my arms around these pillars, stroke them and gaze into the rich darkness of the wood. That great bed was a different place from the ordinary world. The deep pillows and the wide eiderdown were a haven of luxury and indulgence. One of the privileges of being ill was to be moved from my thin-skinned iron bed to lie in splendour in the big bed, to be cosseted and made special. There I would float in absolute happiness, knowing that I was in the safe centre of life.

My brother John was three years older than me. We slept in the back bedroom, which we shared with a tall linen-press like an open-fronted chest of drawers and a large wickerwork laundry skip which crackled and clicked to itself during the night.

Other sensations came back: the rich taste of the leather pram strap which I chewed, the delicious cold flavour of a Wall's penny Sno-frute, the smell of roses. Daisy had a wide blue bowl in which she would float big roses from the garden. This stood on a table just below the height of my nose, so I could lean on it and gaze across the wide landscape of roses, watch some luckless insect clambering from petal to petal, and sniff my heart full of the glorious scent.

There was music too. In the downstairs back room stood a tiny piano-like instrument called a Dulcitone. Our housekeeper Elsie would sit at it and press the keys with one finger. For her it would play 'Baa, Baa, Black Sheep' in delightful tinkly tones, like a carillon of chiming clocks. It wouldn't do it for me. However hard I hit the keys and shouted the words, it refused to play that song or any other. I hated it.

The front room, which we weren't always allowed to go into, had a powerful smell of its own. It was a darkish room, lined entirely with books, and it contained my father's intriguing roll-top desk, which had pigeonholes and sliding drawers and strange interlocking containers. I remember the day my brother and I discovered, third along in the bookshelf to the right of the fireplace, a heavy German book called *Die Erotik in der Photographie*. The text was of course incomprehensible but the many photographs of interestingly undressed ladies were deeply fascinating. Some of the photographs were printed side by side in pairs. I discovered that if I held the book up and allowed my eyes to look right through these photographs, beyond them and away into the distance, the images would merge until at last a voluptuous three-dimensional form materialized on the paper. I was proud of this accomplishment and with the right glasses on I can do it to this day, but sadly the allure of the coy Teutonic lovelies has diminished.

On a tall table in the window stood a gramophone with a magnificent polished-wood horn. Sometimes, late at night, this could be heard playing scratchy German tangos.

The smell of that front room lingers to this day in the drawers of my father's desk, which is now in my study. It is the smell of briar pipes and tobacco, mixed with the rich scent of cigar boxes. It brings back clear memories of the place, but not of the people.

But there is one incident in which I can recall the people – both myself and another person – with dreadful clarity. I was standing on the doorstep of the house next door where John's friend, Russell Wright, lived. I banged on the door as usual. Mrs Wright opened it. As usual I said: 'Can I come in?' Mrs Wright looked down on me sternly from a great height and, unexpectedly, said: 'No. You can't.' Then she added: 'You don't come knocking on other people's doors saying "Can I come in?" That's rude! That's what rude, naughty children do.' Then she slammed the door in my face.

I stood there, profoundly astonished.

From that moment on I think I began to be more aware, or perhaps more wary, of people; certainly so of Mrs Wright. I think my wariness may have taken the form of an anxiety to please. I know I liked to try and find things to say that would interest people and so cause them to feel friendly towards me. Little pieces of information would lodge in my otherwise unoccupied mind and when what seemed to me an appropriate moment came up, I would bring them out.

On Saturday mornings the milkman always came to collect money. He yodelled, 'Milk-oh,' as he came up to the door and clanked his metal basket on the step. I ran to open the door and, while Elsie went to fetch his money, I leaned nonchalantly against the door-post to have a chat.

I said: 'You don't look like a dog.'

He said: 'I'm not a dog.'

I said: 'Muvver says you are.'

'Does she?'

'Yes. Muvver said the milkman's a dirty dog because of the short change, and you're the milkman.'

This incident caused a lot of noise, and later a lot of head-shaking and glaring was done at me. I felt profoundly guilty and very ashamed, a feeling that was made worse by the fact that I didn't actually know what it was that I had done wrong.

Perhaps if I had known that this pattern was going to be repeated throughout my life I would have taken more notice, but at the time I think I put it out of my mind quite quickly and went to watch the milkman's horse, whose behaviour was more reliable.

While he did his deliveries along the street, the milkman would leave his horse and cart outside our house. He would put a nosebag on the horse's head. I would watch the horse sniff and snort into the bag of bran and oats that was fixed over its nose and then, suddenly, throw its head and the bag high up into the air in a cloud of dusty chaff. Then it would lower it gently to the ground and go on munching.

I have since learned that horses do this for a reason. They do it in order to bring the heavy oat-grains up from the bottom of the bag so that they can eat them. That was a disappointment: I thought it was just *joie de vivre*.

II. Wonders.

Even though I can remember their names, Elsie, Amy and Peggy, and I know I was fond of them, I can't recall exactly what our housekeepers looked like. But – even though she wasn't always there and when she was it wasn't always easy to attract her attention – it was my mother Daisy who was my refuge and haven. I would like to be able to describe her as she was in those very early days, but it is quite impossible. As I try to picture her I find myself folding softly into her safety, which was a place from which no comparisons could be made, a place where it was good to be, a place where there were good times.

Bathtime was particularly good. It was presided over by a large copper-coloured geyser at the far end of the bath. This had a sort of swivel tap which Daisy would turn on and light with a match. A bright finger of blue and yellow flame would spring from it. Daisy would turn on the water tap and then deftly swing the flame round into the interior of the geyser. There came a moment of thrilled anticipation and then the whole geyser went 'WOOF' and seemed for a second to be so full of flame that it must burst. After that it settled down to a gentle roar as the hot water poured out of its spout and splashed into the bath.

In those days the bath seemed much larger. There were lots of waves and drifts of foam, a rubber duck, elusive soap to slither after, a long scratchy loofah and Daisy's huge sponge which drank up so much water that you could hardly lift it. My brother would be at the other end making even more waves and ill-treating the duck. Then, after the bath, there would be big warm bath towels and running about with nothing on and after that sitting up in bed in flannelette pyjamas being told a story.

Taking a bath was never a particularly private activity in our house. John and I would wander in and out of the bathroom while Daisy was in the bath, to talk of domestic matters or make enquiries about anatomy. This was quite ordinary.

I think my father, Ray, may have been a bit less hospitable. I can only remember once seeing him in the bath. He was very hairy and his body seemed to fill the bath almost completely. It occurred to me at the time that he didn't need a lot of hot water for his bath and that if he had been truly bath-shaped a couple of jugfuls would probably have been enough to cover him quite adequately.

Ray is almost as hard to describe as Daisy. He was very large and very warm, with a roughish pelt that smelt faintly of tobacco smoke. Being an author, he was usually busy in his study but even so he did observe certain ceremonies. Every Saturday I was given my 'Saturday Penny'. Ray would solemnly make the presentation and then he and I would put on our coats and walk along to the sweetshop to spend it.

Ray had a large woolly overcoat and a large furry-backed hand. When walking beside him I liked to get my head between his hand

and his coat and hang on to two of his fingers. This was a very comfortable arrangement because his hand was as warm as a hot-water bottle and it also kept the wind off.

The sweetshop had a marvellous array of cheap goodies. It was amazing what you could buy for a penny – four round gobstoppers which changed colour and flavour as you sucked them, or four liquorice bootlaces, or two blocks of solid lemonade or one chocolate-covered ice-cream cone, which didn't have ice-cream in it but pink marshmallow, or even, I think, a yellow sherbet-fountain with a liquorice tube in the top. This looked a bit like a firework and behaved in much the same way when you sucked at the tube and suddenly found yourself with a mouthful of explosive, prickly tasting sherbet.

Sometimes we would be taken shopping, to Golders Green on the top of a rattling, roaring open-topped bus, an experience I always hugely enjoyed because I was fascinated by all forms of transport. We would get off at Hoop Lane and walk along the wide pavement of the shopping parade. There we would often see a three-piece brass band: three strong-looking men wearing medals and playing golden instruments while another capered and saluted and smiled, rattling a box for pennies. I expect they were out-of-work ex-soldiers, but they made a lovely noise.

In the draper's shop with its broad mahogany counters all was calmness, efficiency and respectful servility, but high up, close to the ceiling, the money-jars were whizzing backwards and forwards like frenzied bats to and from the cashier, a lady in a high round desk at the centre of a web of wires.

One amazing shop had fires burning in the window with perforated tins rotating on the top. They made smoke, but this was no ordinary smoke, it was the smoke of roasting coffee; powerful, pungent stuff. I wasn't sure I liked the smell but it was devilish exciting.

The fish shop had a cold smell which came from a marble slab where wet dead fish were laid out, and also from a deep metal tray in which live eels were squiggling.

In those days quite a lot of ladies wore foxes around their

necks. These animals were very thin, with sparse hair and eyes as bright as beads. Eventually I decided that they weren't really alive but I still didn't want to touch one.

Occasionally we travelled on from Golders Green to visit our cousins the Coles, who lived in a tall house in West Hampstead.

To do this we travelled on the queen of all public transport – the tram.

Trams were tall and thin and had a special smell. This wasn't smoky and oily like the smell of buses, it was clean and almost fresh. As it started to move, a tram made a rich metallic grinding noise, *Gerdoing – gerdoing, gerdoing, gerdoing* ... which rose in pitch as it speeded up until it became a steady song, accompanied by clangs, clunks, creaks and graunching noises as the tram swayed and pitched on its narrow rails. When it came to a sharp corner the tram would jerk sideways and lurch as if it had been barged by an elephant. To this day I don't understand why trams didn't just fall flat on their sides at every corner.

One evening, on our way back from the Coles', I saw something quite unexpected. It was dusk, almost dark, which was the best time to travel on the open top of a tram. Being above the lampposts the deck was dark except when the tram-pole spluttered and gave off white sparks as it rolled, hissing, along its wire. You could hold on to the rail and look down on the stream of cars and vans and see the people moving busily on the pavements, lit by the bright shop windows. It was like being high in the rigging of a tall ship. Standing there, scanning the view from side to side, I suddenly observed, or perhaps I should say, noted the predicament of, what I could only conclude must be a hitherto unknown section of society.

Along the Finchley Road, as along many other big roads in London, there were parades of shops, all brightly lit and thronged with people. From the top of the tram I could see that the shops themselves had dark flat roofs. Behind these, on a level with me but invisible from below, was a line of windows. Many of these were brightly lit and as the tram passed I could see straight into each room from corner to corner. I saw families having tea, people sitting reading, a boy doing his homework, a mum ironing on the table, even a thin man and a fat lady playing cellos – all life was there for me to look at, set out in single bright boxes.

This was quite fascinating, but gradually an awful thought occurred to me. These upstairs people had no front doors. They were totally isolated. They had to live their upstairs lives in an upstairs world which was completely separate from ours.

Amy, our housekeeper, was in the cabin below. I ran down to tell her about it. I explained to her how the rooms were set side by side for the whole length of the shopping parade, so there was no way out on that level, and there was no way in or out downwards because the dark flat roof was in the way and underneath was all shops, and shops had counters which you weren't allowed to go behind and shops were often closed. I was alarmed about this but Amy didn't seem to think it was very serious. She said she was quite sure the upstairs people had ways to get in and out if they wanted to.

Eventually I had to agree that this might be the case. But even so the anxiety must have remained in my mind because, years later, I noticed some unobtrusive front doors squashed between the shops on that part of the Finchley Road, and I remember feeling distinctly relieved.

In 1930 I was five and it was time for me to go to school. I wasn't enthusiastic about this idea, mainly because it meant I had to master the intricacies of dressing in school clothes. I had to put on a thick vest with short sleeves and a grey tuck-in shirt. The rather long and complicated underpants had loops on the side through which the leather tabs of the braces had to be threaded before they were buttoned to the grey flannel short trousers. If you forgot to do this, one side of the pants came down, which made walking difficult. But I mastered the procedures and, to my surprise, found I quite liked school.

This was Woodstock School, a private school with about two hundred pupils in a spacious house and grounds on the Golders Green Road. The school was run, and perhaps owned, by a Dutch couple, Mr and Mrs de Vries.

The atmosphere of the school was friendly, gentle, respectful and firm. In general we sat still and learned things, like how to read and write and do sums, a grounding for which I never cease to be grateful. The teachers, and sometimes even Sir (Mr de Vries), were genuinely pleased if I did something well, and awarded stars for good work, stars which Sir liked to draw all over the page in elaborate patterns and many coloured crayons till they looked like bursting fireworks. The teachers were equally unhappy if the work wasn't good and didn't hesitate to sling it back and have it done again if it wasn't up to scratch. I didn't really mind that either. I liked to please.

Reading my first school reports I see that: '... his drawings are interesting as they frequently deal with the mechanical workings of things, particularly with water works', that I had a bad stammer and was nervous and easily upset and also, rather nicely, that: 'He is a lovable wee fellow and has delightful manners.'

The member of the staff that I remember most clearly was a lady who came in to teach us Art. I think her name was Miss Horrocks. She looked quite old, wore a long dress and beads, and spoke in a slightly wistful manner with a dark, croaky voice. The fascinating thing about her was that her hair grew in the form of intricately woven circular pads which covered each ear like earphones.

Miss Horrocks showed us pictures of people with straight noses and lots of floating hair who wore lovely flowing clothes and lived in dreamy decorated landscapes. These, she told us, were Art. I found it truly wonder-full, deeply imbued with rich but unknown significance.

What Miss Horrocks liked us to do for her was make copies of designs which she called 'tile patterns'. She had stacks of cards of these which she would hand out for us to look at and copy. As far as I can recall the patterns were mostly of formal entwinings of leaves and flowers, but the one I remember most clearly, perhaps because I thought it was a bit sinister, looked something like a partially deflated ace of spades surrounded by limp black snakes, which seemed to be fainting in coils on to the floor.

Looking back I have the impression that Miss Horrocks may have been a genuine surviving disciple of William Morris, or even of the Pre-Raphaelites, and I feel rather honoured to have met her.

For the first year or so we were taken to school and collected by Amy. Of all the various housekeepers who looked after us at Hendon, she is the one I remember with particular affection. We had even been to stay at her parents' tiny house in Leiston in Suffolk. The house and the neighbourhood were fascinating, especially the water supply which was brought from a well in shiny buckets, but I saw little of the place because I almost immediately came down with measles.

My body became very pink and knobbly and I was put to bed. I think Ray and Daisy may have been away in Paris at the time, so my grandfather, George Lansbury, who was a member of the Cabinet in the newly elected Labour Government, was alerted. Perhaps as a result of this a uniformed policeman was sent to the house to ask after my health. This event caused great excitement in the neighbourhood but it was nothing to the excitement that came a day or two later when Grandad himself turned up, really just to pat me and wish me well because by then I was over the worst of the measles. Being in bed I didn't witness his arrival but apparently the reception was fairly rapturous. These were poor people and they all knew George Lansbury.

III. Grandad.

Poor people were George Lansbury's life. He was a founder member of the Labour Party, a militant pacifist, a lifelong campaigner for social justice who had become a much loved and revered figure, known as the uncrowned king of London's East End. He it was who, accompanied by a brass band, had led the whole of the Poplar Borough Council to the High Court and on to prison, for refusing to implement the Means Test.

My mother Daisy was George's seventh child (he had twelve in all) and she was brought up in 'the movement', where there was

exciting work for all to do, including, for her, the task of imperson-
ating, and being arrested for, Dorothy Pankhurst, the Suffragette
leader.

My father, Raymond Postgate, who came from a formidably
academic family, had turned against the academic life and had
embraced socialism. He became a conscientious objector in the
1914–18 war, and was imprisoned and disowned by his father. He
went to work for George Lansbury when he was editor of the
Daily Herald, and married his secretary, and daughter, Daisy.

Grandad played an important part in our lives. Well, no, he
didn't exactly play a part, he was just there, a godlike personage
hovering somewhere above us, likely to appear unexpectedly at any
moment. I can see him standing in the doorway. He was huge. His
bowler hat over his big white-whiskered face and massive black
overcoat completely filled the door. He also had the largest ears I
have ever seen. They didn't stick out, they just covered a large area.
I distinctly remember sitting on his knee and admiring them.

I already knew that Grandad was an important man, both in
the family and in the world, but I didn't know that he was a truly
great man, nor that he would one day stand up in the House of
Commons, reprove Winston Churchill for behaving like God
Almighty and tell him to hold his tongue.

Once or twice Daisy took us to the House of Commons to see
Grandad at work. The great palace was guarded by policemen but
they each greeted Daisy by name and had a joke with her as we
passed. Daisy walked through the sombrely magnificent halls and
corridors of the House as if she lived there, and at every corner
the officers smiled at her and spoke. I felt very proud.

Grandad was pleased to see us and took us all to tea on the
terrace that overlooked the Thames. From there we watched the
tugboats pulling lines of barges loaded high with planks of yellow
wood. Grandad knew the names of the timber merchants and
where the cargoes were going. I was very impressed by that but I
also remember feeling a bit anxious about my important grandfather, sitting on the terrace having tea with us. It occurred to me
that he was supposed to be in Parliament making laws, not wasting
his time having tea with children. I raised this point with him and

he took me into an inner hall of the tearoom and showed me a machine that was making ticking noises in short bursts and issuing paper tape. He lifted a piece of the tape and read it to me. Apparently it told him what was going on in the Chamber. He explained that he was allowed to go wherever he liked whenever he liked so long as he came and looked at the tape now and then to see what was going on, and if he was really needed in the Chamber to vote, a Division Bell would be rung to tell him it was time for him to go back in.

Once we actually went into the Commons Chamber to hear part of a debate. Daisy took us up into the Visitors' Gallery, from where we looked down on the lines of green leather benches and saw a few Members sitting here and there. We saw the golden mace on the table and the Speaker on his throne, wearing a wig.

Daisy shushed us because something was happening. A voice muttered: 'Mr Lansbury' and I saw Grandad rise quite slowly and look around. I was so nervous for him I felt quite sick, but he seemed perfectly at ease as he began to speak. At first he spoke quietly, but then he gradually warmed to his work and his voice swelled to a sort of musical baying, which caught and carried my imagination along and would perhaps have moved me greatly if I had had the slightest idea what he was on about. Then, quite suddenly, he stopped and sat down. Amazingly, there was no applause or cheering. A few Members shifted the way they were sitting, and grunted. Then one of them, who seemed a bit angry, jumped up and began to yap like a terrier. That caused several of the Members to get up and, rather rudely I thought, walk straight out. The debate proceeded, but we didn't stay.

My grandfather's work in Parliament, making laws, seemed to me very august and remote from our own lives, but at other times and places we had a real part to play. In his capacity as First Commissioner of Works Grandad often had to attend ceremonial engagements. As these tended to be a bit solemn he liked to bring along a grandchild to lighten the proceedings and do small tasks, like cutting tapes.

I had the honour of assisting him at the opening of Lansbury's Lido, a section of the Serpentine lake in Hyde Park which he had

had adapted for the people of London to swim in. On this occasion I became a shade over-excited and inaugurated the swimming season myself by falling in, a gesture which was much appreciated by the onlookers, less so by my mother who had to borrow a towel from the changing-rooms to dry me.

By far the most alarming thing that had ever happened in my short life took place by accident on May Day in, I guess, 1931. There was, as always, a great rally in Hyde Park, at which, as always, George gave one of his huge rousing speeches that was received rapturously by an enthusiastic, loving crowd. At some point, after he had finished speaking and was leaving, I became separated from the party. The situation was that Daisy and Gran-dad were in a taxi with the windows open and I was on the grass about twenty feet away from them. This would have been no problem if I hadn't been stuck in the middle of a solid cheering crowd that was mobbing the taxi to shake his hand. The crowd was shouting: 'Good Old George!' George was shouting: 'Thank you, Brothers and Sisters!' and: 'Keep up the good work!' My mother was shouting: 'That's my son over there!' and I was shouting: 'Help!' I was only at waist-height in a tight press of people that was moving as a single cheering mass, carrying me with it. I had to hang on to the arm of the man beside me to save myself from going under and being trampled.

By pure good luck the man saw me and caught my mother's eye. In an instant I was lifted bodily into the air and passed from hand to hand like a long parcel over the heads of the cheering crowd, to be posted head-first in through the window of the taxi, amid laughter and cheers of relief from the crowd, and tears of fury from my mother.

IV. The Green Bench.

As I was looking at these memories my feet had taken me away from the house in Hendon and along old familiar streets to what Ray had called 'the Recreation Ground', a small park about a quarter of a mile away.

I sat on a particular green bench in the top corner of the park and looked around. The view from it was no more inspiring than the sight of the house had been – I saw a small, fairly drab area of worn grass divided by smooth paths and clumps of blackish-looking trees.

So this was the wide space where John and I and our friends used to play. We played football with coats for goalposts, rounders or one-ended hit-and-run cricket. We had quite big teams, so we must have played with other boys as well but, apart from Russell Wright and Jimmy Thwaites and Kenneth Collins, I couldn't bring any of them to mind. I do know one thing for certain – we never played with girls!

Girls, I remembered, were different. John and I had girl cousins and of course we treated these more or less as people, but girls as a race were creatures apart, strange and unpredictable – as I had already found out.

When I was quite young, about four or five, there had lived, in the house opposite, a golden curly-haired Shirley Temple called, I think, Desirée. One day she expressed a desire to have me over to play with. So, through the good offices of go-betweens (their maid and ours), I was duly procured, brushed down and delivered into her amazingly pink and frilly house. There seemed to be nobody else there. I remember myself as being dumb with embarrassment. Desirée may also have been embarrassed, but she was voluble. Her discourse was a continuous paean of elaborate self-praise, punctuated with prods and interspersed with small items of scorn about me. I believe at one point she proposed an activity which at the time struck me as being a bit rude. I didn't cooperate and quite soon, when grown-ups reappeared, she had me sent home for being, in some serious but unspecified way, naughty. I was deeply ashamed but very, very relieved to get away. We never spoke again.

I don't think I minded about that. Her paths were not mine. John and I now had important projects that she probably wouldn't have enjoyed – like damming the River Brent. This was no more than a broad, shallow brook, with a bed of black slime-covered things, some of which were stones. Wearing shiny Wellington boots we dislodged these and used them for building dams and diversions, a fascinating task which we did well and enjoyed a lot, even though we often got into trouble for coming home smelly. But for me, personally, the main attraction of the River Brent was that it was edged with patches of untamed jungle, lost land which had been left by the developers and had gone to waste.

Here the terrain was generally steep, with scrubby trees and bushes, bramble patches and rocks of broken concrete. In places there were branches to swing on and small smelly waterfalls that glugged out of the ends of pipes and flowed down muddy gorges to the brook below. But there were also precipitous paths that led to dark leafy bowers where, in summer, one could sense stillness, feel oneself far from civilization and even hope to see a rabbit. These sylvan glades, so near to home but so different, were awesome and full of magic.

Sitting there on the bench, I wondered what sort of boys we were. Were we wild? No, I think we were pretty tame. We didn't scratch the paint of the cars or let down the tyres or break off the wipers. We didn't steal, we didn't break-and-enter, didn't mug old ladies.

We went to the Saturday-morning cinema, of course, and at home we could sometimes be quiet. There was no such thing as television to watch or home computers to play with, but we did listen to the wireless and we played games, cards, board games, paper games, or made models with Meccano. We also read books, *Alice in Wonderland*, *The Wind in the Willows*, *The Midnight Folk*, *The Amulet*, etc., but these were not as essential to our lives as the comics and adventure weeklies – like *The Wizard* and *Hotspur* – which my father called 'penny dreadfuls' and deplored. So if necessary we had to read these under the bed-covers, by torchlight.

As the years passed John and I gradually became larger, louder, more enterprising and more of a nuisance. This was made worse by the fact that we didn't really get on.

After some initial reluctance he had become, with reservations, reconciled to the fact of my existence and was even willing to use me, occasionally, as a menial accomplice, but not as a companion.

I was untiring in my efforts to procure his acceptance and approval, while he was not only determined not to give it himself but was also anxious to prevent my getting any from anybody else.

In our dealings with grown-ups John and I were strictly in competition and loudly jealous of what we thought were our rights. I also remember spending a lot of time whining at whoever was there, trying to get them to *make* John play with me, while John was probably whining at them to get me off his back. The rest of the time we spent noisily bickering.

I have the feeling that 'they' – Elsie, Amy, Peggy, even Daisy – came to see the pair of us as a single agglomeration of squabble, nuisance and overcrowding, and became thoroughly fed up with it. So it must have been a great relief, if the weather was reasonable, to be able to send us to play in the Recreation Ground.

As to our characters, what John and I were like personally, there is a better reference than my cloudy memory. In about 1934 Ray wrote a novel called *No Epitaph*, which was, as he admitted, largely autobiographical. Included in it were thumbnail sketches of the hero's two sons, James and Richard. He wrote:

... They were good-looking children, in fact as well as in his prejudiced eyes. James' dark colouring was unlike either of his parents. His complexion was olive, his hair black, his eyes bright and dark brown. His most attractive feature was his bright, white-toothed grin. Inattentive, rampageous and greedy, he got himself forgiven innumerable escapades by his cheerful smile and instant assumption of a false penitence ... James held a larger place in his father's affection than Richard, a year younger. Richard was not indeed so apparently lovable a child ... With one year's gap in everything, Richard had had to strain always, and learned to ascribe his failure to cheating by his brother, to ill-luck, to insufficient self-advertisement, to anything rather than his natural inferiority ... Because his elder brother grabbed all the attention that he could, Richard had formed the habit of talking almost incessantly, so that he might break into any pause in the conversation and for a minute secure the centre of the stage. Once started on his way, it had become an obsession with the child: he thought aloud like an old man. 'Vere is,' he would say – he had retained one or two childish mispronunciations – 'a man in ve park who gives sixpences if you run fastest in races. Yesterday I ran faster van James and he gave me sixpence. I know he is vere and and it is true. He always gives sixpences and he wears a brown hat. I can run faster van James. When I have forty sixpences I shall buy a bicycle. Arfur, James' friend at school who doesn't like me, was bought a bicycle by his faver...' Anne was too conscientious a mother to rebuke or punish Richard for 'lying', but his incessant stream of small imaginings was a minor nuisance, battering on her half-attentive ears day after day. It obscured Richard's sweet and generous nature and his puppy-like affection. He was far more unselfish than his brother: give him a quarter of chocolates and he would scatter them around his friends (or rather his brother's friends, who would conde-scend from their attitude of contempt to him just long enough to rob him completely) while James would stuff himself silently in a corner...*

Although the age gap is different I'm sure that James was John. I also have evidence to confirm that Richard was me, and there is no reason to doubt that the piece is a fairly accurate account of how our parents, or at least our father, saw us. When I look back at myself the picture I get is very similar to the one Ray gives, but seen from a different angle. It is that of a child constantly scrambling for acceptance, like somebody frantically trying to clamber on to a crowded raft, hoping somehow to be allowed a place. Fortunately, I could also see that the child knew nothing of this. He never lost hope, never gave up trying, bore no grudges and took whatever small mercies came his way with innocent delight.

That is all ancient history but there is one small piece of evidence with which I would like to set the record straight. The green bench I was sitting on was the one which the man in a brown hat had sat on when he *did*, once, give me sixpence for winning a race. His hat *was* brown and, dammit, I wasn't lying.

---

* R. W. Postgate, *No Epitaph* (Hamish Hamilton, 1932), p. 98.

I got up and walked away from these disagreeable memories. There were more pleasant ones to entertain.

John and I were not stuck in that poky house for all our time. Ray and Daisy were great travellers and they took us to France almost every year, and once on an epic journey to Spain.

They would often go for short visits to Paris on their own. Daisy had even flown there in an airliner, a Handley-Page Heracles, from Croydon Aerodrome. The adventure had frightened her terribly but I, with my passion for vehicles, thought it must have been terribly exciting.

Daisy's younger brother, our uncle Eric, had had a different aeronautical adventure. He was to fly in an airship, but he was lucky enough to miss his flight because his car broke down. The airship was the ill-fated *R101* which, that night, crashed into a hill in France and burst into flames.

I saw the newspaper pictures of the crumpled skeleton of the airship and heard the reports on the wireless, and I know I wondered what I would do if I were on an airliner which was about to crash. It occurred to me that the obvious thing to do at, or just before, the moment of impact, was to jump vigorously into the air. In that way one would be going upwards, not downwards, and would land gently, as one would from such a jump. I wondered whether anybody had thought of doing this. The idea stayed in the back of my mind, along with the car which had small wheels in front and large wheels at the back so that it would be going downhill all the time, thus eliminating the need for an engine.

V. Another Place.

When they went to Paris Ray and Daisy usually left John and me at home with the housekeeper or, quite often, they would send us with her to a left-wing holiday camp called Treetops. Once or twice we stayed with Grannie, Ray's mother, sometimes with other relations. Only once did we spend a long time in a completely strange environment.

This happened at the beginning of 1933 when Daisy had

arranged to become a film star. No, that's an exaggeration. What happened was that Rudolph Messel, who was a very rich young man as well as a socialist, had formed an organization called the Socialist Film Council, which was going to make *The Road to Hell*, a film about the evils of unemployment and the Means Test. Everything was set up for this and shooting was about to start when Amy, our housekeeper and the king-pin of the family's life, had to go back to her home in Leiston. This was a serious crisis because somebody had to look after John and me.

So, towards the end of March, we were sent to Woodstock School as boarders.

Woodstock School only took about half a dozen boarders at a time but that was quite enough because Mrs de Vries, the headmistress, saw to them herself. We slept in tiny rooms high up under the roof, we had our meals and were left to play in a large, uncomfortable, bare room with a floor of brown linoleum, and each weekday morning at a quarter to nine we simply went to school, but through a green-baize door in the hall, not through the main entrance.

I was lonely and miserable so I was quite glad to be taken over by a slightly older girl whose name was, I think, Laura. She was very shocked to discover that I had not been taught to pray because she knew it was essential to 'pray for God', as she put it, every morning and evening. She explained that if I didn't do this God wouldn't know I was there and consequently wouldn't be able to look after me. She showed me how to kneel at the foot of the bed and told me what to say. I remember I felt a bit dubious about the whole procedure but this didn't interest Laura. Her only purpose was to get me to do what had to be done. What I thought about it was irrelevant.

In fact I didn't think anything about it. I mean, as far as I know, I had no previous acquaintance with the subject. Ray and Daisy were simply not religious, they didn't talk about God. Nor, as far as I can remember, did Amy. So Laura had a clear field.

I asked Laura a lot of questions about God and also about Jesus who, she said, was also God but not quite. Her answers weren't really very clear but I was able to piece together a picture of a white-haired old man, a bit like Grandad, but cross. He was sitting on a white cloud surrounded by glory, which was gold-coloured and shiny. I wondered where He was. Laura said He was everywhere, which didn't seem very likely, and that He could do anything and see everything, and that He moved in a mysterious way.

I knew about that. I had once seen my parents' friend, the novelist Naomi Mitchison, 'move in a mysterious way'. She was playing charades I think, wearing a wide hat and a cloak. It had been very impressive.

I observed the rituals Laura required and also consented to do a ballet dance with her in front of everybody, or, to tell the truth, half a ballet dance, because she had dressed me in a sort of frill, like a vestigial tutu, and after the gramophone ran down in the middle of the dance I refused to go on with it on the grounds that I was making an idiot of myself. After that she gave up her charge of my life and let me be.

But the question of the existence or otherwise of God remained in my mind. As far as I could tell He didn't seem to be taking a very active part in my life because cause and effect seemed to be proceeding according to what I assumed to be natural laws. However, it was worth while finding out, so, roaming through the empty school one chilly afternoon, I decided to confront my maker and test His mettle.

I looked out of a window and said: 'All right then, try this. If that bird gets to the telegraph pole before the red bus reaches the pillar-box there *is* a God. If it doesn't there *isn't.*'

This was a very fair test because the bird and the bus were going at about the same speed and, as far as any human could estimate, were going to pass the pole and the pillar-box at about the same moment; so it would only require a minute twitch of omnipotence to slow the bus down a shade and let the bird win. Nobody else would notice.

In the event the bus and the bird arrived exactly simultaneously. This told me that if God was there He probably wasn't paying attention. So I repeated the tests a few times. God scored one, Non-existence two, with three draws.

Then it began to snow, which was unusual in April. I watched the big white flakes swing slowly down and melt away on the wet ground. They fell so thickly that I could hardly see the road, let alone the pillar-box. It suddenly occurred to me that God, if He was there, might have decided He'd had more than enough of this carry-on. So I rather quickly turned away and ran back down the empty brown lino corridor to find the others. I was cold and I wanted, more than anything in the world, to go home.

VI. Bloomsbury-on-the-Marsh.

For all its pokiness, our house in Hendon was far more full of life than the bleak impersonal school house. Although John and I didn't see all that much of our parents, even I could sense that this was because Ray and Daisy were busy people, joining enthusiastically in with, if not an actual 'movement', some common social purpose which they shared with their friends.

However, we were sometimes able to take more of a part in their world because Daisy had obtained a car, a second-hand bull-nosed Morris, with an open top and grey-green oilcloth seats. Its gearbox sang a different note for each gear and its bulb-hooter didn't just go 'HONK' when you squeezed it, it went 'SqueeeA-HONK' like an outraged sea lion. Most of the trips we took in it were fairly local but occasionally we took longer journeys, real holiday journeys with luggage, to stay with their friends in the country.

I guess the first time Daisy drove us to Bloomsbury-on-the-Marsh must have been in about 1931. She took us up the Cambridge road, turned into Essex and drove through Toppesfield to Bradfields, which was the country house of Francis and Vera Meynell.

I had never consciously seen a really old house before and I was astonished. It looked as if a giant had sat on it. All the walls were crooked, either leaning in or leaning out, and the roof was bent and dented, like an old hat.

The Meynells' garden was large and glorious, the grassy side of a hill, rolling down to a stream with a bridge at the bottom. Under some trees at the top of the garden was a large pond. Beside this was a patch of lawn with a wooden diving platform, and it was all surrounded by a modest hedge.

But, once I was sure it wasn't going to fall in on me, it was the house that I found really fascinating. None of the doors was quite door-shaped and they didn't have handles but latches. The floors were particularly alarming because they sloped in all directions and the boards were odd-shaped, but they smelled most sweetly of beeswax.

Also, while they were there, our parents and their friends seemed to be so full of fun that the house rang with laughter. I hoped we would be able to go there often, which indeed we did, for many years.

Needless to say there is no such place as Bloomsbury-on-the-Marsh. The name was probably invented much later by some wit, but it could be taken to refer to an undefined area covering part of the south of Suffolk and the north of Essex in which some of the better-off, cultured, vaguely left-wing lot seemed to have bought themselves country houses.

Our host and master of ceremonies, Francis Meynell, was a large, loud, exuberant man. Born in 1891 to a family of distinguished poets – his mother was Alice Meynell, his godfather Francis Thompson – he grew up into the world of the literary avant-garde in Bayswater, in a house where well-known poets and authors came and went, where there was much singing and poetry reading and endless literary talk by his mother's devoted admirers.

Francis's political life was forged in the same revolutionary fire as that of Ray and Daisy. George Lansbury was his hero and, later, his employer. Like Ray he had been a conscientious objector in the First World War. He worked on the *Daily Herald*, and later smuggled diamonds into the country in jars of butter for the Soviet trade delegation. Once, to Lansbury's embarrassment, he brought in a Soviet contribution of several thousand pounds to the funds of the *Daily Herald*, a gift which, to everybody's regret, had to be declined.

After that their paths diverged. Ray went on to his life in history and politics, Francis to his lives in poetry, typography and publishing and to his loves, which were cricket, tennis, sociability, games, fun and women. Although Daisy could be a bit sardonic about the last of these, he remained my parents' close friend throughout their lives.

It was said that Francis knew everybody. That wasn't meant to be taken literally, I think it meant that Francis knew everybody who was anybody in the many fields in which he was interested. That was probably fairly true and it was also true that a lot of them lived in the neighbourhood, or turned up there as weekend guests.

Thus it happened that the short wide frenzied man with a squeaky voice, who bullied people to play games and hated losing, turned out to be H. G. Wells, and the elderly man with a thin ratty voice who was treated with a certain cautious respect was, I was told, Bertrand Russell. I drop those names here out of pure retrospective snobbery, but at the time they didn't mean a thing to me. I just saw them as fellow guests who were there, like everybody else, to have a good time.

I had already got the message that my parents had come here to have fun and enjoy themselves in their way, and that I was welcome to do the same, in my way, which could be to join in the fun, or not, as I wished. I found I had no quarrel with this situation and was, I believe, fairly sparing in my demands for their attention.

I do remember being a bit of a spoilsport about the nude bathing at the pond. I decided to wear bathing trunks and was ridiculed for my genteel modesty, but I persisted, not because of modesty but because of water-beetles. I had been to murky ponds like that before. I had caught water-beetles in my net and I had noticed that some of them had jaws like bolt-croppers. There was no way I was going to take my unprotected private parts, vestigial though they may have been, within their reach.

But, apart from necessary reservations like that, I was in a very neutral situation and quite happy to be an unnoticed spectator. Francis seemed to take the healthy view that other people's children were OK to have about so long as they didn't get in the way and spoil the grown-ups' games; which was fine by me. His own son, who was a year or two younger than me, didn't get off so lightly and was constantly subjected to applause and admiration. Surprisingly perhaps, I didn't envy him.

Looking back, I think I can see why that time and place has left such a powerful flavour in my memory. It may have been because, although London was the place where Ray and Daisy and their friends were serious, anxious for the world and busy at their work, the Meynells' was where they laughed, put aside doubt, were frivolous and played – and maybe one gets a clearer picture of what people are like and how they feel when they are talking spontaneously together and having fun.

The people we met there were altogether motley, with no shared characteristics except that of being individuals. If they had anything in common it was that they seemed to have in their manner a certain underlying confidence. When they talked they talked as thinkers and innovators. I can see that they were people who quite naturally set the agenda for their own lives. In fact I think they saw themselves as setting the agenda for the future of the world, a future which they were already helping to bring about, a future in which agriculture was going to eradicate hunger, in which Socialism was going to make personal greed a thing of the past and there would be no more rich and no more poor, in a golden age that was already on its way.

I sensed that there was a lot of gladness about, and quite right too! The dragons of moralism, snobbery and conformity had been vanquished. Love, life and liberty were all new, wrested by their own courage from the iron grip of Queen Victoria. They had come into their kingdom and taken their places as part of the new cultural elite, which indeed they were, because the cultural elite was much smaller in those days and quite a lot of it lived in the neighbourhood. So there was no shortage of genuine literary giants to lead them prancing in sandals and Liberty prints through a magic William Morris forest, ringing with licentious laughter. And perhaps the pranciest and most licentious of them all was Francis Meynell.

Of course the future didn't work out as they had hoped, and I dare say that away from the Meynells' they could already see that it wasn't going to. Stalin was turning the Soviet dream into a bloody nightmare, Hitler was rising to rekindle a different, perhaps even more bloody, ambition. But all the same, I think that to have lived at that time, with those dreams, must have been very glorious and exciting.

2

A HOUSE, THREE SCHOOLS
AND A WAR

I. Finchley.

In 1935 we moved from Hendon to Finchley, a distance of about four miles. Our new house, which had conker trees in the front garden, was immense. Well, it was only immense to my eyes which compared it with our little box-house in Hendon. Nor was it new. It was Victorian, made of dirty greenish-brown bricks.

Ray unlocked the wide front door and led us into the house. The hall was dark and dusty and smelt damp. He led the way up the wide, handsome, creaking staircase. The main landing was as big as a whole room in our Hendon house. He opened a door and showed me into a very large empty room with walls of mottled brown and mauve. There was nothing on the floor except some bits of whitish clinker that had once spilled from the broken fireplace.

'This will be your room,' he said.

Then John and I were let loose to roam through the great house from the two big attic rooms to the coal-smelling cellars. I found the idea of living in a house that I could actually run about in very exciting. The same was true of the back garden. In Hendon the back garden was a small patch closely overlooked by other people's windows. This one was large and secluded. Quite a lot of it was metalled over with cracked asphalt because it had been the playground of the school next door, but there was a large grassy hump right across the back of it and it was lined all round with old pear trees and overhung by a very big walnut tree.

Having more space, John began to collect pets: white mice, white rats, rabbits, small snakes and lizards, even a very large goldfish that had cost five shillings and lived in a sink in the garden until some predator got it. After it had disappeared, Queagh, our cat, helped us to look for that goldfish. He made a great show of turning over the dead leaves and searching the shrubbery all around the sink. That didn't fool us. He had eaten it.

Queagh was by far the most clear-cut character in the family. He was surly, with crumpled ears and an evil sense of humour. His pleasure was to sit in front of the vivarium where the snakes and lizards lived and gently stroke the glass front with his paw. This would cause the glass to inch itself along its groove until the reptiles could squeeze out. He didn't try to catch them; he was content just to sit and watch them slither and scuttle across the garden, knowing that the neighbours would soon be ringing up in a state of panic to demand the removal of our revolting creatures from their nice rockery.

Taken all in all the new house was a great improvement, partly because it was so spacious but also because it was convivial. Ray and Daisy had given dinner parties at Hendon but the pokiness of the house had been a constraint. The Finchley house was broad and welcoming. I can see the fire in the long room, bright with a mountain of Coalite, and I can hear the dining room ringing with laughter, not embarrassed, strained or forced laughter but the happy, genuine laughter of people fully at ease with each other in an atmosphere where all undertones of suspicion or anxiety had been dispelled and replaced by whole-hearted trustful enjoyment.

As a neighbourhood, Finchley suited us much better than Hendon because we had family friends and relations nearby. In fact the suggestion that we should move had originally come from H. L. (Lance) Beales and his wife Taffy, who lived in an even larger house about a hundred yards away. Their children, Mary and Michael, also kept a lot of pets, mainly rabbits and guinea-pigs. John used to take his rabbits to visit Mary's and they would give them the freedom of the grass tennis court for their meeting, or Jamboree, as they called it. John and Mary would run about the court trying, for some reason, to prevent the rabbits copulating – an absurd ambition!

Down Hendon Avenue and across the brook lived Douglas and Margaret Cole with their children, Jane, Ann and Humphrey. They had moved from West Hampstead to Freelands, a wide rambling house with a couple of acres of garden around it. A new hard tennis court had been built beside the house and in summer we used to go there almost every Sunday afternoon to left-wing tennis parties where there was good intellectual conversation, indifferent tennis and an unending supply of China tea.

Tennis was *the* game in the thirties. Unfortunately our asphalt back garden wasn't big enough for a court, so Ray and Daisy marked it out with silver paint and bought a badminton set. Ray also bought a small pickaxe and a wheelbarrow so that we could have the pleasure – and it was a pleasure – of prising up parts of the crisp asphalt skin to expose the earth beneath. As time passed the garden became very fertile, in a wild sort of way, with a forest of giant, very delicious blackberries at the far end. The pride of the garden was a climbing rose that Daisy had bought in Woolworth's for sixpence. Its name was 'Albertine', it grew to enormous size and I worked out that over the years it must have given us a million flowers.

I can see that garden in the summertime, with the crumbly yellowish bricks of the house, the badminton patch deeply embowered in the surrounding trees and the squirrels dropping walnut shells on the players. It is a picture of mellow ease and contentment.

By 1936 I had graduated to long trousers, at least for ceremonial occasions, and John and I had both become very sartorial and particular about what we wore; details which, looking back, seem to be no more than nuances of drabness. Clothes were very dull in those days, but we wore sock-suspenders and put Brylcreem on our hair.

Once or twice a year Daisy would take us to visit the Gents' Outfitters in the Charing Cross Road. The high point of the outings would be Chinese lunch with chopsticks at the Shanghai Restaurant in Greek Street, where the waitress was called Doris and had been no further east than Clacton. Between the Outfitters in Charing Cross Road there were seedy little shops which advertised DAMAROIDS and sold strangely shaped trusses. These were puzzling, but the amusement arcades, where the illuminated bagatelle games thumped and pinged and whistled, were fascinating. Daisy found them boring, so she tended to stay outside and look at the shops. When this happened I was able to nip to the back of the arcade and furtively put a penny into one of the machines marked ADULTS ONLY. These were always disappointing. You peered in and saw an old scratchy photograph. When you turned the handle the photographs tipped over and tottered past like a flicker-book. The pictures were faint and blurred and seemed to concern minor happenings in the lives of well-corseted ladies and rolly-eyed gentlemen in suits.

I didn't really need to be furtive about watching the not-very-rude pictures because Daisy was not in any way a prude – far from it! Perhaps from the music halls, where she had listened to Marie Lloyd belting out her hilarious, ribald songs, she had developed a healthily bawdy view of life and a very vulgar laugh. I recall one spectacular outing on which she took us to see the Crazy Gang at the Victoria Palace. The Crazy Gang were renowned for the high quality of their rude jokes and *double entendres*, many of which were so sophisticated that their import was lost on the nice-minded in the audience. However, that afternoon there was one member of the audience who not only saw every aspect of every gag but was also laughing uproariously at them. John and I got the distinct impression that the Crazy Gang were enjoying Daisy's appreciation so much that they were slipping in particularly fruity jokes especially for her, so it sometimes seemed as if she was the only member of the audience who was laughing. John and I were so embarrassed that we were practically hiding under the seats, but Daisy really enjoyed herself.

Sometimes, if one of us had a birthday, or had Christmas money to spend, we would go to Hamley's toy shop in Regent Street. It was from there that I chose, by grace of Ray and Daisy's friend, Rudolph Messell, who was rich and liked to give big presents, something that was destined to become my most prized possession. This was a Super-de-luxe Conjuring Set by Ernest Sewell. It came in a big box that cost nearly two pounds and contained some very sophisticated pieces of equipment with which I looked forward to impressing rapturous audiences.

Rapturous audiences were not readily available to small boys of eleven, but there would soon be a 'window of opportunity' – Grandad's party.

George Lansbury's seventy-seventh birthday party might have been a rather muted occasion because he was at what must have been the lowest point in his long political career. At the Labour Party Conference in 1935 he had suffered a vicious personal attack from Ernest Bevin, who had, in effect, called him a traitor and accused him of stabbing the Labour Party in the back. The Party faithful had not rallied to his support and he had resigned from the leadership.

Such a shattering blow would have broken most politicians and left them bitter. It is a measure of George's greatness that his spirit seemed to be quite undamaged and he was his usual jovial, grandfatherly self.

Grandad's birthday party had always been quite an elaborate affair which was attended by all, or certainly most, of his large family. Usually thirty or forty people turned up and I am told the occasions could be a bit tense, often for reasons that were more political than personal. Ray couldn't abide Party-line Communists and every year of Stalin's reign made him more contemptuous of them. Equally he had little time for the far right wing of the Labour Party, which our uncle Ernest Thurtle represented. He could also be less than respectful of Labour activists who affected what they thought were working-class accents in order to show that they were down-to-earth trade-unionists. To cap it all, Daisy's eldest sister, Annie, was a Christian fundamentalist. She wasn't really on speaking terms with any of them except perhaps her sister Nellie, who worked at Collet's bookshop and wasn't quite a Communist, though her youngest sister Violet very definitely was. So at one level the party was festive and full of fun, while on another it was fraught with submerged implications, turned backs and barbed references. Apparently John was sensitive to these tensions and found them a bit alarming. I was totally oblivious to them and so, I believe, was Grandad. He and I simply enjoyed the party and joined in with gusto.

At this particular party I was especially excited because, after a deal of campaigning, it had been established that I would be permitted to entertain Grandad and the party with one, just one, of the tricks from my amazing new conjuring set – but I wasn't to muck about and waste time. That was fine by me and I set it all up most carefully. The moment came and my parents, sighing indulgently, apologized to the assembled guests and craved their indulgence while their tedious son showed off with his conjuring trick.

Everybody sat down and I began the trick, which was the best one in the box, involving a tall magic goblet. I didn't waste time. I borrowed Grandad's engraved gold watch which had been presented to him by the Borough of Poplar. I lowered it carefully into the goblet on to a bed of cotton wool and after a few deft passes transformed it into a half a pint of hot coffee. I had in fact improved the trick. In order to add verisimilitude I had earlier slipped a lump of yellow soap into the coffee with the result that as I was pouring it proudly from the goblet into a mug, something round and yellow slurped in with it.

Grandad gave a bellow and shouted: 'Cripes! The little tyke's done it again!' – or words to that effect.

Suddenly there was a lot of noise. Grandad was demanding his watch back, Daisy was shouting for a kitchen towel, Nellie was denouncing me, John was looking on the floor. Everybody was talking very loudly and urgently, while I, the only sensible person there, was fumbling for the soap in the mug of coffee in order to get it out and show that it was only soap. I recovered it successfully but, for some reason, Grandad didn't seem interested in soap and went on shouting for his watch. I could make his watch reappear but not by dismantling the trick and showing how it worked – no proper conjurer would ever do that. I consented to bring it back, but only by going through the whole trick again in reverse.

So then everybody had to sit down again and be still and quiet while I poured the soap and coffee carefully back into the goblet, placed over it the various covers and false tops, intoned the necessary incantations and finally, with a proud gesture, revealed the watch, still ticking, on its bed of cotton wool. It had been a good trick, and I, personally, thought it had gone rather well.

II. Time Out.

You might think that settling down in a large comfortable house might have reduced Ray and Daisy's love of travel. Not a chance. We had hardly been there a year when the time came for us to pack our rucksacks and set off into the unknown.

Our journey started at dead of night. We took a taxi all the way from Finchley to Millwall Docks on the River Thames. There in the darkness we stepped down on to the glistening cobbles of the quay and, clutching our bags, gingerly made our way up the gangplank towards a square of yellow light in the middle of a black shape that was the SS *Margharita*, a small cargo ship bound for Denmark on the morning tide.

I was put to bed in a bunk in a cabin made of painted iron. When I touched the metal walls they were warm and felt as if they were alive with the faint vibrations of the ship. Nothing special seemed to be happening and I may have slept. Then, much later I think, the judder of the engines starting up nearly shook me out of the bunk, and later still, after I had got used to the gentle thudding, the ship gave one blast on its hooter, a blast which sounded in my ear as if it had been blown through the pipe beside my pillow. That woke me with a jolt.

I was too excited to try and sleep any more, so, as grey light had begun to be visible through the porthole, I put on some clothes and, climbing down past my sleeping brother, stepped out of the cabin. I made my way along the iron passage which served the eight or so passenger cabins, climbed a companionway, pushed open a small mahogany door and felt the sharp cold air on my face. The world outside was dark grey – uniform, uninterrupted grey. I shivered. The air didn't seem to be foggy because I could see blurred lights not far away, but it could have been misty. It was too dark to be sure.

Hanging on to the dewy rail I inched my way along the deck. Above me a door opened and a benign face with a peaked cap over it looked down. It was the Captain. He was on the bridge.

'Yerwll ber cerld,' he said, 'erts werm erp her. Cmern erp.'

I must explain that although, like most Danes, Captain Jørgensen spoke good English, he also followed their habit of using only one vowel.

I accepted his invitation and joined him on the bridge. This was a pleasantly warm small summer house with large windows. The only occupants at that early hour were Captain Jørgensen and his Queagh-like cat, who was sitting on the window sill looking out at the greyness.

Keeping one hand on the wheel the Captain reached out with the other and pulled a high stool to the window. 'Yerurly,' he said, 'sert dern.' I sat on the stool, put my elbows on the window sill beside the cat and we sat there, watching the morning arrive.

For no reason that I can identify, this was to be one of the happiest mornings in my short life, and the memory of it has stayed with me ever since. Perhaps this was a special time because at that moment there was nothing else I had to do and no other place where I should be. Of course I could have stayed in my bunk in the oily-smelling cabin, but if I had done so I would have missed the very gradual painting in of form and light that was the coming of the day.

First, very slowly, the slate-grey flatness which was the water took shape. Then I began to notice that a sort of glowing was filling the air, as if it were being lit from the inside, and against it ripples and reflections began to take light and shade and become discernible as moving water. Soon, like slow magic, a dark cut-out shape with silver lines beyond it began to materialize in the distance. It seemed remote and mythical, like a fairy-tale fortress creating itself from nothing at the very edge of time. It was, I believe, a gasworks near Gravesend. As we glided slowly on other shapes began to form on the bank of the river, ethereal factories, groups of silent cranes, long flat walls with bollards and, between them, shining arms of mud and reeds swept away into emptiness as the ship passed a side river.

More scenes materialized. One by one still groups of grey houses, immobile clumps of colourless trees, flat grey fields, broken fences, and complex rusty machines as high as churches, some surrounded by pyramids of gravel, appeared from the mist. These softly offered themselves to our view and slipped away past. They were just suggestions, none of them was real. What was real was the warm rumbling of the ship's engines.

Sometimes we passed tall thin poles sticking up out of the water, each faithfully reflected by another pole, pointing downwards. I suddenly saw a large fruit-like object clear its way through the mist and float quite swiftly towards us. Well, no, I realized it was anchored; we were approaching it. The thing was about the size of an elephant but fat, ugly and very rusty. It seemed infinitely forlorn, alone in the dirty water.

'S'berl-burj,' said the Captain. 'It'll clurng.'

He was right. After we had passed the poor thing and were leaving it behind, the ship's wash caught it and the bell-buoy did indeed go *clurng*... and then *clurng*... again; a rusty reproachful sound which did nothing but cause a handful of roosting gulls to lift off and swoop around a few times before settling again on the now-silent buoy.

A small man wearing plimsolls brought me a mug of sweet tea. The cat turned up its nose at this and moved to another window but I stayed watching as a single line of gold was pencilled across the grey sea and, like a curtain, the mist slowly and graciously moved itself aside to reveal that it was a vertical wall of cloud sitting on the water under a wide, cold, very slightly blue sky.

In the sudden clear light our little ship sailed along below this tall, incongruous cliff. The estuary was now so wide that only the far horizon was edged with dark knobbly land and streaks of heavy cloud. I looked up at the cliff of cloud beside us and noticed that the very top of it was shining with pale gold light. I wondered at this for a moment and then, from straight in front of us, the sun, hoisting itself up from behind the streaky clouds, unleashed a shaft of light, a shaft which lit the whole ship and the sea and all the world around us with glorious sunshine, even reflecting it up into the ceiling of the wheelhouse, where it lit, with dappled moving light, the high cobwebby shelf where dusty bottles and packets were stored.

'Smerning,' observed the Captain. 'Brerkfirst?'

'Oh, yes, please!' I said. Then, realising that I hadn't been very polite, I added: 'And, er, thank you very much, sir, I hope you didn't mind me . . .'

'Nerw,' said the Captain. 'Gerw.'

Nobody had told me that Copenhagen, or Kjøbenhavn as I was expected to call it, was full of canals. Well, no, not full, but there were several, with little motor boats that were buses. Nor did they tell me that it was full of bicycles, very full.

In my memory I can see a wide park with railings. It is sunny and I am standing on the pavement beside a crossroads. The traffic policeman turns and puts out an arm. At once the traffic moves forward, but silently, because it consists almost entirely of persons on bicycles, respectable middle-aged persons as well as young ones. A well set-up matron, with her broad hat pinned securely on, pedals sedately past. The back wheel of her old-fashioned sit-up-and-beg bicycle has a fan of strings stretched from hub to mudguard to save her skirt from tangling with the spokes. In a basket on the carrier sits a poodle. The rider looks slightly Edwardian and very ladylike, except that she is puffing a cigar.

At another time I saw a well-dressed gentleman come past riding a very superior-looking bike. He was smiling and people were touching their hats to him in a friendly way. A short way behind him came two soldiers in uniform, cycling side by side and chatting together. Later somebody told me that the gentleman was the king, but of course I didn't believe it.

I liked Denmark a lot. I remember it as being a gentle, courteous place with people who were always kind and really friendly. Perhaps the local courtesy had rubbed off on us because I don't remember doing much squabbling with John. No doubt I was still very touchy about protocol and 'fairness' but I don't remember being quite as grizzly as usual. If so it must have been a relief to Ray and Daisy and I hope they enjoyed that holiday as much as I did.

III. Conventional Education.

Academically, Woodstock School had turned out to be something of a disappointment so, late in 1936, it was decided that if I was to have a chance of passing the Entrance Examination to a secondary school I should attend a small school a couple of miles away in Friern Barnet which specialized in preparing pupils for that exam.

The school, which I shall call Crumlin House, was run by a North Country family, the Springbottoms, all of whom did their stint of teaching. They may not have been highly qualified but the curriculum was devoted solely to stocking up the minds of the Entrants, as they were called, with the facts and figures required for passing the Secondary Entrance Examination. Mr Springbottom, the headmaster, did occasionally allow himself to take a broader view and tell us that fixed-wheel bicycles were better than free-wheel ones if you were, as he was, a proper cyclist and that it's the damp muggy weather that gives you colds, not proper cold weather, wise saws that we duly wrote down and committed to memory. He also taught us the arcane language of Business Letters, which included passages like:

> Dear Sirs,
>   Yours of the 12th ult. to hand in re of which
> we acknowledge safe receipt of same and . . .
>   Assuring you of our best attention at all times,
>   Beg to remain,
>   Yours faithfully

. . . which I found quite baffling. This was mainly because Mr Springbottom never explained anything. He and the school saw their task as being to impart information and instruction, not to encourage understanding. So to the question: 'Why . . .?' he would answer: 'Because that's what you write.'

The school was also pretentious in a half-hearted way, with rather elaborate uniforms, a school song and long-winded speech-days which dwelt on the Spirit of the School. All this was a bit incongruous in a 'sausage-machine' crammer. I suspect it irritated my parents a bit and this may have caused them not to treat the Springbottoms with quite the respect they thought was their due. Mrs Springbottom in particular would make scathing remarks about the stuck-up children of clever-clever parents, which she made sure everybody knew were directed at me – though I hadn't the slightest idea why.

Things like that weren't important. Life was real and earnest. We had to be ready, fully primed, for the momentous Examination, at which the Entrants from Crumlin House School would sweep the board and honour their Alma Mater by excelling in all ways. As the day came closer the tension rose to fever pitch. Time after time we sat mock exams using previous years' papers. I was very frightened and convinced that I would fail but, when at last we were taken to another school to sit the exam and the paper was laid before me, it had written on it:

1. If A comes before P in the alphabet, put a cross in the square marked Y.

I had no idea what this had to do with the kings and queens and British Empire geography I had stuffed into my head but, as all the questions were as straightforward as that one, I nipped through the paper and waited for the exam proper to start.

It didn't start. That was it. We went home. The rest of the week was free, perhaps for us to recover from the rigours of the Exam. On the following Monday Mrs Springbottom addressed Assembly. She told us that the exam had been a great success and thanks to the valiant efforts of the school nearly all the pupils had passed. She told us that she had had letters of thanks from the parents of all the pupils, except one.

'Except one!' she repeated, glaring at me ... 'Postgate!'

I went forward and stood before her and the school.

'Well?' she demanded ... 'Well?'

'Er, er ... thankyouverymuch.'

'I should think so too!'

I crept back to my place and that afternoon when I returned home I told Daisy that Mrs Springbottom had been a bit cross because she hadn't written to thank her for getting me through the exam and that I had had to say a public thankyou on her behalf.

Daisy seemed a bit cross about this too, but the next morning she did give me a letter to take to Mrs Springbottom. I gave it to her at Assembly and directly it was over she ordered me to collect up my belongings and go home. There wasn't room in my satchel for all my things so she grudgingly gave me a paper bag. Although it split as soon as I was out of the school I didn't feel like going back to ask for another. I found a piece of string in the gutter and tied the things together with that.

I can see, now, that the change from a formal academic examination to a simple IQ test must have come as a terrible blow to the school, but even so I don't see why they had to take it out on me – but then I don't know what was in Daisy's letter.

I had passed the exam and was offered a place at Woodhouse County Secondary School in North Finchley.

Woodhouse School was, I think, a quite ordinary middle-of-the-road school, typical of England in the 1930s. It had a House system comprising four houses, Gordon, Livingstone, Nightingale and Scott, and its school motto was 'Cheerfulness with Industry'. I was a lowly member of Scott House, which was of course the best.

In general we behaved respectfully to the teachers, held up a hand when we wished to speak, attended to what was being said and did our work. In due course I found that teachers could be cheeked and would usually take it in good part, providing one was careful to preserve respect, calling them 'Sir' or 'Miss', and didn't go on too long. All of them would, if approached courteously at an appropriate moment, be willing to give a careful answer to a seriously asked question, and be quite companionable about it, particularly if the question had to do with their subject.

Essentially there were two social orders in the school. The main one was the formal hierarchy, with the headmaster at the top, then the teachers and house-captains. Below them came the prefects, the school and finally us, the newcomers. There were recognized heroes in the hierarchy, mostly distinguished achievers in sport or music, whom we were expected to look up to. The other was the social life of the pupils, lived during unsupervised moments in the classrooms, in the playground, the cycle sheds and on the playing fields during the dinner-hour. As a school, Woodhouse was thought to be a bit 'rough', by which I mean that the coinage of our lives together seemed to be a sort of formalized thuggery, in which the most important thing was to be seen to be 'tough'. Very occasionally there would be real fights between potential top persons in the class but for the rest of us it was a ritual by which we confirmed our position in the pack with small arm-twistings and shoves. Girls, as always, were different. They had a social hierarchy of their own from which boys were excluded, not that we would have wanted to have anything to do with girls anyway.

Of course with a complex institution like a school there were occasional failures of communication. It was as a result of one of these that I could be said to have dived for the House. One of the house-prefects came up to us in the field and said: 'Any of you rabbits dive?' So I, foolish but, as always, anxious to help, admitted that when I was on holiday I had once dived off some rocks.

'Right,' he said. 'You're diving for the House,' and went away.

I was proud, but only for a minute. When I read the list of awesome types of dives that I had been entered for I went, cap in hand, to the Head of House to tell him I couldn't dive and that it was all a mistake. He told me not to be modest and that it was my duty to the House to do my best. I went to the Sports master but he was too busy to talk and directed me back to the Head of House. He again refused to hear that I couldn't dive, told me not to be a ninny and said that they were all depending on me to put up a good show.

The Swimming Sports Day came. The diving was announced and duly took place. Six times I was called and six times I managed to find the courage to drop myself off the end of the board into the water, gaining for my House a total of nine points out of a possible sixty and for myself a red patch all down my front where my body had slapped the water. I was an object of ridicule and for most of my life I have been deeply ashamed of that disgrace. Only very recently have I been able to revise that view and look on the incident with something like pride. I had been ordered to dive for the House and I bloody did it. The fact that it was a complete fiasco was not my fault. I had told them it was going to be – and it was!

IV. Mocking Providence.

For me the spring of 1938 was full of excitement; I had been promised a brand-new full-size bike for my birthday. I had pored over the coloured catalogue of bicycles for hours and, with the expert advice of John and his friends, had eventually chosen a green Raleigh with half-drop handlebars, cable brakes and a Sturmey-Archer three-speed gear. It was priced at £5 19s 6d.

This was quite a large sum of money for Ray and Daisy to fork out but it was all part of a Grand Plan which they were hatching. We were to undertake a valedictory tour of France, on bicycles.

Even for Ray and Daisy, this was an enterprising idea. They were not in the bloom of youth. Ray was ponderous and over-weight. Daisy was in her late forties and rheumaticky. Neither of them was in the habit of taking exercise and neither of them had been on a bicycle for decades. But, with the war-clouds looming, they both felt that this might be the last time they would see their beloved France.

That was one serious reason for the trip. The other was that the franc stood at 1,750 to the pound, a rate of exchange that was not so much advantageous as mythically bountiful. A practical difficulty arose from the fact that our parents were very short of money at the time. Although once we had got to France the living would be very cheap, getting there was going to be expensive. So, obviously, bicycles were the logical choice.

Bicycles were obtained, saddlebags and panniers were bought. Our cousin, Peter Thurtle, and his wife-to-be, Kitty, joined the project and Daisy made divided skirts with box-pleats for her and Kitty to wear. Ray enrolled us all in the Cyclists' Touring Club.

The start of the tour proper was a triumph worthy of Jacques Tati. We left the small hotel in La Ferté Alais, just south of Paris, and proceeded '*en crocodile*' along a quiet wide road. At the edge of the town we came over a gentle hill and rolled down to a roundabout.

Ray, in the lead, put out his arm to signal his intent and rode steadily round the roundabout, to the left. John, knowing better, put his other arm out and rode steadily round it, to the right. I, confused, swung round and rode back towards the others, seeking instructions, but in vain. Kitty followed Ray to the left. Peter followed John to the right. Daisy jumped off and pushed her bike across the middle of the roundabout, shouting. I rode across behind her. The gendarme, his Gauloise hanging from his lip, stood with his hands on his hips observing the spectacle, but in the end chose not to comment.

That holiday has left me with the most glorious pictures. We rode along a set of stone bridges across a wide-spread river and in through the gates of a medieval town. Everything – the sun, the sky, the glittering of the leaves in the lines of trees, the lazy flat river rippling gently over gravel – was part of a fairy tale. Every roof, every dark shadow, every patch of sun-warmed stone in that town was full of glory and magic. I was drunk with amazement and delight and that night, when I went to bed filled with excellent dinner, I wished with all my heart that I could take the feeling of that place with me for the rest of my life.

A few years later I came across the work of Alfred Sisley. He too had seen Moret-sur-Loing and had spent much of his life painting the very scenes that I had taken in that day. When I saw his paintings I jumped for joy, not so much because they were great paintings but because, for me, they were like a magic snapshot album – each painting filled to overflowing with the light and essence of places that I had already seen and loved. In fact I found out later that the whole of that holiday was being painted by the Impressionist and Post-impressionist schools. We rode along the towpaths of canals under the poplar trees and passed slow barges with washing on their lines, gently turning over the brown water as a plough turns soft earth. Camille Pissarro must have been there with his easel. The long straight Roman roads were lined with stalky plane trees leaving dabs of shadow for us to ride through, singing at the tops of our voices as the warm wind blew in our hair. There must have been half a dozen painters there. But I, being pig-ignorant, knew nothing of art. I was scooping in, through my eyes, ears and nose, the impressions that those great painters had immortalized, but I was taking them in neat, for the first time, just as they must once have done.

For John and me the riding was easy. We were both experienced cyclists, light and wiry. Each morning our bicycles were like young horses, circling the yard, eager to be away on the road. We developed a habit of whizzing on ahead, leaving the others to trundle after us at their own speed. Then we would stop at a wayside estaminet, order *vin rouge-grenadine à l'eau de selz*, and wait for the elders to catch up and pay the bill, which would only be about five francs. They couldn't very well refuse such a small sum and the slight tint of rosy inebriation that was my happy condition on those mornings was soon burned away in leg-work.

Lunch was bought – a long loaf, some pâté, tomatoes, cheese, wine and water – in a village, and eaten, with the bottles chilling in the shallows and the toes fingering cool sand, on the green bank of some shady stream.

Towards evening we would come to the designated town. There John and I would drop back, leaving Ray, riding slow and high on his high, slow bicycle, to make his entrance and sniff the atmosphere, but circumspectly, as at dusk a bull elephant approaches a waterhole, leaving the herd to await his signal to follow.

Ray would come to a hotel and heave to outside it. The herd would follow and an important discussion about price and suitability would ensue. At St-Valerien, madame of the hotel came out to greet us. She spoke most highly of her establishment and intimated that if we were to take dinner as well as bed and breakfast all would be felicitous and of good price. The herd acquiesced and madame led us in, shouting orders as she did so to bring the dormant hotel to life. Small children with baskets, on foot and on bicycles, were despatched to the shops. A boiler was lit, bags were unpacked, baths were taken, and after a short cool stroll through the village we came back to find, not just dinner but a proper menu with choices. Later, the sheets were coarse but clean and I slept, as always in those times, still as a stone angel.

Waking up in a French village was always the same and always surprising. The sun would be up first, trying to find a way in through the shutters. It would reflect blurred green and gold stripes on to the ceiling, which would move and change with the passing shadows. Then, as if by a signal, somebody outside would drop a bucket, *clang*, on to the stones. A door would creak, a chain rattle, and then a shrill voice would let fly with a short complicated yell which would echo among the resonant walls. What was it, a greeting or an imprecation? Whatever it was it would be answered by more buckets being thrown and other voices from other directions giving answering yells until it seemed the whole town was out there, greeting the day.

That morning, after a French breakfast of croissants and hot chocolate we said goodbye to madame, and Ray paid the bill which, when converted, worked out at one and ninepence (9p) a head.

Ray, for all his atheism, was fascinated by churches. During the tour we must have seen and examined quite a number of them, but the one which has left the strongest impression with me was the Abbey at Vézelay. There the tops of the pillars and all the odd corners of the stonework are infested with carvings of ribald persons and unlikely creatures doing unexpected things. I noticed them and searched them out, wondering what they were up to, wondering indeed what religion was up to that it gave house-room to such manifestly disreputable denizens.

It soon became clear that we had not come to France for the architecture. Gradually, as we travelled westwards, I began to recognize the names of some of the towns and villages. I wondered why this was, and then I realized where I had seen them before – on the labels of wine bottles. Sleepy little towns like Nuits-St-Georges, Puligny-Montrachet, Volnay and Mersault were approached by Ray with the reverence of a pilgrim – which indeed he was, for in these places the nectar of the gods might still be found and taken. Here the *vin maison* was *premier cru* and the 'good bottle' of the evening was the stuff of dreams.

Although they had made the pilgrimage in a spirit of dread, fearing that the impending war might sweep it all away, Ray and Daisy were not so foolish as to allow the wine or food to be tainted with foreboding. It was a very happy time and I suspect that, if anything, the thought that he and Daisy and the rest of us might be mocking Providence simply added to Ray's delight.

V. When War Comes.

The family returned to Finchley and the real world, a bit saddle-sore but content, to find that the international situation had taken a turn for the worse. At school we no longer said: 'If war comes . . .' We said: 'When war comes . . .'

Then, at the end of September, Neville Chamberlain flew back from Munich waving the absurd document that, he said, ensured peace in our time. Herr Hitler had confirmed that the Sudetenland had been his last territorial ambition in Europe. The threat of war was said to be over.

I remember the enormous feeling of euphoria that swept through us. Hearts were lighter for many days, but the underlying sense that war was still somewhere in the offing was not fully dispelled and I don't think anybody, even among the pupils of Woodhouse School, was really surprised when, in March 1939, Hitler's army marched into Prague and took the whole of Czechoslovakia.

Politics, the international situation, the prospect of war, had never seemed fully real to me, mainly because I hadn't bothered to pay any attention to them, but gradually things began to happen which brought them home.

I watched Anderson shelters being delivered. These were the corrugated iron bolt-holes that householders would assemble and bury in their back gardens as a refuge from bombing. There had been an 'air raid drill' at school and I had been given a gas mask in a cardboard box, which I had tried on and didn't like. There had also been talk of evacuation; of taking children away and sending them to stay with strangers in safe places. All these things concentrated my attention. I still had the idea, somewhere in my head, that war was supposed to be exciting, even heroic, but these preparations seemed peculiarly unexciting, inconvenient and boring. They were also frightening, in a numb sort of way, because they didn't seem to be preparations for anything positive, like riding into battle, but more like preparations for some overall but unspecified disaster that would soon befall us all.

Ray seemed to be fairly calm about it all but Daisy was very frightened indeed. She told me that 'they' now had bombs that could wipe out half a town at one blast, and guns that could fire round corners and seek out their targets, and gas that was invisible but deadly. Her picture of the power of modern armaments was, fortunately for the world, premature; such things were yet to come. She didn't speak of it again but fears for our safety must have been in her mind because she and Ray had made plans for our evacuation.

They had met W. B. Curry, the headmaster of Dartington Hall School in Devon, and he had generously offered to take John and me as day-pupils at reduced fees if the war came. Their old friend Kay Starr was the secretary of Leonard Elmhirst, one of the owners of Dartington Hall. She offered to provide accommodation and look after us. So that was settled; the moment war came John and I were to go straight to Devon.

Meanwhile we made ready for war. We stuck strips of brown paper across the windows. We upholstered the thick-walled cupboards between the kitchen and the hall with mattresses and we listened to the wireless, which told us that crowds of children were waiting at railway stations to be evacuated, carrying their gas masks in cardboard boxes.

On September the first Hitler invaded Poland and Ray said it was time for us to go. Philip and Valerie Beales (Lance and Taffy's son and daughter-in-law) offered to give us a lift in their car. They would be going to somewhere near Cirencester, which was more than halfway to Devon. The offer was gratefully accepted.

It was a nightmare journey. The main roads were packed and the drivers very agitated. The police and the air raid wardens were out in force, shouting at motorists to put their lights out, which they did, and as a result couldn't see where they were going.

We reached our destination at about 4 a.m. and slept on the floor of a mill belonging to the Beales' uncle, who had a beard. His name was Percy and he was, I think, a weaver. Then, quite late the next morning, after mugs of tea and chunks of bread and jam, John and I got on our bikes and rode together into the future.

Well, we didn't exactly ride *together*. John was seventeen and a proper cyclist. I was thirteen and beginning to be a bit overweight, so he tended to be a long way in front of me, getting impatient. My rucksack was heavy and my gas mask case banged against my leg. We stayed at 'bed and breakfast' houses and at a café we heard the wireless say '...no such undertaking has been received and that consequently this country is at war with...'

Then, one sunny morning, we rode up the long leafy drive to Dartington Hall, the grand medieval house and estate that was the great centre of art and progress. Entering the ancient courtyard through the arch, I felt as if I was stepping into a film about knights in armour and maidens locked in towers. I expected a richly caparisoned white horse to ride up to us, bearing a bearded serjeant-at-arms on its broad back. In fact a young man in corduroy trousers and sandals came and asked if he could help us. He directed us to Kay Starr's office, which was through the Great Hall.

The Great Hall was amazing. It was huge and echoey but bright with sunlight flooding in through the tall windows. The walls were hung with bright banners and the floor strewn with rush mats. It smelled sweetly of beeswax and flowers, and had clearly just been made ready for the arrival of a king.

We knocked on a door in the far corner. A voice said, 'Come in.' We stepped down into Kay Starr's office: a tall rather embarrassed-looking youth and a shorter, fattish one, who grinned, both quite grimy and dishevelled.

Kay was a tall, tidy, tweedy stick of a lady, very upright, clean and exact. I shall never forget the look on her face when she saw us. It was dismay, but a dismay so intense and overwhelming that for a few seconds she couldn't speak.

Then she said: 'Oh, so you've arrived, have you?'

'Yes,' I replied, still grinning.

VI. *Progressive Education.*

When I told people I might be going to Dartington Hall School they would sometimes go 'Ooooh!' and look at me coyly, as if there was something slightly risqué about the idea, because Dartington Hall was what was called a 'progressive' school. They had heard tell, they said, that there was no uniform and people sometimes went about with nothing on! From some I heard that there were no rules and no proper classes, that the pupils were in charge of the staff and there was fun and freedom all the time. From others I heard that it was licentious, and surely a sink of sin. Everything that was said about the school was charged with strong feeling. It may seem a bit odd today but in 1939 the very idea of educating people in an unconventional way was slightly outrageous.

Now it was the first day of term and as I rode down the hill towards the school I realised that I had absolutely no idea what I was going to find when I arrived. It might of course be a quite ordinary place like Woodhouse School, with uniforms, prefects and an Assembly. I think I was rather hoping it would be.

I couldn't see anywhere to put my bike so I leaned it against the wall, opened the front door and looked in.

I heard a lot of noise and saw a lot of people milling about. They weren't all children, some of them seemed to be grown-ups but none of these were wearing academic gowns. In fact they were dressed in all sorts of different clothes and were just chattering away together and looking at notices.

I stepped in and stood just inside the door. People smiled at me as they brushed past but didn't say anything. After a few minutes of standing about I realised that nobody was coming to find me, so I had better find somebody myself. I moved along a corridor to the right and saw a door marked 'Office'. I knocked but nobody answered. So in the end I pushed the door open and walked in. A lady was sitting at a typewriter.

'Hallo,' she said, 'I'm Sarah.'

'Postgate,' I said, 'Oliver Postgate. I am here.'

'Yes, I can see. What can I do for you?'

'I'm sorry. I don't know what to do.'

Sarah sighed with resignation, arose and led me back into the foyer. There she pointed to a gigantic timetable. 'Look,' she said, 'you're in C Group. In half an hour you have Art.'

'Yes, but what do I do?'

'Why, whatever you like! You are free, absolutely free! Aren't you lucky!' She lifted her arms in joyful freedom and swirled away, back to her office.

I stood there, stunned. I looked at the board. I turned and looked at the doors. I looked at the people milling busily about, oblivious of my existence. I have never felt quite so lonely and baffled in my life.

How long I stood there I don't know. I remember finding a man looking out of a window and asking him if he knew where Art was. He must have told me because I came at last to the Art Room. It was deserted. I sat at a table.

After about twenty minutes a large girl in trousers walked in. She dumped her things on a table and said: ''Lo, who're you?'

'Postgate,' I said.

'What?'

'Postgate.'

'Poached egg? You a poached egg?'

'No . . .'

Four or five more people came in, all dressed differently; then a thin young man wearing a brown jersey.

'Hallo,' he said in quite a friendly tone, 'I'm Mark. Who are you?'

'He's a poached egg!' shouted the girl.

'No, I'm not,' I whispered.

The Art class didn't seem to begin at any particular moment. Some people had rummaged around and found paper and powder-paints but the rest just chatted. The teacher chatted with them. Nobody spoke to me so I found a piece of paper and a crayon and drew a fish. The class must have ended at some point because everybody left.

For the rest of the day I kept my head down and did my best to follow on behind the others. I clung on to the hope that somebody official would come along to acknowledge my existence, but it didn't happen.

Late in the afternoon I noticed that people were going into the dining room to eat. I wondered whether I was supposed to join them. I didn't know who to ask so I went to the Office to ask the typing lady if it would be all right to go home. The Office was locked, so, feeling cold with misery, I got on my bike and rode back to Kay Starr's house.

John had had a different but equally daunting time. Notice had been taken of him and he had been told to wait for some sort of 'tutor', who simply didn't turn up. So where I was feeling baffled and lost, he was healthily angry. He noted in his diary that it was a silly school and he asked to be taken away from it as soon as possible. Very soon he was staying with our uncle Richmond in Exeter and going to a school there.

*

My first day at Dartington Hall School had not only been very different from my first day at Woodhouse School, it had been quite different from anything I had been able to imagine. In all my conjectures about what Dartington might be like I had always wondered what sort of *school* it would be, how we, the pupils, would be controlled and directed. It had never occurred to me that there mightn't be a *school* there at all, that I would have no desk, no place to go, and that nobody would tell me what to do next. But that's how it was.

From the moment I had arrived at Woodhouse School, I had been fully involved in the organized life of the school and had felt quite secure in the place I held in that benevolent authoritarian hierarchy. At Dartington there seemed to be no benevolent authority, nobody to notice what I did or didn't do. I might as well not have existed.

Although I didn't realise it at the time, I was completely desperate, frantically trying to find a place for myself in a social order that didn't in fact exist. In this I was of course unsuccessful but my behaviour must have been observed, because it was mentioned in my first report:

> Oliver ... started off by showing off in ways that did not endear himself to either children or staff ... both in class and in his written work his chief motive seems to be to gain admiring attention.

Ray passed that report to me with a contemptuous gesture and I remember it hitting me like a body-blow, not so much because it was so casually damning as because it was the *only* comment that had been made. During the term I had been given no clue as to whether or not my behaviour was acceptable. I had spent my time in a sort of ongoing panic because I hadn't been able to get anybody to *acknowledge* my existence, let alone *admire* it.

Looking back, I can get some really embarrassing pictures of the obnoxious way I carried on in that first term. During the first weeks I think I went in for a bit of the formal thuggery and arm-twisting that had been customary at Woodhouse. That simply didn't work. I remember trying to be funny in class. That was a waste of time. Answering back at the teachers provided no thrills and was just ignored. I can see myself clowning and nobody taking any notice. I pretended to be clever and know everything but all that brought was mockery – all these were the standard reactions to a smart-arsed git trying to grab attention. That was fair enough but it was the response, or rather the lack of response, of the teachers to this carry-on that I found completely incomprehensible. At Woodhouse they wouldn't have put up with it. I would have been put in my place in no time (and so would have known my place). Here they took no notice at all. They suffered the inconvenience and looked away. Needless to say, this discouragement simply caused me to redouble my efforts.

In contrast to this rather frantic school life my current home life was very quiet, if not exactly homely. Kay Starr was, I think, kindly disposed towards me, but I knew that she felt very keenly the intrusion and disruption that my presence caused in her life. She was also, in herself, a righteous person, very conscious of the shortcomings of the rest of the world, which she did not hesitate to condemn.

In the evenings Kay would often say: 'Don't let's bother with proper supper, let's just have some scrambled egg on our knees.' Then there would be small pieces of thin toast covered with reconstituted dried egg and perhaps an apple to follow. I would sit very carefully and eat it neatly and when I had finished she would look at me anxiously and her face would tell me that she couldn't think what she was going to do with me for the rest of the long evening. Neither could I.

At weekends I was, as Kay's protégé, allowed to partake of her life in Dartington Hall itself. This was a completely different world from the school. This was an essentially civilized, artistically sensitive foundation which had been created by Mr and Mrs Elmhirst to provide a centre of excellence, where individuals and groups engaged in the arts could be encouraged and supported in their work. There were painters, musicians, sculptors, silversmiths, even a ballet company, all busy working away at their arts, sustained by the loving generosity of Leonard and Dorothy Elmhirst.

The collection of people drawn to that cultural magnet was

amazingly varied and interesting. The atmosphere seemed to be very free and easy but Kay, being perhaps conscious of her position as Leonard Elmhirst's private secretary, was at pains to emphasize the need for me to be as unobtrusive as possible. So I walked on tiptoe through that part of Kay's world, as I tiptoed through every other part of her neat house and her neat life, because I was steeped in long-term apology for being there and being a nuisance and because I was totally intimidated by her, even though she had told me, quite firmly, that we were close friends.

Getting used to life in Kay's cold house was not easy, but it was my life at school that was causing me the most bafflement.

Looking back I can see that what I was having trouble with was the freedom. Freedom was assumed to be the aim and joy of life, and I was sure it was, but I didn't seem to be very good at it. Freedom was presenting itself to me as a succession of choices that I had to make. These were not just choices between set alternatives like: 'Will you have jam or marmalade?' These were more basic choices like: 'Do I want to bother to get out of this chair?' or 'Do I want to find out what the next class is and go to it?'

This unsettling responsibility was complicated by the fact that I truly believed that I was *supposed* to make decisions that reflected my fancy. If I asked somebody which option I should take, I was asked in reply: 'Well, which do you *want* to take?' – a question to which I had no answer, because I had no fancy and no purpose of my own. Today I can see quite clearly that all I really wanted was somebody to be there and mind enough to tell me what to do – and that, alas, was not on the menu.

So I think I just soldiered on and, as children and chameleons do, began to take on the colour of my surroundings. I started to affect the arrogant unconcern that I imagined was the convention, disdained the timetable and tried to follow what I hoped was my fancy. I must emphasize that I was not doing this as a real affirmation of personal independence. Quite the contrary, I was simply doing my best to conform, to do what I imagined was expected of me.

Absurd as it may seem, I think that may have worked. It seems that I did become what was (for Dartington Hall School) a socially acceptable person, because my next report said that I had '*settled down*', was '*becoming more popular*' and that my time was '*for the most part being profitably occupied*'.

There was some truth in the last of these observations because I found a microscope in the biology lab and became fascinated by the underwater life that seemed to appear by itself in ponds and puddles when they became stagnant. I would cycle around the estate collecting smelly jars of it and bring them back to the biology lab. I sometimes think that could have become 'my subject' if I had managed, or even been encouraged, to organize my studies a bit, but that didn't happen. At one time I became very interested in pottery and spent some months doing very little else, but here again my activity was quite solitary, random and disorganized. For a few months a craze for small theatricals swept through the school. At another time people collected pieces of tubing and blew bullets made of modelling-clay at each other.

These peripheral activities were engrossing enough to ensure that the academic side of school life was neglected. I was supposed to spend half an hour each week with my tutor, Boris, to talk about my work. He was the Chemistry master and, like me, an inveterate small-joke-maker. At our tutorial meetings he was icily polite and punctilious but I'm sorry to say he was unable to conceal from me the fact that he disliked me intensely and found the task of discussing my educational future distasteful. I didn't care a lot for it myself because I, being fifteen years old, had found other interests, so I tended to miss tutorials. When this happened Boris would remind me of the possible academic consequences of neglecting my studies, but he did so more in resignation than in hope.

The other interest I had found was not pottery, pond-life or play-acting. It was sex, or rather, the distant prospect of sex.

Many people tended to assume that because Dartington Hall School was 'progressive' and free of restraints, the life of the pupils would inevitably be an ongoing orgy of sexual indulgence. That wasn't true.

Quite a lot of fairly heavy petting went on but, as far as I remember, not much else.

The general policy of the school seemed to be one of non-interference. There were no organized house-based activities, so the pupils were mostly left to stew in their juice, which probably explains why the social life was so obsessively sex-centred. Looking back I can see that although it may all have been a bit overwrought, I don't think it was unhealthy, just children growing up.

My position in this social life was marginal. Being a day-pupil meant that I was always a sort of visitor in the boarders' houses. This made me slightly uncomfortable. Also I was still very much in awe of girls and knew that if they were not treated carefully they could give you a nasty bite, though their bites were of scorn and derision.

At Dartington, girls began to take on a new light. They became objects of desire and they glowed with thrilling but unspecific allure. I became infatuated with girls in general but I was also in love with one girl in particular. This girl shone in my sky like the full moon. Every ordinary movement she made was steeped in sensual magic and as I watched her I knew that my sole aim in life was to approach her and be as near to her as possible. My infatuation was made all the more intense by the fact that I had no clear idea where my feelings were supposed to lead. I had hardly reached puberty and, although the rabbits had taught me that the sole purpose of courtship was sexual intercourse, the very idea of having to do anything so ungainly seemed to me quite unthinkable and I quickly put such thoughts from my mind. Doing this did not diminish my ardour, it allowed it to be pure, which was a relief. It also allowed it to be private, something which nobody else knew about. Thus it came as a shock to discover that everybody, including the beloved, knew all about my feelings, and that her very natural efforts to avoid my cowlike gaze were being aided and abetted by most of her friends, who were watching the farcical carry-on with derisive amusement.

This was a disappointing introduction to romance, but not surprising. The idea that a girl might value my attention and be pleased to receive it had simply never crossed my mind. I knew for certain that girls were by nature always hostile to advances and I assumed that my role as a suitor could only be that of the plaintive lovelorn swain, ever hopeful but always unworthy. The assumption may sometimes have been accurate, but it was never attractive.

VII. The Home Front.

Returning home from school for the Christmas holiday in 1939 was a happy anticlimax. In September we had fled, as refugees, from the terrors of the war that was to come. The war had come and had brought no terrors, at least not to 45 Hendon Lane in Finchley. Like Mole in *The Wind in the Willows* I returned to my home and was deeply moved to find it miraculously unchanged, exactly as I had left it. The windows were still striped with brown paper and at night fully covered by heavy blackout pads made of cardboard and black cloth.

Ration books had arrived but were not yet to be used. We looked at them closely and tried to divine what amounts of the various foods we might be going to receive but to no avail. Otherwise there was not much war to be seen. The only bombs that went off in London were put there by the IRA. So I painted huge frogs and Chinese dragons on the blackout pads and settled down to enjoy Christmas.

Although the house was unchanged, the atmosphere was quite different. Dread had gone, or been shelved for the moment, and there was gaiety about. War had not, after all, wiped everything away and it was good to be alive and able to enjoy ordinary things.

Only at dusk, as darkness fell and the blackout was complete, did a sense of menace return. Then no man-made light could be shown, in case the German eyes lurking in the sky should see it. Even the air-raid warden's torch was sparingly used – flashed on to see something and then off again at once. There were very few cars about and their headlamps were intricately shielded so as to shine a very little light down on to the road. Without any street-lights or house lights the streets were in a world separate from people, a place where everything was still and sharp-edged. Even when it was absolutely black, at times when there was no moon, the stars were clouded and I was truly blind, I discovered that I could tell where I was by interpreting the subtle echoes of my own footsteps. I had first noticed this faculty at Dartington, where every night I walked back from Foxhole over the hill to Kay's house near the Hall. I had found that on pitch-black nights I could walk back almost as briskly as on clear nights, so long as I didn't think about it too much and remembered to sing.

In the spring of 1940 I heard that Grandad was very seriously ill and, in May, that he had died. I would have liked to go to his funeral but for some reason this wasn't possible, perhaps Dartington was too far from London, I don't know.

Dartington was also a long way from the war. Kay and I listened to the news on the wireless and saw the maps in the newspapers, all covered with arrows, but the reality of the war only really came home to me when I returned to Finchley in the summer of 1940.

There the sky was very noisy and was often decorated with circles of smoke as the aeroplanes fought out the Battle of Britain. The air-raid sirens sang at all hours and from time to time the earth would shudder underfoot and a heavy *crump* would be heard. The kitchen at 45 Hendon Lane was dark because the windows were heavily sandbagged. The cellar had been shored up to make an air-raid shelter and a long escape-way had been dug under the long room to a trapdoor in the garden. As ration books were now in full use and food was short, the honorary post of head of household had fallen to Daisy. She held the books and took to the task of feeding the flock in the midst of shortages with a mixture of enthusiasm and dismay.

With her father's death an era of great activity in Daisy's life had suddenly come to an end, so I think she found this challenge to her very considerable skill as an organizer quite rewarding. Her originality and resourcefulness as a cook was certainly a great joy to the rest of us.

I returned to Dartington at the end of the summer holiday fairly confident that our lives were charmed and that although war would probably be interesting, it was unlikely to be dangerous. I was wrong about that. A couple of days later a bomb fell in Hendon Lane, blowing out all the windows and damaging the house.

I came back to Finchley for the Christmas holidays of 1940 to find that life there was different. It had become very busy. Daisy was now fully in charge of what was, in effect, an extended-family boarding house. Kate (who used to be called Kitty), lived there, as did Peter when he was on leave from the RAF, also our uncle Eric with his wife Emily and their three boys. Daisy's younger sister Nellie had gone back to her little flat in Gray's Inn after a night-shift and had found it not there, just a hole and a heap of charred things, so she was in residence. John was back at his old school at Kingsbury, studying for Oxford Entrance, and I was back from Devon.

The house itself had changed quite a lot. The window glass had been replaced by a sort of oiled buckram which let in some light but you couldn't see through it. The cellars had become two bedrooms with camp beds. Even Matilda the cat had given up nocturnal outings and spent her nights lying on Daisy's feet.

Our night-time procedure was fairly standardized. John and I would go to bed in our own bedrooms as usual but as soon as the air-raid siren went or, when I became more blasé, as soon as I heard the sound of bombers or gunfire, I would jump out of bed, roll up the bedding like a Swiss roll with the pillow in the middle, pick it up and prance lightly down the stairs into the cellarage, where I would unroll the still warm bed on a camp bed and climb in. Once I pranced very lightly indeed because a bomb fell quite near and I took the last flight of eighteen stairs at a single bound and landed squarely on the bedding. I didn't hang about to check for broken bones, I was down and unrolled and had my head under the covers in a matter of seconds.

I was frightened by the bombing, but so was everybody else, and as it was quite obvious that there was nothing to be done about it, people just went on with life as usual and hoped one wouldn't drop too close. I was also slightly thrilled by the danger and excitement of it all. This was a bit childish I suppose and the feeling would probably have evaporated if I had been really close to a disaster and seen people killed or lying dead, but, perhaps fortunately, I was lucky enough to miss that experience. I did see other unnerving sights, like bombed houses with their insides on the outsides. I remember looking up and seeing flowered wallpaper and tiled fireplaces on the outsides of walls four storeys up. One fireplace had a picture of a stag over it and the ornaments were still in place. Above it a large bath hovered, hanging on its pipes in midair, like a hippopotamus diving off a cliff.

To come home on a late tube-train through the London stations with their lines of steel bunks was a strange and moving experience. Each family brought small living-items with them: cushions, bedding, books, torches, cans of water, bowls, all personal bedroom things, and made their bunks into a piece of home. Coming alongside and waiting quietly, I was like a ghost passing through their private lives. I felt enormous affection and care for them and prayed silently for their safety, but I was also glad they took no more notice of my presence than they did of the bright trains that roared in and out, stopping less than a yard from their beds.

One night we heard the distant sound of many planes and gunfire. We went outside into a world lit by what seemed to be a sunset in the south-east. On the horizon the distant houses and trees were silhouetted black against a sky glowing golden red and flickering softly. That was the city of London being burned by incendiary bombs.

The war moved eastward. Hitler postponed his plans to invade Britain and started on the second part of his great war plan: the invasion of Russia.

I was sixteen and the School Certificate Exams were looming, but even so I remained fairly uninterested in academic study. I had already found out, by reading my reports, that I was not thought to be *'higher education material'* and that an art or craft career was recommended. Simply in order to get shot of the task of choosing, I settled on stage design, which I thought might interest me if I was ever going to have a career.

The school had no facilities to teach me stage design and no wish to try. The Art teacher had already dismissed my efforts in Art as '*showing a lack of clear thinking*', and being '*aimless work that could be described as a slow disintegration of an idea into a pleasant façade*'. This was a valid comment which might have been very useful if it had been made to me at the time, but it wasn't. As usual it was just sent to my parents in an end-of-term report.

Since then I have often wondered about this phenomenon: the contrast between the outspoken and generally damning reports sent to my parents and the carefully noncommittal and evasive attitude of the teachers. Some years later I had an opportunity to talk about this with an ex-member of the school staff, one who was, incidentally, the author of one or two of my reports. He explained that, because there were no rules or any discipline to support them, the teachers were inevitably vulnerable and at a disadvantage in their dealings with their less-than-endearing pupils. These could be as foul as they liked without any fear of reprisal, while the teachers, bound by the theory-driven education method, could not answer back. This situation did not allow them to be spontaneous in their responses to their pupils, nor did it encourage them to form genuine relationships with them. Luckily, he explained, they didn't have to. Freedom was seen as being the 'cure-all'. So long as the pupil had freedom, the teacher could look away, remain cool and detached, and leave them to their fate, saving their real comments for the parents' reports.

I could understand that, even sympathize with it, and it went some way to explaining why, at Dartington, I had sometimes felt I was in a zoo rather than a school. In the light of it I now cherish the thought that, although at the time I had slunk shamefully away, I did, once, cause W. B. Curry, the headmaster, to lose his cool.

Curry gave evening seminars in Philosophy for interested pupils at his house. At one of these he told us that we would be discussing 'good'.

'Good!' I said enthusiastically. 'Good what?'

'What d'you mean, good what?'

'That's what I mean,' I answered. 'What are you going to talk about that is good?'

'No,' he explained. 'Not good anything ... The Good. Good as a quality in its own right.'

W. B. Curry went on to discourse on Plato's Essences, on the nature of Good and Truth and Beauty, and all the time I found myself becoming more and more agitated and, no doubt, huffing and puffing and tearing my hair. In the end Curry turned to me and said: 'All right, then. What's biting *you*?'

I said: 'I'm sorry, but it doesn't work.'

'What do you mean?'

'I don't think what we are talking about is there. I mean, I don't think I can think about Good as if it were a *thing* because I don't think it is.'

'Well, what *do* you think it is?'

'I don't know. I don't see how a quality can exist all on its own. I think it's the name of an adjective, an aspect of whatever it is describing, an observation *about* something.'

'Is that really what you think?' asked the headmaster.

'Yes, I think so.'

'Right, then!' he snapped, his eyes blazing. '*FUCK OFF!*'

3

STIRRING IT UP

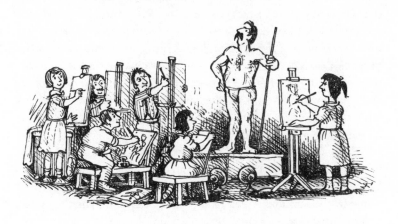

I. Growing Pains.

Back in London in the spring of 1942 I noticed that the bomb sites were a riot of colour. A flower, I think it was willowherb, had invaded the tops of the broken walls, coated the heaps and was springing out from between the floors where the torn wallpapers flapped, softening the hard edges and making everything part of a garden.

I had left Dartington having, by some miracle, passed my School Certificate Exams. Well, it wasn't quite a miracle. A friend and I had spent the last fortnight before the exams in the school library going through the whole syllabus. After they were over I had joined the Home Guard – a gesture that had caused much amusement at the school. When I returned to Finchley I was assigned to what was known as the 'Offensive Section', though a milder band of shopkeepers it would be hard to find.

I got on well with the Offensive Section but in myself I was feeling glum and uncomfortable. Well, worse than that – I was angry. I don't think I was angry with any particular person, not all the time anyway, I think it was more that I was violently discontented.

If there was a rationale to what was happening I think it was that I was slowly becoming aware of myself. Throughout my early life I had been glad enough to be allowed just to be there. I had been innocently happy when loved, innocently miserable when oppressed, bearing no grudges and keeping no records. I hadn't questioned my place at the bottom of the pile and had grown into, and later even played into, the picture of myself that I had got back from the others – that of the clever/stupid, facetious show-off who had to be kept down.

There was a very simple reason for this. Burned right into my bones was the basic knowledge, learned perhaps at my brother's knee, that anything I said or thought was automatically, solely by virtue of the fact that it was *I* who was saying or thinking it, certain to be stupid and therefore unacceptable. As a result I spent my time frantically searching for something to say that would be *more* interesting or *more* funny than what I would ordinarily have said, because only that would stand a chance of being worth listening to.

This is a fairly commonplace condition, one felt in some degree, I'm sure, by most of the human race. The trouble was that I'd had enough of it. I'd had enough of being at the bottom of the pile. I had had enough of being sneered at and enough of playing the idiot.

Of course my unfortunate parents weren't really sneering at me, not on purpose anyway. I think they were actually a bit nervous of me. Daisy hadn't much liked the effect that Dartington had been having on me and her manner towards me had become guarded and slightly defensive. She would say significant things like: 'I don't expect going up to the shop to get me some carrots would be the sort of thing that would interest you.'

These were small, very forgettable, barbs which up to then I hadn't bothered to notice. Now they really got to me. I became touchy and darkly explosive. I noticed again that my Aunt Nellie (who in her day had been firmly installed at the bottom of the pile in George Lansbury's family) possessed an absolutely reliable reflex action. The family would all be at table, talking. If, at a lull in the conversation, I should start to say something, she would recognize this as a signal that the floor was clear, and cut straight into the middle of my first sentence. She did this every single bloody time and, as far as I ever knew, nobody (but me) even noticed. But I had been, and still was, too half-baked to object.

Needless to say the joker that hung over everything at that time, making nonsense of everybody's personal purposes, mine included, was the war. In about a year, when I reached the age of eighteen, I would be due for call-up. So there really wasn't any point in doing anything connected with a long-term future, because even if I was going to have one – which was by no means certain – there was no telling what it might be.

Still hanging on to the possibility that I might one day become a stage designer, I enrolled at the Kingston College of Art.

This meant that I had to travel daily from Finchley to Kingston, by tube, Southern Railway and number 65 bus. This journey, an hour and a half each way, could have been boring and a burden, but I remember it as a delight. It was time out of life, time in which there was nothing I had to do but sit there and let the train carry me on. Sometimes I read, but mostly I just sat and thought. Since those days I have looked forward to long train journeys just because, as the world slides busily past outside, one can be alone inside one's head and free to roam.

Goodness knows what I was thinking about on those rumbling journeys but the process of thinking was itself a great joy. I suppose I was looking for, finding and maybe fitting together, the pieces of that immense, unfinishable 3D jigsaw puzzle of the spirit, called *How things are*. My mind would go ranging away, swinging from branch to branch, yodelling like Tarzan through marvellous forests of huge ideas and wide vistas of glorious realisation. Nowadays, alas, I usually go to sleep.

Kingston College of Art was run as a college in that the students were regarded as being adults, but I think many of the young people who started with me in the Foundation Class must have come from quite authoritarian schools, because they appeared to be absolutely in awe of the teachers and took the comments and advice they received as direct instructions, to be followed exactly. I, on the other hand, had no automatic respect for the teachers' comments and didn't know I was supposed to have. I regarded what they had to say as a contribution to my own thinking about what I was doing and acted accordingly. Some members of the staff didn't seem to mind this, others seemed a bit put out. But, unexpectedly, my fellow students hated it. They were outraged, not so much by the fact that I had the temerity to argue with or even disregard the teacher's instructions, as by the fact that doing so didn't seem to require any daring on my part. To them the very thought of rebelling against the teacher's authority called for outstanding courage. My being able to do just that, apparently quite casually, showed that I either possessed superhuman courage or was some sort of monster, so grossly arrogant and conceited that I had no grasp of the situation.

The latter view seemed to be the one that prevailed, the one that caused them to flick ink-pellets at me when the teacher was out of the room and, once or twice, to scrawl nasties on my drawing when I wasn't there.

That was the first really clear signal the outside world had given me that there was something about me that was seriously unacceptable. It wasn't just that I didn't show proper respect to the teachers. It was more fundamental than that. I could sense that there was something in the way I walked, in the way I spoke, in the way I looked, which instantly proclaimed that I was a bit 'off'; that I was peculiar. But I had no idea what it was. I found this very disturbing, so much so that I mentioned it to Daisy, who said something like: 'Well what do you expect? It's all that stuff you picked up at Dartington, isn't it?'

Oh. Was it? I didn't know what she was talking about. I was still convinced that Dartington was irreproachable. I had had the privilege of receiving its enlightened form of education. The idea that the effects of this could be anything but wholly beneficial was unthinkable.

However, the hostile signals I was receiving were so clear that I had to consider the possibility that something might have been wrong with, or missing from, my education. That set the seed in my mind, but it has taken me many years to get a clear picture of the after-effects of my time at Dartington.

I had left the school in 1942, happily assuming that my personal acceptability in the social circles in which I would find myself would be decided by the relevance of my thinking and the value of my opinions and contributions. I thought, in fact I knew, that my intentions were friendly. I was careful to be, in my fashion, courteous. I liked to be helpful and was glad to contribute useful ideas to any discussion and would occasionally go out of my way to tell people useful things – like, for instance, how to do their jobs.

In fact my happy assumption could not have been further from the truth. Acceptance had to be earned. Without knowing it I had been let out into a world which, in 1942, was far more rigid and intolerant than it is today, a world in which whether or not I was going to be allowed into the pack was going to be decided by how diligently I observed certain infinitely delicate nuances of behaviour with which I was supposed to signal my appreciation of the worth and position of my betters and thereby, in their charity, be accorded my place.

This was a world which any well brought-up wolf or chimpanzee would, by virtue of the early conditioning of its pack, recognize without hesitation, but, unlike Woodhouse School, Dartington had no hierarchy in which one could learn to 'know one's place', and consequently that essential piece of education had been missed out.

W. B. Curry, the headmaster of Dartington, once described the education he purveyed as 'education for discontent', and as far as I was concerned he was right about that. Dartington not only omitted to teach me any manners, it gave me precious little proper education. It also, and this is something I have reason to resent to this day, *gave me no practice or training in doing things I don't want to do!* This I believe to be one of the basic purposes of education because, after all, one spends most of one's life doing things one doesn't really want to do simply in order to clear the space to do what one *does want to do*. Dartington ignored this as part of a deliberate, theory-led policy, and it did so without asking me or telling me. So I had no way of knowing what was going on.

No doubt I am being unjust as well as tiresome in my comments. I have friends who were there with me who felt, and still feel, that the time they spent there was valuable and idyllic, and that (although perhaps they are too courteous to put it so crudely) if it wasn't like that for me it was probably my own fault. I am sure there is some truth in that and I dare say many of the difficulties I experienced there arose from regrettable characteristics that were probably well formed by the time I arrived there. Nevertheless, at a different school I might have learned or been taught my way out of them, but, apart from sending sneering reports to my parents, Dartington Hall School took no interest in them, or in me.

However peculiar my life at school may have been, and however unwelcome and uncomfortable I may have been feeling at the College of Art, they were as nothing compared to the shemozzle that was going on at home.

Disdaining the family rooms, I had made a kingdom of my bedroom in which I spent my time frantically drawing and painting pictures. This was a waste of time because in the house I was too overwrought to think properly about what I was doing. I declined to show the pictures to my parents and threw them away. I remember Ray observing that I threw them away because: '. . . they are unworthy of his genius!' That was probably meant as a joke and, perhaps because it was a joke, it stung, and made me frantically hostile.

But I can also see that I wasn't really feeling hostile towards them as they were at that moment, I was trying to get away from something else, a collection of ghosts that, over the years, had occupied the inside of my head and had made me what I was. Ray was in there, with his back to me. John was there too, flapping me disdainfully aside and looking over my head. Kay Starr was there, tall and aghast. And Daisy was very much there, her heavy

Lansbury eyes drilling rays of loving anxiety that could cripple at fifty yards.

My behaviour was fearsomely overwrought, an effect, no doubt, of the quantities of new hormones that were pounding through my seventeen-year-old veins. I suspect that, had I but known it, what I most needed to do was say I was sorry, and maybe ask something like a blessing for the changes that had to happen.

But that would have taken a rare courage. Too bad we have to do our growing up when we are young.

II. Playing the Joker.

The number 65 bus was my salvation. Faithfully every morning I had boarded it at Surbiton Station and climbed to the front seat of the upper deck while it took me along the accustomed route, past houses and shops, to the stop by the bridge over a small dirty river called the Hogsmill, a couple of hundred yards from the undistinguished block that was the Kingston-upon-Thames College of Art. There I would get off.

Only one day I didn't. I looked across out of the nearside window and saw the College waiting there with its Foundation Class beating out mock-jazz on the table tops, and Mr Kisby, for whom we had to draw tiny squares of a million fine lines to make patterns for pin-stripe shirt material, and I said: 'Er ... no. Not today, thank you. Today is different.'

That said, I sat back in the captain's seat and looked out at the world ahead. The engine revved up, the gears clanked. The bus began to move. Two trumpeters beside the portal of the County Court blew a long fanfare in our honour, and the day began.

I can't tell you what a glorious lifting of the spirit came from that small decision. For a moment the ghosts of conformity peered reproachfully up at me, but I was firm. I said: 'No, I am not playing truant ... all right, yes, I am, but I am not running away. I am a free person and I have just decided not to go to College today. I may decide to go there tomorrow, in fact I'm sure I will, but today . . . today I shall go to . . .' By peering through a tiny oval window in the top of the destination-box I could just see the word. '. . . Leatherhead. I wonder where Leatherhead is.'

The number 65 was an enterprising bus. It didn't just pootle around the suburbs. Once it was clear of Surbiton it stretched its wheels and headed out into the country. The houses dropped away behind and the road went on through open common-land. One by one the passengers got off and when all the fares were taken the conductor came up and sat on the other front seat across the aisle.

'S'all right down this end,' he said.

'Yeh, 'tis,' I replied.

It certainly was. In fact it was marvellous. It was the eighteenth of February 1943, with the sun heading up the southern sky like midsummer and the air as clear as ice.

Leatherhead turned out to be a proper small country town, neat and compact. I left the bus in its yard and wondered what to do.

My legs told me they wanted to walk.

'OK,' I said, 'which way?'

They said: 'Towards the sun.'

'All right, then. Get on with it!'

Oh! What it was to have seventeen-year-old legs. My goodness, they were full of life! We strode off towards the sun into a piece of country the like of which I had never imagined.

To the right lay a broad meadow below which a small river accompanied the road – well no, actually it was flowing the other way. Beside it was a modest railway line and behind that rose a broad sweep of brown field in which the young green corn was beginning to sprout. Just a field it was, but its extremities were edged with tall leafless trees, their twiggy outlines spread sharply against the sky. Among them jackdaws, black as commas on a page, swooped and played, clunking conversationally to each other.

To the left the road led towards steep wooded chalk hills, and over the top of it all arched a bright blue sky, singing with larks.

The February air was cold and in dark places under the trees and hedgerows a faint bloom of white told of last night's frost –

there's nothing in the telling of this that could impart the huge sense of freedom and escape that I and my legs felt that morning.

I said: 'It'll be a long walk.'

They replied: 'Just leave it to us. Leave it to us, and sing.'

So I sang, and on they went, rejoicing.

The valley narrowed in as we reached the wooded hills. There the houses were stacked right into the valley wall and behind them patches of white showed places where the hillside had slipped and become a cliff. The main road swung to the right here, following the river, but I found a pub and bought two cheese rolls and a bottle of beer. My legs wouldn't let me stay and sit, so we took a small road to the left. This led into and along a tree-lined valley past old houses set deep in their gardens and on upwards, into the folds of the downs, following the lines of their smooth shapes in curves and swings, past clumps of dark evergreens sheltering in valleys, and copses of tall bare beech trees clinging to the slopes. Then we took a broad, steep, well-worn track, white chalk in close velvety turf, that led on up the smooth back of the hill, through a clump of mixed beech and evergreens and out on to the top, where three roe deer were standing, gazing at me in rapt astonishment before bounding away.

This was the top of the world. There I stood face to face with the sun and could look down on a miniature England and see a silver railway-line snaking through the shadowy valley where fields and hedges and villages squatted in the hazy light, quite still among the smooth hills.

Beyond, beneath the sun, the haze was luminous as on a summer's evening, with only subtle tones to show more hills and plains lying in the distance. But the sun itself was quite clear of the haze and bright as summer ... hot!

'This is it,' said my legs, 'make the most of it.'

So I did, took off my shirt and vest and lay on a soft south-facing slope of turf. I chewed my cheese rolls, drank my beer and with the sun lighting up my closed eyelids, I slept, my arms spread wide, surrounded, held and warmed by the golden light.

Not for very long. It was February. A small wind which had

scooped a little air from some dark frosted corner sent me no more than a single breath.

I shivered and sat up. The sun was already shifting apologetically down into the haze. 'Don't worry,' I said. 'You did well.'

I scrambled into my vest, shirt, pullover and jacket and was for a stately saunter, but my legs wanted to run. And they did, straight down the hill, bounding from hump to hillock, whizzing through small copses and slithering down the skiddy bits where strangely shaped white pebbles with holes through them lay among the chalk chips.

By the time we reached the black and white hotel beside the river the valley was already in shadow, and the rest of that day has fallen from my memory. No doubt the Southern Railway provided a branch line to take me to Waterloo.

Perhaps the place was magic. I know that Box Hill spurred Keats to write the last five hundred lines of *Endymion* in record time. I wouldn't be surprised if the same Spirits and Speculations that inspired him in 1817 were still about in 1943.

Magic or not, something was changed in me that day. Perhaps I had turned away from worry and badgering and not being sure, and had found broad space and clarity. There was no going back on that and if the world didn't suit? Well then, I would make another one.

The next day I went to college and found that everything was going on as usual in the Foundation Class, including the shirt-patterns. I was pleased to find that my absence had not been noticed.

Then, one morning, as I was sitting at a table in the canteen drinking tea, a rather worried-looking young man came up to me and said: 'Good morning, my name is Bruce. I am a painting student.' I rose, we shook hands. I invited him to sit down and we had a perfectly ordinary conversation. He was a painter. His mind and heart were deeply involved in the art of painting, in form, space and colour. He told me his father was a taxi driver and that he was an anarchist, a great admirer of the work of Herbert Read.

Bruce seemed to be a careful, baffled sort of chap, but passionate and definitely his own man, answerable finally to himself.

Next time we met, at the same table, other members of the painting class came and talked, including a tall attractive girl whose name was Dorothy. We met many times and although I can't remember what we all talked about, I know the conversation was both respectful and emotional, in that everything was real and everything mattered enough to be savoured and thought about carefully.

It was a time for such things. My season ticket allowed me to break my journey in the centre of London, so I haunted the National Gallery where the War Artists' paintings were on show, and the bookshops, where I remember buying copies of T. S. Eliot's newly published *Four Quartets* (paper, one shilling (5p) each) and being deeply but incomprehensibly moved by them. In those days my response to everything I saw or read was immediate, intense and complete, not clouded by doubt or muddled by fashion.

I discovered music. Big music, like Beethoven's third symphony, which sang of glory and tragedy, swept through me like a forest fire. I bought a set of second-hand 78rpm records of it and played them at full volume on the huge mahogany electric radiogram in the long room, sometimes with my head close to the loudspeaker as if to get inside the music, sometimes leaping about the room like a balletic orang utan. I found ancient, scratchy one-sided (80rpm) records of Enrico Caruso that my parents had bought new when they were young. These filled me with a heartrending excitement and delight that no later recordings by other great singers would ever match. Dvořák's ninth symphony, hackneyed perhaps today, sang to me then of breezes combing the cornfields, of birds swooping in sunlight and of life, rolling, ongoing, joyous life. I knew every note by heart and it could be heard, somewhere in my head, through all that golden idiotic time.

There really must have been something golden about the spring of 1943, at least in Kingston and along the banks of the Thames, because, and I remember this quite clearly, the sun shone all the time.

Dorothy, who was just as uncomfortable in her ordinary world as I was in mine, became my companion and girlfriend (though, sensibly perhaps, not my lover) and we went to find our other world. We would turn and walk softly out of the unseeing College, slink down the path by the Hogsmill stream, cross the main road and walk hand in hand along the banks of the Thames. The pictures I have of that time are full of ease and forgetfulness. We bought cherries in Kingston market and flicked the stones from the bridge. Sometimes we hired a punt and poled up the river to lie shady under the overhanging willows. We fed ducks and when the water was high we tickled the edge of it until small fishes rose to nibble our fingers.

Dreaming, we wandered through royal parks and along riverside paths, invaded timber barges and explored strange unused grounds where broken walls were lost in thickets of alder. For long sun-soaked hours we would lie in private clumps of tall grass, kissing and cuddling and talking of brave, absurd ambitions in the making of our world, a world that would unplug itself from civilization so that it could start again. There was no aggression in these dreams, some derision perhaps but no hate against authority, only a gentle wish to be away from it.

To show that I was serious, I formally left home. With a small tent, a sleeping bag and a book of poems, we took up residence under some trees beside the River Mole. A small boy in a boat rowed in to talk to us and share our tin of baked beans, heated up on a tiny bonfire of broken boxes. It was nice to have our own place where we could entertain friends. Later Dorothy went home and I slept there in the tent. But, though I packed everything together into a bundle and hid the bundle high in the branches of a tree before leaving for College the next morning, by nightfall it was all stolen. So I went home.

Once or twice I took Dorothy to Finchley for weekends to meet the family. This wasn't a very welcome gesture. Daisy did her best to have chats with her but Ray was icily polite, visibly, and I suspect intentionally, failing to hide his contempt behind a charade of over-elaborate courtesy. I think this must have made me angry because I remember telling Ray and Daisy that Dorothy and I were thinking of getting married. Daisy said: 'Don't be ridiculous.' So I told Dorothy I was thinking of asking her to marry me and she said: 'Don't be ridiculous.' So I didn't raise the subject again.

Term ended. Ray and Daisy, gluttons for punishment, took their two adolescent sons to the Lake District for a wet summer holiday in a boarding house. The holiday was uneasy and we were glad to return to Finchley, where I found an order to attend a Medical Board examination prior to my being called up. This I did and was pronounced A1; entirely fit for service.

Nothing further happened, so I returned to the art college and tried to pick up where I had left off, but somehow, for both Dorothy and myself, the steam seemed to have gone out of our hopes for new worlds.

At about the same time my college work had become more comfortable, or at least more interesting. I had been promoted from the Foundation Class and the shirt patterns to the Drawing Class with real people to draw. There, somewhat to my surprise, I very much enjoyed the life-drawing sessions and found the process fascinating and deeply concentrating. I'm sorry to say I came eventually to disagree quite profoundly with Mr Hockey, the drawing teacher. His recommended method of drawing figures was to analyse the separate forms of the model's body and fit them together like pieces of subtle dough, with all the angles and curves carefully shaped. The end product was a very correct-looking body which seemed to me to have about as much life as a piece of shaped dough. I wanted to do a drawing that had some life to it. For a long time I was turning out stilted, unsatisfactory work and then, one afternoon, it all fell into place.

This happened in a rather unexpected way. I liked to draw in ink but, in the middle of the war, I couldn't find a pen which exactly suited my purpose, so I made one. It was carved from bamboo and it worked quite well, giving a line which, as the nib dried out, became lighter in tone. Unfortunately I couldn't find an ink which had any richness of colour, so in the end I collected some pebbles, an old caviare-pot, a handful of apple-wood soot and some gum-arabic, and made a crude grinder, driven by an old gramophone motor. After several hours of grinding and straining I achieved about a thimbleful of very black ink that thinned out to a scrumptious walnutty tone.

That afternoon I was really only trying out the new ink, concentrating on the way it was working, when I suddenly noticed that the drawings which my hand was doing – a set of quick sketches of a mountainous Frenchman called M. Letailleur – were good. They were full of life, exactly the sort of drawing I had been hoping and trying to do all along. Mr Hockey, bless him, cheered me on and for the rest of the afternoon my hand was directly connected to my heart and could do no wrong.

Those drawings told me something important. This was that on that afternoon the capacity to draw had been *liberated* as an effect of the fact that my anxious unconfident conscious mind was otherwise engaged in technical matters. This showed that my capacity to draw did in fact exist and had been waiting there, and also that it had worked well *simply because* I had spent so many hours painstakingly training my hand until it had become physically capable of putting down on paper exactly what my heart was telling it to – without having to consult my head on the way. That is a marvellous feeling, something I expect musicians come to when, after much practice, they no longer have to think about what their fingers are doing and can just play the music.

I could see that in the past, when I had been drawing or painting, there had always been a temptation waiting beside me, a temptation to latch on to spontaneous effects that were in fact accidental (and had really only happened as a result of my failing to do exactly what I had intended) and, because they were attractive, keep them and pretend to myself that I had meant them. That made nonsense of the original intention while at the same time allowing me to get away with slovenly work. I began to understand what the art master at Dartington had meant when he wrote in my report that my efforts were *'aimless work that could be described as a slow disintegration of an idea into a pleasant façade'*.

That afternoon and those few, not really all that marvellous, drawings repaid all the frustration and muddled thinking that had gone before. I felt that I had begun to understand what I was doing at the College and could, at last, begin to feel at ease there.

It was a bit late to be feeling at ease anywhere.

I went to the canteen for a cup of tea and told Bruce that I was waiting to be called up. He thought for a few moments before answering. Then he said: 'You aren't going, are you?'

I heard myself answer: 'No.'

'They'll put you in clink,' he said.

'I expect so.'

There didn't seem to be a lot more to be said at that moment, so I finished my tea, said goodbye and went away.

There was in fact a great deal to be said and it was being said, loudly, inside my head. I had heard myself answer 'No' and from that moment a thundering row had been going on. There was no doubt that I had meant what I said, but why had I just blurted it out like that without proper consultation?

'What d'you mean, proper consultation? We've been thinking about it for weeks.'

'Yes, but you know what our thinking is like. It's all muddle and fancy. You know it is.'

'This isn't. And anyway, it's true. I'm not going to join the army.'

'But they'll call you a coward; shoot you.'

'I don't think so.'

'They'd have every right to.'

'That's true. That's very true.'

'So what are you going to do?'

'I suppose I had better tell Ray and Daisy.'

Telling my parents turned out not to be as difficult as I had feared. Daisy's reactions were essentially practical. She simply said: 'But you can't. You've already had the Medical Examination.' I replied that I didn't think that would make a lot of difference, just make things a bit more complicated.

Ray's reactions were also quite straightforward. Speaking from the point of view of a conscientious objector in the First World

War, he told me why he wasn't one in this war, giving reasons which I respected. I tried to tell him what I was thinking but I remember feeling that the case I was making sounded pretty muddled and lame.

Ray made no attempt to argue with me and we simply discussed my situation. He said he thought there would be some 'procedures for the treatment of conscientious objectors' laid down, and he recommended me to consult the Quakers, who had helped him a lot in the First World War. I was relieved and grateful for this and very touched because he had, perhaps for the first time, actually listened to what I had to say. I felt I had been treated as a grown-up.

What he and Daisy really felt I don't know. Neither of them showed any sign of ordering me out of the house, never to darken their doors again, but I hadn't seriously thought they would. The tradition of dissent in both their lives was too well established for them to bother with gestures like that.

John observed, almost in passing, that in a country whose survival depended on food brought in by ship and whose ships were regularly being torpedoed by U-boats, there was no reason to assume that society would feel obliged to feed people who were not contributing – a thought which was never out of my head, and probably never will be.

The aunts were, I think, fairly noncommittal, though Nell, I remember, denounced me, not for being a conscientious objector but for being fanciful and changing my mind.

My call-up papers came in November, instructing me to report to the Household Cavalry at Combermere Barracks in Windsor on the ninth of December.

I collected a leaflet from the Peace Pledge Union which outlined the procedure. I would have to join the unit and refuse to put on uniform. The army would then court-martial me and send me to a civil prison. From there I would go before a tribunal.

I wrote to the Commanding Officer of the Household Cavalry at Windsor, politely letting him know that I would not be joining his regiment on the day appointed but that in order to avoid inconvenience I would present myself for arrest at the gates of

Combermere Barracks at 11.30 in the morning of 13 December 1943.

On the thirteenth of December I packed a small bag, said quite a fond goodbye to my parents, and took the North London Railway from Finchley Road to Windsor.

My goodness, that was a slow railway! I sat in an empty unheated compartment in an antique train that must have crawled into twenty little stations in cold dismal suburbs I had never heard of, and at each one I said to myself: 'Oh please, may I get off here and just go home?'

Eventually the train reached Windsor and, on leaden legs, I made my way to Combermere Barracks, where, at 11.30 a.m. precisely, wearing a brown raincoat, I stood outside the gates and waited.

III. Uncertainties.

Nothing happened. I stood at the gates of the barracks, duly making myself available for arrest, by appointment, as arranged, and, dammit, nobody came to arrest me! I was affronted. I had travelled a long dreary way and I was cold. Also the hope that it might all be a mistake, that I had got the day wrong, that they had decided not to do it after all, was bounding about inside me like an unruly dog. It was all a bit bloody much!

Then I saw an armoured car, a vehicle like a small tank with wheels, coming towards me. The officer in charge was standing high in the turret looking around him.

'That's a bit elaborate!' I thought.

The armoured car drove straight past me. 'Thank you very much,' I said.

So then I did what I should have done in the first place: just walked in through the gates. Nobody stopped me. The nearest building looked like a guardhouse. I peered in through a window and saw a soldier sitting at a desk.

I tapped on the window. He looked up and waved to me to come in through the door, which was open.

'Hallo,' I said, 'I've arrived.'

'Yes?'

'I've come to give myself up.'

He looked up. 'To give yourself what?' he asked.

'Up.'

'Up what?'

'No, not exactly.'

'You've come to join up?'

'No, not really.'

'Got any papers?'

'Papers?'

'Look, you can't join the army if you haven't got the proper papers.'

'No, I'm not here to join the army.'

'What then?'

'I'm here *not* to join the army.'

The soldier thought about this for a moment. Then he said: 'You know, I'd have thought you would have been better off doing that somewhere else.'

'Oh, dear,' I said. 'May I sit down?'

'Help yourself.'

I sat down on a folding chair and tried to marshal my thoughts.

'I have come here to be arrested,' I said, quite slowly.

The soldier looked at me in silence. Then he picked up the telephone. 'Got a right one here, sir,' he said. 'Civvy. Says he's come to be arrested ... Sir ... Sir!' He put his hand over the mouthpiece. 'Duty Officer's compliments, and by whom was you wishing to be arrested?'

'The Household Cavalry ... I thought. I thought it was all arranged. I wrote to ...'

'... Hang on, hang on!' The soldier spoke into the telephone. 'Household Cavalry, sir ... Right, sir ... Sir!'

He put down the receiver. 'Orders is to arrest you, if you insist, only Major Whatton-Burby says why don't you just push off out of it?'

That certainly was a temptation, but ... 'No,' I said, regretfully, 'I think I'd better stay.'

'Please yourself. Perhaps you'd come this way.'

The soldier ushered me into a cell at the end of the guardroom. There were three truckle-beds in it, each with a mattress, grey blanket and dark-grey shiny pillow.

'I'll leave the door unlocked, if you don't mind. Less formal, if you know what I mean.'

'Thank you.'

'Cup of tea?'

'Ta! That'd be nice.'

I sat on one of the beds. The soldier brought me a mug of very sweet tea. 'Make yourself at home. There's plenty of time.'

He was right about that. Nothing happened. Well, no. At dinner time he brought me bangers and mash with Brown Sauce on an enamel plate and, later, he rather diffidently accompanied me to the door of the WC out at the back. 'Regulations,' he said. 'Persons in custody.'

'Of course,' I said. 'Got to be careful.'

'S'right.'

After lunch I put my feet up. The shiny dark-grey patina on the pillow seemed most likely to be impacted Brylcreem or something of the sort. I decided it wasn't dangerous and put my head on it. I hoped I would doze off.

'Warner's pissed off again!'

I sat up with a jerk. Gales of laughter were coming from the guardroom.

'He's not! How'd 'e do it?'

'Slipped off detail. Spud-bashing. Hopped it.'

'Be down the Dilly by now!'

'What's doing? Sending after him?'

'No such luck. Major says: leave it to the Redcaps.'

'Pity. Could have done with an airing.'

'Yeh.'

Then quiet again for about three hours. The day grew dark.

The sound of steps outside. Stamping, muffled shouts. The guard detail was called to attention. Louder stamping noises. The soldier marched into the cell, followed by an officer.

'Pris'ner .. Shun!' he bawled.

I began to get up off the bed.

'Oh, no need for that,' said the officer kindly.

'No trouble,' I said, 'no trouble at all.'

I stood up, attentively.

'Ah, er . . .' The officer seemed embarrassed. 'Could I perhaps have your name, please?'

'Richard Oliver Postgate.'

'Oh.' He looked at a notebook.

'I wrote to the Commanding Officer,' I said.

'Did you? . . . Colonel Sir Alastair Mews?'

'I don't know the name.'

'He'll be in the Cairngorms.'

'Ah,' I said.

'Well, er. Can you sort of put me in the picture?' he suggested. 'Please, do sit down.'

We sat on separate beds and I told him that I had been supposed to report on the 9th but didn't because I was a conscientious objector, and had been advised that in order to save inconvenience I should present myself for arrest at a later date.

'That's extremely civil,' he said, and laughed slightly, perhaps at the thought of its not being military.

'What exactly are you to be arrested for?'

'Being absent without leave?' I suggested.

'Oh, yes. Yes, of course. Well, that should be no problem. You were supposed to be here last week, then?'

'That's right.'

'So you'll be on the intake roster for the 9th and posted as not-arrived, absent without leave?'

'I dare say.'

'Well, that's fine, then,' said the officer, standing up. 'We'll just do the paperwork for that and I'll, er, leave you to it.'

'Thank you,' I said.

'Carry on, Corpr'l-o'-th'Horse.'

'Sir!' The guard detail stood to attention as he left.

Later there was shepherd's pie and baked beans. Later still there was more stamping and a tiny officer, accompanied by a huge

Corporal of the Horse, appeared. The officer couldn't have been more than about fifteen years old.

He looked up at me. 'Any complaints?' he piped.

'No, no, I don't think so, everything's fine, really . . .' I began, but he had already turned round and walked out before I'd even begun to speak.

I was furious. A great rage welled up inside me. The rudeness! The appalling impertinence of that fancy-dressed twerp! I marched to the other end of the cell and viciously kicked one of the beds, hurting my foot. That gave me something to swear about.

Nothing more happened, except a mug of cocoa and a quick supervised wash out at the back. There was absolutely nothing wrong, everybody had been most courteous. That tiny officer was probably a boy from the OTC of one of the local schools, like for instance Eton. I couldn't think why I had got into such a rage at him. Looking back I can see why. I was just petrified.

Back in the cell I used my spare vest as a pillowcase, and kept my underclothes and socks on under my pyjamas. Just as well I did, it was a cold night. I doubled the blanket on one of the beds and climbed under it.

'You'd better sleep,' I said to myself, without much hope of it happening. I was wrong about that. I must have fallen asleep almost at once.

Through my dreams I heard stamping feet. A door slammed open. A voice shouted: 'Pris'ner SHUN!'

A bright electric light bulb was shining in the cell.

'Pris'ner SHUN!' roared a soldier standing by the doorway.

I sat up. 'Yes, right-ho, hang on a minute.'

A different tiny officer marched in. 'Any complaints?' he piped.

'Oh, er well, no. I've only just woken up as a matter of fact. You don't happen to know what time it is, do you?'

But he was gone.

The soldier remained. I didn't recognize him.

'Good morning,' I said, 'if it is morning?'

'ABLUTIONS!' he shouted.

'Oh yes?'

'C'mon! UP! UP! UP! UP!' he punctuated this by smacks on the blanket with a short leather-covered stick he was carrying. 'UP! UP! UP! UP!'

I jumped out of bed.

'Right! Out the BACK! One-two, one-two, one-two!'

I grabbed my towel and walked quickly out to the wash-house. The soldier followed close behind shouting 'One-two, one-two . . . Come on! Get at it now!'

'I'll have a pee first, if you don't mind.'

'There'll be no Pee-if-you-don't-mind where you're going! Get at it now! I haven't got all day.'

I washed as quickly as I could, which was very quickly because it was dark, outside, December, cold water and no soap. The soldier started shouting again and I walked back to the cell, taking care not to walk in time to his shouts. This was quite a different soldier from the one who had been there the day before. This one was podgy-fat with a shiny white face and a mean-looking moustache.

I went into the cell. He slammed the door shut and locked it.

The cell was dark. There was no sound from the guardroom. I had no idea what the time was. I felt for my clothes and got dressed. I stood there in the dark, feeling very cold and wondering what to do. I got back into bed again.

This treatment was more like what I had been expecting. There was absolutely no reason why the army should be courteous and accommodating to me and quite a lot of reason why it should feel hostile and unaccommodating. The important thing, I thought, was that I should behave courteously and accommodatingly to the army, while making it clear that I was doing so by choice, not because I had given way to the impulse to obey when shouted at. It was all very well my deciding what I had to do, quite another thing to do it.

'The bugger's gone back to bed!'

The door slammed open. 'UP! UP! UP!'

I scrambled out of bed.

'He's got all his bloody clothes on! Slovenly! That's what you are! You're a disgrace, lying in bed all day!'

'What else was I supposed to do?'

'Stand to attention when you speak to me!'

'. . . No,' I said, and sat down on the bed.

'Oh!' said the Corporal of the Horse. 'Like that, is it? Having a tantrum, are we? Well, you'll see. You'll see.'

He turned on his heel and marched out, slamming the door. I sat exactly where I was, trembling, but at the same time feeling that making the gesture of defiance hadn't really been very difficult.

The day grew lighter. I grew hungry. Through a spy-hole in the door I could see a table with a plate of fried bread with baked beans on top. Eventually I heard the Corporal of the Horse say he was going out. Then one of the other soldiers nipped in with the plate and a mug of tea.

'He's a hard one,' explained the soldier, 'Corp'ral-o'-th'-Horse Morris. You want to keep out of his way.'

'Fat chance I'll have of doing that.'

'Fat chance any of us have. Mind out!'

He slipped out and locked the door as the Corporal returned.

Cold baked beans on cold fried bread was not my favourite breakfast but I ate every scrap. Then I lay on, but not in, the bed.

Apart from a supervised visit to the WC, nothing happened for several hours. The day began to darken.

Then the door slammed open.

'Pris'ner Shun!'

I sat on the edge of the bed, waiting for somebody to appear.

'On your feet!'

'What for?'

''Cause you're insanitary. That's what for.'

'Insanitary?'

'On your feet! You're going to be dealt with. You're a disgrace. Come on. One-two, one-two, one-two. Right turn.'

I walked out of the cell, through the guardroom and into the cold air of the yard. It was a dismal day.

'Straight ahead. One-two, one-two . . .'

'Yes, all right. Don't keep shouting.'

'You'll be shouting, where you're going.'

We came to a door in a wall.

'Open the door and enter,' ordered the corporal.

I opened the door and entered; into what looked like a hairdresser's saloon without the advertisements.

'No nonsense now! Sit in the chair.'

'What if I say no?' I asked.

'In the chair, one-two, one-two.'

'What if you were to say please?'

'Don't come that stuff with me. You're a disgrace. Lying about all day with your hair down over your ears. A bit of self-respect, that's what you need.'

While saying this the Corporal of the Horse did not lay hands on me. Holding his arms tight to his sides, he bumped me with his belly towards and into the chair. I sat down.

The hairdresser deftly covered me with the white apron.

'How do you like it, sir?' he asked.

'Oh, high on top, I think, with a blue rinse.' We both roared with laughter. The Corporal glared. The hairdresser snipped.

The wind was cold about my shorn ears as we walked back to the cell. Later another midget officer came asking for complaints. I mentioned to him the hippo in the WC but he was on his way.

Then all was quiet for what seemed like several hours. Lunch having been overlooked, I was very hungry. I was also agitated, pacing up and down. I wished something would happen, like for instance, supper.

Supper didn't appear, Warner did. Having been recaptured by the Redcaps, he was marched into the cell by Corporal of the Horse Morris.

'Oh, look!' he cried, 'And there's this gorgeous boy to keep me company. Oooh, you are *darlings*!' The door was slammed.

Warner flopped down on one of the beds. 'I have had the most *awful* day,' he announced. 'There was this lovely man, rich as Christmas cake and not a bit kinky, well, except . . . you know. And you see, there we were, in this rather pretty bar, him in his Homburg hat and twinkly eyes and me with my rubber fronts in, and we were doing fine, just sort of getting around to the real questions, when in came these four Redcaps and literally dragged me out, without a word! I mean, it was humiliating. All I could do was wave!'

Warner stopped speaking and looked at me. He was a fairly ordinary-looking young man wearing a crumpled uniform. He had a smooth face with traces of mascara around the eyes.

He said: 'I'm rabbiting on again. Lionel Warner, Trooper, of this regiment, God help it.'

'Oliver Postgate.' We shook hands.

He said: 'You're in a right two-and-eight, aren't you?'

I nodded, unable to speak.

Warner said: 'Listen. Don't take any notice of me. I'm all mouth! I mean, I'm, well . . . you know.'

I nodded.

'Right,' he said. 'Well, anyway, what I'm saying is . . .' He seemed embarrassed. 'Er . . . you don't have to worry.'

'Oh . . . thanks.'

'You've got other things to worry about, I dare say.'

'A bit, yes.'

'Tell me.'

I gave him a brief rundown on my situation and prospects.

He listened in silence, then he said: 'Hmm. It *sounds* all right. Quite a long journey, though. You could hit trouble on the way. But I'll tell you one thing: you're in the right place, here.'

'Am I?'

'Oh, yes. This lot, they're ornamental. All spit and polish and do it by the book. They're all into careers and they are dead scared 'cause if they put a foot wrong, just once, they'll be posted to the Second Regiment in North Africa. You've only got to threaten them with the "proper procedures" and you'll have them eating out of your hand. So don't worry! Come on, smile!'

I smiled. 'I could do with eating out of something. I'm ravenous.'

'Now that,' said Warner, 'will be attended to. I have friends in high places. I have but to rub the lamp and behold . . . Oh dear! There should be a puff of green smoke and a crash of cymbals.'

Nothing happened, but a few minutes later the door opened softly and a soldier slipped in carrying two plates of dinner.

'Sorry I'm late,' he said. 'Morris was everywhere. I'm afraid they're a bit untidy, the dinners, but I got three from the cook-house and sort of amalgamated them. Guessed you'd be hungry.'

'You were right,' I said. 'Ta!'

I don't remember what the food was but I wolfed it down.

Later there was cocoa and decorous, supervised ablutions.

'Ugh!' said Warner, with feeling. 'That's the one thing I can't stand about this place, the black pillows.'

'I've got a hanky you could have,' I suggested.

'No, don't bother.'

'It's no trouble. At least it's clean.'

I gave him my spare clean handkerchief. He laid it carefully on his grimy pillow.

'That's nice,' he said. 'Be of good cheer.'

'You too. Good night, Lionel.'

'Good night, Oliver.'

In the morning he wasn't there any more. Vanished as if he had never existed. But he had. The hanky had been folded and was tucked under my pillow.

Corporal of the Horse Morris opened the door.

'Where's Warner gone?' I asked.

'Mind your own business,' he replied.

I could have hit him. But I didn't, which was probably just as well.

This was the beginning of another day, one which was interesting only because I was taken to the cook-house to do some spud-bashing and had a pleasant chat with a nice lady cook called Mrs Murch.

I was taken back to the guardhouse and in the evening I told yet another tiny officer about the wallaby under the washbasin, but he didn't seem to mind.

The next day the Duty Officer I had met on the first day popped in to sit on the bed and check a few details. He said that absent without leave wasn't a sufficient charge on its own. I explained that that was just the hors d'oeuvre. The next move would be to charge me with refusing to put on uniform. He seemed to get the hang of that and pottered away.

Another day passed and the following afternoon Corporal of the Horse Morris and another soldier marched in.

'Come on! Smarten up a bit! Can't you do something about your personal appearance?'

'What for?'

'Interview.'

'What interview?'

'Never you mind. Do something about your hair.'

I combed my hair and shook out the jacket I had been lying on. I retied my tie. 'How do I look?'

'Horrible. Have to do. Come on, outside! One-two, one-two . . .'

Morris and the other soldier marched one each side of me, across the yard and into the main door of a big building. I found I had great difficulty in not walking in step with them, but I managed it.

They marched me up the stairs and into a room where a very senior-looking officer was sitting writing at a big desk. I finished up standing in front of the desk with Morris directly behind me.

The officer looked up. He was elderly, with full walrus whiskers.

'You are 306346 Trooper Postgate, R. O.'

'No.'

'Stand tattention! Address supiorofficers SIR!' barked Morris, prodding me in the kidneys with his stick.

'My name is Oliver Postgate.'

'Address supiorofficers SIR!' prodded Morris.

Colonel Walrus and I looked at each other balefully for a moment.

'I would be very happy to address you as sir, if you'd like me to,' I said, 'but it's a bit difficult to think straight while that chap behind me keeps prodding me with his stick.' (Or words to that effect. Let me not give the impression that I was cool and calm. I was practically speechless.)

Colonel Walrus flicked a glance at Morris. Then he spoke.

'Trooper 306346 Postgate, R. O. You have been medically examined by the appropriate Medical Board and found fit for combatant service with His Majesty's Forces. Consequently you are now deemed to be a soldier. Do you understand that?'

'I hear what you say but I don't agree that it is so.'

'Whether or not you agree is immaterial. You are deemed to be a soldier and you are required to wear the appropriate uniform. Consequently I order you to go into another room and don the said uniform.'

'Pris'ner SHUN!'

I was conducted to an adjoining room which had four chairs and a table in it. A uniform was laid out on the table.

'Come along, then! Get it on!'

I sat on one of the chairs. The two soldiers stood over me.

'Oh, come on,' said Morris quite kindly, 'make it easy for yourself. Put it on.'

'No, I don't think I will, thanks.'

I sat for about five minutes. Then Morris said: 'Do you refuse, then?'

'That's right.'

They led me back to Colonel Walrus. He repeated the order, with variations. I was led away again. This time we all sat in the chairs.

The third time, as we entered the room with the uniform, Morris asked: 'Are you going to?'

'No.' So we just turned round and came out again.

'Trooper Postgate,' said Colonel Walrus, 'you have three times been given a legitimate order by a superior officer and three times you have refused to obey that order. So you are charged with insubordination and will be dealt with accordingly. You understand?'

'Er ... yes.'

'Dismiss!'

'Pris'ner SHUN! About turn. One-two, one-two.'

'... Oh and by the way,' said Colonel Walrus.

We stopped in the doorway.

'It'll take a day or two to set up, but I think we've got the drift of it. Did you do anything about a Friend?'

'Friend?'

'The prisoner may have either a defending officer or a Prisoner's Friend.'

'Oh, I see. I haven't thought about that. I can't think of anybody I would actually think of as a friend. Trooper Warner is a pleasant sort of chap but, you know . . . sir.'

At this Corporal of the Horse Morris gave a snort of laughter and nipped smartly out of sight behind the door.

Colonel Walrus said: 'It should be somebody from outside, don't you think? You chappies have some sort of organization, don't you? Isn't there a society of some sort?'

'There's the Society of Friends, sir. They're Quakers.'

'Society of *Friends*, eh? Sounds ideal.'

'I think they have a Meeting in Windsor. Or there's Friends' House, that's their sort of Head Office, in the Euston Road.'

'Well, that'll be it, then, won't it? Off you go.'

'Pris'ner SHUN!'

The next day was a Saturday, which was uneventful. Then on Sunday afternoon a rather nervous young man came to call. He was a Friend from Windsor Meeting. He had come to offer to be my Prisoner's Friend for the forthcoming court martial. We went through the procedures together. It all seemed fairly cut and dried and there wouldn't be a lot for him to do if all went according to plan.

The court martial went quite smoothly. Four officers sat behind a table, Colonel Walrus and two other oldish ones and a young one who was very quiet and seemed anxious. The charge was read out. I pleaded guilty and was sentenced to three months' imprisonment.

It was all over in a few minutes and we were led away. Corporal of the Horse Morris, almost affable, gave my Friend and me mugs of tea by the guardroom stove. Then we shook hands and our Meeting was over. The Corporal and I watched him go.

'By the way,' I said, 'what did happen to Warner?'
'Pissed off again,' said the Corporal.

IV. Absurdities.

I had worked out what prison was going to be like. After the uncertainties of the Guards' barracks I thought it would be a pleasure to have a quiet cell of my own and live a well-ordered life with perhaps a few mailbags to sew.

I was wrong about that. My time in the nick turned out to be far from quiet. I was delivered to Feltham Juvenile Prison, where the inmates, of any age, wore short trousers and were paraded outside in the freezing wind. I was taken to a place called West Tech., which was a large disused classroom containing thirteen bed-boards. This was where the conscientious objectors were housed.

The 'conchies' were thirteen young men of markedly different characters and backgrounds. As far as I remember there were two Quakers, two Seventh-Day Adventists, two Plymouth Brethren, one Church of England evangelist, three Jehovah's Witnesses and three non-religious persons, one of whom was an educational psychology student, another a cinema projectionist from Swansea and the last was me.

Each of the religious sects was visited once a week by its minister, who conducted whatever service was appropriate in the side room. The Quaker visitor was a very kind, warm-hearted man who quaffed his mug of prison cocoa with gusto and said: 'Ah! that was good!' This was a hearty, well-meant gesture, but unconvincing. The cocoa was indisputably foul.

The other services took place in private, though I did once inadvertently go into the side room where the Jehovah's Witnesses were conferring with their minister, who wore a trilby hat. I was intrigued to observe that they were huddled together, underlining selected passages in their Bibles in red ink, and chuckling with glee.

One evening, the Prison Governor came into West Tech. He said: 'Anybody here know anything about the theatre?'

Like a fool, I said: 'I do, a bit.'

The next morning I found myself in the Governor's Office, accompanied by a principal officer, who was a sort of sergeant-major of the 'screws'. To his disgust the Governor invited me to take a seat in his nicely furnished office while he outlined his scheme.

The Governor, a crisp-voiced upright man with a decisive manner, told me he had invited a local dramatic society to come to the prison in about three weeks' time to perform its current play, *Badger's Green*, by R. C. Sherriff, in the assembly hall of the prison, and that I was to prepare the stage.

'Ah, I see ... Yes. But I'm not exactly a free agent, sir.'

'No worry about that. You shall have a blue armband. That gives you access to all premises. The Institution has ample work-shop facilities and services. My officers have orders to give you every cooperation ... understood?

'Yes, sir,' I said.

'Understood, Mr Saunders?'

'Yessir!' barked the outraged Principal Officer.

'Right, then. Off you go!'

The Principal Officer marched me out of the office and along the corridor. 'What am I going to do about that, then?' I asked.

'I'll tell you what you're going to do, lad. You're going to watch it. That's what!'

'I'll have to do the job, though.'

'Frigging stupid if you ask me. Always coming up with these fart-arsed fancies. Gives me the squitters. Gives us all the squitters! All right, then. You can't bloody help it. I can't bloody help it. It's got to be bloody done.'

'Yes, I know that. But how do I set about bloody doing it ... sir?'

'That's your bloody problem, not mine. I give you a blue band, OK? I put the word about among my officers that you've got a charmed life, that you're carrying out the Governor's direct instructions and can dance through the place like the queen of the frigging fairies, OK?'

The officer took me to a store, where I received a blue armband.

'That's it then,' he said, 'I've done my bit, so if you come a cropper, don't come bloody snivelling to me.'

Mr Saunders walked away down the corridor, leaving me, an inmate, standing alone and free to follow my fancies, in the middle of one of His Majesty's Prisons, an institution created and administered solely for the purpose of preventing such activity.

As always there was no alternative but to have a go and, in the event, it worked out quite well. I was able to get some lighting rigged up and, apart from a couple of disasters, like blowing a sub-station fuse and getting myself accidentally locked in the assembly hall for the night (a fate which I avoided by ringing the Riot Bell), things came together very satisfactorily, and members of the prison staff, once they came to terms with the incongruity of it, enjoyed joining in with the project. I can see the Governor, in full dungarees, painting in a grove of cypresses and complaining that the house-painting brushes from the store were no good for detail work. I did suggest that I could nip into town and get some from the art shop. He was already putting his hand in his pocket for the money when he remembered there were reasons why that idea wasn't altogether practical.

Badger's Green was a pleasant play, but it was about the politics of village cricket. In the evening, when it was performed before the assembled felons, all my fears were realized. From the moment the curtain went up the audience greeted the play with cat-calls and made lewd contributions to the dialogue, some of which caused the jeune première to blush quite prettily – much to their delight. Later in the performance a semblance of order was restored, but only because the Governor and Principal Officers were silently patrolling the aisles.

After it was over I was back on hoeing carrots and laying tiles, which was almost a relief, but my sentence was nearly up and quite soon I was sitting in the Reception Block waiting for the van to take me to Wandsworth Prison, from where I would be taken to the Conscientious Objectors' Tribunal.

Mr Saunders, the Principal Officer, came past. He looked at me sitting on a bench. I was wearing handcuffs and not enjoying it at all.

'Ah,' he said. 'Given up being a genius, have we?'

'None of my doing,' I said.

'That's true.'

He spoke to the Transport Officer: 'This gentleman here's not a villain, he's a genius. Take the cuffs off.'

Wandsworth Prison was more like the sort of prison I had imagined – old, fairly dirty, fairly uncomfortable, quite impersonal, but peaceful. I did sew one or two mailbags but not very well. In any case I was only going to be there for the inside of a week in order that I could be escorted, in a taxi, wearing my own clothes (such luxury!) to the tribunal.

The tribunal was a fairly perfunctory occasion. In a large panelled room sat a number of people on folding chairs in front of three elderly people sitting at a table on a small raised platform.

When my turn came, one of them asked after my aunt Margaret, with whom he had been at Cambridge. I promised to give her his good wishes. The tribunal conferred and announced that I was to be discharged from His Majesty's Forces and sent to work under-ground in a coal-mine.

I didn't hear any of the next case because I was taken straight back to Wandsworth Prison and later that day put into a prison van, a Black Maria. It isn't possible to see where you are going in a Black Maria, so when I was finally set down I hadn't the slightest idea where I was.

However, with sinking heart, I recognized the place. It was Combermere Barracks in Windsor.

'What the hell are you doing here?' cried Corporal of the Horse Morris.

'Buggered if I know!'

'Cripes! I thought we'd seen the last of you!'

'Wish you had.'

My disappointment was as nothing to the embarrassment of the Household Cavalry. The Duty Officer came rushing over at once to explain to me that they were very sorry but they couldn't accommodate me in the guardroom cell because I had committed no offence. They couldn't put me in the dormitories with the men because I wasn't in uniform and, you know, not one of them, as you might say ... They couldn't send me back to prison because I had served my sentence and they couldn't discharge me because the papers hadn't come through.

'What am I supposed to do?'

'Jiggered if I know,' said the Duty Officer.

In the end they consulted the Quartermaster's storeman, who was an expert on improvisation. He put up a camp bed for me in the storeroom. As to what I should do with my time, nobody had any idea, nor any suggestions. I think they hoped I would dematerialize. So I just wandered about the barracks or did a bit of potato peeling for Mrs Murch. I don't think I was any trouble to anybody but I did feel a bit of a gooseberry standing about in my old mackintosh.

I think it was the next day that I came face to face with Colonel Walrus. For a moment I thought he was going to explode.

'What the blazes are you doing here?' he roared.

'Er ... Jiggered if I know,' I said. 'I seem to be sort of left over.'

'You're not being left over here!' said the Colonel. 'Why don't you push off out of it?'

'I'm not allowed to, am I?'

'Rubbish! Can't have you hanging about the place making it untidy. You're going on leave.'

'Good ... when?'

'Now! Immediately! This minute! Come along!'

We marched together, this time in step, to the guardroom. There the Colonel signed dockets.

'Here's an open rail warrant and a ten-bob note.'

'Thank you sir,' I said, and held out my hand.

He shook it firmly. 'Now push off!' he said.

I walked out of the gates and across the road to a phone box. I rang Daisy.

'I'm out,' I said.

'Oh, are you?' she replied. 'Will you be in to supper? It's only corned-beef hash, I'm afraid.'

I can sit here, fifty years on, and look back at that muddled, wilful young man, or rather, overgrown boy, of eighteen, trundling eagerly back to Finchley on that dreadful suburban railway, and I confess that as well as embarrassment (which really only comes from the fact that we still share the same life), I have a sneaking admiration for the oaf. He may have been wrong in what he did, and it is easy to say with hindsight that he was, but he saw what he thought was true and in a morass of doubt, guilt and fear, he stood by it. Oddly enough the times when he was most confused and unhappy came when he didn't know what to do next. Once he was committed and clear about the path he was going to take he was surprised to find in himself a previously unknown serenity of mind.

His view of the situation, one which I recognize and would, with some dull reservations, support, was much the same as that of his grandfather, George Lansbury. He saw that Hitler, though a monster, was a product of history – if you put a nation into the state of penury and shame that Germany was put into by the Treaty of Versailles, then a Hitler will rise to rekindle its anger and wreak vengeance on the world. Like his grandfather he could foresee no end-product of the war but another round of the cycle of oppression, retribution, aggression and devastation.

Although he was called, and sometimes even called himself, a pacifist, and although he would, I believe, have died rather than kill, he recognized in himself the instincts that fire the blood to battle and understood the general feeling of the time – that Hitler and fascism were an evil that, for the sake of freedom and democracy, must be fought and destroyed at any cost, even if that cost was the outright destruction of everything and everybody, by modern weapons used in the rage of battle. He wholeheartedly respected society's right to choose that course and did not campaign against it, scorn it, or harbour the illusion that pacifism could be seen as a popularly acceptable policy. Not being encumbered with absolute principles he had even admitted that if somebody had put a rifle in his hand and Hitler in the sights he would probably have pulled the trigger.

When, as I have often done, I confront him with this and say: 'If you would have done that why would you not fight?', I think he replies: 'Because of arithmetic. There are good ways to die and bad ways to die, some can give their lives gladly, some, perhaps most, are wholly innocent, not even knowing what the war is about. They have their lives unjustly torn from them. But in the end death is death and can be counted. Fifty million people were to die in that war. If I had killed Hitler personally many of those millions might have lived. If I had gone out and joined in the killing, then even more would have died, and for what? Was there ever a political cause that was worth the death of fifty million people and the destruction of an entire continent – with, as far as I could see, every likelihood that nothing would come of it at the end but another turn of the wheel and the next generation slaughtered?'

But I am putting words into his mouth. Perhaps he would say something simpler, like: 'You are old and you aren't remembering right. I was eighteen. I was not *sure* of anything except that I was being commanded to take a particular course which involved my having to go somewhere and kill people I had never met and had no quarrel with. I did have a choice. I could either do as I was told and kill them, or I could, if I was willing to take the consequences, refuse to do that. As an immediate decision was required I chose the option that did not involve killing people.'

In the event, as we have seen, the consequences I took were far from unpleasant. Even though I was frightened out of my wits, the procedure was conducted in a way that was unexpectedly considerate. That was a relief but, nevertheless, there was not a moment in that time when I was not aware, somewhere in my heart, that I had defied my country, had refused to come to its aid, and by that act had become a stranger.

By virtue of its inherent goodwill and kindness my country had allowed me to continue to live and eat. It had not only allowed me to stand by my convictions, it had respected them. After that I knew I could not, in good conscience, refuse to reciprocate that generosity; that I would always have to respect the convictions of others even though I might disagree with them. I don't expect I have managed to do that all my life, but I have never forgotten that I am living here as a guest, a welcome guest perhaps, but none the less a visitor. I don't regret this. It sets a good curb on righteousness.

There would be time for thoughts like that later. For now I was a free man, with ten bob and an open rail pass in my pocket, and I was heading for home and corned-beef hash.

4

RURAL PURSUITS

I. The Shires.

Ray and Daisy were glad to see me in one piece and the corned-beef hash was lovely. Corned-beef hash always is lovely, but in 1944 it was a rare delicacy.

For me the pleasure of being home and at liberty were tinged with uncertainty about what might be going to happen next. My guess was that the Ministry of Labour would now come after me quite swiftly and try to send me to the coal-mines.

This suspicion was alerted when, within days of my return, I received an instruction from the Ministry of Labour to attend for a medical examination but, as it turned out, I was mistaken about the purpose of the examination. The Medical Board kept me waiting all day, which was not unusual, but when they did examine me they did so very thoroughly for a long time, which *was* unusual. It seemed as if they were determined to find something wrong with me. In the end I grew weary and drew the doctor's attention to some slight adhesions under my shoulder-blades.

'Got it!' shouted the doctor. 'That will do. Thank you. Please get dressed now. Good afternoon.'

I later received from Dr Dunlop, our GP, who was associated with the Medical Board, the intriguing information that the Ministry of Labour had clipped a note to my file to the effect that it would be obliged if they would find something, anything, wrong with me which would confirm that I was unfit for work underground in the coal-mines.

I was grateful for that unexplained mercy but even so there was no certainty that the Ministry of Labour had really given up on me. I decided that my best move would be to get myself a job on a farm.

Daisy's brother Eric knew a family who kept a dairy farm in Dorset. He very kindly approached them and the farmer offered me a job as a general farm labourer for 35 shillings a week.

So, sometime in April 1944, I took my bike and my rucksack on the train to Sherborne in Dorset and started on my new career as a farm worker. As usual I had allowed myself to look into the future and had, in my mind's eye, seen the peaceful idyllic life of the English countryside with the lowing herd winding slowly o'er the lea, the ploughman plodding homeward in tune with the eternal rhythm of the seasons.

I was mistaken about that.

Bob, the farmer I had come to work for, was a thin tight-lipped man who ran everywhere and wouldn't look me in the eye. He was without humour and failed to respond to attempts at conversation. I persevered, but there was always an atmosphere of electric tension in the air, the sort that comes between people who have quarrelled. If he *had* to speak to me I saw his hands trembling as if with terror. It was clear that he genuinely and sincerely hated me. I was quite relieved when I discovered that he also hated almost everybody else.

I hoped to find some other friends, but the local people,

though not actually hostile, didn't want to have anything to do with me.

After a few months it suddenly occurred to me that I was a free man, that I didn't really have to go on with the wretched business if I didn't want to. So I gave Bob a week's notice and left. He didn't even bother to say goodbye, but I didn't expect him to.

I went home to Finchley for a few days and approached the Quakers to find out whether they would accept me for one of the Friends' Ambulance Units. They wouldn't, so I looked for another farm job. Once again I made the contact through friends of friends and found an informal job with Giles, a well-bred young man who was calling himself a farmer and growing some market-garden vegetables on some land near Oxford. Giles's heart wasn't in farming. It was in celebrating his manhood at sessions of rural dalliance with various young and not-so-young women who moved in to help with the farming.

I myself received offers of dalliance from one or two of the lady guests. These were flattering but I declined them, partly out of nervousness but mainly on the grounds that one stud bull on the premises was enough.

I think Giles took the same view, because he gave me a task which kept me well out of the way – clearing some acres of woodland below the house. He told me to go to the horse-sale and buy the cheapest strong-looking horse I could find and an old collar and chain that would just about last for the job of hauling out the cut wood.

The horse I chose looked fine to me but he was named, ominously, Rocket. I noticed, as I was walking him away from the sale, that the men in flat caps who had sold him to me were chuckling together, gleefully satisfied that they had found a sucker and unloaded a practically useless animal on to him.

They turned out to be wrong about that. Rocket soon became a good friend and we worked well together. He was happy to munch peacefully for as long as it took me to assemble a bundle of cut saplings and brushwood, but, once harnessed to it, he remembered his days with Ben Hur and charged off through the undergrowth at a wild gallop. The only way I could keep up was to ride the bundle, hauling at the reins and shouting. At the edge of the wood he would stop and hang his head, panting heavily while I undid the chain and carefully looped it over his back. The first couple of times I waited for him to recover his breath before walking back into the wood, but after that I left him there, telling him to follow me when he felt up to it – which he did, a few minutes later.

Rocket was also great at pulling out trees. I climbed as high as I could into the tree and hauled the chain up with a piece of washing line. I fixed it and led Rocket out until the chain was tight. Then, hauling on the washing line with all my might, I called him to do his bit. I think he took this as a personal challenge because he whinnied and, with nostrils flared, reared up like a charger, dropping his whole weight forward on to the collar and following it with all the power of his legs. The tree didn't stand a chance. It came over with a crunch and a crackle and he dragged it nonchalantly away.

I can see that with his temperament Rocket wouldn't have been much use for all-day plodding work as a farm horse, but I'm sure he could have had a great career in B-movies.

The year moved on. Without telling me Giles sold Rocket, so I left.

I tried the Friends' Ambulance Unit again, but without success. November was not a good month in which to look for agricultural work and as I had collected a small income-tax rebate – something like £8 – I decided to stay at home until the weather improved.

For years, perhaps for all my life, I had enjoyed thinking. When doing a traditional job, one which called for a lot of manual effort, I would often go off into a dream in which I would try to conjure up a tool or a machine that would do the job for me.

Sugar-beet lifting was probably the most back-breaking job on the farm. I designed a machine for doing that but it was rather complicated. Muck-spreading came a close second. The dung had to be forked off the cart on to the field in heaps. Then the heaps had to be spread with heavy long-handled forks. The machine for that was simple. I have somewhere a sketch of a cart that has long screws holding a loose plate that goes right across the interior of the cart. As the cart moves across the field the screws are slowly turned (by being connected to the wheels), which causes the plate to shove the dung slowly off the back of the cart, where it falls on to spinning paddles which slap the clods of dung and hurl them in all directions.

I showed this sketch to the farmer in Dorset. It caused him to give one of his rare laughs and gleefully tell me that it was obviously ridiculous and that I was completely mad.

However, back in London in the winter, I discovered the fountainhead and true depository of all such fancies – the Patent Office Library. In a huge room, the size of a small cathedral, were thousands of volumes of the most marvellous testaments to human ingenuity, ranging from the absurd to the sublime. I would go there quite early in the morning and look for previous Specifications of whatever device I was thinking about. I had learned how to use the catalogue and codes, seeking out *Vehicles, agricultural, adapted for specific purposes ... etc.* And there it was: my muck-spreader. OK, so somebody had already thought of it. That meant it was a good idea.

Apart from the pleasures of the Patent Office Library, the winter of 1944–5 was fairly uneventful. I spent quite a lot of it mooching around the streets of Soho and drinking endless cups of tea in the Swiss café. So when spring came I was quite glad to get my third farm job.

This was with two Czech brothers named Drexler, who ran a large market garden near Kidlington in Oxfordshire. The work there was fairly boring but in my spare time I was able to go into Oxford on the bus and haunt John and his friends at Balliol College.

It didn't last. In June the gods sent a thunderstorm with hailstones the size of golf-balls. With great courage I put on a steel helmet and rounded up the Drexlers' pigs and horses, who were squealing under the bombardment but too stupid to take cover. Alas, my heroism went unrewarded. The pigs and horses were all right but the uninsured greenhouses were totally shattered, which meant that the Drexlers were bankrupt and I was out of work again.

At my aunt Emily's suggestion I moved to Essex and took lodgings in Wethersfield with their friend, Son Wicks, who was a builder. There I got my fourth farm job, as a general farm labourer on a large local farm.

Ray and Daisy were fond of the country. I knew that they would have liked to be able to afford a country retreat, especially one near Bloomsbury-on-the-Marsh. I mentioned this to Son Wicks and he immediately suggested a vacant cottage at Penny Pot, which was only about four miles from Bradfields, the Meynells' house near Toppesfield. Ray and Daisy bought their cottage for under £600, including renovations, and were very happy indeed.

One day I had an unexpected stroke of luck – I found a motorbike. It was blocking up a gap in somebody's hedge. I was able to buy it for £3 and an old iron bed-head, which went into the hedge in its place. Under the dirt it was a 1926 New Imperial 350cc side-valve chain-drive motor-cycle with a square tank.

It was a good bike, in its fashion. It never went faster than about 40 m.p.h., it always did at least 120 miles to the gallon and it had absolutely no springs. Riding it was like riding a pneumatic drill, but it was my own and I loved it.

My memories of that summer are hazy: mainly of work, of hot harvesting, of stooking the sheaves of wheat after the reaper and binder had passed, threshing out horse-beans, curry-combing the two big Suffolk horses. And riding blissfully along deserted lanes in the cool of the evening, the engine going sweetly, sounding like a clapped-out sewing-machine with asthma.

One memory is very clear. It was a morning early in August. I was in Son Wicks's yard getting my motorbike out when his wife, Olga, came out with a newspaper.

She said: 'We've dropped something nasty on Japan.'

For some reason the news that an atomic bomb had been dropped on Hiroshima filled me with an absolute physical terror, as if, for a moment, I had seen the end of the world. Reading about it was like hearing a scream inside myself, a scream which silenced everything else in my head and left it numb. After it came an extraordinary sense, a conviction that somewhere in my mind I had known about it and had been waiting for it to happen. That was completely impossible, of course. The only prior connection I could recall was Daisy's remark, made six years earlier, that 'they' now had bombs that could wipe out half a town. I hadn't forgotten that. They didn't have them then. Now they did.

There was nothing to be done except get on my bike and go to work as usual, wondering what was to become of us.

II. Engines.

The cottage in Essex celebrated my parents' accession by producing a magnificent crop of sloes and greengages, which Ray and Daisy carried back to Finchley and made into wine.

The sloe wine was particularly delicious, dark red and crystal-clear, strong and not too sweet, with a long, mellow, exotic aftertaste of, well, tiny bitter plums. The family wines were a solace and delight in the dark years of deprivation. And for Ray a source of reassurance and hope for the future was to be found in the very last page of the Ministry of Food Handbook on Home Winemaking, whereon it was written ... A GOOD WINE CAN ALSO BE MADE FROM GRAPES.

Buck's Farm was sold and I was sacked, but I still hoped it might be possible for me to join either the Friends' Ambulance Unit or one of the relief teams that were being set up to try to help reorganize life in the ruins of Europe. I asked the Red Cross and other organizations but was turned down, on the perfectly reasonable grounds that only people with specific skills were being sought. So I was back in London for the winter of 1945–6, mooching about and looking for something to do, or make.

Daisy suffered a lot from fibrositis in her arms and shoulders. Any heavy activity would cause her pain, so I decided to make her a washing machine. I knew more or less how they worked. A washing machine was a round metal tub on legs that had in it a

sort of three-cornered paddle which rotated backwards and forwards, sloshing the clothes about in the sudsy water.

It occurred to me that if the whole tub were to be rotated
backwards and forwards, the paddle could be part of the tub. This
would simplify the design and avoid the problem of how to make
a leak-proof hole in the tub for the paddle spindle to go through.

I pictured a large deep container, a milk-churn in fact, with a
smooth piece of wood three inches (75mm) square and about
eighteen inches (45cm) long, bolted to the wall of the churn on the
inside. When the churn was rotated backwards and forwards with
suds and clothes in it, the piece of wood acted like a breakwater,
creating the amount of sloshing necessary to loosen the dirt from
the clothes.

The rest of the design was purely mechanical. I made a strong
four-legged wooden frame with an open top in which the churn
could sit. I balanced it on a pivot at the centre of its base and held
it upright with four small rubber wheels fixed to the top of the
frame. Thus the churn could be rotated in an upright position
inside its frame. After that all I had to do was buy a large electric
motor with a gearbox from the army surplus shop in New Oxford
Street and fix it to the frame, coupling the churn to a crank plate
on the motor-shaft by a connecting rod. It functioned correctly;
when the motor was switched on the churn rotated backwards and
forwards a quarter of a turn each way at a rate of about sixty
sloshes a minute.

It also worked triumphantly as a washing-engine. It washed the
clothes really well, beautifully clean and quite undamaged. It would
even rinse them if you ran water through it with a hose from the
tap.

Daisy was absolutely dismayed by it. Just looking at the thing,
standing like a home-made cannon in a corner of the scullery, filled
her with dread. Hearing it in action alarmed her terribly, though
both Ray and I thought its noise magnificent, like the sound of
tramcars copulating. This simile, though apt and evocative, did
nothing to improve Daisy's confidence.

However, Daisy was nothing if not loyal to the cause. She
screwed up her courage and consented to use the washing-engine.

She was, perhaps understandably, cautious in her approach to it. She would drop the clothes in at arm's length, fill it with hot water from a hose, reach out and pour in the soap-flakes, drop on the lid and then, with the door to the kitchen held open, flick on the switch and run out, locking the door behind her. I wondered why she locked it. It was almost as if she was afraid the engine, which was going '*Yerk-graunch-slop*, *yerk-graunch-slop*, *yerk-graunch-slop*' to itself in the scullery, was going to clamber out and chase after her.

Daisy admitted that this was precisely what she was afraid of and, I have to confess, her fears, although exaggerated, were not altogether unfounded. The washing-engine did have an unforeseen peculiarity. Due to an inevitable degree of flexibility in the construction of the frame it had a tendency, while working, to walk, or rather shuffle, about the scullery in an idle inquisitive sort of way.

Daisy said that was the worst part; coming back after the engine had been going for ten or fifteen minutes and not knowing for sure where in the scullery she would find it, though often she would hear it nudging softly at the other side of the door as if mutely pleading with her to open it.

One day, as she came back, she heard a different, far more ominous, sound. The healthy '*Yerk-graunch-slop*' had changed to '*Clonk-scrindle-yaaha*, *clonk-scrindle-yaaha*' the last sound being a desperate bubbling sigh. She opened the door an inch and peered in. She saw a terrible sight. The washing-engine had tripped over and fallen. The poor thing had spread its contents on to the floor and was lying on its side, writhing and reciprocating in a heaving pool of foam and underclothes.

Daisy closed the door and ran to fetch me but, even as she did so, the soapsuds reached its electrical works and the ill-fated engine blew the fuses and expired. All the lights in the house went out.

As I removed the debris and cleared up the scullery, I could see that the project hadn't been altogether successful.

Another device, a high-speed food-mixer built into a screw-top coffee-jar, had turned out to be very acceptable. Daisy was pleased with it, even proud of it on my behalf, but alas, that too eventually succumbed to fate. One Sunday morning, perhaps because she hadn't screwed it in properly, the jar came adrift in full flight and distempered the scullery from floor to ceiling with Yorkshire pudding batter.

Apart from a bird-scarer which trapped my aunt Emily and roared at her at two o'clock in the morning, a fan-heater, an inspired toilet-roll holder, the first electric rotary lawn-mower and a simple but appallingly dangerous electric circular saw on a kitchen table in the back garden, I am fairly sure I didn't make any more useful engines that winter, but even so I dare say Ray and Daisy were secretly relieved when, early in 1946, I decided it was time for me to be off into another year of 'work of national importance'.

The year started well. I visited Dartington Hall and had a meeting with Leonard K. Elmhirst, who, with his American wife Dorothy, was the owner of the hall and founder of the estate companies. It was a good meeting. L.K. listened to me rabbiting on about my pet subject, the feeling that the men coming back from the wars were not going to be content to step back into laborious archaic working practices. Power tools and labour-saving methods were going to be needed. L.K. agreed enthusiastically and we got on famously.

As a result of that meeting I got my fifth rural job: as a winch-tractor driver for the Dartington Hall Woodlands Department, with a private brief from L.K. to report in due course on the potential for mechanization in the forestry work of the estate.

For the first time in my life I felt really well set up, as if I was at the start of what could perhaps become a career. I didn't know exactly what a winch-tractor driver did, and I had no inkling that it would turn out to be the most spectacular job I had ever taken on.

The work wasn't being done on the Dartington estate itself but in the woods near their sawmill at Moretonhampstead, a small town high up on Dartmoor. There I took lodgings with a Miss Overdown, who lived in a small house near the mill.

My tractor was a petrol-driven Fordson with a large simple winch on the back which had cast-steel spades attached. These could be dropped down so that when the winch was pulling the spades would dig into the ground and stop the tractor being dragged back. The machine was immensely strong. With the wire-rope hooked around the trimmed trunks of the felled oak trees and using the stumps as pulley-blocks, the tractor was able to haul them across the rocky precipitous terrain and stack them by the track. That was the main part of the job and it was delicate as well as brutal in that one false move could have sent a loose five-ton tree trunk bounding down into the river below. But perhaps the greatest test of the tractor's strength came when I had to pull one of the really big trees out by the roots. This only happened once or twice – I am glad to say – when the tree in question was directly in the way of the track. Once the wire rope was firmly hooked around a high branch and the winch began to pull, the tractor was dragged back like a toy until the spades were firmly dug in. Then the real tug-of-war began. The wire pulled so taut that it thrummed like the string of a double-bass. The huge tree leaned over but held firm. Then, as I opened the throttle, the front of the tractor was lifted clean off the ground and slowly rose until all four wheels were in the air and it was standing on the dug-in spades. I had discovered the trick of playing it on the clutch, lifting and dropping the tractor in rhythm so that the tree started rocking on its roots. I did this until, at last, with a series of cracks like pistol shots, the great tree came away. The winch pulled it half over and then its own weight brought it down, with a swoosh of air sweeping through the branches and an earth-shaking thud as it hit the ground. Rocket would have been proud of us.

III. Roy's World.

Home life at Miss Overdown's residence in Moretonhampstead was, to put it simply, interesting. She was a gross, florid lady, probably in her mid-fifties, who had been, in her day, a much admired and sought-after prostitute in Plymouth. She was not in the least ashamed of her choice of profession and was happy to tell me how she came to choose it.

She said: 'When I were a little girl, my da sat me on his knee and he said to me: "Chloë, my girl, when you'm grown up, you'll choose what you'm a going a do. Now you make sure you do some-en you enjoy!" Well . . .' she giggled, put her finger to her cheek and cast her eyes coyly down, '. . . there bain't naught I enjoy more nor fucking. So there weren't really no choosing to it.'

Miss Overdown's house was small and dirty and, even though it contained very little in the way of furniture, it was a tip. This didn't matter really because although she took in lodgers, these were mostly muddy labourers like me. She had a son, a pasty-faced youth in his late teens, surly and vaguely hostile. When he saw me and was told I would be staying there he said: 'You're stupid staying here. I'm not.' That was partly true. He had obtained a broken-down saloon car and had had it dumped in front of the house as if it was parked there. He spent all his spare time sitting in it, listening to the wireless and eating lumps of bread and jam.

Sometimes Miss Overdown would go to the front door and shout to him: 'Eric, you coming in to tea, then?' To which he would, sometimes, reply: 'I'm not eating any of that old muck!'

That was overstating it a bit but he did have a point. The wartime sausage, the basis of Miss Overdown's cuisine, was never very palatable at the best of times but when boiled in a big saucepan with plenty of water and a few handfuls of macaroni it would swell up into a pallid water-filled bulb. This, when punctured on the plate, would sully the surrounding macaroni with muddy liquid and gristly fragments that imparted to it a very faint flavour, like the smell of wet cardboard. One had to be hungry to eat that.

The only other lodger, Roy, was about my age. He was a contract worker with a gang which did ploughing for the War Agricultural Committee. Roy made a great impression on me because he was the most absolutely ignorant person I had ever met. I use the word 'ignorant' here in the old-fashioned bucolic sense as meaning 'without courtesy or consideration'. Until I met Roy I hadn't realised how simple life could be if you really, sincerely, had no interest in or concern for anybody else at all.

When Roy first barged in through the door of Miss Overdown's front room I knew at once, from the way he moved, that he was a man totally committed to one purpose: getting what he wanted.

Roy didn't seem to have noticed me. He peeled off his grimy shirt and dropped it on the floor. Then he flopped down into the broken easy chair, unlaced and hauled off his muddy boots, revealing shiny dirty bare feet that filled the room with an abominable stench. He sighed with relief and wiggled his toes. Then he shouted: 'Missus! Where's my tea?'

There came no reply. He stood up, dropped his trousers off, followed them with grey underpants, stepped out of them and walked, bollock-naked and smelly, out of the room and up the stairs.

Miss Overdown came in carrying the big saucepan of boiled sausages and macaroni. She looked at the clothes on the floor and shouted, 'What's this?'

'That's yer washing,' came the reply from upstairs.

Miss Overdown kicked the dirty clothes into the hall.

'His rent hasn't come for two weeks,' she said reproachfully.

'Oh dear, I *am* sorry,' I replied.

Roy came in wearing tweed plus-fours, a dinner jacket and no shirt.

He dropped more dirty clothes on the floor.

'What's that?' asked Miss Overdown.

'Yer washing. I'm going out.'

'Your rent's not come for a fortnight.' she said.

'Fuck-all to do with me.'

Roy sat down at the table, slopped most of the macaroni stuff on to his plate and started shovelling it in.

'You can't stay if your rent's not paid,' said Miss Overdown.

'Can't help that. You'll just have to write to the "War Ag" and put in for it, won't you?'

He reached out for the saucepan.

I don't know what I was doing, just standing there. Perhaps I was waiting to be introduced or something. I suddenly came to and, realising that if I wanted any food I would have to act, grabbed the handle of the saucepan and whisked it away.

'Yur!' growled Roy.

'Oliver Postgate,' I replied. 'Pleased to meet you.' I poured what was left of the macaroni stuff on to my plate and started to eat.

Roy looked hard at me as if he was trying to work out what I was.

'You live here?' he asked.

My mouth was full so I couldn't reply.

'I said, d'you live here?' he growled.

'Yesh.'

Roy went on looking at me. Then he belched loudly and stood up, knocking over the chair.

'I'll want the boots in the morning, Missus,' he said and walked out.

Miss Overdown and I looked at each other. She picked up the chair.

I was suddenly angry. 'But ... but ... but, is he always like that?'

'Oh, yes.' She looked at me as if she was surprised by the question. 'He's a pig. They'm all like that; whole family. They'm ignorant.'

'Ah, well, I suppose his mother loves him.'

'I doubt that,' said Miss Overdown.

Roy showed his true mettle a week or two later, when Miss Overdown, who had been limping and sighing for some days, consented to show me what she called 'the place on her leg'. This was a very large ulcer or something that had gone septic. The patch covered half her thigh. It was red and throbbing. She had all the symptoms of advanced septicaemia. I ordered her to bed and ran to the doctor's surgery. It was closed. I stuck an urgent note through the door. I ran to the call-box and rang the hospital in Exeter but they wouldn't send an ambulance without a doctor's say-so. I went to the bakery where her son Eric worked and asked to see him. He came out. I told him his mother was very ill and asked him to go back to the house and wait for the doctor. He looked at me as if I was mad and went back into the bakery.

I went to the grocer and bought some food. When I got back

to the house Roy was there. He saw my basket. 'You doing tea, then?' he asked.

I saw a piece of paper on the floor and picked it up.

'What's this?'

'Dunno. Doctor or somebody came in to look at Missus upstairs. He gave me that. Prescription or something.'

'You going to get it made up?' I asked.

Roy looked blank.

'She'll probably die if she doesn't have the medicine.'

'That's what he said.'

'Right. So are you going to get it?'

'Fuck-all to do with me,' said Roy.

I looked at the prescription. It was for M&B, one of the new wonder drugs, like penicillin.

'I'd better get this made up,' I said.

'Haven't had my tea yet,' said Roy.

'Fuck-all to do with me,' I said and ran off up the road.

The chemist-cum-hairdresser's was closed but I banged on the door until somebody came to open it. The chemist didn't have the medication in stock but he realised the urgency and told me to go round to the vet. The vet made up the prescription and charged me half-a-crown for it.

I returned to Miss Overdown's house. Eric was outside in his car with bread and jam. Roy was sitting at the table in the front room, glowering. Miss Overdown was in her bed, snoring in a heavy, sinister way. I managed to wake her up and got her to take four pills and a glass of water. She fell back to sleep.

I went downstairs. As I went into the front room I said: 'You doing tea then, Roy?' He had opened his mouth to ask me the same question but I had got there first. So he just glared at me.

Then I made a suggestion. I said: 'If you speak to Eric very nicely, he might just let you have a piece of his bread and jam.'

Roy got up at once and walked out to Eric's car. I followed a minute or two later. Roy had forced himself halfway in through the car window and seemed to be shouting in Eric's ear, but I didn't think it likely that he would get any bread and jam.

'Fuck-all to do with me,' I said to myself and walked down the town to buy some fish and chips from the van that came round once a week. I was learning the rules of ignorance. As far as I was concerned Roy could feed himself or bugger off. In the event he buggered off. I never saw him again.

IV. Beatrice.

For the next week or two I did what I could for Miss Overdown. I cooked food when I came home, made breakfast, set out her pills and even bullied Eric into coming home at midday to give her bread and jam. Miss Overdown seemed embarrassed by this attention and so, strangely, were some of the local people, who watched me, nudged each other and sniggered. I found this unnerving and began to wonder whether I had committed some social gaffe. Perhaps, for that time and place, Roy's attitude would have been more acceptable.

At weekends it was a great joy to escape from Roy's world and drive down on my motorbike to visit friends at Dartington. Going there was like stepping out of the dark ages into friendliness and light, from agitation and suspicion into quiet and acceptance.

I had several friends at Dartington but it was a special pleasure to visit Cecily Martin and her family, who lived at Yarner Barn.

On one of those happy weekends I unexpectedly encountered my uncle, G. D. H. Cole, who was also staying with Cecily Martin while he attended a learned conference at Dartington Hall.

Cecily Martin was relieved to see me because my uncle Douglas, though a much-loved friend, was so dry and formidably intellectual that she had completely run out of conversation. She hoped I might be able to think of something to do or talk about that would take his attention.

I was flattered, and of course accepted the invitation but, as I felt the challenge would be more to my ingenuity than my intellect, I suggested to Cecily that Douglas and I should make a much-needed kennel for their dog.

After he had recovered from the initial shock of being

appointed carpenter's labourer, the Chichele Professor of Social and Political Theory and Fellow of All Souls at the University of Oxford put on a leather apron and knuckled down with a will. He took instructions well and was neat and careful in his work, though a shade slow.

However, as the kennel began to take shape it became clear that something was bothering him.

He said: 'It's all very well making a kennel for a dog, but how are you going to explain to the dog what it is?'

I laughed the question aside but he persisted: 'Look!' he said, quite firmly. 'This is a serious situation. The dog is just sitting there. It's a dumb animal. We can't explain things to it. So what are we going to do?'

Indeed the dog, whose name I believe was Digby, was sitting there, but he was not *just* sitting there. He was watching us closely as we worked.

I looked at Digby and said: 'D'you want to try it, then?'

Without a flicker of hesitation Digby jumped up on to the bench, climbed into the box, turned around a few times and then curled up, thus giving us a comprehensive demonstration of the settling-down procedure.

'All right, is it?'

Digby stood up, wagged his tail and jumped down. It was all right.

I mention this simple incident not so much because I found it surprising but because of the effect it had on Douglas. He was, if one can say such a thing of anyone so rigorously erudite, gob-smacked. He stood there, still as a crane, for some minutes while his mind was coming to terms with the implications of this impossible event. Then he gave a loud *cronk* of laughter and, apparently, accepted it wholeheartedly and without argument. From then on he was more than happy to discourse to Digby on the fine details of his kennel, asking his advice about the positioning of the door and roof. This puzzled the dog because he really had no idea what Douglas was talking about. But he understood perfectly when Douglas invited him to assess the exact positioning of the precious aged blanket that was his bed, and was happy to try it several times before they were both satisfied. In fact they were more than satisfied: both Digby and Douglas were really happy and pleased with their day's work.

On another of those slightly magical weekends I made one of the most exciting discoveries in my life.

Rooting through the outhouses at Cecily Martin's farm, I came across something large covered with a cobwebby tarpaulin. I lifted it carefully and found underneath it the car which Daisy had owned and driven so many years before. Of course it wasn't the same car but it was identical, a bull-nosed Morris Cowley tourer with grey-green oil-cloth seats. I squeezed the bulb of the horn. Probably for the first time in years it went '*SqueeeeeeA-OINK*', just like Daisy's used to. Wildly excited I ran in and told Cecily what I had found. 'Oh dear,' she said. 'Is that old thing still there? Do me a favour, would you? Get rid of it for me.'

I gave a whoop of delight, jumped on my bike and drove down to the garage on the Plymouth road.

The estimate for putting the car in order came to £37, a small enough charge for the work involved but beyond my means at the time. I telephoned Daisy, long-distance, and told her I wanted to buy something on her behalf for £37 but I didn't want to tell her what it was, yet. She was puzzled, then intrigued and in the end consented.

I told the garage to go ahead. The proprietor warned me that, what with getting parts and so on, the work might take a few weeks. So I swallowed my excitement and returned to Moreton-hampstead.

As requested by L. K. Elmhirst, I wrote a tactfully worded report about the prospects for mechanization at Moretonhampstead. There wasn't a lot of scope there. The main problem was with the lorries and the timber-carriage, which were all road vehicles, with worn-smooth road tyres. These either couldn't get up the rough hills because of wheel-spin or else they got bogged down. This meant that I had to spend a lot of my time using the tractor to pull them out instead of getting the trunks stacked ready for the sawmill.

I sent the report privately to Mr Elmhirst. I received no direct reply but a day or two later I was summarily transferred to a subsidiary company that was planting seedling trees near Newton Abbot.

I was a bit puzzled by this but, on the whole, relieved to be leaving the gruesome realities of life on the moor.

I returned to Dartington and stayed at one of the houses in the junior school which had been turned into an agricultural hostel and general lodging-house. After Miss Overdown's establishment this was a really pleasant place to live, especially because the company there was so varied that conversation could be quite lively and interesting.

The work I was now doing was much more varied than the logging work on the moor. As well as planting seedling trees we put up fences and gates, and trimmed the weeds from young plantations and the dead branches from the trunks of larch trees in the dark woods.

There was plenty of scope for labour-saving devices in these activities and I sketched several out, including a post-hole borer, two fence-post drivers and a steel-wire strimmer. None of these were world-changing innovations but they were all worth looking into. But first there was a small question in my mind that needed clearing up.

My informal mandate from L. K. Elmhirst was to report on the potential for mechanization in the forestry operations with a view to suggesting some ideas. That was fine, but I had noticed, in the small print of the work-contract I had been given, a clause to the effect that any inventions, ideas or patents that an employee might develop would become the sole property of the Company.

I wrote a note to the head of the Woodlands Department mentioning that, as requested, I had been working on some ideas, but before discussing them I would like to have a chat with him to clarify the situation about the ownership of the patents, etc.

The immediate effect of this was similar to that of my report about Moretonhampstead but more final. I received no answer, just a week's wages in lieu of notice and my cards.

I was very rattled by this. I couldn't have been sacked because my ideas were no good, because nobody had even looked at them. I asked to see Mr Elmhirst but was told he was still in America. It occurred to me that perhaps his idea of putting me in to report (spy?) on the Woodlands Department had not been popular. Perhaps, who could say? The only thing to do was write off that great career and go.

So, early one midsummer morning, under a blue sky, I threw my bag on to the back seat of Daisy's open car and wound the starting-handle. As always the engine started on the first pull, and the gearbox sang as I drove away, glad to be gone, happy to be starting another life, but somewhere else.

As I drove I looked back over the recent past. For most young people the years between seventeen and twenty-one are important and formative. Those are the years in which one's character is formed, the years in which lifelong friendships are made, in which one finds out who one is and where one is going. Above all they are the years for passionate relationships and love affairs.

For me – and without a doubt for thousands of others whose lives were complicated by the war – those years didn't work out like that.

I looked back on my time as a farm worker and saw no rompings in haylofts with buxom milkmaids. I would have liked a bit of that and one or two had been very romp-withable, but I was diffident and different and didn't really belong. I usually got on quite well with the people I worked with but, not speaking quite the same language, I never felt fully at ease in their world.

Even so, I didn't regret the years, didn't feel they had been wasted. I was strong, I knew how to work, I did it well, I enjoyed it and I loved the smell of hay and cows and rain. Also, even if I was occasionally tripped into patches of confusion and anxiety, I could think quite well. As for love affairs? There would be time, when there was a place.

I had some money saved up. It was only a few pounds, but I could take life easy for a month or two. Then I would see what the world had to offer, or maybe what I had to offer the world.

But, most of all, as I was bowling along on that sunny day, I was looking forward to bringing Daisy her new-old car.

Daisy was delighted. When she was introduced to the car, she asked me politely what its name was and I heard myself reply: 'Beatrice.' There was no argument about the name and Beatrice was duly welcomed into the family. Daisy and I bought canvas and made her a new hood. We bought plastic sheets and webbing to repair her drop-in side windows. We poured woodworm-killer into the interstices of the bodywork to discourage the death-watch beetles, painted it and polished her brass nose.

Daisy was nervous of driving Beatrice in the London streets so, a couple of weeks later, my cousin Peter, my uncle Eric and I took turns driving her to the cottage in Essex.

Having Beatrice with us in Essex was a great luxury. We no longer had to wait for rare, unpredictable buses or have to get out the old bicycles, which Ray and Daisy were finding hard work. As well as visiting friends we could go shopping or go swimming in Gosfield lake, where the water was warm and brown as Windsor soup.

For Ray and Daisy that summer must have been like coming back to a much-loved time after a long absence. With their own cottage and their own car they were once again fully equipped for Bloomsbury-on-the-Marsh visiting. The question that remained in my mind was whether the Bloomsbury-on-the-Marsh that they had known and loved in the twenties and thirties was still there.

Oddly enough, it was.

During the war Ray and Francis Meynell, along with many other capable, well-educated, middle-aged persons, had become civil servants – and very good at it they were too. Like everybody else they needed somewhere to relax so, albeit more rarely and with some austerity, the weekend parties had continued. Indeed I think Francis felt that to manage to carry on with fun in the face of dreadfulness was almost a patriotic gesture, it showed that war could not defeat them. So, give or take the effects of age and changes in their personal lives, the dream, with variations, had survived.

In 1946 the possession of any sort of car conferred great distinction on the owner, and owning Beatrice, who was a reincarnation of the one she had driven along the same lanes so many years ago, was for Daisy a nostalgic pleasure which she loved to share with her friends.

I remember how excited she was the day she drove us over to a lunch party at the handsome house of a well-known politician, because our host was known to be a lover of old cars. He happened to be in the garden when we appeared through the gates and he came to greet us, rejoicing at the venerable beauty of ours.

'That is a genuine bull-nosed Morris!' he cried.

'Her name is Beatrice,' announced Daisy with pride.

'Ah,' he said thoughtfully. 'Is it? Well, then ... Excuse me. Would you mind just waiting there a moment?'

He walked briskly back to the house and disappeared around the side. I heard the sound of large doors being closed and then he came out and waved us in.

Later, after much lunch and laughter, I asked our host what had been happening when we arrived. He led me through passages and cloakrooms to a door that opened into a garage. There stood a long beautiful Lancia sports car, low, sleek and grey.

'That's it,' he said.

'It certainly is!' I replied. 'But why . . .?'

'The name,' he explained. 'His name is Dante, you see. They mustn't meet, of course.'

'Oh, I see! Of course not,' I said, nodding sagely, and we came away.

Of course I was lying. I didn't see. Being twenty-one and ignorant I didn't know the legend of Dante and Beatrice. When I told my father what had happened he chortled very happily, but the old so-and-so declined to explain to me why it was they mustn't meet.*

*

---

* Beatrice: a nine-year-old girl glimpsed by the poet Dante Alighieri when he was also nine. She became the love of his life and the inspiration of his work but it seems they never actually met. I still don't know why they *mustn't* meet. OP.

That happy, silly, nostalgic, summer flowed by. We returned to Finchley and reality. There, in October 1946, I heard that the Save the Children Fund had accepted my application and was offering me a job as an ambulance-driver for one of the Relief Teams they had set up in Germany. So at last I was off to what was left of the wars, or rather, to what the wars had left of Germany.

5

THE HONEY-BARREL

We crossed the Channel by night, waited on a cold quay in Ostend and then boarded an old decrepit train which bumped along on uneven rails. I was wearing standard army-issue battledress. This, although physically comfortable, was mentally quite a shock, I having refused to put the uniform on during the war. I was also slightly embarrassed by the fact that as a civilian in uniform I had officer status and bore the honorary rank of major, even though the post I was about to take up was that of a lowly driver attached to a Relief Team in the Hamelin town of Brunswick – or rather, Braunschweig.

I must have slept on the train because I remember waking up and looking out of the window to get my first sight of devastated Europe. I saw fields and hedgerows, neat houses and one or two slow-moving people, well wrapped up against the chill November wind, who were pulling tiny four-wheeled carts, rather like doll's cots on wheels, along the rough roads. The countryside didn't look the least bit devastated and the people seemed to be doing what they had been doing for centuries. I saw an ox-cart loaded with dung, the steam from it hung in the air like a mist.

Then the train passed through a town (I don't know its name) and that was flat; rubble. It looked as if it had been trampled by giants. There was no sign of habitation, no sign of any standing building. Every single brick and stone had been broken away and become part of the heap. In places the debris had been pushed aside to uncover streets, showing shallow dry canals with beds of broken cobblestones. Except for one or two slow people pulling their carts along these, the place was deserted. I had seen quite a lot of bomb damage in England, but nothing quite as absolute as that crushed town.

The train didn't stop. There would have been no point.

I laid my cheek on the dirty window and watched the landscape pass, wondering what exactly I had come for, what a Relief Team would do. Where, I wondered, were the people who had lived in that town? Would they all be standing, huddled in some huge pen, waiting for me to come along and give them food, clothes, houses and hope? Possibly . . . I didn't know. I reminded myself that I was here to play a simple part in a huge, highly organized emergency exercise. At that moment I felt relieved that I was just going to be a driver.

Our journey ended at the Red Cross headquarters in Vlotho. There, in the dull light of a overcast November afternoon, I was able to walk out into the street.

The town didn't seem to be particularly damaged, but I had an almost overwhelming feeling that it was near to death.

How could a town be near to death? I stood and looked at it. Everything I saw was old, worn out, or broken. The road was pot-holed, with cobbles lying loose. The street-lamps were rusted and bent. Guttering hung from the chipped eaves. The cracked and tilted pavements and the crumbling house walls were worn and grimy, as if dirty things had been dragged against them for years. But there were no things there; there was nothing to show that this was a place where people lived, just bare steps, bare paint-peeled doors, hinge-pins sticking out of cracked gate-posts to show where there might once have been wrought-iron gates.

A tall white-faced man was walking in the gutter. He was handsomely dressed in a leather cap and a leather greatcoat with wide lapels and carved bone buttons. As he came closer I saw that from the knee down his coat was in tatters and that string was wound around his polished boots to keep the soles on. In his little cart was a large, ornately carved barometer. He stopped and gave me an emaciated smile.

'*Zigaretten?*' he suggested.

'By all means,' I replied, taking out a packet of cigarettes and offering him one. He took four, smiled, bowed, put them carefully into his pocket and then, absurdly, picked up the barometer and tried to push it into my hands. I remember thinking it was peculiarly ugly.

'Oh, no, no, no, I already have a barometer,' I explained, untruthfully.

The man looked distressed and thoughtful. From an inside pocket he slowly withdrew a rectangular object wrapped in faded cloth. It was about the size of a small book, but when he unwrapped it I saw that it was a very thick picture-frame, moulded in the form of fat leaves and fruits. These were brightly painted and embellished with gilded edges and purple spraywork. In the centre of it was an oval glass covering a faded sepia photo of a whiskery man wearing a helmet with a spike on the top. I had seen pictures like that before.

'But that's come off somebody's grave!' I said.

The man stood up very straight. '*Finckelglockner!*' he said proudly, and clicked his heels.

'Oh, is it?' I said. 'A relative, perhaps?'

'*Zigaretten?*' he suggested.

I held out the packet. He took four more cigarettes, looked long and fondly at the portrait and then, turning his head away, reached out as if to hand it to me.

I didn't take it. I fled. Muttering good wishes I backed off and made my way briskly to the Red Cross headquarters where there was laughter and chatter in the canteen.

That was my first encounter with '*die grosse Knappheit*' (the great shortage), the period just after the end of the war when money lost its value and cigarettes became the only real currency. I had heard about this in England and, although I didn't smoke, I had been advised always to carry cigarettes because sometimes that was the only way to pay for things.

The Save the Children Fund Relief Section that I was attached to was accommodated in a large house in a pleasant suburban street which had somehow escaped the bombing. Braunschweig was a patchwork of almost undamaged areas and areas of total devastation – one just walked, or drove, through the dead bits. The team drivers, myself and a young man named Chesley, were billeted in a couple of rooms over the team's garage on the outskirts of the town.

The Relief Team consisted of a team leader, who was absent when I arrived, and about eight other individuals, each one with a special interest – youth groups, the blind, children's homes, etc.

The team's transport fleet had been provided by the army – two heavy lorries, two 2-ton Army ambulances and two trucks, all in rather poor condition, without heaters. These may have been standard issue for units on active service, but they were not ideal for taxiing individual social workers about on their visits. Driving in a 3-ton army lorry when it is well loaded can be quite comfortable but with no load it gets thrown about like an empty box. But that's what we had. My job was to drive the members of the team. Their job was to hold on tight and put up with the jolting.

About once a fortnight a delivery of relief materials came. Shortly after I arrived an HQ lorry dumped a large wooden barrel containing honey, and a steel drum about the same size, labelled cod-liver oil, along with a small sack of louse-combs, into the elegant front garden.

As nobody in the team had any idea what to do about these massive items I found myself with the task of working out how to deal with them.

I enlisted the help of our mechanic, Giff. We manhandled them into a truck and took them out to the team's garage. On the way we stopped at the Army Medical Centre where I told them I needed five hundred empty small medicine bottles and a roll of plastic tubing. These were fetched and handed over without question.

At the garage we rolled the drum of cod-liver oil on to a stand, chopped off ten lengths of plastic tubing and, at carefully timed one minute intervals, set up ten separate siphons into ten bottles.

In principle that was an excellent system. In operation it would also have been if the oil had consented to flow at an even rate. Unfortunately some bottles filled faster than others, so we had to watch very closely and pounce on each one as it filled. Sometimes three or four would overflow at the same moment, so if either of us lost concentration for a second there would be a slow flood. Changing the bottles was slippery and messy and the tray we had put under them was soon half-full of spilt oil which had to be baled out with a tablespoon. But we persevered, slurping tubes and bottles in the smelly mess, non-stop for the next eleven hours. When we had screwed on the last bottle-top we tipped all five hundred bottles into the bath to wash them. The whole place stank of bad fish.

Compared with that the task of dealing with the barrel of honey was simplicity itself. Giff and I stood the barrel upright in the back of one of the 3-ton lorries, tied it on securely and smashed in the top with an axe. As I expected, the honey had set hard. I borrowed a strong garden spade, scrubbed it thoroughly, put it in the back of the lorry with a carton of cod-liver oil bottles and the bag of louse-combs, and we were ready to move out and relieve Germany.

Giff and I went back to the house to tell our proud news to the team, but there was nobody there. However, that evening I mentioned to Helen, a nice middle-aged lady whose interest was in Children's Homes, that the goods were now ready for distribution. She was pleased and suggested that we take them out the next day.

Wisely Helen brought one of the sofa cushions with her to ease the journey. That meant we could drive the lorry at a fair speed without causing her to yelp.

The Children's Homes (perhaps we would call them orphanages) were mostly run by the various Churches, Evangelical, Catholic, Lutheran, etc., in conditions of utter poverty and surprising cheerfulness. The first Home we visited was in a large, part-ruined bungalow deep in the country. It stood in an unkempt but well-trodden garden with the front door wide open. We walked in. The inside of the house was smelly, almost completely devoid of furniture and fittings, and full of stick-skinny barefoot children dressed in drab worn-out clothes, who were laughing and singing and running about as if happiness was the only fuel they needed for their lives.

Oddly, they didn't crowd around us. We stood in the hall for a moment and then a small girl came to us, curtsied, said good morning, and skipped away to fetch the Home-keeper.

The Home-keeper was a thin, old, wispy-haired man wearing a dark suit. He looked pale and serious but when he saw the honey-barrel he clapped his hands with delight and sent children scurrying for a container. They brought him a long oval saucepan, a fish-kettle I think, into which, with great difficulty, I managed to scrape three or four spadefuls of sticky honey. The children bore it away in triumph.

As I was sorting out some bottles of cod-liver oil a woman came out of the kitchen to watch us. She was young but her face was hard. She looked at me fixedly with such implacable hatred that I could only turn my eyes away. The man had noticed. He spoke to me softly in English: 'It is not bad. Her man has been in Russia,' he explained. 'It is often so.' He touched my arm and smiled very gently. 'Please do not worry.'

I stood still for a moment. Then, in my school German, I said: 'It is good here.'

'Oh yes,' he said, 'we live well.' And he laughed.

'Is there anything you miss?' I asked.

'Oh yes, brandy, and coffee made from beans. But that is so long ago I have forgotten.'

Helen came back from explaining to the woman about using the louse-combs in wet hair. 'We must be off,' she said.

'Oh no!' cried the man. 'We must sing to you. We know a very correct English Christmas song. Come!'

He led us into the chilly sparse hall where he sat at a creaking harmonium and played the introduction to the song.

'What's the tune?' I whispered to Helen.

'I know it, but I can't place it,' she muttered.

Then the cheerful reedy voices of the children came in with the words:

'I'm dreamink of a vite Crischmas . . .'

I stood there and wept like a river.

There seemed to be a multitude of Children's Homes in the area so, after a few more bumpy excursions, I was entrusted with the task of distributing the honey and cod-liver oil and louse-combs on my own. I had also looted some coffee beans and small paper bags from the army stores, and poured glasses of my Officer's Brandy allocation into some of the unused cod-liver oil bottles. So, fully equipped, I set off each morning with my list of visits, and threw my 3-ton lorry along the pitted roads. One or two of the Homes I visited were gloomy and sorry for themselves, not without reason, but most were like the first one we went to, completely light-hearted, full of fun and genuinely happy to receive whatever was going, even the louse-combs. I could see why. In the fairly recent past times had been very bad, not only because of the physical shortages of food and fuel but also because while the Third Reich had been bleeding to death there had been no future to look towards, only the prospect of even greater sacrifices being imposed in order to maintain the delusion that there was hope of victory. The spadefuls of honey that I brought were not just sweet food, they were also a symbol, a precursor, of better times that were coming, lighting up for them the possibility of a future without war, starvation and fear.

I was entirely infatuated with everything that was happening, buzzing with energy and delight. My school German rushed back into my head, flourishing long-forgotten grammatical tables, whole pages of which would pop up behind my eyes when needed, and in no time I found myself talking fluently to the people I met in a language that may, in part at least, have been German. Apparently the language was serviceable, but I did notice that after a while the people I was talking to tended to dissolve into fits of giggles, in which I usually joined.

Having another, necessarily simple, language to use with my new friends was not in any way a drawback; quite the contrary. My ridiculous German was not encumbered by my past. It was free of the anxieties, inhibitions and social nuances that silted up my use of my own language. I could express simple direct thoughts and feelings in a way that would, if I had been speaking in English to a group of English people (like for instance the Relief Team), simply have caused embarrassment to everybody, especially me.

Let me say at once that I have every respect for English reticence and understatement, and for the exactness and subtlety of the English language. I also know the danger, and the power, of the sweeping simple expressions of emotion that German can deliver – Hitler was a master of these – but even so, at that moment in my life, the German language, such of it as I could use, helped to liberate my silly diffident spirit and allowed me to join wholeheartedly with the happiness that was all around.

I felt I could have spent the whole of my life, like some mythological spirit, bounding along broken roads in the aftermath of wars, dispensing honey and hope with a spade. Alas it had to end. The barrel was suddenly empty and I was back with the team, doing my bit as a driver.

Well, not quite. The Team Leader came back off leave and immediately fell out with the Transport Officer, who stamped his foot and resigned. As a result his very undemanding job fell to me and I became Acting Transport Officer. In that capacity I was able to do a magnificent deal with the Transport Officer of the Control Commission by which I borrowed two Volkswagen cars and a motorbike in return for the use of our 3-ton lorries. This was strictly against orders but it made travelling much more comfortable, especially as the winter was now setting in.

Now that the team had a leader I looked forward to seeing the huge highly organized emergency exercise that I was playing my humble part in swing into action. The Team Leader had brought back some excellent gramophone records from the UK. We listened to these with pleasure but otherwise everything went on as before.

That was disappointing but at the same time it wasn't easy to see what else the members of the team could do. What was needed in Germany at that time was food and clothes, shelter and, urgently, fuel. The Relief Team did not have such things to offer.

I reminded myself that mine was not to reason why. The team members needed to come and go from the house and I, who knew nothing of their purposes, was there to drive them. However, Bob, who was a very large man connected with the Boy Scout organization, would often talk about his work. He was enthusiastic about reviving, or recreating, the Christian Youth Groups that had existed in the 1920s and early 30s, before such things were taken over by the Nazis. He felt that for the great task of reconstruction that the German people had before them it was important to foster a spirit of cooperation, comradeship and common purpose among young people.

I remember going along with Bob to an evening get-together of the *Evangelische Jugendgruppe* (Evangelical Youth Group).

This was quite a noisy occasion, but with a certain formality about it. The young men would walk briskly up to each other and, each gazing sternly into the eyes of the other, clasp hands to forearms in a Roman handshake, stamp a foot and shout: '*FREUNDSCHAFT!*' (Friendship!)

The girls seemed watchful and subdued. I noticed that one of them was obviously quite ill, flushed with fever and hardly able to stand, so I offered to drive her home at once. She was very grateful but the chief young man said no. He said she could not depart because it was not proper that she should do so.

I said that she was ill and that I was going to drive her home. The young man – no older than me – glared. I glared back. But I was not only the guest, I was also, in his eyes, the conqueror. In the end he turned and walked away, sat down in a corner with his back to the room.

I helped the girl into the truck and drove her to her home. The night air did her no good at all and by the time we got to her parents' makeshift house she was practically unconscious. So I put her over my shoulder and carried her in. I remember thinking how surprisingly light she was.

I drove back to the hall. As I drew up I heard the sound of a guitar and voices singing. Looking through a window I saw the young men sitting together. Flushed and glazed with nostalgia, they were singing one of those rousing gut-wrenching songs of glory and conquest that had fired the blood of the Wehrmacht and led it to its death. The words may have been changed but the song was still the same.

As I drove Bob home I wondered whether the same rousing songs had been sung in the 1920s. Probably they had, and certainly they were being sung in the 1930s while Herr Hitler was fostering a spirit of cooperation, comradeship and common purpose among young people for the glorious task that he had in mind for the German people – I shivered and hoped Bob knew what he was doing.

Although I met many German people and made some good friends while I was there, we rarely spoke of Herr Hitler, or of the recently ended war. Only once did anybody deliberately set out to inform me about what had happened. This was a middle-aged lady who, having accompanied her sister to a meeting with the Team Leader, found herself waiting in the sitting room with only me as a companion.

The lady told me that the war had been very terrible. With that I agreed.

She told me that the German people had done terrible things during the war, very terrible things, but that for her the most terrible had been the betrayal of the vision. This was the pure, glorious vision that she and her friends had all together felt in their souls at the great rallies in Nürnberg. That had been a time of truth.

I ventured to wonder whether Herr Hitler's vision had really been so true and pure if it had led to such terrible happenings.

The lady looked at me with affection tinged with pity. She reminded me that she had heard the Führer speak. She had been there with him. For a moment she had clasped his hand and looked deep into his eyes. Oh yes, the vision was pure. She held the light of it holy in her memory, separate from all that had followed. The failures and the betrayals were the work of lesser men and also of other, dirty interferences.

Were these other interferences to do with Communism, I wondered.

She shuddered and told me that Communism was a darkness that spread in the shadows, bringing doubt and subversion to make all things uncertain. To guard the light it had to be swept away.

'And the Jews?'

She was silent for a moment. Then she said. 'Oh yes. Oh yes. Terrible things were done. Hurtful, hateful things by evil people. But they too were done to guard the light. They were wrong to do and for that we have guilt, but the light itself was pure. It is still so.'

And abruptly she rose and went to sit in the hall, not wishing me to see her tears.

I have no idea how typical that lady's feelings were. Most people I spoke to were far less forthcoming and usually confined themselves to asking how soon I thought we would be going to start fighting the Russians. That, they said, was the inevitable next move, and once we realised who our true enemies were, we would be looking to Germany for help . . . wouldn't we? . . . Yes?

I tended to duck out of that sort of conversation.

At the beginning of December the temperature dropped to minus eighteen degrees Celsius. I had never been in cold like that before; it bit my face and numbed my extremities through layers of clothing. The streets seemed to ring with cold as if the walls and pavements, even the trees, had frozen hard as glass. Even the antifreeze in the vehicle radiators froze to a mush.

The team house and my room over the garage were warm because our fuel was supplied through the army but I wondered how the people of the town were managing. When I asked Giff if he knew how fuel was delivered to the people, he laughed and said it wasn't delivered.

'Do you mean there are no fuel supplies to the town?' I asked.

'Oh yes, coal comes in but it doesn't get delivered.'

'What happens to it?'

'It gets pinched. Come tonight, I will show you the *Kohlenklau* (coal pinch).'

Just after midnight, in the pitch dark, we drew up quietly beside the railway yards at the other side of the town. I could see nothing except the black silhouette of the sheds. Giff turned the 15cwt so that its nose was pointing into the yard. Then he turned the headlights on.

I saw a train of coal trucks on the siding. The chutes had been opened so that the coal had slipped in heaps on to the track. Clambering over the heaps were literally hundreds of people, furtively scooping the coal into baskets and bags. What impressed me was the fact that so many of them were well dressed and that the rucksacks they were stuffing with coal were expensive framed types, the ones that mountain climbers use. Fearing the light they scuttled around to the dark side. So we came away.

Soon after that the snow began to fall. About two and a half feet fell in the night. It brought complete silence and, for a while, immobility. Very efficient snowploughs came out and soon the town streets were navigable. Then we could get about, but only locally. Life in general slowed down and the members of the team spent quite a lot of time sitting about in the house trying not to get on each other's nerves.

I took the opportunity to take a few days' leave. I had borrowed a pair of skis from the Military Police quartermaster and I was eager to try them. They were terrible skis and my first attempt, in Bad Harzburg, was a disaster, but later, in the ski-resort, I managed to master the skis and had a marvellous, invigorating holiday. I also recognized, and had a drink with, a young Guards officer who turned out to have been on my court martial. 'I was very nervous,' he said. 'It was my first court martial.'

'Mine too,' I replied.

I returned, full of zeal, and went to offer my services to an

American religous relief team which was looking after refugees coming in from East Prussia. To my surprise I was roundly denounced by them for 'doing God's Work' when I was not a 'True Believer'. They appeared to assume that as I had rejected the Love of God I had a duty to live a life of sin and debauchery and not go pinching the heavenly Brownie Points that were rightly theirs. I got away in time, just as they were about to forgive me and welcome me into the brotherhood of repentence.

I had an even more alarming encounter a few days later.

Politics had started up again in Germany and, because it was proving to be a vehicle for passions, grievances and antagonisms that must have been brewing up under the surface for years, we had been warned to keep out of the way of any demonstrations.

I remembered the political meetings and demonstrations at which my grandfather had spoken. They had been moving, power-ful occasions but essentially warm-hearted and enthusiastic. I wondered what a post-war German demonstration would be like.

I took the rather asthmatic motorbike I had borrowed from the Control Commission and pottered through the town towards the park where the demonstrations were likely to be held. As I was passing through one of the bombed-out areas where the road was lined with ruins and rubble, I saw coming towards me a mass of angry-looking people. They were shouting and waving their arms. They were singing as they marched. They were throw-ing stones and turning over parked cars. Like an eruption of red-hot lava from some volcano of hatred the riot was flowing towards me, glowing with rage and roaring some huge muddled song.

I turned the bike for a quick getaway and sat astride it, knowing that I could kick-start it and escape, but daring myself to stay as long as possible. Then, as I saw the whites of the eyes and the shining ecstatic faces of the young men leading the crowd, I kick-started the engine.

It didn't start.

I kicked and kicked at the starter pedal and the engine rotated, but it didn't fire.

The riot came closer. They were only a few yards away. I turned to the crowd. 'The damn thing won't start!' I shouted.

'English shit-bike!' shouted one of the men.

'You should get a BMW!' shouted another.

'Jump on, we'll give you a shove!' shouted a third.

I jumped on and four of them ran forward and pushed the bike. The engine fired at last and they gave a shout of triumph.

'Ride on to England!' shouted one.

'I shall!' I replied, and at that moment I meant it.

One or two of them may have thrown the odd stone, just as a sort of token, but I was away like a bat out of hell.

I couldn't drive properly because my head was too confused. So once I was far enough away I stopped the bike and sat on it, shaking from head to foot, trying to sort out what had happened. What was confusing me was the realisation that from the instant I had spoken directly to them, the young men had, in my eyes, completely changed. They had ceased to be the fangs of a gigantic dragon of rage and had turned into a crowd of excited youngsters having a great time throwing their weight about. Something had been seriously wrong with my perceptions. They had not been reliable and that had rattled me almost as much as the encounter.

Eventually I recovered my composure and, freezing cold, kick-started the bike. This time the damn thing started first kick and carried me back to the team house where I sat with my hand on one of the radiators to thaw out my blood.

Then, in February 1947, the thaw came and we had to deal with the river behind the team house. This had become jammed with ice-floes and was threatening to flood, so we all had to go out on to the bridge and pick at the floes with long bamboo poles tipped with heavy spikes. That was tremendous fun, especially when the floes finally cracked and sidled away under the arches of the bridge in a gurgling rush of grey water.

Not long after that, at the end of February, the spring arrived. You could smell it in the air. People smiled and soon they had food in their baskets, sometimes even, I was told, jars of honey! A thought that had been in the back of my mind for some time now came to the surface. Germany's own economy had begun to recover. I could see that its progress would benefit far more by my absence than by my continued presence.

I resigned, wrapped three bottles of gin in my bed-roll and returned to England and the future, whatever that was to be.

6

TREADING THE BOARDS

I. The Academy.

In 1942 I had been severely admonished by Ray and Daisy's friend, the painter Stella Bowen. At the time she had been painting a portrait of me holding one of John's rabbits on my lap. This meant I had to stay very still and quiet, concentrating on the hope that the rabbit, whose name was Snowball, was not going to pee on me again. In this situation one does feel rather vulnerable. Stella said: 'You'd better make up your mind what you're going to *be*. If you fritter away your life on fancies you'll end up being a player at all trades and master of none!' A few years later I might have argued, but I was seventeen and the condemnation in her voice was so absolute that I took it on the chin, vowing that if I should ever come to know my mind I would be sure to make it up, and *be* . . . something or other.

So, in 1947, coming back from frittering my life in Germany, I repeated my vow and determined to make up my mind and decide on a career ... or something of the sort ... I wasn't sure what.

I had definitely concluded that stage design was not for me but I was still attracted by the idea of working in the theatre, perhaps as a stage manager. Then I thought: why not go the whole hog and *be* an actor?

An actor? ... Yes, it had a simple decisive ring to it. I firmly proclaimed this intention to my friends and family. Ray, taking the cue, consulted his friends at the Savile Club and was told by a distinguished knight of the theatre that the only place to go for training was the London Academy of Music and Dramatic Art in Earl's Court. I duly wrote to the Principal and was offered a place at the Academy.

So I came to another first day at school. Carrying a pad and pencil and a bound volume of Shakespeare's plays, I diffidently entered the shabby portals of an imposing house at the corner of the Earl's Court Road and Cromwell Road. I crossed the brown lino of the hall and sat on a folding chair in what would have been a very elegant large drawing room if there had been any decoration or furniture in it.

My fellow students were a motley collection, ranging from exquisite, languid starlets being groomed for fame by the studios that owned them, through serious-minded teachers of drama in the making and fairly mature ex-service people, to rumbustious teenagers just out of school.

The Academy was run economically. The Principal was not an actor, nor was he directly connected with the theatre. He did no teaching and as far as we could tell had no views on how drama should be taught. In the main his policy seemed to be to invite professional people, usually out-of-work actors, to give lectures on acting, or whatever they chose to call it – and let them get on with it.

The actor/lecturers would come to the Academy, play their parts as lecturers (which were often entertaining and instructive to watch), and then go.

The interesting, and to my mind rewarding, characteristic of this system was that although what the lecturers had to tell us about the art of acting was usually very clear and definitive, the instruction they gave was often incompatible with, and sometimes contradictory to, what we had been told by another lecturer the day before.

It would have been good to have had an opportunity to discuss this phenomenon with the lecturers themselves, but that wasn't what they were being paid to do, and in any case they were legging it out of the building the moment the session was over.

I don't see this as a having been a deprivation. On the contrary I see it as a benefit, because it meant that we, the students, were forced to take on board the contradictory instructions we received and then have to work out for ourselves, among ourselves, where the truth lay; or rather, were able to find out that there was no absolute truth, that we each had to find our own way to deliver the goods. It may be a novel approach to education but I would recommend it.

Not all the lecturers were passers-by. Beatrice Forbes-Robertson, of the great theatrical family, who was in her eighties but still light as a feather, brought Shakespeare to life for us through her own delight. Trevennen Peters, bearded and sardonic, was as likely to talk on philosophy as on acting and had once, I remember, thanked me for bringing a note of proper disrespect to his lectures.

But the empress of Friday afternoon was a really great lady: Frieda Hodgson. In her presence one was lifted and carried forward on a deep warm tide of encouragement and possibility. She had a close personal relationship with every one of her students, a relationship that was far from indulgent. Her eye was clear and critical but at the same time she gave each student the sense of being both supported and appreciated, and from that sense came the courage they needed to lift themselves over the threshold of diffidence.

Technically I'm not sure that Frieda was a very exact teacher, at least I found that if I listened too closely to the words she was saying they didn't always make a lot of sense, but that was not her role. As an inspirer Frieda was without peer and many distinguished actors and actresses in the theatre today have reason to cherish her belief in them, and pay tribute to the part she played in bringing them to success.

At LAMDA I played a love-sick fairy and the king of the ants in Karel Capek's *Insect Play*, and provided shiny carapaces for the dung-beetles by turning my father's overcoats inside out. We played a scene from Shakespeare's *As You Like It* in an imaginary railway station, complete with hand-luggage and tickets. I also, to my shame, played a piece of delicate, elegant, Restoration comedy (from *The Rivals*, I think) wearing American army boots.

The time I spent at LAMDA was, in some ways, one of the happiest in my life. In that acceptive community of individuals I was able to be at ease and make some long-lasting friendships, as well as learning something of the craft of acting.

My heart, which had seemed quiescent for the last few years, was moved again. I got to know a nervous, tearful girl named Ro, who happened to live near me in North London. We became close friends and I slowly fell in love with her. Our relationship was not easy, mainly because she didn't feel the same for me, but it was to prove durable.

The course at LAMDA was for two years. At the end of the first year I took the Gold Medal Examination, for which I did my piece from *The Rivals* (in the boots). The adjudicator that year was Peter Ustinov, which was slightly confusing because at the time he was married to one of my relatives and we had met on family occasions. We greeted each other warmly, he overlooked the boots, and awarded me the Gold Medal for Acting, which I treasure to this day.

When we saw the curriculum for the next year at LAMDA, I and some of the other post-war-service students noticed that it was to be an exact repeat of the first year. This fact was confirmed by the Principal, who saw no fault in it. Several of us did see fault in it, and promptly left the Academy to seek our fortunes in the real world of the theatre.

II. The Playhouse.

As I turned to go, the agent said: 'Do yourself a favour, lad. Don't go flashing that gong about. It doesn't signify.'

'Oh, right-ho,' I said lightly, putting my Gold Medal for Acting back in my pocket, 'you'll be in touch, then, will you?'

The agent looked at me sadly without answering, and I left.

Being an actor in 1948 didn't often involve acting. Mainly it involved climbing many flights of narrow smelly stairs to importune bored theatrical agents. It involved endlessly poring over the small advertisements in *The Stage* and it also involved something else, something invisible and imponderable: having inside knowledge of where to go, what to do and who to be seen hobnobbing with in order to be at the centre of the theatrical scene – the place where, one assumed, the jobs were being handed out.

There were no jobs being handed out in London, so I was lucky to spot an ad in *The Stage* from a big production company that was casting actors and staff for a group of first-class theatres in the south of England. I applied and was called to an interview with the producer. He warned me that he was taking a great risk in doing so but he was going to appoint me actor/stage-director for their Brighton company – at £3 10s a week.

I was over the moon. I bought the necessary dinner jacket and bow-tie from the Fifty-shilling Tailors. I travelled to Brighton, found myself cheap lodgings and, as instructed, presented myself at the first-class theatre. This was called the Playhouse and was situated in a back street in Kemptown, the poor end of the town.

The door of the theatre was open, so I went in. The auditorium was small, but long and thin, presumably because it had been built as a cinema. The stage was a bit shallow, which was OK, but behind it and on each side of it there was hardly any space, just a wall at the back and a wall on each side with an ordinary door in it. I saw a pencilled note stuck to the box-office window: 'QW rehearsal Sunday 2.30 p.m.'. It was now 11.30 a.m.

I wandered about Brighton for the next hour or two, feeling very keyed-up and wondering what QW meant. Then at 2.20 p.m.

I entered the theatre and walked straight into a loud row that was going on between the producer and a large middle-aged lady with a fat, sad face. The producer saw me coming and, to end the row perhaps, turned his anger on to me. 'Oh, there you are. About bloody time. We're relying on you, you know! Listen everybody, this is Oliver Post ... er, thing. Our new stage-director. So from now on all questions go to him. Come on, let's get on with reading this play. From the top ... Oh, just mime the telephone for now, dear. We'll need a telephone for rehearsals, Oliver, see to it. Come on everybody. Settle down now, we've only got a week!'

They started to read the play – *Quiet Wedding*. I stood there, stunned with agitation. What? Just *what* was I supposed to be doing?

I survived, and managed to do my job. Some of the plays were fun but the romantic lead was always played by a middle-aged lady called Mona. This was because the 'big production company with a group of first-class theatres' was a fiction. Mona's husband, a chemical manufacturer, owned the Playhouse.

We put on some surprisingly elaborate productions, including Noël Coward's trilogy of one-act plays, *Tonight at Eight-thirty*. One of these was *Brief Encounter*, in which a young actor named John Teagen and I played the comic relief – two half-drunk soldiers in the station tea-room. After the show a fast-talking gentleman called Mr Jobson came round to see us. He said we were a great act and he offered us a spot in his forthcoming pantomime, *Aladdin*, which would be touring number one dates in the south of England at Christmas.

What a piece of luck that was! And providential too, because after *Brief Encounter* the company was dismissed. Gossip had it that Mona's encounters with the leading man, both on and off the stage, had been briefer than she would have wished and as a result she had decided she didn't want her toy any more. So the chemical manufacturer closed it and the Kemptown Playhouse reverted to its original function – showing rude films.

III. Pantomime.

Mr Jobson was as good as his word. He came to tea in John Teagen's room in Earls Court and talked tremendously fast and enthusiastically about his Christmas ventures. We gave him hot buttered toast to eat but that didn't slow down the torrent of words, it just gave them substance.

Mr Jobson was by trade a scenery contractor. He had, he said, huge warehouses full of gorgeous scenery and full set-pieces, from which he supplied all the most glittering shows in the south. For his own ventures he had the pick of the best scenery and the greatest talent in the world at his fingertips. He told us of the marvellous acts that he had booked for the show, how he had managed to engage Tubby Blackwell and Zelda! We had heard of them of course – best 'Big Wheels' in the business! And the Great Ernest Watson, whose dog, Lily, did those amazing card tricks. And did we know Armand and Heloïse, Apache dancers extraordinaires? We must! The verve, the vitality, the passion! Oh, hot stuff, strong stuff for a panto, a bit sexy, but WOW! And the dancers, COR! The Mavis Bewley Dancers . . . tap, ballet, speciality, Lat'n American, they could do it all, and sing too, big chorus numbers, marvellous! But we were to have real music as well, with a real musical director, young but really talented, and a full three-piece orchestral ensemble.

'What about *Aladdin*?' I asked.

Uninterrupted the flow went on. He had got the best Principal Boy there ever was and a great Abanazer. The Emperor was a wow and the Princess . . . Oh! The thought of her beauty almost silenced him for a second. She was a stunner, gorgeous, but so delicate, so vulnerable, so pure. And we, we two were going to be a smash hit. We did *real* acting. He was, he declared, a great respecter of real acting. He had seen at once that we had the true spark. Not just the tinsel glitter of show-biz but the real thing, the clear light of great art.

We found this outpouring of praise, flattery and buttery toast-crumbs quite irresistible. We readily agreed take the part of a pair of Chinese policemen at £15 a week for the Act, which was twice what we had been getting at the Playhouse.

The rehearsal room above the Rose and Crown in Tooting was large, with some chairs set out and some stacked by a piano at one end. As in a doctor's waiting room a number of ordinary-looking people were sitting around the edge of the room. John Teagen and I entered, smiled and took seats next to the door.

After a while I had the feeling that we were being scrutinized. People would look at us, then turn to each other and quietly say something. Then they would look at us again.

A tall man with slightly military bearing rose and came over. He was holding a paper.

'Teagen and Post?' he said.

'I beg your pardon?'

'It says here Teagen and Post, on the cast list. Chinese policemen.'

'Oh, right. This is John Teagen. I'm Oliver Postgate.'

'So you are Teagen and Post. Got your music?'

'Music?'

The man looked at us in silence and then marched out of the room. He could soon be heard talking angrily on the telephone on the landing. The other people watched us anxiously.

Sitting together at the other side of the room was a middle-aged couple, she knitting, he reading a magazine. To break the silence I got up and walked over to them. 'Good morning,' I said. 'My name is Oliver Postgate. This is John Teagen.'

The lady smiled. 'Pleased to meet you. This is Gerald Worple. I'm Amy.'

'May we join you?' I asked.

'Oh, please do.'

So John and I sat down and we had a quiet chat. Amy and Gerald Worple were in fact Armand and Heloïse, Apache dancers extraordinaires.

'Do you know what's going on?' I asked.

'We'll just be doing the moves, I expect,' said Amy. 'In fact I think we'll do ours now. Come on, Gerald.'

Amy took a sheaf of music out of her bag and gave it to a young woman who took it to the piano.

Then the place seemed to come to life. The Apache dancers' music was exciting. The real Parisian angry-passionate stuff. Gerald and Amy checked the tempo, got into the beat, and took their places for the dance. 'Right. From the top, please,' said Amy.

What Gerald and Amy did next *was* extraordinaire. They walked briskly forward to meet each other, held hands for a second and then turned away. She waved her arms and stepped back. He walked around behind her and lightly tapped her on the head. She stooped slightly, turned around, and they walked backwards together across the room, took hands and circled slowly, nodding to the music. She touched the top of his head, he stooped and stood still while she walked across the room.

We watched, fascinated. The music swooped to its fiery end.

'Lovely,' said Amy. 'Have to watch out for the rallentando. We can't hold it for ever. How was it for time?'

'Thirteen eleven,' said the pianist.

'I think it'll stretch a bit,' said Amy.

She and Gerald came and sat down, not even out of breath.

'We're thinking of opening a guest-house in St Leonards,' said Amy.

'Are you? I've got an aunt lives in Hastings.'

'Can't keep young and fit for ever!' laughed Gerald. 'Got to make provision for our old age. By the way, how d'you reckon it went?'

'Fantastic,' I said. 'Marvellous music. Strong stuff. Tell me, though, what were the taps on the head? You know, just now and then.'

'Oh, they're the trays,' said Amy. 'We do the trays, you know.'

'The trays?'

'Yes. Gerald's the waiter. I'm the tart. In this French café. We slam trays about. We use those cheap tin trays. They just crumple up. You must have seen it done!'

'No, never,' I said. 'Sounds fantastic. I can't wait.'

'We can't wait, neither,' said the tall man, who had been standing over us. 'We'll do your bit now, OK?'

'Er ... right-ho.'

John Teagen and I stood up, feeling as if we were about to be sentenced. We stood in silence while the company looked at us.

'What's your act, then?' asked the tall man.

'Well, er ... nothing worked out.'

'What do you do? Rolls and falls? Stage-slaps?'

'A bit ... at the drama school.' That got a laugh.

'Do you dance? Tap? Soft shoe? Speciality?'

I shook my head.

'Can you put across a number?'

'A what?'

'Can you sing?'

'I don't know.'

'So we're going to have to teach you, are we?'

'I don't know.' I was near to tears. 'May I go home, please?'

'No. Sorry. You two have got work to do. Take off your jackets and put these on.' The tall man reached behind the table and brought out two toy policeman's helmets.

'Just a minute,' I said.

'Yes, what?'

'Who are you?'

'Me?' The man seemed puzzled.

'Yes, you. Do you by any chance have a name? What do you do?'

'Trevor Prangley. I play Abanazer. I also produce the show. OK?'

'Ah, thank you. Very pleased to meet you, Mr Prangley. My name is Oliver Postgate. This is John Teagen.'

'I know that. It's written on the cast list. You're Teagen and Post. Well now, that's settled. I wonder if you would do us a favour and put on the helmets. Then we'll do some slaps.'

Abanazer was sounding almost conciliatory so John and I rolled up our sleeves and put on the helmets.

To do a stage-slap, one person slaps the other, but just stops short or just misses. At the apparent moment of impact the person slapped secretly claps his hands to create the sound of the slap. It's easy once you've rehearsed it, and very convincing. Rolls and falls are something else. The essence is to appear to be knocked over but in fact to propel oneself, relying on the orchestra to provide the noise. Neither of us was exactly athletic, or supple. We were both clumsy, deeply embarrassed and nervous.

'Anybody would think,' observed the Principal Boy, a podgy lady who chain-smoked, 'that we had performing seals.'

She wasn't referring to our clumsy falls but to the lino where, at every fall, my sweaty hands had left a pair of slithery flipper-marks.

Soon, thank goodness, the helmets were casualties. Trying to do a forward roll, I had landed squarely on the point of mine and rammed it so hard on to my head that the papier-mâché had to be peeled off in pieces.

Abanazer was scathing about our knockabout act, but he said that with the help of the orchestral effects, the whizzes, bangs and claps, we might just about get away with it.

That evening we went our ways bruised, aching and disconsolate.

Rehearsals continued and after a while Abanazer turned his attention to the song and dance routines. There, he said, we had first-class material to work with.

The first dance routine was classical; Egyptian. We had to stand dead sideways, holding strange gestures to imitate the figures in the hieroglyphs of Ancient Egypt, and shuffle across the stage, whipping round at the end of each line and shuffling back in a different posture. The music was weird, there were no words and I couldn't really see what any of it had to do with Chinese or policemen. When I asked Abanazer he said it was all Oriental and anyway what difference did it make?

The rehearsing of *Aladdin* itself, the play, was fairly low-key and perfunctory, partly because most of the cast had played it before, and partly because the ones doing speciality acts, being otherwise engaged, didn't turn up till the last day.

The Princess, whose beauty and delicacy had so moved Mr Jobson, also turned up on the last day of rehearsals. Although her acting was limp and her manner lethargic, she was indeed strikingly beautiful and, strangely, type-cast for the role of the cloistered princess whom none may set eyes on, because she was squired by a heavy man in a double-breasted suit who couldn't keep his hands off her. He watched her, and glared at everybody else, throughout the rehearsal and whisked her away in a big car the moment it was over.

Eventually the time came to move. I went ahead and fixed up cheap lodgings for John and myself in Ryde. Then I walked out to find the cinema, where the glittering show was to open. It seemed sad, with only a stand-up board outside and some curled photos of the cast pinned up in the foyer.

Looking at these I was intrigued to notice that the Great Ernest Watson wore full evening tails and a top hat, and his dog, Lily, a frilly collar for their act. Tubby Blackwell was, it seemed, a fixed-bar acrobat and Zelda wore skin-tights covered with sequins. I didn't recognize Gerald and Amy from their photograph. At that moment the picture of the handsome, sullen waiter, Armand, and the perky, flaunting Parisian tart, Heloïse, posing against the Impressionist café background seemed more alive and interesting than *Aladdin* or, come to that, Ryde. I was really looking forward to seeing their act.

On the afternoon before the show was due to open there was a run-through of the play, but most of the time was spent sorting out the scenery and props for the speciality acts. Gerald and Amy had their own café cloth. The Great Ernest had a massive chromium and black set-piece like a nineteen-thirties cocktail bar. Tubby and Zelda's fixed bar had strong guy-wires that had to be hooked into holes which Zelda had drilled into the corners of the floor of the stage with a brace and bit. *Aladdin*'s scenery, the street in Old Peking beside the Emperor's Palace, included various wing-flats, one of which was a fish and chip shop and another a piece of Baroque church. I mentioned this to Gerald who explained that, as Mr Jobson was a scenery contractor, all the good stuff went out at Christmas, to paying companies. His own productions had to make do with what was left over.

The Mavis Bewley Dance Troupe, a collection of local school-girls aged between eleven and fourteen years, was everywhere, winking and flaunting and squeaking. Mavis Bewley played for them herself. She chose a position out of the audience's sight behind the corner of the proscenium from which to play her accordion. As it was a very large accordion, her left arm and half the instrument would move in and out of the audience's view. As this was happening in time to the music the effect wasn't particularly distracting.

As the afternoon wore on and curtain-up time came closer I felt the familiar first-night excitement rising in my blood. Everything seemed to be in hand. There was one moment of emergency: Gerald and Amy's trays hadn't arrived with their skip, so somebody had to go out and buy some – but that was not my job.

The half was called. As I put on the costume and the make-up I could hear the rustling and chatter of the audience coming in. John and I wished each other good luck and we moved to our positions, one on each side at the back of the stage.

The girls were already on. The orchestra – piano, drums and trombone – was doing a good job with the plinky-plonky overture.

The end chord came. The curtain hissed as it went up its wires.

'Sing up, Gels!' shrilled Mavis as she hauled at her accordion.

The clear untutored voices of the girls sang out:

'Hail mighty Emperor of China

Of noble birth and ancestreee.

Gladly we bow before thee,

Voicing our love and loyalteee . . .'

It had started. They were doing well.

As the song ended the Emperor in his fine robes strolled in, followed by his Grand Vizier. He strolled a bit slowly because for some reason the girls were being a bit slow moving out. The orchestra vamped a few bars until most of them were off and then the Emperor spoke his first line:

'Well, Chung-k'ing, what entertainment have you prepared for me this lovely morning?'

That was the first time I had heard the Emperor use his full voice. It was very impressive.

The Grand Vizier did his imitation of Winston Churchill, which the Emperor (rightly, I thought) rejected, demanding stronger stuff. That was our cue. We fell across the stage. John did his snatch of cod-opera. We did our knockabout act, but as the chap in the orchestra doing the whizzes, bangs and claps couldn't actually see us, he did them at the wrong times. That didn't help. Then we went straight into our number. The Egyptian piece was very mysterious and, I suspect, baffling.

I felt mounting despair as the music went on and on, but, eventually, the number ended. It was received with respectful silence by the audience. The Emperor, as he was supposed to, ordered us away. We chased off and he was able to start his ominous song about what would happen to anybody who caught sight of his beautiful daughter, the Princess.

'. . . to compensate,
How sad his fate,
He'll perish,
mis'rableeee . . .'

The last note was rich and deep. Awesome stuff!

The play was doing well. The girls were still having difficulty getting on and off the stage for their chorus numbers. This was because the scenery had been set too close and they had to hop, one at a time, over the struts. So they were queuing at the back of the stage, giggling, but that didn't seem to matter. The acting was very strong and the drama unfolded. Aladdin met the Princess. They fell in love. They kissed and were discovered. The Policemen were called in to arrest Aladdin. He was about to be dragged off to execution when Abanazer stalked in (my goodness he was frightening!) and brought the thunderous power of his magic to bear on the situation:

'. . . and under my magic spell,
you shall all stand where you are,
and let the boy and I
go WHERE we WILL! . . . AHA!'

Abanazer snarled and threw the magic sequin dust. We all froze in absurd positions waiting for the thunderclap, the flash and the blackout, during which the halfway cloth of the next scene, the Road to the Cave, would be lowered in.

Unfortunately none of these things happened. We stood there bathed in golden light for, it seemed, minutes on end.

Then the Emperor exercised his authority. 'Well, sod that!' he said loudly and walked off. We all relaxed. At that moment the halfway cloth dropped in like a bomb. Luckily Abanazer and Aladdin were on the front side of it. Book-wings in the shape of rocks were shoved into each side and the scene was set. Abanazer and Aladdin were at last able to go on with the play, at least until the end of that scene, when they discovered that they had been boxed in by the book-wings. There was no way out.

Abanazer dealt with that small problem very promptly. He reached down, picked up the whole bottom-batten of the cloth and, lifting it high in the air, courteously ushered Aladdin underneath it. He followed through and dropped the lot behind him with a crash. For this he received tumultuous applause.

The curtain came down for the end of the first act.

The second act opened with Tubby and Zelda's fixed-bar number. Tubby was an amazing athlete. He wasn't tall or handsome; he was like a tennis-ball made of solid muscle. He swung and circled and somersaulted in perfect time to the music. Watching from the wings I could see what Mr Jobson had meant when he said he had the best 'Big Wheels' in the business. Zelda curtsied and posed as he did it, looking very glittery in her sequins.

Watching from the wings I noticed something else. The boards which the guy-wires were hooked into were lifting. Each time Tubby performed a grand circle they seemed to spring a bit more. I looked across and caught John's eye. He nodded and we both stepped boldly on to the stage and stood one on each side with our arms folded, looking like policemen.

Zelda saw us and skipped lightly across. She gave me a flashing smile and hissed: 'Piss off out of it!' I opened my mouth to speak but she pirouetted and fluttered across to John: 'Sod off! This is our act!' she whispered and kicked his ankle.

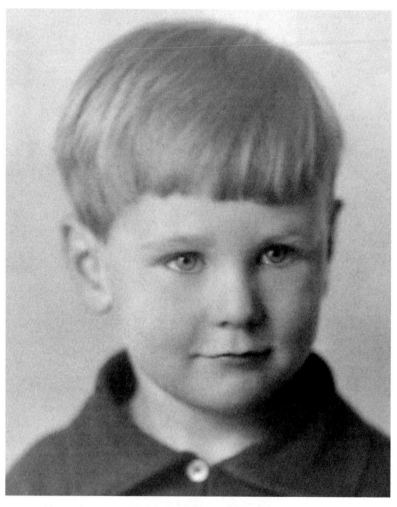

Portrait of the young person, taken in 1928.

Me, my mother Daisy and my brother John, in the garden at Hendon in 1927.

My parents, Ray and Daisy, properly
dressed for a walking holiday in 1927.

Our family holidays were often spent
at Wissant, on the coast of France
near Calais. There were miles of
sandy dunes and the wind was cold.

Me, John and Daisy at Wissant in 1932.

The Rt. Hon. George Lansbury PC MP. Grandad was by far the *largest* man in my small life!

Daisy and me on the deck of the SS *Margharita*, bound for Denmark. I don't know why I was wearing a suit with long trousers and looking gloomy. Perhaps I was just trying to be grown up.

In 1937, on the way to our cycling holiday, we met the Thurtle family at a café in Dieppe. From left to right: our cousin Peter, his wife-to-be Kitty, Uncle Ernest Thurtle MP, Daisy, Daisy's sister Dolly (lately Mayor of Shoreditch), me, Ray, our cousin Helen, and the bicycles.

Me, making a pot. In about 1942, I would guess.

This is me on the ancient motorcycle which I found in a hedge in Essex in 1945. It was a 1926 New Imperial with burned-out valves and no springs.

Beatrice: the 1924 bull-nosed Cowley that Cecily Martin gave me in 1946.

Lunch in the shade of the big walnut tree in the garden at Finchley in 1955. My sister-in-law Mary is at the table. My brother John is holding their daughter Selina. Cousin Kate is in the background and Ray is carving the joint. It is an idyllic memory. The squirrels in the trees would drop walnut shells on us as we ate.

Some friends:

Me with Albertine, the 1930 Austin Seven which I bought in 1953. She was the joy of my life even though she had almost no brakes.

Jill thinking.

Bob Auf der Mauer considering the prospect of lunch.

Keith wondering.

Not a friend. This is the virtuoso pig that in 1950 failed to bring me fame on television.

My new family: Prue with her five
children at a picnic in 1960. Kerris and
Kevan are on either side of her at the top
and below them Krispian is wrestling with
our twins Simon and Stephen.

Simon and Stephen on the beach
in front of our house in Whitstable.

1965. Daniel, our
youngest, in the garden
of our new old house,
an ex-pub on the road
to Canterbury . . .

. . . known as Red Lion House.

Work:

Our first television programme,
Alexander the Mouse, in 1958.

Ivor the Engine, 1959.

Our first single-frame puppet film,
The Pingwings, 1961.

1964. The witch from *The Pogles* –
too frightening for the BBC!

Pogles' Wood, 1965. Mr Pogle with Pippin,
Mrs Pogle and Tog setting out to earn our living.

Meanwhile Tubby, apparently unaware of any problems, was whirling in the air like an indiarubber Catherine-wheel. Zelda crossed in front of me and jabbed me in the solar-plexus with her elbow.

'I'm holding the floor down!' I gasped.

'Fuck off! Go on! Do it now!'

I caught John's eye and we both stepped back. Ten seconds later, with a crack like a pistol shot, one of the guy-wires broke out. The fixed bar came unfixed. The audience gasped but Tubby was a genius. He let the bar go, whipped into an airborne somersault and landed on his feet beside Zelda. They smiled and took their bows.

As they came off Zelda was weeping. She glared accusingly at John and me. 'He could have broke his poor neck!' she wailed, and ran to her dressing room.

The audience took that disaster, as it took everything else, in its stride. But as the debris of Tubby's equipment was whisked away in the blackout and the drama went ahead, I prayed that the spirit of the Marx Brothers that had somehow got into the performance would at least be gentle from now on.

For a while it seemed that it might be so. Widow Twankey, a skinny old man with an ingratiating manner, tried fervently to persuade the children to believe in fairies but they, equally fervently, told him to get stuffed. The cocktail bar, with the Great Ernest in it, was found incongruously in the streets of Old Peking. His dog Lily, though obviously anxious to please, muffed a couple of her card-tricks, but the audience forgave her and, far from blaming, loved her for it. All seemed to be well.

The last act opened with the Apache dance extraordinaire. That was what I had come to see. I posted myself in Mavis's place to have a good view. Their backcloth was old but very striking. In the pools of light the white bamboo café table and chairs appeared to glow with an inner light. The years had fallen from Gerald and Amy and, in their costumes and make-up, he truly was the lustful jealous Armand and she the teasing coquette, Heloïse.

The fierce music brought them suddenly to life and they

swung into their routine. It was recognizable as being the one that we had seen in Tooting, but now, where they had walked, they flew, where he had lifted, he threw. They clinched and whirled, fled and were recaptured. Heloïse seized a tray from the pile, swung it and brought it down on his head with a crash. He staggered, pretended to fall and then leapt up again, grabbed her, swung her round and over his head and, taking another tray, clouted her with that. The dance went on, full of fiery lust and primal savagery, but slowly, something – could it be age? – began to tell. Their movements faltered. They staggered. They wavered and recovered, swung their trays, missed and, as the music swooped to its climactic end, they sank to the floor and collapsed, together at last in each other's arms. It was a very original and moving performance.

The audience was in raptures. It rose and cheered, but it was several seconds before Armand and Heloïse were able to stand up to acknowledge the applause. They smiled and bowed, but as they turned I saw that it was Gerald Worple who was taking Amy gently by the arm and leading her away from the stage.

Quite late the next morning I was sitting in the Cosy Café with the Worples. Amy was explaining.

'It's the rage does it,' she said. 'You can't do the act properly if you don't let it get to you a bit. I mean ... it wouldn't look right. But you see, the proper tin trays don't count. They don't hurt, they just crumple up. Isn't that right, dear?'

Gerald nodded. 'That's it. The moment you belted me with that stainless-steel job I just saw red. From then on it was all for real.'

'It certainly looked real to me,' I said.

'Oh it was,' said Amy. 'I was that furious, if I'd had a club I'd have laid him out cold. I would have, really!'

She put her hand over Gerald's and they looked at each other. She patted it. 'Don't worry, love. The proper trays have come. We'll be all right now.' She turned to me.

'What about you two, then? Your whole act has been cut. That really *is* a shame.'

I said: 'No, and yes ... No, I don't mind its being cut. I'm glad to be off the hook. But also ... yes. It is a shame you haven't got a proper knockabout act for *Aladdin*. I'm sorry about that. I feel a bit ashamed.'

'Not your fault,' said Gerald. 'Jobson should never have booked you, not without telling you what you were in for. He's all fancies, and stupid with it. And he's a crook as well.'

Amy patted his hand. 'Now don't say things, dear. We just have to keep an eye open, that's all.'

'Even so,' I went on, 'I feel I've let the company down and they have every right to feel hostile towards us.'

'What company?' asked Gerald. 'There isn't any company. There's a dozen or so people stuck on the Isle of Wight doing their own thing and getting paid for it. They don't care tuppence for you or the play, or for anything except the money.'

That was a comfort. I felt better about the next fortnight. I would be a respectable inscrutable Chinese policeman, join in the songs, arrest Aladdin and be part of the scenery.

Time passed slowly but fairly easily. Audiences dropped away until towards the end we were playing to half-filled houses. Mr Jobson turned up on the last day. He was full of praises and invited us all to join him in the big hotel after the show for a celebratory glass.

We waited in the hotel bar for about a quarter of an hour, feeling a bit embarrassed at not buying any drinks. Then suddenly the Emperor looked at Abanazer, who looked at Widow Twankey. He looked at the Principal Boy who shouted: 'Christ! He's fucking off with the takings!'

Without another word the cast streamed out of the hotel and set off for the ferry terminal to head Mr Jobson off. 'Thank God we're on an island.' sighed Widow Twankey as he puffed up the steps. 'If it'd been on the mainland we'd have had to fish for it.'

IV. Thronging.

The pantomime was perhaps the pinnacle of my theatrical career. From then on it was all downhill.

I got a good engagement as actor/stage manager with an excellent company at the Margate Hippodrome, but that only lasted a few weeks.

I did an audition for the Royal Shakespeare Company, which was embarrassing. I applied for a General Audition for BBC Radio. This took place in an empty studio with a microphone. Perhaps by mistake the people listening in another room had left their microphone on, so I could softly hear them sneering and mocking from the start.

That was depressing and I was feeling sorry for myself when I met John Arlott. He was an old friend who was well on his way to becoming a famous cricket commentator.

John was very sympathetic when he heard about the General Audition and he immediately gave me a part in a programme he was doing about Irish Railways for the BBC Education Department.

I don't think I gave a very good performance. I was appallingly nervous, while the rest of the cast, all full-time members of the BBC Repertory Company, were so appallingly relaxed that they were mucking about and playing practical jokes. One of the members of the cast, a big sporting chap named Greg, played a particularly disturbing trick. While I was reading a rather long paragraph, he stood on the other side of the microphone and vigorously chewed the sleeve of his Harris tweed jacket. That had a very unwelcome effect on my salivary glands. It was all meant in fun of course and as soon as he saw that because I was so nervous the jokes were really putting me off, he stopped and apologized at once. Perhaps to make amends, he invited me to come back to his house for a cup of tea after the recording.

Greg's house was sumptuously furnished, like a Victorian club, with brass fittings, dark wood and deep leather chairs. He also had, surprisingly, a butler. Greg handed the butler his coat and said we would like tea as soon as poss., with toast.

Greg and I sat in armchairs beside a blazing fire. We talked about the hazards of broadcasting and radio work in general. After a while the butler appeared with a large silver tray which he carried to the table beside Greg. He lowered the tray to a point about two inches above the polished table and then, quite deliberately, dropped it. The tray fell with a loud clatter. The butler tossed his head and flounced out of the room. Greg took no notice at all, just went on talking.

Luckily none of the china was broken. Greg poured the tea. The hot buttered toast was excellent. We had a long friendly chat and then I went home. As the butler held the front door open for me to leave, he bowed and said something softly under his breath, but I didn't catch it.

The next time I met John Arlott I mentioned what had happened. He laughed and told me that Greg was, as people now say, 'gay' and that he had a habit, very distressing to his boyfriend the butler, of bringing home attractive young men for his pleasure.

'Oh!' I said. 'I never guessed.'

'Of course not!' laughed John. 'You were perfectly safe. There is no armour like innocence.'

I have since wondered how many times my innocence or, more accurately, ignorance, has guarded my honour. I have no way of knowing.

My next engagement, at a dismal theatre in Southport, was mercifully very short. The producer, a sly spiteful man, had engaged twice as many actors as he needed, with the intention of sacking half of them almost immediately.

Later in the year, it must have been 1947, I mingled with the mighty. I was given the part of First Fisherman in a production of *Pericles* at the Rudolph Steiner Theatre. Pericles was being played by Paul Scofield, and Second Fisherman was played by a young man whose name was Donald Sinden. Unfortunately the production was just a showcase and only ran for a couple of performances.

My theatrical career ended with my last engagement – one day as a film extra. I can't remember the name of the film or anything about the director except that he was Hungarian.

I went to the film studios very early in the morning and was given a nineteenth-century jacket to wear over my ordinary clothes and a cloth cap with a knob on the top. After waiting some hours, I and several dozen other friendly people, equally oddly dressed, were invited on to the film set, which seemed to be a square in some European city at about the turn of the century. In the absence of any direct instructions I think most of us assumed that we were there to give the illusion that the place was populated. So we walked about and met each other and engaged in imaginary conversations, even made purposeful journeys and generally tried not to look like a load of extras standing about on the set.

After a few minutes of this the director addressed us through a loudhailer: 'No, no. It says here please zat you are a *throng*. Now please will you please commence to throng ... Action!'

We moved about rather faster and showed urgency by speaking briskly to one another and pointing at imaginary things.

'No, no, no! Zis is not a cattle-market. Please you are here to throng. Garry, love, I ask you please, why do zey not throng?'

Garry, a nice young man with wavy hair, took the loudhailer and had a word with us: 'Now come along, please. Let's get this together. You aren't just wandering about, you are a throng. Now you lot on the left, you throng in from that side and the ones on the right throng in from this side. OK? ... Action!'

So I thronged in from the right and met a girl I had known at the Drama School who was thronging the other way. 'Did we do thronging?' she asked. 'Not *as such*,' I replied as I passed on.

'No, no, no! Zis is not country-dancing, please. Garry, please, they must *throng*!'

Garry had another word with us and next time we thronged in from the four corners, meeting in the middle in a polite apologetic scrum. I raised my cap to my friend.

She said: 'We did do self-realization in music and movement.'

'Not quite the same thing perhaps,' I suggested.

'Is no good!' wailed the director. 'Cut, please. For zis we must have a throng, not a football Rugby. Now please Garry if zese people cannot, send zem away thank you and fetch me people who will properly throng.'

Garry took the loudhailer and said: 'Right, then. We'll break now for coffee. Thank you, folks. Please call in at the office as you leave.'

I came away with £3 in my pocket and it was only a quarter to eleven in the morning – not a bad rate of pay for unskilled thronging.

7

RATTLING THE BARS

I. The White Knight.

By the beginning of 1950 life in our house at Finchley had changed completely. John and his girlfriend from Oxford days, Mary Stewart, were married in October 1948 and had gone to live in Twickenham, and all the wartime lodgers had moved on. Having been captain of a busy ship all through the war, feeding the hungry relatives and dealing with every emergency as it arose, Daisy now found that the emergencies, apart from the boring restrictions of food rationing, were over. Except for my intermittent presence, she and Ray were alone and, as she put it, '... rattling about in that damn great house'.

I had things to do. I had long ago realised that the one essential thing an aspiring actor needs is another source of income. So I was trying to find a market for my designs for agricultural machinery. Nobody would look at my mechanical sugar-beet lifter but one firm showed interest in my bouncing fence-post driver, the cork-screw post-hole digger and the over-arm jib which I had worked out for lifters and excavators. They were fascinated by the over-arm jib but in the end they decided that all these things were too outlandish ever to take on, and returned them, but with a small cheque, which was gratefully received.

I could see that I should be offering simpler ideas, ones for which capital costs would be low and the financial returns fairly swift. That obviously ruled out my favourite inventions – various rotary engines, the jet-lifted hovercraft and the giant silent toc-toc boat.

On the other hand there was hope for the alarm wristwatch that didn't buzz or ring but silently tapped on the wearer's wrist. And of course for the windscreen wipers for motor-cyclists' goggles, a pair of which I had actually made and worn while riding my push-bike – much to the amusement of passers-by. I think it was these which caused my father to observe, slightly ruefully, that he was surprised to find that he was the father of the White Knight.*

It occurred to me that one field in which small ideas would probably be welcome would be toy-design. So, quite deliberately, I settled down with a pad of blank paper and a pencil to try and think of new ideas for toys.

I was attracted by the idea of remotely controlled mechanical toys. Radio controls already existed for model aircraft but they were expensive and limited in scope. It seemed to me that toys could be controlled from a distance but not necessarily by invisible means. An unobtrusive wire would do.

There were some tiny cheap reversible electric motors on the market. I bought some of these and used them to make some wire-controlled toy vehicles, which could be steered like tanks. The toy I finally made was very peaceful – a remotely driven fork-lift truck. This would buzz about, picking up small things like cigarette packets or cups and saucers, lifting them up and stacking them in

---

* The White Knight is a character in Lewis Carroll's *Alice Through the Looking Glass* who invents particularly unlikely articles.

neat piles. I loved it and played with it for hours, becoming so skilled that I could work all the systems at once, so that it behaved almost as if it were alive.

I took this one to the managing director of a major toy manufacturer. I didn't say much. I simply put it on his desk and we watched it begin to gather his papers and pens and scissors and thing-holders, carry them to the edge and drop them one by one into the waste-paper basket. He pressed the intercom and said into it: 'Everybody in here.' Then he sat back in his chair and watched the procedure with great satisfaction. His colleagues filed quietly into the office and they too watched in respectful silence. I felt rather proud. When the desk was clear I called it on to my hand.

'No office should be without one,' said the managing director.

The demonstration had been very successful. Everybody was full of fun, but in the end the firm didn't take the toy.

None of this was making me any money. I realised that if I wanted a quick return I would do better to be a craftsman, making and selling finished articles.

Like what, for example? There followed a period of frenzied enterprises, many of which I have forgotten. I spent a lot of time making Batik scarves and hand-painted materials. These were very attractive and might have gone well today in Carnaby Street and the craft markets, but in 1950 the buyers in the big stores sneered at them.

It occurred to me that there might be some future in making animations for television, so I made a flat pig which played 'Parlez-moi d'amour' on a violin, interspersed with squeals and grunts. The effect of this on the BBC Television Office at Alexandra Palace was totally hysterical – far more devastating than I had dared to imagine. They howled and wept and begged me to stop. They fell completely in love with the gross article and insisted that I leave it with them, being sure that it would be the inspiration of great things.

I heard no more about the virtuoso pig, or about anything else, so I concluded that there was no future for me in television. By the autumn of 1950 I also had to admit that the theatre, or rather my ambitions to have any part in it, had receded so far that I could no longer, with any honesty, describe myself as an actor. This distancing was not so much due to my not being any good as an actor – there hadn't been much chance to find out about that – as to my lack of commitment. I didn't live for the theatre. My sole interest and raison d'être was not centred in the West End. I didn't spend the whole of my time badgering agents, mingling with the hopeful and exchanging theatre gossip. That wasn't in my blood and, in the theatre of 1950, if that wasn't in your blood there was little chance of work coming your way.

I had also had a problem with the language. I had an unforgivable habit of saying what I thought was true before I had really thought about what would be wise, or kind, to say. The language of theatrical flattery does have meanings but these are coded and cushioned by elaborate tact, simply because, in a world where life is being sustained only by far-fetched hopes and carefully tended illusions, words of cold reality are just poison. I am ashamed not to have been able to learn that language, but perhaps that too was in my blood.

Having concluded that I wasn't, after all, cut out to be an actor, I couldn't go on pretending that the casual projects I had been dabbling in were just an auxiliary sideline which I followed while I was 'resting' between engagements. They were my only work – and very potty they seemed to be.

I see that I have been writing about this period now, forty-five years on, almost as if, at the time, I had been coolly and single-mindedly pursuing my prospects and purposes. That is not how it was. As I lurched desperately from one project to another I was also lurching, inside myself, from one picture of myself to another, from confidence to contempt. It was a very uncomfortable and overwrought period in my life.

In 1950 there was a vogue for mechanical shop-window displays. These were often mysterious, being based on optical or mechanical illusions.

I made several of these, mostly based on magnets. My favourite was a box on which, with no visible means of propulsion, a small reclining figure (with a hole through it) was busily pedalling itself round and round on a sort of trolley, and holding up a placard with the words UNFAIR TO HENRY MOORE written on it.

I took it along to Harvey and Goodman Ltd., who specialized in point-of-sale displays. The man there looked at it for a long time. Then he said: 'OK, so who is this guy Henry Moore?' I tried to explain, but he had lost interest.

Depressed, I returned to the theatre, took a job as a flyman at the King's Hammersmith and later did some scene painting in Harrow. Neither job lasted more than a couple of weeks.

Towards the end of 1950 my sister-in-law Mary suggested I should show some of my gadgets to the husband of one of her University friends. This was Tony, a young man who ran a firm which specialized in designing and setting up exhibitions and displays and was interested in the idea of offering his clients animated displays for their exhibition stands.

Tony invited me to join his team of freelance designers who were working from his new offices in the Cromwell Road. Having been at a loose end for so long I eagerly accepted his invitation.

The office was an empty room with loose papers and bits of handbag fittings left by the previous tenants when they fled, and for a while it was plagued by debt-collectors and bailiffs. Tony's 'team' was a bit sparse. It consisted of himself, a rather tense young lady who had to be addressed as Miss Page, me and, sometimes, a man who drove a van. Also, he explained, the business was starting from scratch, so any money that came in initially would have to be ploughed back in, though of course we would have a share of the grand final profits of each project. Although he didn't put it so crudely, this meant that for the moment we would be working for nothing. That fact did not stop Tony representing his organization as being substantial, fully equipped and well established, a habit that led to some embarrassing misunderstandings.

Quite soon a real break came. Tony was offered a contract to supply and set up the interiors of a set of showcases in one of the pavilions at the great Festival of Britain that was due to be built on the south bank of the Thames in 1951.

These showcases, which were intended to extol the virtues of plastic materials, included no less than four animated displays – three fairly simple rotary devices and one bubble-machine. The bubble-machine was, in essence, a large diagram depicting a flow of materials, the flow being marked out by thin glass tubes through which coloured liquid, regularly interspersed with air-bubbles, would travel slowly along – rather like a moving dotted line. Bubble-machines were quite frequently installed at exhibitions but, although I had seen them, I didn't know how they worked.

This sudden access of business greatly enhanced Tony's view of the status of his company and caused him to invite a designer to join the team. The designer's name was Robert Auf-der-Mauer. He was a first-rate graphic artist and a sensible chap. He was to be a great companion in the difficult times that were to come and a great friend for the rest of his life. I remember telephoning to arrange to meet him at Gloucester Road tube station. 'How shall I recognize you?' I asked. 'You can't miss me,' he replied. 'I look like a friendly goose.' Which indeed he did.

Never having worked in the field of Exhibition and Display before, I hadn't appreciated the remarkable delaying and stultifying effect that having to deal with important design-persons would have. The job we had to do could have been worked out and finished in a few weeks if we had been given the necessary data and the opportunity to do it. Unfortunately, each single item of visual design had to be discussed, conceptually pondered and elaborately negotiated by a hierarchy of pretentious self-important overseers, each determined to stamp his own personality on the work. Tony, who didn't actually do anything, was quite at home in the posy world of meetings and discussions but, for Bob Auf-der-Mauer and me, who were eventually going to have to deliver the goods, the sheer absence of decisions or workable instructions was a nightmare.

I had another nightmare of my own. I was committed to supplying the bubble-machine and had blithely assumed that I could either find an existing pump mechanism or at least get some information on how they worked. My efforts to locate either a machine or an expert were a complete failure and I was left with the prospect of either admitting that I couldn't do the job – thus jeopardizing the whole contract – or settling down to work out from first principles how to make one. I had to choose the latter.

It seemed to me that the mechanism necessary to provide the flow of alternate bubbles and fluid along the tubes could possibly be fairly simple in that, given the right situation, the division of the flow might occur automatically. I set up a number of different rigs in the hope of making this happen, but they weren't successful.

One morning, after having spent the whole of the previous day failing to produce anything but small floods, Bob suggested that we should take a more basic and mechanistic approach to the problem: that we should make up a machine that would take hold of alternate doses of air and water and just stuff them into the tubing so that they would shove each other along. So we resorted to force.

I made an air-pusher from a sawn-off bicycle pump and found a small gear-pump to deliver small amounts of coloured water.

We fitted a glass T-junction tube to the top of the circuit in the specimen display panel we had made and connected the air-pump and the water-pump to that. Then Bob and I knelt in front of it, he with the water-pump and I with the air-pump, and we took turns squeezing small bursts of air and water into the system. In a sense it worked. Air and water did go into the tubes and after we got into a rhythm the air and water did go into the circuit in approximately equally spaced doses, but these did not proceed in a stately fashion along the tube. As the pumps pushed and pulled, they hiccuped back and forth with such violence that the bubbles broke up. After some hours of trying different speeds and manipulations of pressure we had to admit that force was not going to work.

Feeling thoroughly fed up, Bob and I hung up the various bits we had been holding, left the thing to stew in its juice and turned to go out for a beer and a sandwich.

As we reached the door Bob put a hand on my arm. 'Turn around very slowly,' he whispered.

I turned. Travelling with stately dignity along the top tube of the display was a procession of alternate one-inch red and white bubbles. We watched them turn the corner and busily proceed back along the next section with the bubbles perfectly even and intact.

We tiptoed back to the display and once again knelt before it, watching fascinated and praying that we would be able to divine the mystery of its functioning.

We gradually came to see that the secret lay in a delicate setting of the flows of air and water into the T-junction at the top of the circuit. These had, purely by chance, been left exactly right.

So that was it! We went out for a jubilant beer and sandwich and then came back. It was still working, and it burbled away contentedly for the rest of the day.

That was a glorious end to one of our problems, but more were to come. The main characteristic of work for the Festival was that nothing that was supposed to happen happened when it was supposed to. Our material was finished and ready on time but the building it was to go into, the Power and Production Pavilion, was, to put it simply, not there. It was eventually made available to us exactly a week before the Festival was due to open, whereupon we discovered that, for reasons we knew nothing of, the showcases had not been made according to the plans we had been working to.

There was no time to argue about this and no point in doing so because nobody was taking responsibility. Bob and I just set to and, sustained by Benzedrine and knobs of sugar, worked, nonstop, night and day, for the whole week.

Even then I didn't quite finish. As the King and Queen and the two Princesses came through the pavilion, viewing the exhibits on the formal Opening Day, they might have thought that all the ingenious animated displays were electrically driven. Not so; I was lying on my back underneath one of them, winding it by hand.

Once I was sure the Royal Legs were heading towards the exit I overcame the temptation to drop off to sleep where I was, scrambled out, staggered to the tube and found my way back to Finchley, where I fell into bed. I remained there for the next forty-eight hours, lifting my head at regular intervals to eat large meals brought by Daisy and then falling back into sleep.

When, eventually, I woke up properly and found out what day

it was, I hurried back to the Festival to finish installing the animated display and check the rest of the devices.

Everything seemed to be in order, so I wandered off through the Festival to view the wonders that were on offer. I marvelled at the Skylon and the Dome of Discovery and enjoyed the impressive water-scuttle fountain that looked, behaved and sounded like a heap of giant cooking pans tumbling off a wet draining-board.

The exhibit which, as Quakers say, spoke most strongly to my condition, was in the Lion and Unicorn Pavilion. In this was a full-size effigy of Lewis Carroll's White Knight, who muttered encouragement to himself and carried with him certain inventions that had clearly been chosen for their absurdity. Among these, I noticed, was a pair of goggles with windscreen wipers. Perhaps Ray had been right after all.

II. Silver Linings.

The work was completed and the Festival of Britain was under way but, strangely, no profit came to Tony's team. After a disagreement about the cost of a display clock I told Tony I was resigning.

'What? After all I've taught you!' he cried.

'No. After all the money you've never paid me,' I replied.

I went on to make some animated displays on my own account. These were profitable but not frequent enough to constitute a profession. What I needed was a proper job.

Once again I was lucky. By a sequence of coincidences I fell into a job. One of Ro's friends from her ballet-school days was a South African girl named Clementina. She had met and married a young comedian who was, at that time, taking the world of showbusiness by storm with his brilliant use of a sink-pump and a chair-back – his name was Michael Bentine.

One day when Michael and Clem came to see Ro and her parents at their house in Hendon, I happened to be there and happened to have with me the toy fork-lift truck that I had made. Michael was delighted with this and said at once that I must show it as soon as possible to a fellow member of a gliding club that he belonged to.

That being so, a meeting was arranged. I took the fork-lift truck and one or two other devices to meet Ralph Furness in the office of his firm, Kays Industries Ltd., which was a small room over a shop in Ealing.

My animations were of little use to Ralph in his business, which was perspex fabrication, but his reaction to them was refreshing. He took them seriously. He respected them, and me, and gave serious thought to the question of how they could be developed.

He suggested that if I could design and draw the parts for a perspex prototype of my toy fork-lift truck he could have it made up by a model-maker.

Ralph also told me about a new process that he was thinking of taking up. This was a method by which small plastic articles like buttons and brooches could be coated with metal – copper, silver or brass – by electroplating.

Well, there was just one thing I knew about electroplating and that was that the object to be electroplated had to be able to conduct electricity. It was quite impossible to electroplate plastic articles.

Ralph handed me a large gold button. It felt very light in weight but it was, undoubtedly, gold.

'This can't be solid gold,' I said.

'No, it's brass, electroplated on to copper.'

Ralph took a pair of pliers and cut the button in half.

'Brass-plate over copper-plate over a silver lining on pink plastic,' he said, handing me half of the button. The metal plating was as thin as card on the pink plastic but it was definitely metal.

'So you are a true alchemist,' I said. 'You can turn base materials into gold.'

'Not quite, but I hope to be able to coat base plastic with chemically deposited silver and then plate it with copper and turn it into antique-finish copper, silver or golden brass, for the rag trade. There's a big fashion for metal-finish buttons coming up and I've not only bought the process but also the aged chief chemist who originally developed it.'

'How far have you got with it?' I asked.

'I've rented an empty pub in Baker's Lane.'

'Is that all?'

'We know that it has already been done. We know the exact sequence and nature of the processes and treatments the buttons must go through to get their coats. We have the expert to brew up the chemicals and the button-manufacturers will give us all the buttons we need. What I need next is somebody to design and put together a production line big enough for us to do bulk sample runs.'

'When do I start?'

'Now.'

'How much?'

'Twelve quid a week.'

So that was that.

Turning from putting together fiddly animated displays to designing a complete manufacturing process was like turning out of a bumpy side-lane into a broad main road, getting into gear and opening the throttle.

Though I didn't know it at the time, what I was helping to put together was not just a process. It would grow and become, for several people as well as me, a place of work and a way of life.

Setting up a button-plating plant for Kay's Industries was in many ways similar to putting together an animated display. There were processes that needed to be done and I was going to work out how to do them. Then I was going to prepare the place in which they were to be done, in the sequence in which they had to be done, in a way that would be appropriate for the people doing it – that last consideration was in some ways the most interesting because people, unlike machines, could become bored or tired and consequently careless, as well as unhappy.

The process of coating the plastic buttons with metal was complex and involved the use, in exact sequence, of various bulk-handling machines: rougheners, washers, chemical dips, sensitizers, jar-rollers and some very subtle electroplating barrels. Also, for finishing, burnishing barrels, lacquer-dips and a spinner.

The unit we put together was relatively small, just enough to provide a good flow of samples for the commercial travellers to take to the button-dealers in search of orders.

The orders came in so fast that Ralph had to face the moment of truth that comes to all such projects – the prospect of having to raise working capital in order to invest in a large-scale factory plant designed and properly made by competent engineers. Fortunately Ralph didn't do anything so unwise. The prototype installation was working perfectly well, so we simply replicated it, turning it from a one-barrel to a six-barrel plant, still using the same sort of makeshift devices that I had put together for the first one but on a larger scale. At the same time I moved imperceptibly from being the creative designer to being the general manager, master button-silverer and occasional tea-boy for a very unorthodox factory.

This evolution took place over several months, a period during which my own life also evolved and changed. I became quietly contented, mainly, I think, because my mind was engrossed in the work. There was so much hard thinking to do, so many designs and methods to work out and so many problems to overcome, with the growing satisfaction of seeing the scheme slowly come to fruition. My greatest excitement was to collect and carry away the open boxes of finished work, boxes brim-full of gold and silver buttons, bright, rich and numerous as an *Arabian Nights* treasure. When I brought them to the office where they would be packed up and despatched, I would lift a box and pour a glistening stream into the weighing machine. I would dip my hands into the shining pool, letting the polished buttons flow through my fingers, like a miser rejoicing in his wealth.

By about 1953 the button-plating had settled down, and work was flowing through in a steady stream. At the workshops, a converted stable in Hanwell, a suburb to the west of London, we employed an experienced electroplater, whose name was Harry, and his assistant, whose name was Eric. Although nineteen years old and quite fit, Eric was 'a bit slow' and lived in a local 'home'. There was also Wally, a policeman who turned up when he was off duty to do odd jobs, and Claude Gillett who was Welsh and a window-cleaner. He did some odd jobs but more often just came in for a chat. Our chats were a great part of my life and we became good friends.

I remember that place and those times with great affection. The work was dirty and sometimes dangerously smelly but there seemed to be no need for hassle or shop-floor politics, life just flowed along at its own pace.

I bought a little car, a 1930 Austin Seven tourer. I named her Albertine after the sixpenny Woolworth's rose that flowered so profusely in the garden at Finchley. I painted her lemon yellow and shiny black. She was neat and comely and very strong. I loved her dearly. Sometimes after work I would drive down to Weybridge to spend the weekend with Bob and Margery Auf-der-Mauer and their ever-growing family. Working at Kays Industries left me so filthy that Margery always kept two towels for me. One old one that didn't matter for the first wash and an ordinary one for the second. My memory of those visits is misty – just days of forgotten ease.

All these things should have been enough to keep me quiet, and in most ways they were, but once the plating works was complete and running there was no urgent thinking to do, no more problems to be solved and nothing more to make. So I suppose my mind began to wander again – not that it had ever stopped. Thoughts, possibilities, ideas, grew on me like mildew. Although the plating process was all right, I didn't much care for the patterns of the buttons that were going through, so I put together a crude injection-moulding machine with which I could make plastic articles using home-made metal moulds. I then began to produce buttons and brooches designed especially for electro-plating – medallions, and replicas of antique coins which I thought would make very distinguished fashion accessories. I metallized these and finished them by hand. They looked really handsome and authentic. I showed them to Ralph's travellers and to one or two of our contacts in the button-trade. They all hated them, were certain there was no market for them and that there never would be.

They were probably right. I tried a couple of other patterns and then gave the idea up. Oddly enough, once I was quite sure something wasn't going to work out I never hesitated to scrap it – so long as nobody else was involved. I didn't mind wasting my own time on uncertain follies but I was embarrassed if I wasted other people's. So as far as possible I worked on my own. The only person exempt from this reservation was Keith Hutcheon.

I think I met Keith at one of the club theatres, perhaps the Watergate, where he was doing some wiring and I was helping Ro. He was about my age but, unlike me, he was a proper, qualified engineer. Fortunately he was tolerant of ignorance and shared my appreciation of elegance and originality in mechanical objects and designs. We started talking about this and that, about the insides of rotary pumps, about the similarities between conventional and gas-turbine engines, about alternative sources of energy, etc. – all the sorts of things that swilled about in my head but which would unfailingly put most of my friends to flight if I talked about them. Keith and I talked for several hours that day and have continued our conversation without interruption, except by time and space, ever since.

III. Public Stomach.

My having a proper job had a happy effect on my life at home. I became noticeably less agitated and was able to enjoy the company of my parents in a way that hadn't been possible before. In their eyes I had ceased to be 'a problem' and, in certain fields, had even become worthy of respect. I was able to look at them with affection and pay a bit of attention to their lives.

As I have mentioned, Daisy had felt the ending of her active role in family life very keenly. She was now in her late fifties and her rheumatism was painful. We all encouraged her to do something independent. We even managed to persuade her to start on what would have been some really exciting memoirs, but she lost momentum very easily and didn't keep it up. Having been a first-rate secretary all her life, I don't think Daisy really was an originator – she was a coper.

Ray, on the other hand, had been going from strength to strength. With the war over and a Labour government in power, he now felt able to move away from active political work. He was fast becoming an expert on wine and was addressing what he saw as a major injustice of the time – the wilful ill-treatment of food.

Ray's contention was that although during the war, and the years of austerity that followed it, housewives and home cooks had learned to be enterprising and innovative with the sparse, monotonous food that was available, commercial caterers had more or less given up. Their standards, which had never been high even before the war, had sunk to a level where the restaurants were, in Ray's view, cheating the public by spoiling perfectly good food through careless, slovenly cooking while at the same time fending off criticism with excuses about austerity and shortages which were often long out of date.

Ray wrote articles about this in *The Leader* magazine and *Lilliput*. These brought into existence the Good Food Club, an institution which, as he explained, had no existence except in the minds of those who were moved to write to him with recommendations and comments on their experiences of eating out.

Letters poured in. *Lilliput* couldn't cope with them, so in 1952 Ray brought the lot home to Finchley where the spare room became the office of the President of the Good Food Club.

Daisy, complaining loudly, waded straight into the task of managing the office. She marshalled the helpers, organized the complex filing system, even keeping a separate, confidential 'Bad Food Guide' containing denunciations, some so withering as to be unpublishable, that unlucky members had sent in. She also, as always, fed everybody.

Meanwhile Ray would be at his desk, evaluating the reports and composing the concise, witty entries that were to become the hallmark of the *Good Food Guide*. He also, as always, poured wine.

There wasn't a lot I could do to help because I was in full-time work but, being on the sidelines, watching Ray becoming celebrated and lionized in the slightly precious world of gourmets and wine-writers, was a great pleasure. Daisy, remembering perhaps the revolutionary commitments of their youth, remained affectionately sardonic about these new distinctions and this may have saved him from becoming too carried away. I, rather carelessly, coined for him the title 'Public Stomach Number One'. He affected displeasure at this piece of disrespect but couldn't resist quoting it.

Beatrice, the old bull-nosed Morris car, had been sold into retirement, so when the Good Food Club needed inspections of restaurants in the home counties, Daisy commissioned me to buy her a replacement. The car I found was a 1938 Hillman Minx tourer (it had to be a tourer because Daisy liked to drive with the hood down). She named the car Miranda, on account of the need to remember which inn she and Ray were heading for.*

Sometimes, on summer days when Ray was in town at some gastronomic 'do', Daisy and I would take Miranda out to lunch. We didn't bother her with inns, we would raid the fridge and the larder, purloin a bottle of Ray's rather-better-than-*ordinaire* claret and, with tablecloth, glasses, table napkins, plates, knives and forks all heaped together in a basket, take ourselves off for a very excellent picnic under willow trees beside a small river somewhere in Hertfordshire.

These were happy outings for both Daisy and myself. I have the impression that we both felt deeply affectionate towards each other but also, in the service of that affection, respectful of each other's privacy. My fearsome behaviour as an adolescent had no doubt made Daisy wary of enquiring into the frustrations of my private life, while I, though well aware that her current situation – that of being a spare part at the margins of Ray's hyped-up career – was less than satisfactory, was careful not to badger her about doing something about it. We just sat in the grass and enjoyed the wine. For two outspoken, tactless people, renowned for always saying the first thing that came into their heads, we did rather well.

---

* 'Do you remember an inn, Miranda, do you remember an inn? . . .' ('Tarantella', a poem by Hilaire Belloc.)

IV. Feasts.

The rituals that most fully caught the spirit of those Bacchanalian times were the bottling parties. Ray, through his connections with the wine trade, would select a hogshead of wine. He couldn't afford, let alone drink, a hogshead of wine, but he only had to mention his intent to friends at the Savile Club for them to apply eagerly to subscribe,

The barrel would be shipped and delivered to the out-house, where it would be jacked up on to a specially made stand called a scantling. Meanwhile the subscribers would be gathering up used wine bottles, removing old labels and washing them out with bottle-brushes. Ray would confer with his typographical cronies, elegant labels would be printed and, on the appointed day, corks would be soaked and Daisy would oversee the setting out of a magnificent cold collation on the big dining table. In the evening the sub-scribers would arrive in their handsome cars and when all were present and attentive the barrel would be ceremonially broached.

Tasks were allocated among the subscribers, as fetchers, fillers, swigger-corker, carriers, labellers, packers etc., and bottling would commence.

Ray had obtained a massive antique bottle-corker made of solid cast iron. It weighed as much as an early printing-press and had a similar handle. If carelessly used, this could shatter bottles like eggshells, so I, being used to it, usually manoeuvred myself into the post of swigger-corker – the swigging part of the job being the necessary adjustment of the level of wine in each bottle before fitting it into the corker and slamming in the cork.

The system usually ran well for most of the evening but gradually a certain confusion, bordering on hilarity, would creep into the proceedings. This would be due to various causes. A certain amount of innocent tasting had been going on and the alcoholic fumes of open and spilt wine were quite affecting, but the main cause of jollity was simply general bonhomie, the happi-ness of good friends engaged together in a common joyful task.

*

Ray's bottling parties were very jolly occasions, but for sheer magnificence there was nothing to compare with the ceremonies which he attended in France. In 1951 Ray had been honoured by the Jurade de St-Émilion, a prestigious guild of wine-growers whose function was to judge and maintain the quality of the wines of the region. He was appointed its first overseas *pair* (peer) and was thereby entitled to assist at its ceremonies.

The town of St-Émilion is ideally suited to such purposes because it spreads along the curved slope at the end of a valley like an amphitheatre with, at its centre point, a tall square solid-looking tower, Le Tour du Roi. The town also has two churches. The new one in the square dates from the thirteenth century. The old one underneath it, whose belfry tower sprouts incongruously out of the ground, was originally a cave in the solid rock which had been inhabited by the saint in the eighth century.

The Fête de Printemps of 1954, which Daisy and I had the good fortune to attend with Ray, did not just involve the use of a hall or a hotel, it involved the use of the whole town. It started in the morning with the Jurats, a body of portly gentlemen in scarlet robes trimmed with white, assembling before the War Memorial to lay a wreath. They were followed by a similar number of other well-built gentlemen, including Ray, wearing good suits and *épitoges*, which were ornamental shoulder-stoles to show that they were *pairs*. After them came the *prud'hommes* who, as far as I remember, wore no badge of office. From the Memorial they walked in procession through the town, accompanied by Les Compagnons du Bon Temps de Sarthe, a group of tall men in hunting caps and pink jackets carrying, or rather wound into, golden French hunting horns. These blasted rousing fanfares at each corner as the procession made its way through the town and down steep paths to the cavern of the Old Church, where, by the light of flaming torches, the wines of the year before were poured from bottles without labels and, in the presence of the spirit of the saint, judged and pronounced upon. After that the procession broke up and moved to the banquet.

My memory of the banquet is confused. It was laid on white-covered trestle tables with folding chairs in a wide stone room, arched but with a low ceiling. Perhaps it was an undercroft or crypt. What assailed me in that echoing place was the ear-shattering noise generated by a couple of hundred happy French people engaged in ordinary conversation. The banquet itself was magnificent but, I must say, not very well organized, so that the food was served slowly and arrived rather cold. However there were some lively speeches, including one in which the Premier Jurat welcomed, as Guest of Honour, the Paris Chief of Police, and hoped he would soon have time to enjoy a long and well-deserved holiday away from the bustle of the city. As the Chief of Police was at that moment under investigation for alleged corruption, this invitation was taken to be particularly apt and was rapturously applauded.

As I didn't know a lot of French, much of this hilarity went over my head. So after some hours I slipped away to get some air and have a look at the Tour du Roi where the judgement would be promulgated. On closer inspection the tall tower turned out to be less solid than it had seemed. It was in fact completely hollow. A staircase with a flimsy hand-rail was built against the inside of the walls, and this led up to a narrow walk-way around the top of the tower, the centre void being lightly roofed with tiles.

I heard the sound of hunting-horns and, realising that the banquet must be ending, I turned to walk back. After a few paces I came face to face with Daniel Querre, the Procurer Syndic du Jurade, panting down the hill in advance of the procession. Daniel was our host, a short man but bulky, indeed almost spherical. His eyes lit up with delight as he saw me.

'Ah! What chance!' he cried. 'One pushes!'

Knowing my duty I got behind him and, with as much courtesy as the procedure would allow, literally shoved him up the narrow staircase and out into the cold air at the top. I turned to go back down again.

There was no going down. A single line of scarlet persons could already be seen puffing up the awesome staircase, led by the vast M. Chaillot. As he neared the top I saw his face, grey-pale against the scarlet of his robes, and I reached a hand down to help him up the last few steps. He took it in a vice-like grip and, using both hands, clambered up me like a ladder.

'One excuses oneself,' he muttered humbly, 'You know, the vertigo!' Indeed I did know the vertigo.

More and more rotund persons were emerging on to the narrow parapet and slowly filling it all the way round. Finally the Compagnons with their golden horns emerged and took their positions. From a distance the tower must have looked as if it was wearing a soft crown of scarlet and white bobbles, trimmed with spots of bright gold.

I, quite terrified, had backed into a corner and was crouched low. Through the battlements I could see that the whole town was out there watching. Lining walls and balconies, streets, parapets and windows, the people of St-Émilion were eagerly awaiting their moment of truth.

The tower had been fully wired with loudspeakers so, when he came to make his speech, Daniel Querre's magnificent voice rolled out into the amphitheatre of the valley and echoed away into the distance.

He told them he was there to bring them the great good news that the wine of the year before had been appraised and found truly worthy to bear the Great Seal of the *Jurade* on its barrels and so take its place among the prestigious vintages that bore the holy name of the saint, to whose glory and to the glory of God this vintage was now dedicated, with all the honour and love of the people there assembled, '. . . and of our friends the dead, beneath the stones . . . and even the birds of the air . . .'

As he said these last words, hampers at the foot of the tower were thrown open and a multitude of white doves released. These circled the tower and rose around it in a white cloud. As they did so the evening sun caught them and their flashing wings shone white-gold against the darkening blue sky. The town cheered and laughed and wept. Les Compagnons sped them on their way with golden fanfares and, as the shining birds flew high and turned away towards their lofts, the ceremony ended at last – apart from the delicate and nerve-racking task of getting the Jurats down the dreadful stairs.

V. Friends.

Ever since the days at LAMDA I had remained close to Frieda Hodgson and her family, who also lived in Finchley. Frieda held open house every Sunday evening, gatherings to which any and all of her friends from LAMDA were always welcome. I really enjoyed those evenings because they were filled with the warmth and ease that had characterized her Friday afternoon sessions at the Academy. There diffidence was suspended and joyful appreciation prevailed. There people sang and danced, recited their poems, told stories. There I could make an exhibition of myself without any hint of embarrassment, because the attention was always entirely on what was being offered and never on the temerity of the person offering it. I was even, occasionally, persuaded to sing the blues, God forgive me. There I met several gentle people who became lifelong friends – though where life has taken most of them by now I don't know.

Among those friends the closest, I think, was Jill. She was light, moved delicately and was full of laughter – most of the time. Not all of the time, though. I remember sitting with her at one of Frieda's soirées, both of us feeling glum from the sorrows of our love lives. She was in love with Frieda's eldest son, Charles, and I was, as ever, in thrall to Ro. Things were not going well for either of us.

I said: 'My car isn't all that fit at the moment but next Tuesday I shall have the firm's van. How about we go to the Norfolk Broads?'

'Yes ... let's.'

So we did. I collected Jill at six in the morning in the mists of what was going to become a bright spring day. The van ran sweetly, chewing up the miles till we came to Newmarket. There we saw shifty-looking men in flat caps leaning on hedges, peering at distant racehorses through gigantic binoculars the size of quart beer-bottles. These, I heard later, were tipsters' men, 'spying for form'.

I can recall very few details of that day. We ran along raised paths between wide expanses of water. We lay in long grass looking at the sky and listening to the larks. We laughed a lot and gladly resisted the temptation to pour out all our troubles to each other, because time was too good to waste on boring things like that. We were simply happy to have that day to enjoy together without expecting, needing or looking for anything from one another except to feel the sunshine and be able to share the pleasure of being alive.

In the evening we drove quietly home again. Nothing special happened that day, but it was a day that neither of us have forgotten or ever will forget.

I treasure a slightly puzzled astonishment about the happiness of that day-out-of-life. Certainly it bore no resemblance to the tense anxieties of what, at the time, I thought of as my love life.

I must say I feel a bit diffident writing about my love life, not because it was dramatic but because it was uneventful. As I mentioned earlier, I had met Ro at the Drama School in 1947 and we had formed a rapport which, on my part, soon became an infatuation, a state of feeling which Ro did not share.

Such relationships aren't particularly unusual, but they are usually ended fairly quickly. For some reason this one went on for several years. I confess I don't know for sure why Ro put up with the nuisance of my importunate presence for so long, but I suspect the answer was simple – she was engrossed in her own important purposes and sadnesses which took priority over all other considerations. Also she found me useful, especially once I had got a car.

As for me, I think I remained attendant because I chose to. I couldn't shake off the infatuation, so I put up with it. The situation was ridiculous but in a way it suited us, because Ro was always anxious to receive service and I was a chap who was always glad to drop whatever he was doing and help. Also, although attending Ro in her purposes was unrewarding in some ways, it was not in itself a burden. Quite the contrary, her world was interesting.

Ro and her friend Hilary had teamed up to offer a property-making and costume service to the small shows and 'intimate' revues that were being put on in the many little club-theatres that in those days existed in London. This was a fascinating episode in the history of the theatre because the shows, produced on a shoestring budget, were able to attract a more sophisticated and intellectual audience than the big West End theatres could.

The little theatre I remember best was the Watergate Theatre Club. This was a series of rather grim converted cellars with a tiny auditorium and stage, which could become an uproariously delighted place when a really good revue was on. Most of these were written by Peter Myers. Peter was a plump and particularly single-minded man. In fact he was a power-house of drive and purpose, all centred on the theatre and the productions he was preparing. Like a general, he commanded everybody and, as if he was a general, they obeyed. He and his wife Prue and their three children lived a few doors away from us in Hendon Lane. So, quite apart from meeting them at the theatre, they were our neighbours.

Prue, in particular, became a family friend. She was a tall, slightly ungainly looking young woman, a year or two older than me. Ray liked her a lot, and would often suggest that I should invite her to dinner parties – 'to make up the numbers' as he put it. This I was happy to do because I also liked her, though I confess I was a bit puzzled by the picture I got of her family life. Peter, her husband, seemed to treat her like a servant, while she was quite open and vocal in her condemnation of the overbearing and completely inconsiderate way in which he carried on.

VI. Serious Events.

In February 1956 a late, bitter frost hit the whole Bordeaux region, including St-Émilion. Hundreds of acres of vines were frozen; vines which for decades had produced some of the greatest wines in the world were now pieces of frozen wood. The exact damage could not be assessed at once but it seemed likely that most of the older plants were done for. This was a source of grief and anxiety for Ray – until something came to wipe it from his mind.

One morning in March, Daisy came down to breakfast fully dressed. Ray and I didn't comment on this, assuming that she was going out somewhere. She was: to see the doctor. She was diagnosed as having cancer of the cervix and was taken straight to St Thomas's Hospital to undergo a serious operation.

Ray and I walked about that big house like zombies, having slightly stilted conversations about trivial matters. The wary affection that had grown between us in recent years did not, alas, allow us to share grief and fear, only to respect it in the other. However, there was plenty to do, including buzzing backwards and forwards to the hospital.

The operation went well and was declared a success. In due course Daisy came home to recuperate. Amid rejoicing a barrel of wine was bought and bottled with a special label celebrating her recovery. Daisy was dubious about the gesture but enjoyed the wine. Before long life was more or less as usual again, apart from the unspoken shadow of a recurrence that always follows such an operation.

I think we were all, in our ways, very rattled by this brush with mortality. I know I found myself looking quite closely at my own life, wondering, once again, what I was doing with it. One thing was quite clear: Kays Industries was going into decline. The metallized button trade had passed its peak and was beginning to drop away. Before long my job would come to an end. The time was coming when I would once again have to find something else to do.

For some years I had been interested in photography. I loved the work of photographers like Cartier-Bresson and Robert Doisneau, whose pictures had a clear intensity, capturing a single instant of life in a simple composition. Typically I wasn't content just to enjoy their work, I wanted to have a go. I bought a 35mm camera, took lots of photographs of people and places, some of which I got paid for, and was considering the possibility of doing some freelance photo-journalism for picture-papers like *Picture Post* and *The Leader*.

Although the frost in Bordeaux had been a serious tragedy, I had noticed that the event had not been widely reported in the English press, and I wondered about doing some sort of article on it.

That idea came up again in the late summer of that year, when Daisy was fairly well recovered. Without mentioning that it might be their last chance to do so, Ray proposed that we should take a trip to Bordeaux to visit their friends. I suggested that it might be easier for Daisy if we hired a car in Bordeaux so that I could drive them about on their visits. Then, at other times, I could use the car to take some photographs of the frozen vines and perhaps put together an article that I could offer to one of the picture papers.

We had a very good holiday and I was also able to travel around in the hired car interviewing the farmers, who were using oxen to grub out the dead vines. I took lots of photographs, some of which looked fine to me as illustrations to the article, but in the event the editor of *The Leader* turned them and the article down, saying, 'Very nice, but not quite up to our standard.'

After that I started a new round of doomed projects. I did some specimen book jackets and record sleeves, all of which were admired before being turned down. To Ray's contacts in the office machinery trade which he had overseen during the war I offered a hydraulic typewriter – a concept that filled them with horror.

Keith Hutcheon and I proposed and discussed several ideas for cars including a 'fuel-consumption warning indicator' and an 'average speed indicator' to go on the dashboard. The first of these would warn the driver when he was using the accelerator extravagantly and the second would show, on a dial, how many minutes late or early one was on a pre-determined schedule for a particular journey. As usual we enjoyed the thinking but didn't succeed in developing the ideas to a point where they could be offered for sale. All these ideas are long extinct because nowadays such things would be done with electronics.

Just to see if I could do it, I wrote some short stories. I wrote one about a cat that dreamed it was a tiger. I liked it and read it to people, who also liked it, so I wrote another about a milkman who had a magic day. It had no real plot and nothing much happened, but it wrote itself, the words running down my arm to the pen in my hand, with my head racing along behind trying to keep up. It was the same sort of feeling that I had had in the art college when

I was doing those drawings of M. Letailleur in 1943. It was as if I couldn't go wrong.

I was nervous of showing the stories to Ray but I needed his opinion, which I knew would be absolutely honest. So I left the typescripts on the chest in the hall. They vanished and the next evening were back again with a note pinned to the second page.

It read: 'These are a lot better written than most of the rubbish I have to read nowadays, but watch out for clichés. You know how to recognize a cliché? . . .' Ray went on to discourse on ways to ferret out these dreaded forms.

I asked about 'style' – was the style of my writing OK?

Ray said: 'Style isn't something *else*. If you write what you have to write as clearly and readably as you can, that's enough. That will be your style.'

Much elated, I wrote more stories and sent them to magazines like *Argosy* and *Reader's Digest*. Then, suddenly, I had to stop. Another, far more urgent call on my time had come. My car had just fallen apart.

This wasn't my first car, the wild sweet Albertine. She had died a year earlier and I had written an elegiac poem in her honour (which I still cannot read without tears). This was another Austin Seven, a Ruby, whose bodywork had split in half, making it impossible to close the doors.

I rebuilt it as a sort of jeep, with a high windscreen and an open body made from sixteen-gauge aluminium. It was very ungainly and had the air of being, well . . . accidental, as if it had been bashed together out of aluminium sheet in somebody's front garden. It did have one magnificent piece of equipment: a mechanical Klaxon hooter from the ship's chandlers in Shaftesbury Avenue. This had a brass knob on the top which, if you thumped it with your fist, would give a squawk like a gigantic chicken, a noise so astounding that it would stop an *Evening Standard* van in full flight.

This mucking about with home-made cars was all very well, but it wasn't going to provide me with a way to earn my living.

Reader's Digest and *Argosy* sent back my stories. I didn't mind too much about that. I had had a go at writing stories and knew I could do it. In fact I looked at one or two of those first stories quite recently and they are among the best things I ever wrote. But at that time I couldn't see that story-writing could ever earn me a living. So, almost as a last resort, I turned back to the display trade.

VII. Hitting the Buffers.

I had never really severed my connections with the display trade. I was still occasionally making and installing bubble-machines and other animated displays. Now, rather than looking for individual display jobs, I decided to aim for some small-scale manufacturing. I had in mind to develop one absolutely basic component which I could manufacture, assemble, sell and deliver more or less by myself, without any intermediaries. This was quite a sensible idea, or would be if we could find the right article to manufacture. I first thought of a simple iron-cogwheel electric motor that could be used to power shop-window displays. In consultation with Keith Hutcheon I made a couple of prototypes and they worked quite well but then, one day, entirely by chance, I came across something much more immediately useful.

This was a tiny battery-operated magnetic pendulum that would do something simple – like, for instance, moving the arm of a pig playing a violin – for three weeks nonstop on one torch battery. This seemed to fill the bill exactly. We could manufacture the pendulums, incorporate them in runs of shop-window displays and also, possibly, sell them as a product. I checked the patent situation and it was clear, so Keith and I designed a plastic version of the pendulum and in due course drew a moulding tool in which the impression could be milled out of a solid block. That would be cheap and the parts could be moulded on the injection-moulding machine I had made for the ill-fated antique-button project. We went ahead and turned out some samples. I offered them to a display firm in Pimlico, which gave me an order for fifty, to be delivered the next week.

So life suddenly became real and earnest. With Keith's help I set to and moulded a batch of pendulum parts. We set up a kitchen-table assembly line to wind the coils and fix on the metal bits, and at one point, I remember, we had a dozen of the little clickers tick-tocking away. The order was delivered and another one taken. Great industrial empires had grown from such tiny beginnings. I felt I might be on the brink of becoming a real businessman, owning the means to produce simple articles for which there would be an assured market, prospering at last in the world of commerce!

I remember the feeling very well. I was walking down Victoria Street carrying a batch of pendulums to deliver to the display firm. I came to Horseferry Road and stood there, waiting to cross. As I stood there my legs sent up a message: 'We aren't going.'

I said: 'Cross the road. I'm going to cross the road.'

'No you're not,' they said, 'not without us.'

That was true. So I backed off and sat on a bit of wall.

All this sounds absurd, but it is as near as I can get to describing what happened. I couldn't make myself cross the road. Something was wrong.

I had to sit there and conduct meaningful negotiations with my body in the hope of persuading it to resume normal working. The points it was making were quite simple: 'You are going down a blind alley. The path you are taking is not for you. You would be useless and miserable as a commercial person. You are a lousy craftsman, a hopeless salesman, a rotten work-getter and an even worse businessman. Also, plying a trade like that – as an itinerant vendor of devices that customers don't even know they want – calls for a level of single-mindedness, persistence and self-confidence that you just don't have. And, above all else, you aren't really interested! You don't want to be tied to producing potty pendulums through all eternity. Pack it in!'

'What shall I do?' I asked, much chastened by the truth of those observations.

'You've got to do what you said you would do, of course. So we deliver the pendulums, finish out any other orders, do what has to be done, even new things if necessary, but *you*, you get out of your head any delusion that this is the field you want to work in because it just isn't. OK?'

'OK,' I said, and we crossed Horseferry Road. I must say the legs felt a lot better for the confrontation and my step was light.

8

STARTING AGAIN

I. Stopping and Looking.

To be forced to realise that in a major part of one's life one has been working one's way into a dead end is, to put it mildly, unsettling.

I could see that I was no stranger to dead ends. My involvement with Ro had long since reached and passed the point where I was more trouble to her than I was worth, there was no doubt about that. But also the last few years were strewn with ideas and projects that I had taken just so far and then, at the first hint of discouragement, abandoned, telling myself that there was no future in them. Sometimes that had been true, but had it been true in every case? Certainly it wasn't true of the pendulum project. That was surely viable.

Didn't I want to be an individual entrepreneur? Didn't I want to be a success and show the world I was right after all? If, now that the knitting up of ideas, setting up of methods and costing out of the work was done, my heart wasn't in the task of taking the project ahead and becoming a prosperous manufacturer of small pendulums, then what the hell was it in? Did I harbour some concealed reluctance? Had I always secretly hoped my projects would fail? Why couldn't I do what other people did – just decide what I was going to do and get on with it?

I had no answer to these questions. Asking them made my head ache.

I had another difficulty: I wasn't interested. I didn't want to have anything to do with any of it. All the ideas I had had seemed to have been solitary schemes, private flights of fancy which might or might not be successful but which were all, in the end, directed towards the advancement of me. And at that time I was, to put it bluntly, thoroughly fed up with me. I was fed up with what might be called my 'personality', with the ingratiating, overwrought jokey chap, who was full of far-fetched notions and fancies, and in an almost constant state of submerged agitation. I can see that I didn't so much *dislike* the image I wore, it was more that I was profoundly *bored* by it.

Years earlier I had overheard Mrs Hodgson say, almost in passing: '. . . but of course you never really begin to live until you are committed . . .' At the time I hadn't understood what she meant, but the thought had stayed in my mind as something that might one day turn out to be important.

At that moment, however, one thing was very clear to me. The prospect of committing my life to the single-minded pursuit of the trappings of my boring image – personal success, wealth, dignity, respectability, membership of the Round Table, ulcers, a Mercedes – was not just uninteresting, it was frightening and peculiarly lonely, like spending one's life decorating one's tomb.

Meanwhile, life shuffled on. I went on with what was there – doing the silvering, installing a bubble-machine at Olympia, making up pendulums. I don't think anybody, except perhaps Daisy, noticed that my customary gloom level had deepened and had begun to rumble.

Sometime in October or November 1956, Prue Myers and I arranged to go to the Lyric Theatre in Hammersmith to see *Look Back in Anger*, the new play by John Osborne.

I don't recall the details of the play but I do remember that I found it very moving. In the interval Prue and I talked about our lives, comparing them with those of the people in the play, and I took the opportunity to ask her something that had been in my mind about her life with Peter. She had, as I mentioned earlier, been fairly outspoken about her dislike of the way he carried on. I now asked if I was correct in assuming that, like many married couples who on the surface appeared to be hostile towards each other, she and Peter really shared some deep-rooted bond that held them together.

She thought about this before answering. Then she said: 'No.'

I waited for her to say something more and after a pause she added: 'No. The children hold me, but not to Peter. I would get away if I could.'

The bell went and we returned to our seats. After the play we had a drink in the bar. I looked straight into her eyes, which was something I don't think I had ever done before.

Then we went back to our houses in Finchley. I knew something extraordinary had happened but I wasn't at all sure what it was.

II. Marriage.

About a year later, in November 1957, Prue and I were married.

It had been an eventful year, difficult and complicated, especially so for Prue, and for me it had been explosive. Most of what I thought I knew about love and life was turned upside down.

I mentioned earlier that a level of agitation had always been present in my mind. That wasn't strictly true. There had been isolated occasions and circumstances in which I had been completely quiet. Some of these had been internal: for instance, when I knew I had made my decision to refuse to join the army I had been very frightened but, inside myself, incongruously serene. I had been quiet too, on brief occasions like the outing to the Norfolk Broads with Jill. There had been other, similar times and, although there was no doubt that they had something to do with gender, in that my companions had usually been women, these times seemed to me to have had nothing to do with sex and everything to do with friendliness and acceptance.

In my small experience, sex was something quite different, an alluring minefield into which, under the spell of the loved one's attractions, one was inexorably drawn towards some deeply fraught encounter, which just might turn out to be a lustful consummation but was far more likely to be a scornful rejection.

I had got that wrong. With Prue I was completely free of agitation, safe in a world which not only had everything to do with affection and acceptance, but also, just as strongly, with love and sex. In this world I knew something for certain – that it was where, in due course, if it could be arranged, I would like to spend my life, or rather, we would like to spend our lives. And that knowledge, in itself, brought me complete serenity. Whether it was going to work out that way or not didn't really matter, what we felt for each other at that time was a simple warmth, a roaring tenderness that would take whatever came.

For a while I wasn't sure what Prue's ambitions were. Although we were quite clear about our feelings for each other, I was not asking her to break her marriage. I would go along with whatever future she chose. Nothing else would have been appropriate.

In the end she chose; asked me if I could really want to take on a rather ugly woman and three rumbustious children and I replied: 'If you can disentangle yourselves and come to me free and freely, there is nothing else I want in my life. And besides, you're not ugly, or not very.' So she hit me, but not very hard, and that was that. As I walked home in the moonlight that night, I was thirty feet tall and I plucked the street-lamps like daffodils. Fourteen years earlier, as I had slithered down Box Hill, I had said that if I didn't like the world as it was I would make a new one. Now I was ready to start.

There was certainly a lot to be done. First I had to part company with Kays Industries, the display industry and Ro. I also left home and went to stay with Denzil, my old friend from Drama School, in a flat in Earl's Court. My emotions, which had been crouching for so long in a glum rut, were suddenly riding a roller coaster, swooping from tears to laughter, from joy to despair. Sometimes a tide of self-doubt would wash into me – what on earth did I imagine I was doing, dragging Prue and her children into my follies? How could I possibly imagine . . . etc.?

Prue had her times of anxiety, of course. Naturally she was centred on the welfare of her children and anything that might put that in jeopardy was dangerous. In particular she refused to have any truck with my occasional bouts of self-doubt, dismissing them out of hand as ridiculous. Sometimes our anxieties coincided and then tensions and misunderstandings could brew up. But always, underneath the troubles, lay the still certainty that we only wanted to work through them and be together, and with that certainty came, for some reason, time. There seemed to be plenty of it about. We had all our lives to come. We could be calm.

We needed to be calm, or at least firm of purpose. Prue had a very difficult job to do and it was one in which I could only play a peripheral part. Having decided quite slowly, over a period of years, that if the opportunity should arise she was going to leave Peter, she was now doing it, which meant that she had to negotiate a divorce and generally clear a path for herself and her three children to get away.

First there was a pantomime to play. Although Peter had been far from faithful, Prue was legally the guilty party, so she and I were required formally to furnish 'evidence of adultery'. The scene was set by Peter's solicitors who required us to have a romantic assignation in a certain room at a particular hotel in Russell Square. There, in the morning, we were to be discovered, in flagrante delicto, by a private detective.

The assignation was more embarrassing than romantic and, I'm sorry to say, neither of us was able to take our role seriously. We caught a glimpse of the private detective as he crept in behind the maid with the breakfast trolley and immediately nipped into the en-suite bathroom where he lurked, breathing loudly, perhaps to make sure we knew he was there.

The maid left. We wondered what we ought to do next. Our poached eggs were on the trolley, on warm plates under round silver domes. It seemed a pity to let them get cold, so we sat on the edge of the bed and ate them. They were excellent. Then we had toast and marmalade. I think the detective may have taken the crunching of toast as his cue because he very slowly appeared round the bathroom door and removed his bowler hat.

'Aha!' he said significantly.

'Yes, indeed,' said Prue. 'Cup of tea?'

He gave her a reproachful look and took out a notebook. He gazed severely around the room, licked his pencil and began to write. Then he pointed the pencil at us and told us to identify ourselves.

We suggested various names which he found difficult to accept so, to prove that she really was Brünhilde, Prue jumped up in her nightie and, holding the two silver domes to her bosom, sang him a few bars from Wagner's opera.

This behaviour seemed to cause the detective great distress. Hurriedly assuring us that no further identification was required, he literally ran from the room. We were a bit worried by his sudden departure but it turned out that in spite of our levity the legal requirements had been fulfilled and the divorce proceedings were able to grind on.

Fortunately the proceedings were not complicated by strife. Prue's two elder children, her son Kevan, who was twelve, and her daughter Kerris, who was ten, were fairly enthusiastic about the idea of leaving Peter. He hadn't allowed their existence to inconvenience him and he definitely wasn't popular with them. Although they may have had some reservations about my becoming their stepfather, I believe they took the general view that it was likely to be preferable to the status quo.

The younger boy, Krispian, known as Pip, was four. He had more complex reservations. He said he was entirely in favour of Prue leaving Peter, and he never wavered in this, but he didn't want her to marry me, or anybody. He wanted her to wait and marry him – a perfectly understandable ambition with which I had every sympathy.

I had known Prue's children for some years as neighbours, so we weren't strangers and, although it took Pip quite a long time to become fully reconciled to my presence, we all managed to get along quite well, largely I think because I didn't attempt to take on the emotional role of father.

Nevertheless, I had taken on a role. I had moved imperceptibly from being alone and at odds with myself and the world to being, if not the actual father of a family, at least its loving protector; a position to which I found I was entirely and joyfully committed. This commitment was not the result of a conscious decision on my part, it was just there. My attention had moved away from myself and I could just get on with doing whatever had to be done next. I had begun to live.

I recall one particular incident that showed how far my state of mind had changed during 1957. It was in September, I think. Ray and Daisy had been to France and on their return Prue and I went down to meet them at Charing Cross Station.

As we walked down the platform I saw Daisy coming towards us. I looked at her face and, as I did so, what felt like a bow-wave of pure agitation seemed to sweep down the platform and roll over and through me. The sensation lasted a second or two and was gone, leaving behind the old familiar state of generalized worriedness, the urgent sense that something, somewhere, had either gone wrong or was going to go wrong, and that it was my fault.

Nothing had gone wrong. Greetings were exchanged. I took the bags and we all walked towards the forecourt where Miranda was parked. As we walked I realised that the wave of anxiety I had felt had originated as much in myself as in Daisy. I also realised that whatever anxiety she may have felt about me came from her affection for me and that my vulnerability to her anxiety was a measure of my affection for her. So that was OK. If necessary I would look after Daisy and Ray the same as I looked after Prue and her children. There was nothing to worry about there.

By that time the divorce situation had more or less sorted itself out. The outrages had been roared, the recriminations hurled, the collusions plotted, the resignations shrugged. Having left the family home, I was living in Earl's Court, and Prue had moved, with the children, into half a house in North Finchley.

I think the one who most enjoyed that move was the dog. A highly intelligent, socially perceptive mongrel bitch of no breeding,

Bach had overseen Prue's bringing up of the children. She had always kept out of Peter's way and although at first she had been suspicious of my presence, the day after Prue told Peter what was going to happen she had bounded up to me, full of welcome. We became great friends and after the move I had the pleasure of meeting her special friend, who was an elderly single lady called Doris who lived in the council flats round the back. On Sunday afternoons Bach would call on her and invite her back to the house for a cup of tea and a chat with Prue, and then see her safely home again.

It was a comparatively quiet time. All we could do now was wait for the divorce decree and hope that it would come through in time for the wedding. It very nearly didn't. On the morning of the wedding Prue showed great presence of mind by borrowing a fiver from Ray and taking a taxi to Somerset House. There she demanded the 'decree absolute', obtained it, and raced with it to the Kensington Register Office. Thus, in the nick of time, she saved us from the embarrassment of having to attend the rather sumptuous reception which Ray and Daisy had laid on at Finchley, *before* the wedding.

III. Small Time.

It was all very well my feeling ready and eager to do whatever had to be done next. The trouble was finding out *what* to do. I had to earn money. It didn't matter a sausage what I did so long as it had a pay packet.

Quite early in 1957, just to keep the wolf from the door, I had found a source of casual work as what was called a stage manager in an independent television company – Associated Rediffusion Ltd. A stage manager was a sort of programme director's labourer, a spare body to do odd jobs and attend to small matters as they arose. Stage managers were engaged by the day, for which they received £3, not a lot, even in 1957, but if one did the job fairly well one could be sure of some continuity.

On the whole I think I was quite a good stage manager – once

I had learned the two basic rules, both of which were completely alien to my temperament. One was: Never make suggestions. The director has enough to do without being lumbered with other people's bright ideas. The other was: Don't bump into people. This was more subtle. Bumping into people wasn't necessarily a physical act. From my days as a stage manager in small theatres I had brought a primal sense of responsibility to the production and a watchful eye for potential disasters. If the scenery looked as if it was going to fall down I would run and hold it up. When I did this in the television studio the scene-shifters went on strike. I had to learn to stand back.

Those were the straightforward parts of a stage manager's job. The unexpected parts were, naturally enough, the results of situations that had not been foreseen like, for instance, trying to arrange for the removal of Sylvia, who was a camel, or the more difficult task of obliging a temperamental choreographer who stamped his foot and ordered me to go and punch the nasty costume-designer on the nose. Oddly enough I couldn't afford to refuse the order because stage managers were day-labourers and if I had I wouldn't have been booked again next day. So I went and asked the costume designer for permission, and he very kindly inclined his nose my way so that I could gently carry out my duty. He also, not unexpectedly, suggested other intimacies, which I declined.

For a while after starting work with the ITV company I entertained an ambition to become something in television – a director, perhaps. I even considered going to night school to study for a qualification, but I soon realised that I was temperamentally unsuited to a job which depended on decisiveness, coolness and confidence. However, other qualities in my character must have been observed, because when it came to a real crisis the programme makers knew who to turn to.

A director I had never heard of rang me at home one day.

He said: 'Sorry to trouble you, but they tell me you can supply us with a collapsible soufflé.'

'Do they?' I asked, playing for time.

197

'That's right.'

'Who are "they", may I ask?'

'Oh, you know, people ... directors and so on.'

'Ah.' I felt a small flush of pride.

I said: 'But of course ... Certainly ... I hope so ... Wait a minute! What the blazes is a collapsible soufflé?'

'Well, what it is ... a soufflé that collapses, you know, like they do. It's for Bebe Daniels in *Life with the Lyons*. She makes this marvellous soufflé. When she takes it out of the oven we can see that it has risen beautifully. But then, as she carries it in triumph to the table where everybody is waiting, it slowly sinks, you know, like they do.'

'Oh, yes, I know. When do you want it?'

'Tomorrow afternoon.'

'OK.'

Thank goodness a collapsible soufflé is quite easy to make. I pinched one of Daisy's baking tins, glued a piece of soft rubber sheet into it so that it lay loosely across its top, and pulled the sheet about till it was really out of shape. Then I drilled a hole in the base of the tin and fitted a rubber-sheet flap inside it to act as a valve to keep the air in. When I blew into this hole the rubber top rose up like a soufflé. I painted it and rubbed sand on to it until it looked very like a risen soufflé. The paint and the sand also made the rubber sheet slightly heavy so that all Bebe Daniels had to do at the right moment was secretly push her little finger into the hole in the base and press in the flap to let the air out. The weight of the sand caused the soufflé to collapse most convincingly. I was very proud of the article, especially when I saw the entry in the Property Master's stock-list:

'Soufflé, collapsible ... qty: one only. For Bebe Daniels.'

One Thursday afternoon when I was at my friend Tyrer Copple's joinery works in Battersea, a phone call came through from Geoffrey Hughes, the director of a series of science programmes called *New Horizon*, which was presented by Dr Bronowski.

Geoffrey said: 'Listen carefully ... You take a cube and stand it on one of its points ... OK?'

'Yes. I can picture that.'

'Right, so holding it dead vertical you cut it horizontally across the middle, exactly halfway up. Can you picture that?'

'Yes, I think so.'

'Good,' said Geoffrey. 'So what shape are the faces of the two halves that you have cut?'

'Cor! . . . Buggered if I know.'

'That's fine,' said Geoffrey. 'I want one, about the size of a football, tomorrow afternoon.'

I asked Tyrer Copple the question. He couldn't visualize it but being a practical chap with his own joinery works, he sorted out a ten-inch cube of timber and we blocked it up on the bed of the band-saw so that we could saw it through the middle, as requested. The cut faces – as if you hadn't already worked it out – were perfect hexagons.

New Horizon was a rich vein. I was engaged for the series as stage manager, which provided a small but regular wage. Also most of the productions called for some special visual devices, many of which I provided. I remember a rotating hydrogen atom whose electrons (torch bulbs) jumped (switched) across and turned it into a helium atom (or was it the other way around?). I remember several sets of optical illusions and a very baffling collection of wheels behind slots which illustrated something a visiting Belgian professor called 'Causalité'. My favourite item was a plastic dodecahedron which could be assembled in front of the cameras from a heap of magnetized pentagons.

This small trade – supplying unlikely articles – continued as an occasional sideline for some years. On 4 November 1963 I was asked to supply a full-size effigy of General de Gaulle to be burned on the bonfire in David Frost's firework-night programme. It meant working all night but it looked magnificent. The ITV company sent a large car to collect it and I heard later that as they passed the House of Commons a policeman recognized the General sitting in the passenger seat and saluted him.

That was perhaps the most prestigious article I supplied. I think the most spectacular came from a cubic metre of fresh seaweed, urgently culled from Whitstable beach and stuffed into black dustbin bags. The programme, grateful as it was for the prompt service, said it could have done without the several worried crabs that emerged from the weed because they ran about the studio, molested the scantily clad sea-nymphs lying languidly on the plaster rocks, and sent them shrieking off the set.

V. Of Mice and Magnets.

This work I was doing for television – itinerant stage manager and occasional property supplier – was just about as peculiar and inconsequential as anything I had been doing before, but it seemed to be providing enough for us to live on from day to day. That was OK but precarious. I definitely needed either a full-time job or a freelance way to earn a reasonable living.

While I had been doing a stint on children's programmes, I had come to see that quite a lot of the material that was being sent out was pretty thin stuff, just about adequate to fill the time.

So, on the basis that I probably couldn't do a lot worse, I sat down one morning in 1958 and took pencil and paper to write a story-series for children's television.

In the event I was lucky. A title occurred to me almost at once: *Alexander the Mouse*. That sounded promising. I wondered what it could be about. Obviously a mouse, but a mouse of distinction, royal perhaps? Yes, but perhaps he didn't know it. Aha! There's a fairy-tale: *The Mouse Born to be King*. Yes, but king of where? Where is a mouse kingdom? Under the floorboards and in similar lost places. OK, so that's the bones of it, but what's the story? What happens? How does it begin? ... Well, with his name, of course. His brothers and sisters have proper mouse names like *Eeek*, *Gleek* and *Pleep*. How come he is lumbered with a mouthful like *Alexander*? So he wants to know. That is the quest.

'All right, that'll do for now,' I said to myself. 'Start writing. We'll see what turns up.'

I hadn't quite expected that. I thought I would have to work everything out to the last detail and then go through the mundane task of writing it down. I hadn't realised that at the same time as I was doing the mundane task with the front of my mind, another far more efficient department in the background could get on with brewing up and fitting together the story. It was a good morning, indeed a good week. The words came running down my arm as fast as I could write them and by the end of it I had the six episodes of the story on paper.

I took it to Michael, who was Head of Light Entertainment. He called me in the next day and told me that he liked it and that he thought it would make an excellent vehicle.

'Vehicle for what?' I asked.

'For our new, marvellous, magnetic animation system!' he cried, his eyes lighting up with enthusiasm. 'The most exciting development in motion-portrayal since film itself! We have the inventor under contract. He will oversee the production. You will like Shamus.'

For some reason Michael's enthusiasm was not instantly infectious, and I couldn't help thinking he might have got the 'vehicle' bit the wrong way around, but I was delighted that my story had been accepted and was genuinely enthusiastic about that.

'You get on with it,' said Michael. 'You liaise with Shamus, get yourself an artist to do your pictures. You tell the story on air. Find some music in the library or see if Steve Race has got something that will do.'

Reeling slightly but highly elated, I came away.

Shamus was an eager Irishman, full to bursting with the wonderful potential of his invention. The basic idea was to have a flat picture, laid on a horizontal table with a very thin, non-magnetic surface, like aluminium. Lying on this picture, as part of it, would be a flat figure made of thin card which had a thin magnet sellotaped to its underside. If you held a magnet under the table so that it locked onto the magnet on the flat figure, you could move the figure across the picture by pulling the magnet across. There would be two special tables, each with its own skilled animator. Each table would have a mirror above it which would be set at forty-five degrees, so that the television camera could look directly into the mirror and so down onto the table. That all seemed pretty straightforward.

Finding an artist willing to do over twenty different backgrounds as well as several cut-out figures for a fee of £30 an episode, seemed likely to be a more difficult task. Then I remembered my friend Maurice Kestelman, who was now Head of Fine Art at the Central School of Art and Design in Southampton Row. I went to see him and he suggested one of his lecturers.

Thus it was that I came to meet Peter Firmin and his wife Joan and their three girls, Charlotte, Hannah and Josie (who was only a few days old and very pink). They lived in a ground-floor flat in Battersea.

Peter was a bit dubious about working for television. It didn't seem like proper illustration, and there was rather a lot of it, for very little money. He wasn't so much bothered about the lack of money as about whether or not he would be able to get through the work in time. But in the end I persuaded him and he agreed to have a go.

In the event Peter drew the first batch of pictures quite quickly. We laid out the mice and the camera rehearsals for the first episode of *Alexander the Mouse* began. They were a nightmare.

The system worked, in the sense that the animator could reach under the table with a magnet and, once that magnet had locked on to the mouse's magnet, move the mouse along. That was fine but if the magnet didn't hit the exact spot (which was invisible underneath the table), the mouse would zip across the picture to meet it. Or worse, if the magnet was the wrong way around, the mouse would execute a somersault to bring the north and south poles together, or worse still, if the animator's magnet was the wrong way around but it came up exactly in the right place, the mouse would be lifted bodily off the table by magnetic repulsion, turn over in the air and come down again back to front and underside upwards. Then all the animator could do was reach a hand into the picture in full view of the camera and turn it the right way up. Also the magnets sometimes just let go, leaving the mouse stranded. Then the animator would have to back-track with the magnet and cast about to try and pick it up again.

At the first rehearsals we regarded these difficulties as being teething troubles, but they were not. Hardly a programme went out without some incongruity – a hand coming into shot or a mouse coming adrift. I sometimes felt really relieved that once they were transmitted the pictures were gone for ever.

In spite of all these vicissitudes the programmes were well received by the company. The story was OK, a bit muddled, without much action, but full of good pictures of a mouse-angled world. The last episode ended with the coronation of Alexander, which took place in the mouse-cathedral under a warehouse down by the London Docks. It was a glittering occasion in which the choir of poor church-mice sang the anthem 'Lo, the mouse in triumph comes, see him in his glory', and I gave a solemn commentary in the manner of Richard Dimbleby. After it was transmitted Michael reeled into the studio smiling and full of congratulations.

He said: 'That was one of the nicest programmes I have ever seen and if we aren't arrested for lese-majesty, we'll be done for blasphemy!'

We were all very chuffed by that, and I was even more chuffed when, a few days later, the Contracts Department rang me and ordered twenty more episodes of *Alexander*. We were in business.

Peter and I started on the next batch of *Alexander*s. He now had plenty of work because his skill had been noticed by other producers and he had been offered similar contracts for other programmes, for which he had rounded up several assistants, so their flat in Battersea was fairly buzzing.

I wasn't doing too badly either but I had nothing in my head to follow Alexander. So I was quite relieved when Michael asked me to suggest a programme for deaf children. That narrowed the field a bit and the limitation triggered off an idea. I suggested a slow Chinese story about a small boy and a water buffalo.

Michael liked the idea but he and I were both fed up with the magnets. A different form of animation was needed.

I suggested making the programmes on 16mm film by single-frame animation. Michael rejected that because the budget of £150 for each ten-minute episode wouldn't begin to cover the cost of filming the series.

Wouldn't it? I wondered. Making films was usually quite costly, but the money went on all sorts of things I wouldn't need, like film crews, lights, locations, technicians and sound-recording facilities.

If I was going to make on film the same sort of programme as we were making with the magnetic animation, I wasn't going to need much more than a camera capable of taking single frames (i.e., able to expose one frame of the film at a time), and a table on which I could move the flat card figures in single frames (i.e., moving the figure a tiny distance, shooting one frame and then moving it again), which was the basic process of single-frame filming.

I consulted the Company's film department about the project. They laughed it off, saying that even if I *could* raise the capital costs of setting up a studio, all the profit would go on paying the interest.

Even so the idea wouldn't go away. I could make an animation table. I could put together an editing device, I didn't need a studio, there was a spare room in the half-house in North Finchley where we were living. The arithmetic of the project was a bit daunting, but possible. I located a producer friend from the BBC who had become an honorary Chinaman and was doing authentic Chinese paintings. He liked the story and said he would be willing to do the artwork for £30 an episode and wait for payment until I was paid. There was no need for sound equipment because the film, being for the deaf, was to be silent. So it looked as if, for that film at least, I would need almost no capital.

I did the sums over and over and then, one day, went to Michael and said: 'If you can find £175 for each episode and pay on delivery, I can make *The Journey of Master Ho* for that.'

'All right,' he said, 'go away and do it.'

I came away from Michael's office feeling very alarmed indeed. Just what had I been idiotic enough to let myself in for now?

The answer was simple: a lot of hard work that had to be done very quickly.

Meanwhile Peter, equally disenchanted with the magnets, had moved in a different direction. For certain shots in *Alexander*, the ones that had to be reliable, he had made cut-card mechanical animations with sliders and moving panels worked from the back. These were only ever seen once, which was rather a waste. Peter felt that the principle had a lot of potential and he set about developing it.

At I believe Joan's suggestion, he made some card-pictures with whole nursery rhymes on them. One had a cat actually playing the fiddle in one corner, a cow which jumped clean over the moon, a dog falling about with laughter and a roguish dish, who grabbed the coy spoon and ran away with her – on little rotary legs! These card-pictures were real works of art, especially when seen from the back, where all the intricate, ingenious sliders, handles, springs, cottons and rubber bands can be seen working.

The television company was delighted and they invited a young Australian singer called Rolf Harris to bring his accordion and do a programme in which he would sing the nursery rhyme while Peter worked the reveals and sliders in time to the song. Peter also made smaller, even more complicated animations in which he could cause the characters to sing and play instruments to pre-recorded, sometimes speeded-up, songs, for which Rolf persuaded Peter to sing the harmonies. Later Rolf sang a song about a kangaroo and hit the big time, but a young Country and Western singer, Wally Whyton, took his place and the programme, which was called *Musical Box*, continued for some years.

9

SMALLFILMS

I. Small Miracles.

The animation table and camera gantry went up in the spare room. The Chinese paintings arrived and with them the moment of truth. My assertion that making animated films was simply a matter of pushing pieces of cardboard about under the camera was about to be tested. Was it true?

The answer, as is often the case, was more complicated than the question. Yes, with great patience you could reconstruct motion in terms of tiny movements each taking one twenty-fifth of a second, there was no doubt about that, but whether or not I was going to be able to do it convincingly was yet to be seen. The only way to find out was to do it. So I just got on with it.

I got through it. The films were delivered, accepted and paid for. I settled my accounts and owned the equipment. The film I had made was really quite bad. It was a great improvement on the magnetic animation but it was juddery and uncertain, poorly paced and ragged. However, as the filming went on, the technique seemed to settle down until, in the later episodes, the slightly stilted formal movements of the characters appeared to be quite congruous to the Chineseness of it all.

As well as being transmitted on television *The Journey of Master Ho* was shown to deaf children in their special schools and, I was told, they enjoyed the films. So that was something done.

But there was more to it than that. I have indicated that the process of making a cartoon film was slow and laborious. What I omitted to mention was that it was also tremendously exciting.

I remember the very first test-piece of film I ever made. I loaded the camera and chose one of the Chinese backgrounds. I assembled the card-pieces for a side view of Master Ho, the Chinese boy, and jointed the flat arms and legs to the body with bits of cotton and sticky-tape. I did the same for the pieces of the water buffalo and laid the two of them in position on the Chinese landscape background so that they made a good picture.

I placed the picture on the table, lined it up under the camera and shot about five seconds of film. Then I sat on my stool and, using a small pointed screwdriver as a pusher, moved the legs and body of Master Ho a millimetre at a time across the picture in what I imagined might be an imitation of the way he could have walked – remembering to shoot one frame of film between each movement. After about an hour of this Master Ho had reached the water buffalo, so I stopped moving him along and, frame by frame, let him bow to the buffalo. For good measure I let the buffalo bow to him. Then they both straightened up.

I had the film processed, brought it home and laced the print into my Moviscop editor, which had a screen like a tiny television set. As I wound the film through by hand I saw the Chinese landscape with the boy and the water buffalo standing in it. It did look very good. Then, suddenly, by God! ... the boy actually walked across the picture and bowed to the water buffalo, and then, look! . . . the buffalo bowed back! I wound the film in reverse and they did it backwards. Then I wound it forwards again quite slowly and watched them do it again.

That was all, but I was fizzing with excitement. It didn't matter what the picture was of. It didn't matter that Master Ho had stumbled rather than walked . . . I had done something momentous. I had opened up another dimension to the still picture. I had given it the extra dimension of time. I had made it come to life.

Seeing Alexander the Mouse being pulled along by an invisible magnet had been interesting and fun, but seeing Master Ho walking across was different, and astonishing, because it had never happened in real time. I had built the happening piecemeal by hand, using tiny building-bricks of time, each one twenty-fifth of a second in length – three hundred and forty-three of them to be exact – and I had done it by myself, in the spare-room, on a home-made animation table, using a camera worked with pieces of Meccano and a string.

My body, which always understood much better what was going on than my head, was dancing about, sending up waves of idiotic delight and conjecture. 'This way,' it shouted, 'you could make whole worlds, complete places full of people, and with your love you can give them life!'

'Now take it easy.'

'And you have absolute power, absolute control, over everything in those worlds. Pigs can fly, forests can walk. The river can sing and flow uphill. At your command the world could blow itself to dust and ice.'

'That'll do, that'll do. Any moment now you'll be inventing dragons.'

'Oh, any amount of dragons. Dragons are two a penny. Peter will draw them and you will make them roar and blow great blasts of paper fire, for which, by the way, you'll need a double-exposure.'

All that exuberance may seem a bit overstated today, but forty-two years and two hundred films later, if I were to lace the rushes into the projector, and see for the first time the work I had done the week before spring suddenly into life, I would still feel exactly the same thrill.

And in a sense it was all true. Peter Firmin and I did make worlds, nearly a dozen of them, down to the last nut and bolt.

But that was all to come. In 1958 all I knew was that I had the tool to do a particular sort of work. Now I was faced with the task of finding, from somewhere in the sky, the happenings and places, the stories, that I would use it for – and sell them to the television company.

Let me say now that anybody who thinks that making a living by writing original stories is an easy happy sort of life is, to put it politely, mistaken. There is nothing so numbingly terrifying as a blank piece of paper on to which you are committed, by contract, to write a whole complex piece of yet-to-be-created life.

Sometimes a brainwave would come, but more often I found myself scouring the inside of my head trying to imagine the *sort of thing* that heads of TV departments might fancy.

I remember asking myself if there was one particular sort of creature that everybody could feel unashamedly sentimental about. Was there something somewhere that would surely touch their heartstrings? Not cuddly bunnies or cute dollies, that was for sure. Dogs? Horses? Hmmm ... Cars? Motorbikes? Boats? What did every boy of my generation want to be when he grew up? An engine driver, of course. I knew an engine driver, or rather an engine driver's mate.

Denzil Ellis, my friend from Drama School, had been an engine-fireman. He had fired the *Royal Scot* (or was it the *Flying Scotsman?*), shovelling coal into its firebox as it roared along the track. He once told me how his day used to start. At some unearthly hour in the morning he would have to go and wake up the engine, clear out the firebox, take paper and wood and light its fire, just as you or I would light a stove or a kitchen range, so that the engine would be boiling nicely by the time it was due to set off for Edinburgh. I had been touched by that story because it seemed to give a human dimension to the glowing hundred-ton steel power-machine thundering up the main line.

So, all right. A railway engine. What sort? Where would it be?

Where? ... That wasn't too difficult. Wales was the place. In Wales the railways don't run straight across flat ground at high speeds. They wander up and down the valleys and along the tops of the hills, and in my mind Wales was already a magic place, a place of glorious eccentricities and unlikely logic. I knew this because I was intoxicated by the writings of Dylan Thomas and had been carrying a copy of *Under Milk Wood* in my pocket for years.

All right, then. A Welsh railway engine. So what does a Welsh railway engine do for a living? Pulls trucks with things in. A bit dull, really. Hardly the stuff of legend. Wasn't there something a bit more interesting for it to do?

The answer came – wait for it – while I was in the bath. I muttered 'Eureka,' climbed out dripping wet, and telephoned Peter. I said: 'He wants to sing in the choir.'

'Of course,' said Peter, as if it was a matter of course that in Wales a railway engine would want to sing in the choir.

That single thought provided the touchstone for the world of *Ivor the Engine*, that ordinary world in which the extraordinary was just going to be part of the landscape.

'What landscape?' I asked myself.

'Well, you know, the pictures I'm going to put in front of the camera and make a film of.'

'Now wait a minute! You don't know the first thing about making *films!* All you've done up to now is cobble together a story to replace a barbaric form of magnetic animation. Now you're proposing to commit yourself to making a set of proper films, real films, which will be judged by experienced film-makers who have been on courses, who are qualified, knowing about camera angles and style and pace and fashion. The Art of Film-making is something people study and write books about. You don't know anything about any of it. Why do you imagine you can just walk in and do it?'

Why indeed? I took this very real anxiety to my friend Mary Beales (now Mary Orrom) and her husband Michael, who were both experienced professional film-makers. I sat with them in their flat and told them, in a muddled way, with hoots and puffs, the basic story of *Ivor the Engine*.

They enjoyed the story, so I asked them the question: 'Could I seriously think of myself as being qualified to take on a contract to make a film of it?'

For a moment they didn't seem to understand the question – then they laughed.

Michael said: 'You've got the "visuals" in your head and you know how they follow each other and know who is going to say what to whom, and where. In fact, you can see this film in your head, so you can make it.'

Mary and Michael went on to give me some advice that I have never forgotten. They told me not to bother about what anybody else in the film world was doing or had done. I should just concentrate on what I myself was doing, which was to show the story as clearly as I could. At the end of the day the film might not be the most stunningly impressive example of the film-maker's art, but it would do its job, which was to bring the story to life.

'But,' I said, 'what about the Art of Film-making?'

Mary and Michael had no opinion of the Art of Film-making. They said there were only really four things to know about making films and they are just common sense – and I can't for the life of me remember what they were! I do remember that they told me that the camera, the film, the equipment and the whole pretentious mystique of the Art of Film-making were there for one purpose and one purpose only, to serve me and help me to tell the story as clearly as I could. And they added: 'So you might as well get on with it.'

Heartened by this encouragement I plunged straight into writing the story.

I clearly recall sitting down and writing the first lines:

Not very long ago, in the top left-hand corner of Wales, there was a railway. It wasn't a very long railway or a very important railway, but it was called the Merioneth and Llantisilly Rail Traction Company Limited, and it was all there was. And in a shed, in a siding, at the end of the railway, lived the Locomotive of the Merioneth and Llantisilly Rail Traction Company Limited, which was a long name for a little engine, so his friends just called him Ivor.

Now in the morning, Jones the Steam the engine driver would come down over the hill, jump the stream beside the shed and open the door.

'Morning, Ivor! Jumping cold this morning...'

The story unfolded quite slowly: Jones lit Ivor's fire and when the boiler boiled, made himself a pot of tea from it. He took Ivor out of the shed and down to the water tower, where he filled his tank with water, and then on to the signal box, where Owen was still asleep. They woke him with a whistle and soon they were on their way along the top of the hill above the sea towards Llaniog, where Dai Station the stationmaster was waiting for them, looking fed up as usual...

Then, just as suddenly, I stopped. In spite of Mary and Michael's enthusiasm I felt I wanted to complete one small piece of film for us to look at and maybe show to the ITV company as a sample. I did some sketches of what I imagined would be the backgrounds for the shots and actions, put together a sort of story-board alongside the piece of script and took them straight down to Peter in Battersea.

Apart from small details like the height of Ivor's funnel, Peter's vision of Ivor and his country was perfectly in tune with my own. When, after a day or two, Peter came up with the drawings for the first two minutes of film, I found them completely satisfying and was delighted to have my first view of the place and people with whom my imagination was going to live and work, on and off, for many years.

I filmed that first two minutes and, somewhat nervously, took the print along to the television company, where we showed it to the head of the department, the senior producer and some of their staff, in one of their viewing-studios. The film was of course silent so I told the story as it appeared on the screen, played all the parts and included all the puffs, hisses, clonks, scrapes and whistles that I could manage. I am happy to say that they were not only highly delighted with the film but also falling about with laughter, partly, I suspect, in response to my impromptu pantomime of vocal sound effects.

The ITV company bought the series on the spot, so I was in business and going to be busy. Fortunately, now that I had the pictures in my head, the people, Jones the Steam, Owen the Signal, Dai Station, simply turned up for work. I didn't have to invent them, they came off my pen as if they had been there all along, waiting to be called. It was the same with the places: Llaniog, Tan-y-Gwlch, Grumbly Town, Llanmad,* Tewyn Beach. I could see them all, clear and complete, as I came to them. And, as had happened with *Alexander*, somewhere in my head the story was forming itself while I was writing it.

The actual filming still presented some technical problems, mainly arising from the fact that unlike *The Journey of Master Ho, Ivor the Engine* was to have sound. My impromptu performance had been fine for an audition but the final film would have to have a complete sound-track recorded on to it. I would have to make the film and then take it along to a sound studio and record the sound while watching the picture, more or less as I had done at the audition.

That seemed reasonable enough but I suddenly realised that it wasn't going to work. *Without a sound-track, how was I going to know the right number of frames to shoot for each incident?* This was an absolute problem. Unless I knew exactly how many twenty-fifths-of-a-second frames were available in the sound-track for a particular piece of action, I simply couldn't begin to film it!

I eventually dealt with this by making a rough sound recording of the whole film, leaving time for the various actions and incidents to take place. Then I timed each sentence and section of it so that I knew how many seconds they took to happen. Then I converted the seconds to numbers of frames and wrote the numbers on to the script.

That process sounds laborious and complicated, and it was,

---

* Ray suggested 'Llanmad' because Dylan Thomas's town in *Under Milk Wood* was named 'Llareggub'.

very. It was also unreliable because if the film and the sound didn't come together properly at the final recording the script would have to be revised or the film edited on the spot, and this would involve extra studio time at the recording labs, the cost of which could quickly gobble up our meagre profits.

Even so I really enjoyed those final recording sessions. Reading the script, bearing in mind the character I was speaking for, watching the picture in order to anticipate the animation so that the words and actions would fit together, called for intense concentration. But then, after it was done, to sit back and watch the section being re-run with the sound, was (if I had got it right) another small miracle, because where there had been cardboard figures waving their arms about, now they were alive and talking, their gestures punctuating and expressing their words. And when the cotton wool puffed up out of Ivor's funnel it went *Psst-koff, psst-koff, psst-koff* and was real steam. That was a special pleasure.

The last, but certainly not the least, small miracle was still to come. That was the music.

Steve Race, who had composed a piece for *Alexander the Mouse*, suggested a bassoon for a small Welsh engine, and he put me in touch with Vernon Elliott, who was a professional bassoonist and also a composer.

Vernon Elliott was a bit diffident about composing music for a Welsh railway engine because he had never done anything like it before. I explained that I had never made a film about a Welsh railway engine before, so we were both in the same boat. I gave Vernon a script and he promised to try and think of something.

A day or two later he rang me to say that he thought he had something that might do. I went over to his house to listen to it.

The tune was short and simple and absolutely right, a beautiful, marvellously evocative theme that brought Ivor and his world instantly to mind.

Then, suddenly I remembered something – The Grumbly and

District Choral Society! 'Vernon, do you happen to have a Welsh choir?'

'Well, yes,' said Vernon, 'as a matter of fact I do. There's a choir in North London I work with sometimes. They aren't all Welsh but I'm sure they'd love to sing for a Welsh railway engine.'

That was a marvellous piece of luck. Vernon recorded the bassoon solos at the sound studios and a week or two later I recorded the choir singing 'Cwm Rhondda' in a Catholic Church Hall in Hampstead. The choir wanted to do the recording for nothing but Vernon, being a professional, persuaded them to accept a modest fee. I was more than glad to pay it because the sound was heartrendingly beautiful.

I came away with two reels of tape and a small feeling of pride, which came from the sense that I had caused and helped some glorious music to exist. Little did I know how significant the effect of that recording of 'Cwm Rhondda' was to be, nor did I realise that Vernon and I had just begun a collaboration that would bring us both years of delight.

II. Mass Production.

Looking back at 1959 I find myself wondering how on earth we got through the sheer volume of happenings.

First I had the six *Ivor the Engine* films to make. How long this was going to take was uncertain, because although a particular shot might take an hour or more to film in single frames, it could take even longer to set up initially. The background would have to be chosen and lined up with the camera, the figures would need to be assembled and have their limbs attached with tiny pieces of sticky-tape and cotton. Also, although making the film was essentially a simple task, it was also subtle. Objects, especially living things, don't move at constant speed. A body has weight. If you move the object exactly the same distance in each frame, it stops and starts suddenly and looks as if it was made of cardboard, but if you graduate the movement correctly it can look like a person walking or a railway engine moving off.

I also found myself thinking very carefully about the choice and sequence of the shots.

In the same way that writing a story is not simply a matter of writing lines of words, but calls on the writer to assemble the sentences in such a way that the reader receives them in the right order for stacking in the mind, so too the task of filming the story in pictures calls on the film-maker to present the pictures in such a way that the feeling of what is going on is delivered and the viewer has the sense that it is actually happening. Luckily I was usually able to visualize the shots in my head and make my choice before filming and, even though my choice was never consciously analytical, the sequences were usually pretty satisfactory. But even so it all took time, as did the occasions when I had to nip down to Battersea on the tube to collect the odd cardboard arm or leg or railway carriage that Peter and I had forgotten to include in the list.

Piecing together my diary for the spring of 1959 I see that although Prue was in the late stages of pregnancy, so I was holding the fort, I was also still doing odd days of stage-managing and providing props for ITV. Apparently I was also designing a gear-train for a new off-set litho printer for Ralph Furness and a Mr Groak (I've no idea how I came to be doing that). There was also litigation on the children's maintenance to sort out and Bach's latest litter of puppies to find homes for – and all the time I was wondering what I was going to do after I finished filming *Ivor the Engine*.

That time was fast approaching, so I went to see Mary Orrom's friend Violet Drummond, who wanted films made of some delicious children's books which she had written and illustrated about a rather posh young girl called Little Laura, who wore a Mouflon hat and was looked after by a nanny.

A few days later, while I was at the sound studio recording the sound-track of the last episode of *Ivor*, a call came through from Barnet Hospital to tell me that Prue had given birth to twin boys. I dropped everything and hared off to the hospital. It wasn't proper visiting time, but I stole into the ward and saw Prue sitting up looking very pleased with herself, with two small basket-cots, one on each side of her bed.

I looked in one of these and saw a small perfect young person who was, miraculously, my son. I touched his face with the back of one finger, but very softly so as not to disturb his important sleep, and felt an enormous emotion, of pride, awe and affection. I then walked round to the other side and saw my other son. I touched his face as well and felt exactly the same emotion all over again.

'But they're exactly the same,' I said.

'Of course they are, silly,' said Prue. 'They're twins. Anyway they're not quite the same. Stephen is six ounces heavier than Simon.'

I didn't have a chance to ask which was which because the fierce ward sister chased me out, ordering me not to return until the proper time. I hared back to the sound studio and, completely drunk with elation and confusion, finished off the sound-track for the last episode of *Ivor the Engine* – which was the end of my work for the series.

It was just as well I had finished the filming because the arrival in our flat of the twins and all their paraphernalia meant that the camera and animation table were summarily banished from the bedroom, the cots were set up and a stream of visits and celebrations began.

Gradually the pattern of family life settled into orbit around the timetable of its newest members. For a while I became incongruously maternal and would drink cups of coffee and have chats with other young mums about the details of looking after babies. Prue said I caused some puzzlement because I had a habit of referring to babies in the plural, as if everybody always had twins.

By now money really was running out so, having negotiated another corner for the animation table and a contract with Violet Drummond, I was able to make a start on the films of *Little Laura*.

At first I was worried about the technicalities of these films because Violet Drummond's characters and her style of drawing, though artless and delightful on the page, were a bit inconsistent and wayward. In reality I was being too particular. The strange filming was perfectly in keeping with her style, and the whole effect was delightful and hilarious.

Meanwhile the *Ivor* films had been delivered and were being transmitted. As Prue and I sat and watched it on our rather blurred television set I found myself wondering what the film was really like. I was so conscious of its faults – the clumsy cuts, the missed sound effects, the juddery movements – that I was quite unable to enjoy the story or gauge its worth.

Television is a notoriously unresponsive medium. There is no audience present at the performance. Nobody claps. Small programmes like ours were rarely noticed by the press. The first inkling I had that our film was being appreciated came when I heard that because the transmission of *Ivor the Engine* coincided with the ITV company's weekly board meeting, the directors had arranged for a television set to be wheeled into the boardroom so that they could watch it. That was very gratifying, but the real moment of glory was yet to come.

Later that year the ITV company assembled a compilation of its best children's programmes to show at a rather luxurious reception for the celebrities of the television and entertainment world. Among the items being shown was the last episode of *Ivor the Engine*. It came fairly near the end of the programme which, up till then, had been received politely by the audience. As soon as Ivor came on the screen I could feel the audience go quiet. As it went on I felt them warm up and begin to chuckle and chortle. Then at last, after Ivor had trundled into the siding at Grumbly Gasworks where the choir was waiting for him, came the coup de grâce ... 'Cwm Rhondda'. The singing rose in a rich wave which no heart, however hard, could have resisted. Vernon Elliott's North London Welsh choir, with Vernon playing Ivor's pipes on his bassoon, had done us proud, and as the film ended the celebrities were laughing and crying and clapping at the same time. It had all worked. I muttered a prayer of thanks to the late Reverend John Hughes, to whose heirs I had just paid a substantial fee for the use of his hymn, and felt very happy.

There was one interesting fly in the ointment. All the other items shown in the programme had been introduced by a presenter who duly mentioned the names and gave credit to the people who had made them. However, when it came to Ivor's turn, the presenter just said that the next item was all the work of one person (which wasn't true), without mentioning any name. Also, at the end of the piece, the music suddenly stopped short because the last picture, which was the end-caption with Peter's, Vernon's and my name on it, had been cut off – so somebody had gone to a lot of trouble to ensure that the audience was not told who had made that particular item.

This omission had not passed unnoticed by that sophisticated audience. Ursula Eason, who was Deputy Head of Children's Programmes at the BBC, came over at the end of the show to congratulate us on the film and commiserate about the absence of credits. She said she realised that the omission of our names was obviously an act of petty meanness, but she made the unexpected suggestion that we should perhaps look on it as a sort of compliment, because it showed that we had made something that was worth being seriously jealous of.

III. Moving On.

As we were to discover would often happen, we came upon our next project as the result of an apparently accidental coincidence.

At different times both Peter Firmin and I had visited the Edward VII Gallery at the British Museum, where we had both noticed a set of Norse chessmen from the island of Lewis. What had impressed us was that, far from being fierce and warlike, it was quite clear that these were essentially kindly, non-belligerent characters, who were thoroughly dismayed by the prospect of contest. Neither Peter nor I had any idea that this impression was going to be significant.

Among the characters in one of the programmes which Peter had been involved with was a wicked baron for whom he had made animated moustaches that twirled most evilly.

One day, while he was travelling through Neasden on his way to the studios at Wembley, it occurred to Peter that the chessmen in the Edward VII Gallery could well have been called Nogs, that their Prince was a Noggin and that the wicked baron with the twirly moustaches could be their wicked uncle, perhaps a Nogbad.

Peter thought of a tale from the Land of Nog. It told of the death of a much-loved king and of his son, Prince Noggin, who had to choose a bride within six weeks, because if he did not the crown would go to his wicked uncle, Nogbad the Bad. Noggin could not choose from among the busty maidens of the North-lands, but a strange bird with green feathers, whose name was Graculus, brought him a walrus tooth carved with the likeness of Nooka, daughter of Nan of the Nooks, the ruler of the Land of the Midnight Sun. (This part of the plot was suggested by Peter and Joan's daughter, Hannah, who was four. She had seen the famous film *Nanook of the North* which was about the home life of the Eskimos and had decided she was a Nook and could not therefore be expected to wear pyjamas in bed.)

The Nogs made a longship and sailed beyond the black ice at the edge of the world to the Land of the Midnight Sun. There Noggin and Nooka plighted their troth and amid great feasting Graculus flew back to the Northlands with the glad news. On the way he was captured by Nogbad the Bad and imprisoned in his castle. Nogbad was on his way to claim the crown when a robin took a green feather to Noggin's mother, Queen Grunhilda. She recognized the feather and sent guards to release Graculus while she went to town to sort Nogbad out. He was duly banished and, as the square sail of Noggin's longship appeared over the horizon, Nogbad slunk away over the high pass to stay with his granny in Finland.

Peter wrote a synopsis and a shooting-script for a couple of episodes, not with film in mind but intended to be shown 'live' with complex mechanical animations. He offered this to the ITV company as an alternative to the magnetic animation but, for some reason, it was turned down. Rather disappointed, he passed it over to me to consider as a film. I thought it was great. We rejigged the pictures to suit the film treatment and I wrote one or two patches of slightly heroic prose to set the tone. We took *The Saga of Noggin the Nog* to the BBC, who accepted it, offering us the princely sum of £100 for each ten-minute episode.

We accepted the offer. Peter agreed that I should write the shooting scripts from his episodes and synopses and we set to work.

Working on the Noggin saga was a bit complicated because in 1959 both families moved house. Peter and Joan and their daughters moved into a farmhouse in Blean, just north of Canterbury, in Kent. This had a spacious farmyard with a range of outbuildings, including a cow-shed, some pigsties and a massive, leaky, thatched barn.

Prue said: 'What about moving down there?'

That was obviously the most sensible thing to do, so we made an offer for a tall thin house in a terrace-block right on the seafront at Whitstable. The house was four storeys high, it had two scruffy bathrooms, a derelict service-lift, a small rough back garden and wide views over the glistening estuary of the Thames with, occasionally, a grandstand view of the yacht-racing from the first-floor balcony. Just the other side of a narrow private road in front of the house was the sea wall and the beach. After the dull flat in Finchley we all thought it was a really exciting place to live.

The move was a turning-point in all our lives. Prue and I now had a place of our own. The children had room to move and grow. The air was good.

By now I was fairly confident that the business was viable. I could see that, with the help of Peter and others, I could make films that would be acceptable to the TV companies, at a price they would be willing to pay, and earn our living by doing it.

The obvious next move would be to expand. I could take on capital and form a proper film company, with a studio, employees and new, state-of-the-art equipment. That was the conventional approach and I could see that if I had personal ambition, if I wanted to make a name for myself in the field of film-making, if I wanted my work to become recognized as world-leading in its excellence and win Oscars, that was the way I would have to go.

Did I want these things? Well, yes, I wouldn't mind, one day, perhaps. But for the moment all I wanted was to be an author, a writer of stories, who just happened to have an extension to his pen, a facility which allowed him to write the stories on to film and so bring them to life. That was ambition enough to go on with.

So all right, what did I need to maintain this facility and make a living from it? It would have been nice to have a Sinclair single-frame rostrum camera and rotary table, a Steenbeck editing suite, a double-headed projector and a host of other glorious devices, but they would have set me back several thousand pounds and I would have had to spend the rest of my life paying off the loan.

One item was absolutely essential. That was a good camera with a rock-steady picture. I had one, a Bolex. The other optical equipment, like the projector and the editing viewer, were auxiliary, things which I could buy secondhand and adapt to my purposes. Everything else I could probably put together myself. The most important thing was to own everything and not be saddled with debt.

The great advantage of the move to Kent was that Peter and I now had a proper cow-shed to work in. There would be no more tube journeys across London to fetch a cardboard leg or half a dozen tiny hands. Also I now had somewhere to work which was away from home.

I had my equipment in the dairy part and Peter had his studio and desk in the end where the cows had lived. Using a piece of scaffold-pole we bashed a hole in the wall overlooking the duck-pond so that he could have a window to work by.

At my end of the cow-shed I built a new, improved animation table, mainly out of scaffold poles and pieces of bicycle, which had a camera gantry that would go up and down. This had several sophisticated facilities, like a piece of dressmaker's tape-measure glued to the back wall to show the height of the camera, side rollers to carry very long backgrounds and a new Meccano drive mechanism for the camera that had an electrically operated release and gave me an exposure of about three-quarters of a second for each frame. This meant that I no longer needed the very bright lights which had tended to overheat the card figures and make them curl.

Then I made the one technical change which completely revolutionized my way of working. I thought again about the sound-recording procedures and realised that I had been working back to front. The business of making rough guide tracks, timing them with a stopwatch and converting the time to frames was not just boring, it was a nonsense.

I could see that if I made the complete, final, finished sound-track with all the music and effects already on it, first, before I even started to film, I could have this dubbed on to 16mm film. Then I could run the 16mm sound-track through the sound-head of my projector, listen to each sound and read off its frame numbers from the frame-counter. Then I would know exactly how many frames each movement would take and could film whole sequences which would match the sound-track exactly!

I was tremendously pleased with myself for inventing this way of working, probably because at the time I didn't know that it had been standard practice in the cartoon film industry for years.

Another, unforeseen, advantage of this method was that I could have a cassette recording of the finished sound-track which Peter and I could listen to before starting work. In order to sort out the shots and pictures, we would sit at a table and run the tape backwards and forwards until we could see exactly what would be needed.

All these technicalities are the commonplace details of small film-making, but for us they were crucially significant to the progress of our enterprise. The price we were getting for the films was so low that for us success did not lie in the expansion of our facilities or in the increase of our reputation, it lay in streamlining the financial shoestring on which we worked, honing each piece of procedure, both in terms of time and cost, so that at the end there would be enough money over for us to live on.

It was a close thing. What with the twins and the move and the reorganization of the way we were going to work, I had forgotten to look for any more work.

Quite suddenly, in the spring of 1960, I discovered that I was practically out of money.

Although the BBC had liked *The Saga of Noggin the Nog* they hadn't yet asked for any more, but I had offered them a set of six films called *The Seal of Neptune*, which was a sort of underwater fairy-tale about the adventures of a sea horse and a shrimp. Ursula Eason was kind enough to confirm their intention to take the series, so, on the strength of that and other suggestions that were in the offing, I was able to borrow some money from Ray to tide us over. However it was a salutary experience, one which reminded me forcefully how precarious our living was. It also served very effectively to concentrate the mind.

IV. Sea Horses and Penguins.

The BBC offered a slightly higher price for *The Seal of Neptune*: £125 an episode. That was still far from generous even in 1960 but it meant that there was a little more money to spend on music. That was good because the story needed music, gentle magic underwater music and dark sinister music to go with the sunken city and the evil sharks.

The opening lines were written with music in mind. You can almost hear it in the background . . .

> Far, far away, a long way from here in the Western Sea, where the palm trees wave behind the golden sand and the coral reefs grow like gardens under the water, where the sun keeps the sea warm and clear and it is always summer, there was a rock. It was a rock made of old sandstone, and the gentle ocean, flowing across and around it for thousands and thousands of years, had worn it into shelves and caves, crevices and crannies . . .

. . . but of course I had no idea what the music was going to be like. I just marked up the script with the places where I thought music would be appropriate and handed it over to Vernon.

Vernon wrote some pieces for harp, clarinet and bassoon that, once again, were beautiful and exactly right. They fitted my hopes and imaginings precisely. Peter's drawings were ideal, soft and watery, in tones of grey with glints of reflection (colour television was still years away). My animation could have been better – inadvertent juddery movements are the bane of hand-done animation. They don't notice too much ordinarily but with characters that are supposed to be floating, fishlike, in an underwater world, they do jar the senses. I was very conscious of them when I saw the films but maybe I was being overcritical because the BBC liked them and paid up very promptly. Indeed the whole project went through very swiftly, partly, I suppose, because underwater persons, seahorses, shrimps, fish, etc. are simpler to animate than people with legs and arms, or railway engines with wheels and puffs of cotton wool.

The films were finished and delivered in a matter of weeks, and soon I was ranging around for the next project. Not that I was completely out of work. Small pieces of film for current affairs programmes were being ordered. Most of these were simple animated films, which I could often do more or less overnight, some were more elaborate and some involved live filming. But these were just odds and ends. I still needed to find the next film series. The inside of my head seemed quite empty. There was no new world waiting there.

I didn't actually think of something for our next series, I happened to walk past it in the Firmins' back garden. Joan had put out some washing, a line of wet clothes dripping on to the grass. At the end of the line, pegged to it by its woolly beak, was a full-size knitted penguin, also dripping wet. I had walked past before I realized what it was but I turned back to take a closer look. I thought how uncomfortable it must be to be pegged out on the line by one's beak with one's stuffing sopping wet. A stuffed knitted penguin would hardly be seaworthy. It would have to be a land bird, unless the wool was very special. Wasn't there some French knitting wool named *Pingouin*? Perhaps this uncomfortable bird was a pingwing. The Firmins kept goats, chickens, ducks, all sorts of livestock in their farmyard-garden. Maybe they also kept pingwings, or possibly they didn't keep them, they just lived there.

The barn and outhouses were so conglomerated with junk that a family of pingwings could live there without anybody noticing.

I looked over towards the open door of the barn and imagined another pingwing, a smaller one, Penny Pingwing perhaps, peering nervously round the door. She seemed very agitated. Then she spotted Mr Pingwing hanging on the line and ran straight across the yard, flapping her short wing-arms and shouting: 'Papa! Papa! Come quickly! Come quickly!'

Mr Pingwing replied, through his nose: 'I carn't cub. I've just bid wodged!'

'You must! You must come at once, quickly! *Mama has laid an egg!*'

Mr Pingwing swung his body so that he could reach the peg and unclip it. He fell to the ground with a squelch. As they ran off towards the barn he left a wet trail on the gravel.

None of this took more than a few seconds to happen in my head but I thought it would do. I borrowed the washed pingwing from Josie, dried it and took a set of photographs of it in conversation with other members of the farmyard. I also made some enquiries about its origin. Apparently that was the only pingwing. Gloria, Peter Firmin's sister, had knitted it for Josie. I rang Gloria and invited her to knit a family of five pingwings – Mr and Mrs, their children, Paul and Penny, and their fluffy (Angora wool?) baby.

Gloria agreed, so I felt confident enough to take the little book of photographs and Josie's pingwing to the Senior Producer of Children's Programmes at the ITV company to ask if they would like a set of nature films about the home life of these unusual creatures.

The Senior Producer said: 'How are you going to film them?'

I said: 'In single frames. The same way as I've been doing the cartoons only I'll be filming puppets, not card figures.'

'Good luck!' he replied, dubiously. 'But yes. I like them. Show us some scripts, of course, and a piece of film, and if they're OK I'm pretty sure we'll buy them.'

I came away from that meeting with the now-familiar feeling

that once again I had let myself in for doing something I knew nothing about.

Could I film puppets in the same way that I had filmed cartoons? There didn't seem to be any reason why not but I wouldn't know for sure till I had tried.

So while Gloria was making the first pingwing skin, I considered its internal parts. I could see that they stood upright but, like penguins, they had flat flipper-feet. For my purposes these didn't need to be attached to the bodies. The pingwings would travel on their bottoms and I could tuck flat feet underneath as appropriate. So they needed very heavy bottoms. I started with a 2lb (about 1kg) weight from a weighing-machine and screwed a length of threaded rod into it. I would fix the skeleton to that.

I tried making a wire skeleton. It was too springy. It would be impossible to gauge the movements exactly. I needed a skeleton that was jointed so that the limbs could be moved into position and stay exactly where they were without any spring-back. The joints would have to be made.

The Clerkenwell Screw Company in Hatton Garden kept every imaginable shape and size of screw and screw-related object in stock. There I found some ⅜in (1cm) diameter brass balls with ⅛in (3mm) threaded screw-holes in them. I have no idea what they were originally meant for, but for me they were to be the artificial hips, elbows, shoulder and neck-joints of the pingwings. I made each joint by clamping the ball between holes drilled in flat steel strips (Meccano) and I made the limbs and body and beak out of wood.

When the first knitted pingwing skin arrived from Gloria, I delicately inserted the skeleton into it, stuffing it inch by inch with chopped soft-plastic foam. I sewed it together under the base and it was made. It felt good. Best of all the limbs stayed *exactly* where I put them.

I set the camera on a tripod. I stood the pingwing on a table, lit it with a spotlight and settled down to an hour or two of single-frame waddling, posturing and peering at things.

Seeing the film when it came back was yet another small

miracle. The squidgy woolly chap waddled and peered about in a very determined and purposeful manner. I must say he seemed a shade puzzled about what he was there for, but I knew how he felt and was pleased with his performance.

So was the Senior Producer. I got the contract.

All I had to do now was film a set of single-frame puppets, out of doors, in Peter and Joan's cluttered yard.

Just in case you should ever be tempted to do so, may I give a word of advice: *do not try to make single-frame films out of doors.* The reason is simple: *because the light keeps changing.* While you are moving the puppets between frames a cloud moves across the sun. That means the next frame is darker than the one before. The effect on the film, as you can imagine, is weird, like neon lights flashing on and off at irregular intervals.

Luckily for me the weather turned out to be fairly dull and drab, which gave me a fairly even-toned film, but there were some days when I stood like Job, holding up my exposure-meter and hurling curses at the sky.

There were other unforeseen perils. I remember filming a conversation between Paul and Penny Pingwing by a low grey wall. It was quite a complicated conversation which took the best part of an hour to complete. What I hadn't noticed was a woolly-bear caterpillar on top of the wall. It wasn't doing anything except slowly looping its way along, looking perhaps for a way down, but of course the single-frame camera only saw it at irregular intervals. So on the film the caterpillar dominated the scene by performing a frenzied fandango. It had to be re-shot.

Some of the shots revealed the presence of the omnipotent ghost that causes everything to happen. The first time I saw this puzzling manifestation I couldn't think what it was. As the Pingwings walked away from the camera they left behind them a wake of crushed, heaving grass. Then I realised what it was – my footprints, which I had left as I walked backwards and forwards between the camera and the puppets.

Vernon's music more or less rescued the Pingwings series. He wrote a 'Pingwings' Walk' which was so apt and hilarious that it imbued their waddle with glorious absurdity, an absurdity so irresistible that it made the faults of animation look like part of the comedy. Vernon also wrote an 'English Country Air' to go over the opening sequence that was, and indeed is, quite exquisite.

The munificence of the ITV company, which was paying £175 per episode, enabled me, at last, to employ an actor. Our friend Stephen Sylvester, who worked in the ITV company, suggested that Olwen Griffiths would be ideal as a pingwing.

I telephoned Olwen and we arranged to meet in the foyer of Television House. 'You can't miss me,' she said, 'I'm vast!'

Olwen was a handsome bright-eyed Welsh girl with red hair and a face full of life and laughter. She wasn't exactly vast; rotund, perhaps. She was also a really professional actress with a quick understanding and an almost unlimited range of voices at her instant command.

Our first recording session at Brent Laboratories sound studio went very smoothly. Olwen got on well with Ron Hussey and Colin Bennett, the recording engineers, and we recorded some good episodes. The only slight difficulty came during the late morning when a sound like faint distant thunder began to be audible on some takes. This was eventually identified and dealt with by Colin, who nipped out to the café to fetch Olwen a cheese roll and a doughnut to stop her tummy rumbling.

Stephen's choice had been inspired. Olwen was a glorious lady. She was to be my referee, collaborator and critic for many years, during which she shared with me, and our other actor friends, the happy task of giving the first breath of life to the characters who inhabited our imaginary worlds.

The Pingwing films were fun. They were light-hearted, homely and not violent, and the music was delicious. The TV company liked them and, although I didn't know it at the time, were all set to buy more of the same. What I do remember is that as we came away from showing them the last episode the Senior Producer said to me: '*Pingwings* are lovely but I am commanded by "The Powers that Be" to order thirteen more *Ivor the Engine* films from you.'

'But that's absurd,' I said. 'The story of *Ivor the Engine* is over. He now sings in the choir. That's it.'

'Well, *Ivor* is their first love and the offer is there. I suggest you think about it.'

'But I've got nothing in my head. It would take time.'

'Listen. "The Powers that Be" want more *Ivor*s. They don't mind waiting. So take your time.'

'Oh, all right,' I said, rather ungraciously. 'I'll see what I can think of.'

10

TAKING TIME

I. The Dogwatch.

It was all very well the Senior Producer of the TV company telling me to 'take my time' to think about the next *Ivor the Engine* series. I didn't have any time to take! I had a living to earn and, unlike him, I didn't have a salary.

I did get one job, an acting job, two days' filming. In this I was a Viennese professor of high repute and great erudition, wearing an old-fashioned bathing-costume and gumboots, giving, in a heavy accent, a lecture/demonstration on the English Art of Boat-punting.

I will expound to you the theme of this lecture, which is concerned mainly with the poling, the method of propulsion. In it I depict what might be called the *classical approach*, in which the punt is loaded with many poles. The method is for the poler to take a pole to the front of the punt, push it down into the mud and then walk back along the boat while clinging to the pole, thus causing the punt to move forwards through the water, the poler remembering always to let go of the pole as he reaches the back end of the boat. He or she will then pick up another pole, walk to the front and repeat the procedure.

For reasons of economy this method has been largely superseded by the *standard approach*, in which the poler does not always abandon the pole when he or she reaches the back end of the punt but deftly recovers it by hauling it up out of the mud and carrying it again to the front for a second usage. This method is far less costly in poles, using very few, sometimes only one, for the whole journey.

Finally there is the *modern approach*, in which the poler does not even walk along the boat but stands at the back end and walks with the hands up the pole itself. This is the most skilled method and has the great advantage for passengers in the punt in that they do not have to be walked upon.

It was a long, lugubrious joke, very Germanic, but lightened a little by the failures and misfortunes of the demonstrator whose actions were often ironical to the commentary and who suffered many of the stock jokes about punting, most of them ending up with me falling in.

This was filmed by Patrick Dowling, who was later to become famous as the producer of *Vision On*, a celebrated programme for the deaf, and it was great fun to do, in a damp sort of way.

After the transmission, which I had to attend because some shots were 'live', an extraordinary thing happened. I was invited to the Reception Room where there were several engineers, some of whom I knew, and also Eamonn Andrews, the famous presenter of *This is Your Life*!

For a moment I wondered whether I might be going to be the subject of the presentation, that 'This' was going to be 'my life' – and I got ready to run.

Thank goodness, it was not. It turned out that I was to receive a presentation. Eamon Andrews ceremoniously handed me a film-can with a label on it. The label was inscribed as THE BBC

TELECINE AWARD, presented by the Telecine Department for the best children's programme of the year 1959: *The Saga of Noggin the Nog* – which was the first film that Peter Firmin and I had made for the BBC.

I was completely amazed and delighted, particularly so because this was an appreciation by technicians, by the people whose job it was to watch programmes all the time. They were usually the most detached and cynical audience of all. To have won their approval was a tremendous compliment.

'Thank you. Thank you indeed!' I stammered. 'This is a singular honour.'

'You're right there,' said Eamonn, 'it is unique. The BBC Telecine Award has never been given before.'

'Hasn't it? Why not?'

'Because they just invented it for this occasion!'

That was a proud moment.

But you can't live on proud moments. I needed work.

I was envious of the situation that Peter Firmin and Wally Whyton were in. They had their own weekly programme, *Musical Box*, which was bringing them in a regular wage. I wondered whether Peter and I might be able to do a similar programme. I couldn't sing of course, but I could make films, live films as well as animated films, and I was set up to do them very quickly. Could we perhaps put together a sort of magazine-type programme with stories and pictures, some of Peter's card-animations and pieces of film?

We could. I proposed the Grumbles Light, which was an offshore lighthouse with me as its keeper. I would need a companion – a seagull? a seal? No something more domestic, a dog perhaps. Yes.

OK, so what would a dog do on a lighthouse? Watch television?

Why not? He could be a watch-dog and spend the dog-watch watching dog-television. Of course there was dog-television. The dog and I would watch it on our steam television set.

Peter and I went through our stock. We found some clips of film and mapped out one or two programmes which really seemed quite possible, even amusing. So we put the idea together and offered it. The ITV company accepted it without demur and we found ourselves committed to conjuring up thirteen weekly programmes called *The Dogwatch*. Starting in November, these were scheduled to be recorded in pairs once a fortnight on the new AMPEX videotape system.

Peter began by making the dog. It was a shaggy cockney mongrel with yellowish mop hair and an eager, puzzled expression. Its name was Fred Barker.

Next we had to find somebody to work the puppet and be Fred Barker. I looked out a friend from Drama School, Ivan Owen, who had already been playing various parts in children's programmes. He quite liked the character of Fred Barker but wasn't sure he wanted to spend his time sitting under a table with his arm up in the air, working a puppet. Still, like the rest of us, he needed the money, so he agreed to have a go.

On the whole I think Ivan made a sensible choice. He gave great life and character to Fred Barker and, long after *The Dogwatch* was over, he was to spend many profitable years working a puppet, but this was not Fred Barker, this was another of Peter's creations, Basil Brush.

Basil Brush took Ivan over completely and became a hilarious TV personality. Ivan wisely maintained anonymity and was only occasionally referred to by Basil Brush as 'the chap who gives me a hand'.

However, all this was yet to come. In the winter of 1960 we had *The Dogwatch* to prepare.

The programmes were very rough and ready. Peter and I would spend the week finding bits and pieces to show on dog-television – cut-out caption stories, glove puppets and model-making. Sometimes I would go out with the camera and take pieces of film, of riding on a miniature railway or going out on an oyster yawl.

Each episode began with Ivan singing a sea-dog shanty, but after that we didn't bother with a script, just made it up as we went along. The dog-serial, which I filmed with cut-out card figures, was a Chicago-type gangster film starring Wilbur Dog who hailed from Doggeville Flats in Utah. It was written in – brace yourself – shaggy doggerel! Awesome stuff!

The effort and stress of putting a new *Dogwatch* programme together each week was very wearing and everybody was relieved when, in the spring of 1961, after twenty-six episodes of makeshift mayhem, *The Dogwatch* was taken off.

That had certainly succeeded in 'taking time' and both Peter and I were looking forward to some less frenzied occupation, like making films.

I did have one moment of anxiety for our future. Just as we were about to record the last two episodes, one of the engineers came to speak to me. He told me that he was the representative of the union, the ACTT, and that they had had a meeting about me and my work the day before.

My heart sank. I was sure I had been doing all sorts of things that only union members were allowed to do, like sound-recording, live filming, electrical work, building scenery. Anything that needed doing I had just done for myself without a second thought.

'I dare say I've been stepping over the mark a bit,' I suggested.

He laughed. 'You can say that again.'

'What's going to happen? Are you going to black the programmes?'

'No, no point in doing that. We like the programmes. It was just a matter of establishing categories, that's all. It was formally moved and resolved that if you stick to doing the sort of things you do, things that nobody in their right mind would ever dream of doing, then as far as the union is concerned you can get on with it.'

'Oh,' I said, surprised and profoundly relieved. 'That's good. Thank you. But tell me, what is this category you have established for me?'

'Madman,' he replied.

11

MAINSTREAM

I. Settling In.

On a bright June day in 1961 I said to the booking clerk at Whitstable station: 'I want a period return to London, please.'

He replied: 'You must be out of your mind!'

We laughed and I bought the ticket, but he was quite right. As I sat in the bumpy train looking out at the sunshine on the green marsh fields and the grey-blue sea beyond, I saw that Whitstable on a bright June day was a lovely place to be and that London was a hole. I didn't regret having moved. Our work could perfectly well be done from Kent.

During the *Dogwatch* period the supply of peripheral work had thickened up. Peter and I had been commissioned to prepare an *Ivor* book. TV Publications Ltd. had started a new comic (I beg your pardon, 'children's weekly'), called *TV LAND*, 'featuring all our favourite TV characters and programmes'. It wanted an eight-frame picture story about *Ivor the Engine* every week. The other London jobs, like stage-managing and prop-making, didn't earn much and were drying up.

These were all sidelines. What I wanted to do was get back to making films. The BBC hadn't yet asked for any more *Noggin* films but the ITV company that had put down its marker for another thirteen *Ivor the Engine* films was still waiting. My own feeling had been that the story of *Ivor the Engine* had finally ended when he sang in the choir, but this had turned out to be untrue because, in order to write the weekly stories for *TV LAND*, I had had to take my imagination to the corner of Wales where Ivor worked. Peter and I had surveyed this area quite fully for the first film series and he had made a map of the line with the stations and main features marked, so in our minds it was a completely real place. When I came to look at the neighbourhood more closely I saw that there were plenty of new people to meet and plenty of events going on, some of which had happened since Ivor had joined the Choral Society. They had won a silver laurel at the Eisteddfod, which Ivor wore on his funnel. The Society's annual outing had been to the seaside at Tewyn Beach, where the railway engineers had laid on facilities for Ivor to have a bathe, with disastrous results. Mrs Porty, the slightly tipsy lady who lived in the big house, had given refuge to a nest of brown birds in a disused cuckoo-clock. Her donkey, Bluebell, an old friend of Ivor's, had been given a private truck to ride on. As the result of a regrettable misunderstanding, Old Nell, the sheepdog, had chased the Rev. Poultry up a tree. The gold-miner, Mr Dinwiddy, had put his gold back into the ground and Mrs Porty, who was very rich, had bought the whole railway, lock, stock and barrel, to save it from being taken over by the Welsh National Railways.

So, having duly reported these events each week in *TV LAND* I came to realise that there was absolutely no reason why we couldn't go ahead and make the next lot of thirteen films right away. The stories were waiting. We took the contract for the films and started work.

I suppose the person who was made most busy was Vernon Elliott. I asked him for several pieces for the Ivor films, including three speeds of travelling music – main, cruising and fast – a donkey-trot and some more songs from the choir.

For the recording sessions Vernon would collect some of his associates, usually professional players from the Philharmonia Orchestra, and we would spend an afternoon at some suitable venue, rehearsing and recording all the music for the series on to quarter-inch tapes. I never ceased to marvel at the players' professionalism, at their ability to look at Vernon's pencil-written music and grasp instantly, not just the notes and the tune, but also the feel and purpose of the piece, before they had even played it.

I always came away from those recording sessions ringing with excitement, clutching the reels of recorded tape and feeling marvellously elated at having had some part to play in the creation of these wonders.

As time passed and we became more practised, the voice-recording sessions became nearly as efficient as the music ones. For the Ivor voices I had two actors to help me, David Edwards and Olwen Griffiths. Olwen was of course Welsh, so her portrayal of Welsh people was always authentic, though her tour de force, the queenly, inebriated Mrs Porty, was extremely English.

We all tried to speak for our characters as simply and spontaneously as we could, avoiding as far as possible using consciously artificial voices and, perhaps the most important of all, avoiding adding extra drama.

By this time Peter and I had had enough of sharing a cow-shed and he had raised and refurbished four pigsties behind the barn to accommodate one taller pig. This was my new studio, and very spacious it was until I started filling it with mechanical junk.

From then on the system worked quite smoothly and, with the production of the second *Ivor the Engine* series, Peter and I knew we were entering into the main part of our lives' work.

I think 1962 may have been our most prolific year. We were feeding the hungry television really well. I remember noticing in the *Radio* and *TV Times* that in one week Peter and I between us had a total of five different programmes listed ... *Noggin the Nog* and *The Seal of Neptune* on the BBC, and on ITV, *Ivor the Engine*, Peter and Wally Whyton's *Musical Box* and their puppet show *The Three Scampies*, which was hosted by Howard Williams – not to mention Peter's puppets, Ollie Beak and Fred Barker, who were likely to appear at almost any time on children's programmes.

One incident in 1962 heralded the approach, not of riches but at least of financial solvency and a bit over. We signed an agency agreement with a nice lady called Angela who worked for Talbot Television Ltd., who would sell showings of our films abroad. She started at once and sold them to the most unlikely places, countries like Cyprus, Israel, Rhodesia and Spain – but the money was very welcome.

Another incident, late in 1962, heralded the realisation of something more subtle. I was standing in Piccadilly Circus tube station buying a ticket. A small boy came up to me pushing an effigy in a doll's pram. He plucked at my trouser pocket and said: 'Penny for the guy, Mister?'

I replied: 'Penny? I haven't got a penny to my name!'

'Course you have!' he cried. 'You've got pots of money. You're *Noggin the Nog!*'

How he knew who I was I don't know, I suppose he had heard me speaking to the booking-clerk or something, but it shook me. For years, like dwarves under the hill, Peter and I had been working away, turning out fodder for the television. I knew children would have watched our films, but it had never really occurred to me that anybody would remember them.

I gave the boy half a crown and, for the first time in my life, felt the taste of fame.

A couple of weeks later the BBC asked for a second *Saga of Noggin the Nog*.

II. The Land of Nog.

'In the lands of the North, where the black rocks stand guard against the cold sea, in the dark night that is very long the men of the Northlands sit by their great log fires and they tell a tale . . .'

So began each epic of *The Saga of Noggin the Nog* and nobody who watched those films in the 1960s will ever hear those words without remembering the slow icy chords with which Vernon Elliott (bassoon) and his daughter Bridget (clarinet) heralded and accompanied that opening speech. The piece of music that Vernon had composed was not only just right for its purpose but thrillingly evocative of the Land of Nog, which was now going to be our next world.

When the request for a second saga came through, it came as a bit of a surprise. It was nearly two years since we had made the first one and the sort of everyday incidents I was accustomed to look for in Ivor's Wales would be quite inappropriate for a saga. I was going to need more heroic stuff, a legendary tale, full of dangers and adventures, one which had a beginning in which disaster would befall, a middle in which a quest would be ventured, and an end in which, by some near-miracle, success would be wrested from the jaws of failure – or something of the sort.

The Nogs themselves were essentially peaceable folk. The only reliable villain was Nogbad the Bad, who was the fountain of all evil. He had been banished at the end of the first saga but who knew what villainy he had been up to since then? Who indeed? I had absolutely no idea. I sat in front of a piece of blank paper and drew pictures of dragons. I liked dragons and I had promised myself some. Dragons are always useful in sagas and epics even though they have a bad reputation for wreaking havoc. Unfortunately there didn't seem to be any about in the Land of Nog. Perhaps they had retired. Perhaps they had become friendly and had formed the Dragons' Friendly Society, an institution with assets of untold wealth, a massive treasure of gold and jewels, locked in some icy cave. Perhaps that had attracted Nogbad's attention. He always had a sharp nose for other people's treasure. Mind you, such a treasure would have a guardian, a dragon of course, but one accustomed to the cold, perhaps an ice dragon.

I don't know in what order I had these random thoughts, but it came to pass, eventually, that a small angry man from the Hot Water Valley, in the far north of the kingdom beyond the Glass Mountains, arrived at Noggin's castle to seek his help in getting rid of a huge fierce dragon that was rampaging through their valley. Noggin, with Thor Nogson and the great green bird, Graculus, travelled to the Hot Water Valley to confront the dragon, who was an ice dragon and not fierce at all. He was of course the treasurer of the Dragons' Friendly Society, who had been smoked out of his cold cave. How Nogbad was discovered and how he nearly escaped with sacks of treasure on Noggin's own sledge and how he was finally apprehended by the now angry dragon and turned into a snowman, are now a part of television folk history.

To tell the truth I had felt very dubious about the basic plot of *Noggin and the Ice Dragon* – it seemed to me quite spurious and worthless – but, as I was later to realise, this was the effect of a sort of mental fatigue induced by anxiety. Once I had outlined the plot to Prue and Peter and Joan, and seen their eyes light up, I was able to see that it would do, and then the details came flooding in by themselves. Even the voice of the Ice Dragon, which was a mixture between Prue's brother Capel and the actor, the late Wilfred Lawson, came by itself, as did Graculus's finding of his long-lost family home, a place that he had never seen but had remembered from the time when he was an egg. Discovering these details, piecing them together and writing them down was a time of great joy in my life and I feel enormously privileged to have been able to bring them to light.

For *Noggin and the Ice Dragon* we were going to need a lot of incidental music. Vernon had written plenty of glorious music to accompany Ivor on his travels, including a delicious donkey-trot, but he was a bit baffled by the Noggin music because this seemed to need to follow the action in a more detailed way. I found a way to help him with this by drawing a sketch of each piece of music. This took the form of an illustrated graph, with a base-line of the overall time, say: three minutes. On this I would draw pictures of the actions and happenings in sequence at approximately the time they would happen. I would give the sketch to Vernon and, as soon as he saw the pictures, he found he began to think of the music. The sketches, as he put it, started him off.

At Prue's suggestion I asked Ronnie Stevens, an old friend from the club-theatre days, to share the Noggin voices with me. His voice was lighter than mine, which was an advantage. He was also very relaxed and professional in his approach.

The sound-track of *Noggin and the Ice Dragon* was a joy to make. When it was finished Peter and I sat with the cassette recorder, listening to it and seeing the pictures. By now our imaginations had become attuned to the medium we were using, so that we actually thought in terms of flat card cut-outs, and animation procedures which we knew were possible. This was in no way a limitation to Peter's imagination – the pictures he produced were magnificent. The music fitted with them really well and the end result was very satisfying. I remember taking the first prints along to the showing at the BBC and thinking: 'These they will enjoy!' They did, quite a lot, so much so that they more or less gave us carte blanche to supply them with Noggin sagas whenever we, or rather they, wished.

If we had followed 'good business practice' that would have heralded the start of a constant stream of Noggin-type programmes 'created' according to a formula.

Even if we had wanted to do that, we couldn't have, because Peter and I had other work to do and, in any case, thinking up reasonable Noggin sagas took time. I needed to be patient and let the story brew up somewhere in my head. The main trouble was that, for a saga, one needs villainy and, after his chilly encounter with the Ice Dragon, Nogbad the Bad seemed to have gone to ground, perhaps in some warmer clime.

However, I was fortunate enough to come across one of the great thinkers of his time, a tall, somewhat obsessive man who was Court Inventor to Prince Noggin. His name was Olaf the Lofty and, it must be said, he was in many ways a thorough nuisance because many of his inventions were more trouble than they were worth. Some, however, were brilliant. Among these was a clockwork-driven flying machine in the form of a longship with leather wings. This, he claimed, would flap up into the sky and bear the Nogs away to the ends of the earth, if they should happen to want to go there.

For most of *Noggin and the Flying Machine* Nogbad is nowhere to be seen, but the small man who arrives rather spectacularly in a jar, bringing a magic carpet, is in the same league as, if not in league with, that evil uncle.

He steals the crown of the Northlands and flies off on the magic carpet. Naturally the Nogs give chase in the flying machine, which of course is wrecked by a magic storm thrown by the small man's snuff.

The flying machine is mended with some stolen feathers. They take off again and come to the Land of Silver Sand. There they are captured by the Emir, another wicked uncle, and at last meet up with their own – Nogbad the Bad, the author of all the villainy

All is not lost. Just as the Nogs are about to be eaten by the Emir's vast black Genie, Grolliffe, the Ice Dragon, is called to their rescue. Complaining bitterly of the heat, the Ice Dragon makes short work of the genie, rolls him into a puff of grey smoke and blows him into an ice-cube.

After I had written *Noggin and the Flying Machine* I found myself wondering whether by including the Land of Silver Sand I had been intruding on other people's territory – taking other people's settings and conventions and using them as if they were my own. I thought about this and came to the conclusion that it was really only a matter of being geographically accurate.

When they, inadvertently, travelled to the Land of Silver Sand, the Nogs entered a country that was just as fictional as the Land of Nog but much better known, being recognizable as the setting for *The Arabian Nights*, and Ali Baba and the Forty Thieves (as well as that terrible dance we did for the pantomime in the Isle of Wight). Once the Nogs had arrived there it was more or less inevitable that they would become involved with such clichés as genies, magic carpets, impersonations and palace intrigues, simply because such things are known to be the stuff of ordinary life in that imaginary country.

So, unwittingly, perhaps I had been derivative, but I suspect that most plots have been used many times over and most of the incidents in them have been derived from, or could be traced to, things that have happened in life or literature.

That is one of the reasons why I have always resisted the suggestion that I have been 'creative'. Very occasionally, ideas that seemed to be wholly original would turn up in my head. When these were relevant I would grab them with delight, but the idea that I had *created* them is, I am sure, quite misplaced. When it was looking for stories, my mind would go trawling through a mud of memory, a morass of experience, life and literature, to see what it could find. It is true that I usually rearranged what came up, perhaps showed it from an unusual angle, but I have always had to respect the fact that *novelty* is not, in itself, either interesting or valuable. Its interest and value lies in the degree to which it is able to give a particular view of the condition that we, as human beings, find interesting and valuable, i.e., being alive. That condition doesn't need to be *created* because it is always there – even if we aren't noticing it.

I am glad to say that while I was writing *Noggin and the Flying Machine* none of these nervous considerations entered my head. What I was looking for was a usable story and, though I say it myself, I got a rattling good one.

Vernon wrote some really evocative music for the flight of the flying-machine and a tremendously exciting accompaniment to the magic storm, but it fell to me to provide the mechanical sound effects – the sound of the huge clockwork engine starting up and the great wings beating faster and faster as they bore the incongruous vessel through the water and up into the sky, where the sound would merge seamlessly into the glorious flying theme that Vernon had composed.

Peter and I spent some hours collecting mechanical bits and pieces and recording their noises. I think we settled on a broken wooden toy lorry as a prime mover. When its wheel was turned it went: *Ker-clonk .. bonk*. This was a bit basic and woody, so we screwed a tin to it with a strip cut down to catch against a knob on the wheel. Now it went *Ker-clonk .. cherrrrnk, tweek-bonk*, the *cherrrnk* being a nice metallic spring-sound. This was still a bit slight for such a large machine so we hung a piece of lavatory chain in the tin and mounted the whole thing on a hinged padded board which lifted and fell as it rotated. Now it went:

Ker plink-plink .. Chernk-tweek plinkaplank FLOMP.

The FLOMP was the flap of the great wings. It still sounded a bit small, like somebody turning a mechanical toy, but when we recorded it and played it back at half-speed it was magnificent. Then we could see the absurd machine surging forward and lifting off into the sky.

The films of *Noggin and the Flying Machine* took off well with the BBC and they let it be known that they would appreciate it if we would kindly produce another saga as soon as possible, like later in the year.

This wasn't easy to arrange because, while I had been filming *Noggin and the Flying Machine* with my hands, in my head I had been putting together stories for the third set of *Ivor the Engine* films.

Luckily I had made frequent trips to our imaginary Wales looking for stories to go in *TV LAND* Weekly, so I was able to report that life there had become quite eventful. A dragon's egg had been found in Ivor's firebox. It hatched out during choir practice and the dragon sang rather well. His presence in Ivor's firebox, while welcome, did present some problems and eventually, after one or two unfortunate incidents and the arrival of another dragon, the mythical beasts decided to avoid publicity and retire to a local volcano. Then Mr Brangwyn's pigeons escaped and, on his way back from helping to lure them down off Miss Price's roof, Ivor nearly ran into an elephant lying on the line. The elephant, which had a bad foot, proved even more difficult to house than the dragons but once again, after some difficulties, help arrived in the form of the elephant's keeper, Mr Bani Moukerjee, who had spotted an elephant's boot on Ivor's truck. He was reunited with his elephant, Mr Banger's Circus arrived, and gave them all a free show.

This was only a small part of what had been going on but it was enough for the thirteen episodes of film that had been asked for.

The Northlands, meanwhile, had gone quiet again. Life there was so peaceful and complete that Olaf the Lofty, walking on the hill, was bewailing the fact that, in Noggin's city, Nog civilization had reached its final peak. Everything was perfect and there could be nothing more to invent. At this the whole side of the hill blew up, throwing out a cloud of steam and a very small man whose eyes were not used to the light. Olaf rescued the man, who was an Omrud, one of the little people who lived under the hill. His name was Groont and he was Court Inventor to the King-under-the-Hill. In return Olaf was given the secret of Groont's latest invention, a method of harnessing the powers of fire and water. This inspired Olaf to build a handsome steam engine to pull Noggin's royal carriage. Needless to say it ran amok and jumped over a cliff.

Noggin and the Omruds is not about a quest, it is about an invasion. By Olaf's alchemical folly Nogbad's crows become the size of cart-horses and they fall on Noggin's castle like vultures on their prey. Once again Nogbad nearly achieves his goal, to take the crown of the Northland, but this time he is thwarted by the ingenuity of the Omruds, and by the time they have finished with him he is too small to do any harm – or so they think.

The garden which the Nogs make for the King-under-the-Hill is beautiful, as is the music which Vernon Elliott wrote for it, calm, elegant and glorious. It seemed very final and appropriate, not only for the ending of *Noggin and the Omruds* but perhaps also for the end of all the *Noggin* sagas. I remember feeling almost hopeful that it might be so. Like Olaf the Lofty, I was beginning to think there might be nothing left to invent.

There followed a period of relative quiet. I say 'relative' because as well as turning out our weekly stories for *TV LAND* and contributions to its Annual, I made a set of films for the BBC programme *Blue Peter*. Ronnie Stevens and I, with Vernon and his musicians, made a Noggin gramophone record. Peter and I also, somewhat incongruously, made some filmed inserts for *The Telegoons*, a strange adaptation of the radio programme, *The Goon Show*. I can recall nothing of this job except a Christmas pudding falling from the top of the Kremlin and cracking the pavement of a Moscow street.

Then the BBC became impatient and said it wanted the next *Noggin* saga.

In *Noggin and the Firecake* we moved into a darker area of myth and magic. There was no quest, no travelling dangerously to far lands, only unknown magic powers, locked by the Sword of the Sorcerer deep in the earth. In this Nogbad's simple villainy is completely outclassed by the power of a stone giant who befriends Noggin's young son, Knut, who had heard it singing under the stone.

Certainly Nogbad's villainy takes him nearly to his finest hour, but even as he reaches it the power that he has unleashed closes in on him and is set to crush him.

But in all this the most dangerous material, *firecake*, was invented by the silliest character, Olaf the Lofty – but that has a more terrible moral than any story.

When I showed her the script Ursula Eason, the Deputy Head of Children's Programmes at the BBC, looked at me quizzically. 'Social comment now, is it?' she growled.

'No, not especially,' I replied, lying. 'Just another saga, like the others.' Ursula laughed and commissioned the films.

III. Houses.

The tall terrace of houses known as Wavecrest, of which ours was number six, stood high above the sea wall, breasting the storms. There was, people used to say, nothing between it and the North Pole, and when the wind hit it at night you could feel the house go *thud* inside itself. On such nights I would sometimes dream that I was standing with my feet on the sea wall and my hands under the first-floor balcony, either gripping the rail to hold the houses down or pushing at the balcony to hold them up. Prue would turn over and say: 'It's all right, darling.' And I would reply: 'It's not bloody all right, you stupid woman. The sea's coming over any moment!'

The sea never did come over the wall, but it didn't need to, it could come under it. The sea wall, like the houses, had been built on the shingle, so once the tide rose high enough to reach the wall, the water just oozed underneath and rose gently through the basement floor. Fortunately that only happened once.

On good days, when the sun shone and the sea-breeze smelt fresh, the place was idyllic. The children would run straight out on to the beach and Prue and I would carry tea down on a tray and sit against a breakwater. Bach especially loved the beach and at low tide she would scamper away, splashing through the puddles to chase small seabirds at the distant water's edge.

It certainly was an exciting place to live but, in the end, too tall and thin. Prue had varicose veins and hauling the shopping up four flights of stairs did them no good. So, late in 1962, we bought an ex-pub on the Canterbury to Whitstable road.

Red Lion House, once the Red Lion Public House, had been built in about 1580, an ancient 'pre-fab' with oak beams that were mortised together and numbered with chisel-marks. It had sloping floors and crooked windows and a slightly disreputable air, as if it had once been a highwayman's haunt. The front yard had been enclosed, so the house now stood a little way back from the road and was set in a large rough garden with a dilapidated garage-cum-barn, two wells, a small copse and a stream with a rope on which to swing across it. The interior layout – public bar, private bar, snug, tap-room etc. – was a bit unusual for a dwelling-house but as we looked around the house, Prue and I knew that this was where we were going to live our lives.

To my great delight I found that the Essex-boarding in the main room was covering up the original varnished tongue-and-grooved boarding of the pub and also that the ugly suburban fire-surround had been set in front of a huge open fireplace big enough to roast an ox. I ripped out the Essex-boarding and the fire-surround and got the builder to lay in a tiled hearth. We did some decorating and then, on December 22nd 1962, moved in.

That was the day the snow began to fall. I remember the family shivering disconsolately in the main room while Prue's son Kevan and I tried to light a fire. We set newspaper and kindling wood in the middle of the tiled hearth and then lit it. The smoke rose lazily and began to roam about the room as if looking for something. We flapped at it with newspapers to drive it back towards the fireplace and eventually it seemed to recognize the chimney and began to move into it. After an hour or so the fire was burning really well, so well that the chimney was drawing in air from all directions, freezing the backs of our legs with icy draughts while the fire was roasting our fronts. We finished up putting paraffin stoves in the kitchen and on the landing to warm the incoming draughts.

In that first bitter winter, when the sea froze and the snow stayed until March, we lived an almost medieval life, centred around the great wood fire. Kevan and I made regular sorties into the neglected woodland at the top of the field behind the house and brought back thick branches and sometimes whole dead trees on our shoulders. The cat, Perdita, who loved these outings, would ride, growling, on the wood. Bach would have loved them too but, sadly, she had died of old age and heart-trouble while we were still in Whitstable.

We sawed the branches into long logs which the fire burned away like tinder. We made a fine sledge-run in the field behind the house and used the metal top of an old dead fridge as a sledge.

Ray and Daisy came down to visit us, taking the precaution of booking in at the Chaucer Hotel in Canterbury. Daisy was a bit dubious about the primitive facilities of Red Lion House but she was delighted with the sledge run. I can see the old lady now, crouching in the lid-sledge, her figure muffled and dark against the white snow and her cigar flaming cherry red as she hurtled down the hill, straight towards the brambles. She was saved from certain scratching by young Will Gollop, who heroically threw himself in the path of the sledge before it reached them. She was tipped out and wasn't a bit grateful; insisted on having another go.

The snow eventually melted and by the time spring came we were well settled in our new old house. I commandeered the Private Bar as my study. That room had the advantage of being relatively soundproof, which was a godsend because although the four-acre field behind the house provided ample rough chasing for the boys, their friends and the dog, the house always seemed to be well filled and brimming with noise.

During the holidays Kevan was with us. Kerris, his sister, was in residence, attending school at Faversham, living the spectacularly inconsiderate life of a vigorous, highly emotional fifteen-year-old girl. Pip, their young brother, was going to the Primary School in Blean and the twins, Simon and Stephen, who were four and a half, were going to nursery-school in the mornings. We had also collected a schoolfriend of Kerris's, Fiona Larkin. She came in to help Prue and look after the twins, who seemed to have a genius for amiable destructiveness. She became an honorary member of the family and has been ever since.

Probably the most joyful occasion for Prue and me was our decision to have another baby. Prue, at forty-one, was thought to be a bit old to be having babies but our GP took the view that having had five already she could probably take having another one in her stride.

Daniel was born in February 1964 at the maternity hospital in Whitstable. I met him when he was about twenty minutes old and yelling. He wore a wristband with his name on it: 'Spontaneous D. Postgate'. That, I remember, puzzled me.

IV. Small Persons.

In spite of the troubles with outdoor light I had enjoyed making the *Pingwing* films. Filming single-frame puppets was less fiddly than filming cut-out cartoons. There were no backgrounds to set up, no figures to assemble and joint, no cotton-wool puffs of steam to move. The puppets were just there. I could choose the shots and camera angles as I went along.

So now I was looking for a new puppet series, preferably one that I wouldn't have to film out of doors too much. I was sure there were other small persons about, perhaps not in Peter and Joan's farmyard, but somewhere. People had gnomes in their gardens, of course, but they were a bit sedentary and rarely seemed to do anything except fish.

Maybe there were low-angle persons in the forest. The trees in the wood behind Red Lion House were mostly scrubby oaks with brambly undergrowth – not a very congenial habitat. But among them, relics of an earlier forest, were several massive beech trees. These had wide spreading canopies of leaves under which no brambles grew and wide boles whose gnarled roots spread out to grip the ground. A hollow beech tree would make a well-appointed residence for some woodland person, or maybe persons, a family perhaps. I wondered what they would be. Not gnomes, garden or otherwise, I disliked gnomes. Hobgoblins? No, a bit malicious. So were hobyars. How about leprechauns? They were wily and Celtic and had to do with tricks and magic. I thought the small persons who would live in the roots of these trees would be ordinary. They would be quiet people who wouldn't want to have anything to do with magic. I tried different names in my head and eventually came up with one that sounded all right: *Pogles*.

Right then. Mr and Mrs Pogle live in the root of a tree and grow beans in their little garden. I looked all through the wood to find a beech tree with a hole suitable for a Pogle's front door, but found none. The only thing to do, in fact the obvious thing to do, was to get Peter to make me one in the studio.

I proposed *The Pogles* to Peter. He liked the project in general and said he would be happy to make the people and the tree-root house, but, like me, he had no idea what the story would be about.

I had only one clue about this: Mr and Mrs Pogle were not magic-type people. They didn't hold with magic and didn't want to have anything to do with it. But suppose magic wanted to have something to do with them. How would small ordinary respectable people fare when faced with magic?

Once again I started writing and left it to chance. Mr Pogle went out with his barrow to look for some old dried beans in the shed of the empty cottage. He didn't find any there but under the hearthstone he found one perfect bean, a bean so large and shiny that he could hardly lift it into his barrow. He wheeled it home to Mrs Pogle, who was not pleased because she wanted to plant a line of dwarf beans in her garden, not one giant bean.

'But look at it, wife! It's a lovely bean!'

'Listen to it, you mean.'

The bean was fast asleep and snoring.

Wondering whether it would wake up one day, the Pogles planted it. Expecting that it would take some while to grow, they turned to go indoors, but before they reached the front door the bean was up and awake, stretching its branches and shouting for its breakfast.

The only breakfast the Pogles could offer the Plant was some bilberry wine. They poured it around the roots and the Plant was much revived and somewhat inebriated. It was happy to oblige Mrs Pogle's wish for dwarf beans by waving a magic leaf and causing them to appear, already planted and growing, in her garden.

Mr Pogle was delighted with this encounter with magic, but Mrs Pogle was dubious. Neither of them knew what troubles their involvement with it might bring. Come to think of it, nor did I.

Obviously I had wandered into another well-worn, well-stocked world, the world of rural fairy-tales. There would be good and evil, probably fairies and witches. The Pogles would have to have a real part to play, however inadvertently, in the drama that was to unfold.

The story, when I finally got it together, was quite straight-forward. It involved a baby in a cot, which the Pogles found in the flower of the Plant, some fairies who did little more than twitter, a tiny silver crown of unknown significance and a witch, who wanted the crown and ill-treated the Pogles in a quite inexcusable way in her efforts to obtain it, tying Mrs Pogle up in a small sack and imprisoning Mr Pogle in a cage of twigs.

Then, after the Pogles had escaped from her with the help of a magic flower from the Plant, they barred the door.

The witch laid siege to their house. First she appeared on the doorstep as a jug of milk, left there, apparently, by Mr Burgess the cow-man. This ruse was thwarted by a clockwork singing bird which, along with a tiny silver crown, the fairies had given the Pogles to calm the baby. As Mr Pogle opened to door to collect the jug the bird flew out, picked it up and dropped it on a stone. The witch ran screaming.

In her second attempt the witch was less subtle: she appeared as an old boot and simply kicked the door in. The Pogles still refused to tell her where the crown was hidden and she was about to turn them into toads when the clockwork bird took the silver crown from its hiding-place and dropped it on Mr Pogle's head.

Mr Pogle, who by this time disliked magic more than ever, now had to have a contest of spells with the witch. As he was wearing the crown of the king of the fairies, Mr Pogle naturally won it hands down. But it seemed that there was nothing he or Mrs Pogle could think of to turn the witch into, without her being able to turn herself back again into a witch. So that was what Mr Pogle turned her into; a nothing: 'no thing at all, no shadow, no thought, no terror, no memory of evil, no touch of cold to foul the night, no thing at all . . . be!'

And there she was, or rather, wasn't. The bird, who was of course the king of the fairies in disguise, thanked the Pogles for their care for his infant son, congratulated Mr Pogle on his choice of destiny for the witch, greeted his old friend the Plant and commanded the fairies to stop twittering and bring them a barrel of best bilberry wine. The Plant grew instruments and they danced a merry jig.

The house-in-the-tree-root that Peter built for the Pogles in my studio was particularly realistic and handsome. It had a stout wooden door with a bell beside it which the hedgehog who called in the mornings would ring, and an upstairs window with shutters. Real ivy was growing up it and the garden was greengrocer's grass. Like all of their kind, Mr and Mrs Pogle were short and stocky and wore very large boots with hinged toe-caps. These contained lumps of lead to stop them falling over.

The Pogles were a joy to work with. For them I developed a very economical and telling way of animating conversations. They would strike postures to express and punctuate whatever they were saying and simply hold them until the next phrase.

I made the films and, as always, sent prints to Talbot Television Ltd., our foreign sales agents, and this prompted Paul Talbot, president of the parent Corporation, Fremantle International Inc., to fly in and pay us a visit.

Paul was a classic American captain of industry, large, bluff, warm-hearted and full of entrepreneurial drive. He and I had a long, wide-ranging discussion in which it transpired that he was interested in our capitalization. His idea was to finance Smallfilms so that we could set up a proper studio and go forward from these one-horse shoestring films and move into making broad-appeal family-viewing programmes. That, he said, was where real money could be made.

I had to think about this. It was probably the best chance to become really rich that we would ever be offered. But I had reservations.

One was that Peter and I were perfectly all right as we were. We had a comfortable market for our modest films, and it was pretty clear that so long as we could find the ideas to feed it, British TV would feed us – with the foreign sales as a bonus.

The other reservation was personal. I couldn't see myself being a captain of industry, even on a small scale. As things were, Peter and I weren't even in partnership. When there was work to do on my films we would negotiate a contract for it on the back of an envelope or something. This established that we each had our own territory, so I didn't tell him how to do the drawings and he didn't tell me how to make the films. That saved a lot of potentially fraught compromises, accommodations and cumbersome policy meetings.

I suppose the real virtue of the situation, as far as I was concerned, was the knowledge that if, one day, I should have no films to make, I could close the door of the studio and walk away. I owed it nothing, except the £1.50 a week which I paid Peter towards the rates, etc., which I usually forgot to pay anyway. No, we had a good working set-up already in place. The job of thinking up the stories loaded my small muse with quite enough anxiety for me. I didn't want to add any more burdens to it.

Paul took the point. We laughed and he bore no grudge. His company went on to sell our films diligently for many years and he and his wife Susan have been our close personal friends ever since.

V. Pogles' Wood.

In the middle of 1965 Doreen Stephens, who was Head of Family Programmes at the BBC, asked me to come in for a meeting about *The Pogles*. She told me the Corporation's view, which was that Mr and Mrs Pogle were very welcome at the BBC, and that friendly magic, as practised by the Plant, was perfectly acceptable, but that witches screaming in the back garden were definitely *non grata*. I wasn't particularly surprised at this, in fact I rather felt the same.

However, Doreen's good news was that the BBC would like us to offer it a set of thirteen Pogle films for the *Watch with Mother* programme for small children and their mums, which went out at lunchtime. Her suggestion was that the Pogles could visit real places and watch rural activities actually taking place. I liked the idea very much but I doubted whether Mr and Mrs Pogle would bother to go and watch such things on their own. I thought they should have a larger family, with young persons who could watch the activities for the first time and ask questions.

Peter and I thought about this. We chose a boy-person aged about six, whose name was Pippin, and a small animal-person, halfway between a squirrel and a rabbit, who was a Tog. I knew in my own mind that Pippin was actually the son of the king of the fairies, now in the care of the Pogles and, consequently, if the witch should ever find a way to cease being nothing, he could become vulnerable to witch-type magic, but I didn't mention this to the BBC. About the ancestry of Tog I had no information at all. He was a bright, sensible chap, even though his speech wasn't very intelligible.

Peter and I put together some synopses and sketches of stories, including visits to the dairy, the beekeeper, the sheep-shearer, the farrier, woodcutter, road-builders, etc., and took them along to Doreen and her associate, Joy Whitby. They were very pleased, said the stories were exactly the sort of thing they had been hoping for, and commissioned the films at once, offering about double the money that they had been paying for Noggin films. That was absolutely fine with us. The only worrisome thought came from Joy Whitby's parting words, which were: 'We'd really rather like it if you would make the Pogles a bit more *quirky*.'

I came away completely flummoxed by this request. I tried to imagine myself going up to Mr and Mrs Pogle like some sort of producer and saying: 'Well yes, darlings, everything's quite lovely, but, and I know it's not easy, but I do have to ask you to be a bit more *quirky* . . . Yes, you know . . . *quirky*. I'm sure you understand.' Of course they wouldn't understand. They wouldn't know what I was talking about. I know that as the writer I had some powers, but these didn't include rebuilding people who were already fully alive and in working order. Wisely perhaps I said nothing and just got on with making the films.

Peter had had his big barn refurbished, so he was able to build me a really interesting piece of woodland terrain on a big table, about two metres wide and three long, in the middle of the barn, with a couple of movable leafy flats for backgrounds. This made a really versatile stage because the camera could look at it from any of four different directions. Every few days Peter and I would cut fresh-leaved branches and lay in tufts of grass, so the set provided me with an almost infinite number of different Pogle walks. The great joy was that the light was artificial and everything was at waist-height, so I never had to get down on to hands and knees or shake my fist at the sky again.

That first set of thirteen films of *Pogles' Wood* kept me busy for over a year. They were closely followed by a second set, *Pogles' Wood II*, which were less rural in content, relying mainly on stories and happenings that could be filmed in the studio. These included a set of pipe-cleaners which came magically alive and were extraordinarily good at making folded paper animals and birds. These duly took life and walked about. There was a documentary film on the growing of umbrellas, and a tale about a queen and a carpenter in which the pieces of wood did their own carpentry. This was cast entirely from the families. Simon and Stephen, our twins, both played the carpenter, Katy Firmin played the queen, Daniel and Matthew White were soldiers and David White was a farmer. There was also a story about a foolish tiger and one about a beautiful princess who stole things. These were all delivered magically by the benevolent Plant.

The films were well received by the BBC and, being a new feature of the prestigious *Watch With Mother* programmes, they attracted some attention from the media. Two very pleasant young people came down from one of the tabloid newspapers and spent a jolly day with us collecting material for a feature.

I saw the headline next day:

CALLING MRS POGLE
She's the homely little woman who hopes with her family to put Andy Pandy's nose out of joint...
ANDY PANDY and Bill and Ben the Flowerpot men have new TV rivals – the Pogles!

I rang the newspaper at once to confirm that it was only a joke. It wasn't. I tried to explain that we were not in any way in competition with Andy Pandy or anyone else, but the editor I spoke to didn't understand. The piece was good, straightforward, incisive journalism. Didn't we *want* to win, didn't we *want* to be seen as triumphant? Didn't we even want the publicity, for good-ness' sake?

Well, actually, no.

VI. Red Lion Cottage.

A day or two before Christmas in 1964 I telephoned Ray and Daisy to wish them well and find out what their plans were. I rang two or three times but received no reply. This was odd because I knew they weren't away on holiday. It was worrying too. So, in the end, I had to get into the car and drive to Finchley.

They were all right. Daisy was sitting in the square armchair in the long room with a glass of gin. Ray was upstairs in his study, sitting at his desk reading a detective novel. They were pleased to see me and each blamed the other for not answering the telephone. Daisy took the view that as the calls were always for Ray he could jolly well answer them himself, and Ray took the view that as he was busy the least Daisy could do was answer the telephone.

I took the view that having to pound seventy miles up the old A2 on a nasty evening simply because the old things were too quarrelsome to answer the phone was a bit bloody much, but I didn't say so out loud. We had a pleasant evening and, very late that night, I drove back to Kent, thinking.

Ray and Daisy had always had their quarrels, and these had sometimes been spectacular, but they had been battles between equals and had always been repaired. This time, seeing them in their separate rooms in that great empty house, I felt that some slow change had been taking place.

I could see that, as well as being physically in poor shape (she suffered a lot of pain from her fibrositis), Daisy was also deeply unhappy. It wasn't difficult to see why. Ever since the war, when she had been queen of the house, her role in life had been slowly diminishing and becoming more marginal. It's true that *The Good Food Guide* had given her quite a lot of work to do, but that had mainly been filing and clerking. Then in 1962 *The Good Food Guide* had been taken over by the Consumers' Association and its office had moved into London. This had saved her some painful filing work but it had ended her usefulness.

Daisy, who had been so confident and independent in her youth, who had taken an active and responsible part in so much political life and struggle, who had made a modern marriage with Ray, a marriage in which both would honour the other's freedom of spirit and neither would ever be a chattel of the other, now found that her life had slowly ground to a halt in a siding while Ray's life, as a celebrated expert on food and wine, had gone puffing away into clouds of fame and flattery.

As I drove home I could see that she was, quite simply, lonely. I could also see that none of this was anybody's fault. Time had just moved on.

I was unhappy about their being so far away. Perhaps I could persuade them to move to somewhere closer to hand – not in the house, but within reach.

In the end Prue and I decided to offer them the outbuildings: the dilapidated garage/barn in the corner of the garden, which they could, if they wished, and if building permission were to be forthcoming, rebuild as a sort of mews-bungalow for themselves over a store-room and garage.

Slightly to my surprise, they jumped at the offer and we went ahead with the project. Ray and Daisy were very clear about what they wanted in the way of accommodation so, after a disastrous run-in with a local architect (who proposed a building which not only ignored their wishes but was also ugly), they asked me to design it for them.

This was an enormously exciting idea. I had always wanted to design a house – not necessarily an extraordinary, innovative sort of house but one for people to live in, a house that would make the best of the necessary limitations and considerations and sit comfortably in the landscape.

I now think that Red Lion Cottage did just about fill the bill. The only serious design fault was that Daisy and Ray had specified a spacious open-plan living room and kitchen, with two smallish bedrooms. That was a mistake because they had become so accustomed to having their own space that they got under each other's feet. They would have been more comfortable with two large bed-sitters and a small kitchen-diner. However, this problem was eased shortly before they finally moved in by our turning the store-room under their house into a library and study for Ray.

Once Red Lion Cottage was built and furnished, Ray let it be known that he wasn't actually intending to move into it until the work he had to do was completed. However, fate took a hand here. He suffered a minor heart attack in 1965, as a result of which he was ordered to walk three miles a day. So he and Daisy took to coming down for quite long periods during which he was able to set up a good working arrangement with Fred.

I should explain that Fred was our second dog, a brown mongrel bitch, and also that Ray utterly abhorred dogs. His fear and disgust of them amounted to such a phobia that he wouldn't allow a dog into the house, or stay in the same room with one. Nevertheless, Fred would appear at a certain time each day and sit at the top of Ray and Daisy's garden, gazing meaningfully at the French windows. Ray would see her and put on his boots. Then they would walk, a respectful three paces apart, up the field, through the wood and along the fire-break to the old railway line. On the way back Ray would sit on the bench at the top of the field and Fred would sit some feet away. Then they would walk down the field together and part company at the fence.

In a guarded way Ray was deeply touched by this arrangement, especially so by Fred's perfect respect for his reservations. As they walked he would talk to her on many subjects and she would wag her tail and smile, but never come within reach.

We too seemed to have hit on approximately the right degree of association between the establishments. Although our houses were adjacent, we visited by invitation or necessity. There were some slight inconveniences, like our 'shared' telephone line which enabled Daisy to cut in and read me her shopping-list while I was talking to the BBC, but in general I have very happy memories of Ray and Daisy's time here in the late 1960s. I can see them ambling across the grass on their way to take Sunday lunch with us in the garden, she carrying a board of excellent cheese and he carrying an even more excellent bottle of claret. On these occasions I think they were quite careful not to be too grandparental but at the same time they seemed perfectly at ease. Daisy would complain fulsomely, but without rancour, about Ray's behaviour, while he would sit happily and smile, or have a separate conversation, glad perhaps that she had another audience. Lunch over, we would sit in the shade with the last of the wine while the boys went chasing about in the field. They would come running in every few minutes, steaming like horses, to tell us something important, take a swig of our wine and then charge away again.

My main concern in those years was for Prue's health. She had developed chronic bronchitis, which would arrive during the winter and stay, wheezing and coughing, until the spring. It would leave her fairly low in stamina until the summer began. Not that Prue didn't lead a very active life. She was a pillar of the Canterbury Meeting of the Society of Friends (Quakers), which she and Kerris had originally joined in Finchley, and much of her spare time was taken up with events and activities connected with the Meeting. I didn't have nearly such an active social life. Being fairly fully engrossed with film-making, I seemed to have little time or headspace to spare. I did have one or two outside interests. I had always loved new visions. In fact I feel really lucky to have shared the wonder of many of the innovations that we now take for granted. At that time I was astonished by Hi-Fi stereophonic sound reproduction. I bacame an enthusiast (and a bore) and made my own loudspeakers. Also, enticed by my bank manager, I helped to found a squash club and, more or less by default, became its chairman.

VII. Serious Considerations.

When he was nearly four Daniel came to me with a serious complaint. This was about the way I treated the puppets.

He said: 'You hurt Tog's nose.'

'Tog's nose?'

'Yes, in the film. You fell him on his nose and the end of his nose is hurtable, very hurtable, falling on it.'

'But, Dan,' I said, 'you've seen Tog. He's just a puppet made of fibreglass and bits of fur. You know that.'

'Yes, of course I do, but the end of his nose is hurtable. Don't fall him on it again.'

'Oh, all right,' I said. 'But, Dan, did you see that Tom and Jerry film yesterday? The one where he gets sliced up with a circular saw?'

'Yes!' cried Dan, his eyes lighting up. 'Wasn't that funny!'

That puzzled me. Why should slicing up Tom and Jerry with a circular saw be uproariously funny when Tog falling on his nose is a piece of grievous bodily harm? I still don't know the answer. Perhaps it is a question for psychologists.

Certainly, for some, the *Pogles' Wood* films seemed to have strong psychological overtones. Tony Gruner, our European sales agent, later sold them to a German television station. He read me a letter he had received through the station. It came from a Consortium of Educational Television Viewers which had noted that the educational approach of our *Pogles' Wood* series did not accord with that of either of the two main schools of Educational Psychology. It wished to know the name, credentials and affiliation of the educational psychologist that we had retained for the making of the films and would we also be so kind as to let them know our interpretation of the symbolical significance of the erect Plant standing beside the grassy hole in the root of the tree?

The enquiry was both hilarious and unsettling. On the one hand my reaction was to treat it as a joke. I wrote a careful reply in kind but Tony Gruner refused to forward it on the grounds that the German market was too valuable to risk offending. He pointed out that as the Consortium was obviously Freudian, it wouldn't have a sense of humour. On the other hand I found myself wondering whether or not I really ought to have paid some attention to the education theorists. The only criteria Peter and I used when deciding whether or not a particular idea or piece of material was suitable for filming were:

1. Did we enjoy it? Was it fun?
2. Did we think children would enjoy it? Were we sure it wasn't nasty, frightening, of evil example?
3. Did we think grown-ups would like it – especially the heads of TV departments who would, we hoped, like it enough to buy it?

I had never given conscious thought to sociological-type considerations like the need for positive racial discrimination, the equitable distribution of stereotypes and the elimination of potential implications of social inequality. Nor had I given thought to psychology, though I can remember hearing people who had studied such things speaking of 'strategies for capturing the cognitive', the 'importance of relevant role-model examples' and the need to 'reinforce the acceptability of established demographic trends'. In fact Peter and I had been personally reproved by a sociologist from the local university who told us we *shouldn't* be making films like *Pogles' Wood*, which showed life in the country as being pleasant, because in future people and their children were going to have to live in conurbations. So we *should* be making films about how nice it is to live in towns.

Fortunately, in 1967, the pottiness of 'political correctness' had not yet infected our thinking. It was to be twelve years before the *Ivor the Engine* books would be banned by Brent Council Libraries for racial discrimination (this happened, believe it or not, not because the stories mocked the Welsh, which indeed they did, relentlessly, but because in one of the books there was an Indian elephant-keeper, an absolutely delightful loving man, who spoke with an accent that might be called 'Bombay Welsh' and consequently his portrayal might have been thought to be in some way less than respectful to persons of delicate racial sensibility).

I think our books received more of that sort of scrutiny than the films, probably because a book could be held in the hand, studied and condemned. This danger wasn't something Peter and I had seriously considered, the books having, as it were, grown out of the television programmes.

The book side of our work was now growing rather well. Eric

Marriott, of Edmund Ward Ltd., who were already publishing the Noggin First Readers, told us that he was a great fan of the *Noggin* sagas which, he said, had 'conceptual integrity'.

Of course Peter and I were pleased and flattered by this piece of praise, but I must confess that I had reservations. I didn't want to enquire too closely into what Eric meant by 'conceptual integrity'. I felt that if I started clambering down into the wells of my imagination to try and find out which bits had 'conceptual integrity' and which bits were 'psychologically or sociologically acceptable', I would muddy them beyond recovery and probably never be able to use them again.

So I smiled and waited for Eric to come to the point, which was to tell us that he wanted to publish books of *Noggin* sagas, at the rate of two a year, for the foreseeable future.

That answered the question of whether or not Nogbad had escaped from Roundhead Valley at the end of *Noggin and the Firecake*. He was going to have to have escaped (if you will pardon the tense) because we were going to need him for the books. He was going to be busy.

Nogbad was going to make a steam-driven island, and a terrible Trojan pie. He was going to grow the seeds of Grundelstein's Greater Gripewort to break Noggin's castle. He would rediscover the game of *Hnefetafl* and use it for his evil purposes, he would steal Olaf's invention and displease a sea monster, he would turn time backwards and make morning follow afternoon. He even threatened to melt the polar ice-cap and drown the world. There was no villainy too vile to serve his dread purposes. Nogbad was a great chap and I'm pleased to have known him. He was popular too. When we did book-signing sessions Peter liked to draw sketches on the fly-leaf for the customers. Most of them asked for portraits of Nogbad.

Peter and I were going to be busy. It was fortunate that we didn't have any film work to do at the time, because there was book work to be done. Peter was in the middle of illustrating *Ivor's Outing*, a second *Ivor the Engine* book, and Paul Hamlyn Ltd. had asked us to make some *Pogles' Wood* picture books. Then, as well as continuing with our weekly contributions, the publishers of *TV*

The Saga of Noggin the Nog, 1963. Noggin, Thor Nogson and
Graculus, the great green bird, take off in their ill-fated flying machine.

Clangers, 1969. These were our first films in colour. They are letting off
the rocket which accidentally brought down the Iron Chicken. The sixpenny
firework that powered it also set fire to the set.

The studio:

Smallfilms' palatial studio was behind the door on the right. It was built by raising the roof and walls of a set of disused pigsties.

'Welcome to my studio!' It was baking hot in summer, ice cold in winter and the inside was always an almost impenetrable mess. Though I did look after some things, like this: my Meccano-driven . . .

. . . puppet animation camera.

Me and Peter Firmin pretending to animate the Clangers for a newspaper photograph.

Other places:

Red Lion Cottage. This is the house which I designed for Ray and Daisy in 1965.

Llechau-Uchaf. This is the cottage in Wales which Prue and I bought with the proceeds of the sale of the Pogles' Wood films in Germany. It was pretty derelict in 1972 but . . .

. . . the view was astonishing!

1973. The year of Bagpuss,
the saggy old cloth cat that
Emily loved.

Madeleine the rag doll and
Gabriel the toad.

Bagpuss in Emily's shop, with Professor
Yaffle and the mice on the Mouse Organ.

1976. Daniel christening the engine,
Dougal, with a bottle of brown ale, at
Llanfair Caereinion.

1974. Prue and our three
sons singing in the field beside
Llechau-Uchaf in Wales. From
left to right are: Simon, Prue,
Daniel and Stephen.

The apartment at Cotobro.

We bought this on the spur of the moment because the climate in southern Spain had so miraculously cured Prue's bronchitis.

Prue relaxing on the terrace.

Sketch of the view across the bay at Cotobro.

1981, at Mount Elgon in Kenya. Prue's particular elephant and . . .

. . . 1982, in Wales, her tree.

Later films:

Tottie, on the steps of the Doll's House. This was a set of films based on the famous story by Rumer Godden, which we made in 1983 and 1985.

Pinny and Victor, 1986. From *Pinny's House*, a set of films written by Peter. These were the last films we made for children's television.

Oliver, Bagpuss and Peter, MA. In 1987 the University of Kent awarded honorary degrees to Peter Firmin and me, but it was intimated that the dignity was bestowed on behalf of Bagpuss. So, by invitation, he attended the ceremony, suitably capped and gowned.

Naomi at the exhibition of the Becket Illumination.

1170. Thomas Becket returns to Canterbury. This is a section from the fifty-four-foot-long illumination of the life and death of Thomas Becket which Naomi and I put together in 1988 for Kingfisher Books.

Later, in 1991, we made another, similar illumination to celebrate the quincentenary of the inadvertent discovery of America by Christopher Columbus.

Christopher Columbus.

This is the detail from the large mural about the history of Kent which I painted for the university in 1992. It shows St Dunstan dealing with the Devil.

France, 1993. The artist at work!

Portrait of the old person, taken in 1988.

Broadstairs harbour in the evening.

LAND asked us to do a complete *Pogles Annual* and left it to Peter and myself to produce all the finished material.

We put together a *Pogles Annual* for each year up to 1974 and I must say I enjoyed them enormously. They were full, rich confections but, like all Annuals, they had their year and were gone. I must say I slightly regret this. There was good stuff in them.

So, by 1967, work was going well. Films had been made and were being sold all over the world. Comics, Annuals and books were growing from them and there was even a Noggin gramophone record – what more could we hope for?

One day Peter came to me and said: 'What exactly is "merchandising?"'

'I don't know. Isn't it something to do with selling things?'

Merchandising turned out to be the selling of consumer products packaged so as to connect them with television characters. Today it is an enormous industry.

Strictly speaking the exploitation of the characters which he had made was Peter's department, not mine. He also had a share in the copyright of several other puppets, including Basil Brush, whose pelt he had made. The BBC had just started its own merchandising department so we made a deal with them and looked forward to riches from the sale of *Ivor the Engine* toothbrush holders and *Pogle* pencil boxes.

Unfortunately, for reasons I have never quite fathomed, our characters didn't really take off into the big time of merchandising.

But the ribald fox, Basil Brush, bless his furry tail, earned for Peter a shower of small cheques which continued for many years.

VIII. Prue and Me.

1968 started badly for Prue. The year came in, as usual, with her bronchitis, and that was, as usual, dreadful. Then, in February, when it was just beginning to ease off, she was called into hospital for a long-awaited operation for her varicose veins.

Prue was now forty-five and I was forty-two. We had been married for ten years, years that had passed with the speed of an express train, years in which there had been so much to do, so many mouths to feed, so many small disasters to attend to, that we really hadn't had a lot of time to take notice of each other.

Prue would occasionally mention, a shade ruefully, that we seemed to have missed out a bit on 'romance', that we hadn't really had the proper honeymoon period, as prescribed in Mills and Boon literature and the women's magazines. In a sense that was true because the circumstances of our coming together had been a bramble-patch of external emergencies. However, the affection and commitment that we had found and forged in that complicated time had proved entirely durable and even without the red roses and champagne our time together was easy and full of fun.

The basic pattern of our life was slightly different from the traditional one. During our early years, when I had been working at home in the flat in Finchley, my work had had to take its chance among the imperatives of looking after new babies. I was quite able to change nappies and I could cook so, when Prue was ill, I had always taken over the running of the house as a matter of course.

I was quite happy to do this when necessary but I sometimes wonder whether, at other times, I may have been a bit too capable. Having spent much of her first marriage frantically having to cope with her first husband's total detachment from practical or financial matters, Prue was happy not so much to delegate responsibility, as to abandon it. Even after we had moved to Kent and I was fully engaged in the production of films, I still didn't have to work regular hours, so it was more or less assumed that I could take time off to deal with household difficulties. I sometimes got the impression that as a result of this the whole family had come to the conclusion that the easiest way to deal with problems was to save them until I came back from the studio and then bombard me with them. So, as I came through the door I would be greeted with cries of: 'Oliver! The washing-machine has been making a funny noise,' or 'There's still a horse in the garden,' or 'Dad, why is there a pond in the dining-room?'

These were small things in themselves and, being by nature and instinct a coper, I naturally attended to them but, and I expect this is probably the lot of all copers, they piled up and I gradually found that because I had had to make the decisions, I was not only held to be responsible for everything that happened but also, by some generally held but unstated assumption, potentially to blame for whatever might be going to happen.

This feeling could be daunting and there were times when old fears would come crowding back. Then I would be reminded very forcibly that everything I had been managing to get away with during the past few years had been part of a dangerously extended confidence trick, a sandcastle based on nothing but my original arrogant presumptions and sustained by nothing but a piece of unwarranted good luck, which was that, *so far*, I had managed to find and write some fairly acceptable stories. Then my spirit would drop like a stone and I would sit, numb, in front of my piece of blank paper.

That piece of paper was, of course, the main well-spring of my anxieties – I was committed to trawling next year's income out of my imagination or down from the sky, or from somewhere. There was no certainty that I would find it. But if I didn't, we were done for.

As I mentioned earlier, Prue had always refused to entertain the idea that I could possibly have any doubts about my abilities. She dismissed such thoughts out of hand and blandly assumed that delivery was automatic. She would say: 'Don't worry, darling, you'll think of something, but if you're passing Cawleys, could you get half a pound of ground almonds? I'm doing macaroons for the Bring and Buy.' This was the opposite of reassuring and it could leave me feeling depressed and isolated.

However, the ship of our life sailed on. My agitations were just part of the weather and, on the whole, I was glad that this was so, because once the particular worries that had given rise to them were dealt with, the anxieties would evaporate and I would be my usual, fairly ordinary, self.

Life in our house was always pretty chaotic, with everybody getting on with whatever they were doing and amiably bawling out those in their way. There seemed to be plenty of time – time for tears to be wiped, time for laughter, time for a cuddle – in fact I only had to sit down for a moment and I would become a climbing-frame. There was room for everybody and there didn't seem to be any need to bother with indulgences, sentimentalities, special togethernesses (keeping the others out), or any of the sad luxuries of emotional competition. Of course there were arguments; egos could be bruised as easily as knees, but it all washed past, was mended and forgotten.

I dare say our life with our children was far from being 'Educationally Correct', but I remember that time, when the family was young, as being a period of broad, easy happiness.

IX. Ray and Daisy.

On a dull day in November 1968 I was in my car on the way to Finchley, listening to a radio programme that I had recorded earlier. The programme was *Desert Island Discs* and Ray was the subject. So he was, rather diffidently, choosing the pieces of music he would take to his desert island. The time was gruesomely apt because while I was driving up the A2 listening to him, Ray was actually undergoing an operation for cancer at St Mark's Hospital in London.

The operation was deemed a success. Ray took it all very lightly and although the doctors hadn't told him or Daisy that he had had cancer, I'm fairly sure he knew, but preferred to maintain the fiction that he had been operated on for, as he put it, 'warts on the bowel'.

Ray recovered very swiftly and was soon in good health. The only significant difference the operation made to his life was to persuade him finally to relinquish the house in Finchley and, having had his study and library installed in the lower part of Red Lion Cottage, move down here for good.

Ray took to life in the country very well and before long he became a member of Peter Firmin's Blean Footpath Group, with whom he spent every Sunday morning treading out the paths and, armed with a walking stick to which I had fixed a cutting edge, slashing away at intrusive nettles. He seemed in general to be content, busy rewriting and bringing up to date the last few years of H. G. Wells's *Outline of History*, a task he had been engaged on sporadically since the mid-fifties.

Daisy had feared that the move out of London would put an end to their social life but in practice the opposite seemed to happen. A steady stream of visitors appeared – according to Daisy, many more than they had seen at Finchley. Daisy enjoyed this but found it exhausting, so she was quite pleased when I sometimes agreed to be their commis-chef and waiter. This meant that after she had done the main part of the cooking – a task which she would not have delegated – I would come in, make the gravy, dish up the vegetables and serve the meal, while she made merry with the guests. It was a pleasure for all concerned, particularly me.

So, keeping our fingers crossed that Ray's recovery would be as complete as Daisy's had been fourteen years earlier, the families seemed ready to settle down to a tranquil future. Ray celebrated the move by negotiating a barrel of wine, which was bottled with due celebration on the terrace at Red Lion Cottage.

Daisy wasn't the only 'Lansbury girl' in this corner of Kent. My Communist aunt Violet lived with her husband in a bungalow near Folkestone but, perhaps for ideological reasons, we didn't see her very often. However, we did see quite a lot of my aunt Nell. A couple of years earlier, at her request, Prue and I had obtained a small fisherman's cottage in Whitstable for her to retire to. Nell was Daisy's younger sister, one of the aunts who had lodged at 45 Hendon Lane during the war. As a child she had always been at loggerheads with Daisy and, although they had managed to get along quite well during the war, I think she may have been a bit daunted by Ray and Daisy's arrival in Blean, because their childhood antagonism seemed to reassert itself. Nevertheless she felt it her duty to call on Daisy fairly frequently and often came in to see us as well, usually to complain to Prue about the awfulness of her elder sister, who would, in her turn, pop in to tell her about how unforgivably irritating Nell had been. I think Prue got the feeling that the number of my elderly relatives in the neighbourhood had increased to a rather unwelcome extent.

12

COLOURING IN

I. Outer Space.

In 1968 the BBC issued a decree which put paid to our ambitions
to make any more *Pogles' Wood* type films. In future all bought films
were to be in colour – not only 'in colour' but 'colourful'. They
wanted something completely new and quite astonishing.

Oh, yes. Well, that was a challenge. For me it meant another
piece of paper to sit and look at. Once again we were going to
have to pull our living out of the sky.

Out of the sky? . . . What about that?

In my youth – the 1930s – the conquest of the air and the
development of the aeroplane had been in the forefront of
progress. Now, in the 1960s, it was the conquest of outer space
and rockets that held the public's imagination. So maybe we could,
literally, pull our next film out of the sky.

So far we hadn't had anything to do with outer space, but

science fiction had been out there for years and whole mythologies had been found, or perhaps planted, in space. I did know a bit about what it was like. I had read H. G. Wells and some of the 'sci-fi' writers and, several years earlier when they were about three years old, our twins, Simon and Stephen, had told me about the moon. Apparently there was a giant called Edward on the other side of the moon who lived on soup, hot soup. I asked how he obtained the soup and they explained that as the moon was quite full of soup, all he had to do was unscrew a volcano and suck it out through a straw. I mentioned that I thought the other side of the moon was thought to be very, very cold and they pointed out that the soup was very, very hot. That was all useful information.

While Peter and I were ranging through our stock, looking for old ideas to recycle, I realised that I had been mistaken about our not having had anything to do with outer space. One of the Noggin 'First Readers' was called *Noggin and the Moonmouse*. In this a small spacecraft about the size of a pumpkin landed in the new horse trough. A small mouselike character wearing a duffel coat climbed out of it. Children and dogs chased it but eventually Nooka made friends with it and found out what it had come for: fuel for the craft. So Nooka and the moonmouse collected oil and vinegar and soap-flakes from the grocer's, poured them into the craft and then, borne aloft on a massive cloud of oily, vinegary soap-bubbles, the craft hurtled away into space.

That wasn't really a lot to go on, but it was worth investigating. It was unlikely that the visitor would have come from our moon because Edward lived there, but there were other moons about and there was no reason why they shouldn't contain suitable soup. Also, because nowadays there was so much space-programme debris whizzing about in the sky, they were unlikely to be living on the outside of their moon. They had probably taken to living in caves. The entrances to the caves would have metal covers over them and when they came out the covers would tip over and clang open like dustbin lids.

Peter and I wondered about the name of this extraterrestrial life form. The Nogs had just called the visitor a moonmouse, but that was a description rather than a name. If we were going to make films about them they would have to have a generic name like . . . what?

I remember the conversation quite well. We tried out names . . . '*Hopkins*? . . *Flomps*? . . . . *Clangers*? . . *Hambrils*? . . *Winglooms*?'

'Hang on!' I said. 'Go back.'

'Go back to what?'

'One of those . . . *Clangers*. I like *Clangers*?'

'Oh? I don't know. It sounds a bit rude to me. Why *Clangers*?'

'Because that's the noise the lids make as they tip over.'

'Oh . . . Oh I see. Yes, all right, then.'

So there they were, somewhere out in space, the Clangers, a small tribe or extended family of civil mouse-like persons living their peaceful lives on, in and around a small, undistinguished moon. No doubt during the several hundred years that had passed since Noggin's time the breed had evolved a bit. They no longer had long tails with tufts on the end, perhaps because the tufts kept getting into the soup. Now they were plump and shocking pink, with noses that were long, perhaps for sucking up the soup. They had round ears which drooped when they were sad and big flat feet with holes in. Joan Firmin knitted them and she dressed the ladies, Mother Clanger, Tiny Clanger and the aunts, in patchwork coats, and Peter made suits of armour plates for the men, Major Clanger, Small Clanger and the uncles.

The chance of the Clangers' lives being quiet and peaceful was not very great. In space anything could exist and anything could happen. Even so, I knew that home life was home life wherever it was, even when it was being confused and assaulted by the unlikely. On a moon which is not protected by a blanket of atmosphere, as our Earth is, any of the various objects that float, whizz or hurtle about in space can simply drop in – and have to be entertained, dealt with or disposed of according to the Clangers' standards of hospitality.

We knew what the moon would look like and we knew that the Clangers lived in caves, but we had no idea what the inside of the caves was like. We didn't have any details about how the Clangers lived, with what furniture, what beds, what food? Here again the page was blank. Faced with it Peter said: 'I just can't see it. I can't see what it is like.' So I drew a very rough sketch of a cavern with a path and a shelf and some bed-holes with covers and a table-block. These must have triggered off Peter's imagination because the places he eventually built, with things that could be put together from existing materials but set in incongruous situations – wheel-bushes, copper-leaf trees, and small thickets of drinking-straws – far outstripped, in originality and completeness of conception, anything I could have thought of.

Once we had established the main scenario in our minds – the interstellar family in its self-contained economy, with the Soup Dragon serving green soup and blue-string pudding – the pattern of their lives became clear and stories began to materialize. A sky-rocket accidentally shot down an iron chicken. The Clangers reassembled it and made it welcome but it had, by Clangers' standards, rather bad manners. However Tiny Clanger was kind to it and so, before flying away to its iron nest, the bird laid an iron egg and gave it to Tiny Clanger as a present. The egg was heard to be playing music to itself. When it rolled away it split in half, revealing that it was full of loose music notes. Most of these were eaten by the Soup Dragon, but Small and Tiny Clanger managed to save two of them and plant them outside. The notes germinated and grew into music trees, which flowered and formed more notes. The music they played was very sweet but it was as a means of levitation and propulsion that the Clangers found music most useful. It was from the music-boat, high in the sky, that Small Clanger was able to do his best magnet-fishing. There he caught the top hat which contained the Froglets, who were conjurers. The Soup Dragon did battle with an engine that manufactured plastic articles. That was very exciting as well as untidy.

Then, one day, one seed from an unknown plant floated down on to the surface. The Clangers nurtured it and it grew abundantly, so abundantly that the whole moon was covered with verdure, and the sky-moos with their great wing-ears had to be summoned to eat it. And of course there was the love affair of the Gladstone Bags – that was true romance. So much was going on that we needed do no more than piece it together into episodes and film it.

When we got the go-ahead from the BBC the first thing we had to do was place the Clangers' moon somewhere in outer space. Although, as I said, I tend to reject the accusation of being 'creative', I suppose Peter and I did come near to being the authors of a genesis when we brought the Clangers' universe into existence.

I remember describing the process to a conference which Peter and I attended in Germany in 1984:

> In the beginning was the void and the void was dark and without form, being "eight by five" sheets of battened hard-board painted midnight blue. And on the first day took we a bucket of white emulsion and big floppy brushes and threw white stars thereon, even unto the extremities thereof. And we looked upon it and saw that it was terrible.
>
> And on the second day we painted it out and started again . . .

That was rather a heavy joke but it was also a fairly accurate description of what we were doing. In the event we managed to make the firmament more convincing, or at least more fanciful, by hanging some strange heavenly bodies, mostly assembled from old Christmas tree decorations, in front of it. Peter built the moon in plaster on a plastic football, with shaped craters and silver painted buttons for the lids. It was pale blue in colour and, as the camera moved slowly across and the majestic orb came into view, floating serenely in the night sky, with its craters sharp-edged in the clear golden light, the impression was truly awesome, especially when accompanied by Vernon's evocative space-music.

While Peter had already started building the sets I had a moment of anxiety: the BBC suddenly decided that it didn't like the scripts.

I should explain that the Clangers' conversation had presented a technical problem. They spoke a language of very articulate whistling squeaks, which needed to be translated from its natural medium of nuclear-magnetic-resonance (there being no air to carry sound) into audible terms. The nearest I could get to that was to write out the script in full and then persuade Stephen Sylvester to help me record the dialogue. We did this as we had done for the Pogle films by reading it, or rather playing the inflections of it, on a selection of Swannee whistles. In this way I was hoping to make a sort of wild-life film in which, by listening carefully, the viewer would be able to understand what was being said and work out what was going on.

Rather nervously I asked Ursula Eason of the BBC what they objected to in the scripts. She replied: 'The bad language.'

I could only think of one piece of bad language. One of the episodes begins with Major Clanger trying to open the big sliding doors of the main cave-mouth. It jams and his first line is:

'Oh sod it! The bloody thing's stuck again!'

'That's it,' said Ursula. 'You know quite well we can't say things like that on children's programmes.'

'But . . .' I said, 'they don't say it. They whistle it.'

'But surely people will know?'

'If they have nice minds they will hear him say "Oh dear me. The naughty thing is jammed again."'

'Oh, all right, then, I suppose so, but please keep the language moderate.'

I moderated the expletives and hoped the scripts would now be acceptable. However, the BBC still had some reservations, and these were in fact more sensible. They weren't happy about our relying solely on the whistles to tell the story. They said they didn't think young children would listen carefully. They would just turn away and ask their mums to tell them what the Clangers were saying.

So, rather reluctantly, I made a separate voice-over tape, a sort of intermittent running-commentary on what was going on. It worked quite well but I have always wondered how the films would go in their original form.

I did try it once. I took an episode of *The Clangers* to the 1984 conference in Germany and showed it to the participants without my voice-over. Afterwards I asked them whether they had been able to understand what the Clangers were saying.

'But of course,' said some. 'They are speaking perfect German.'

'But no,' said another. 'That is not so. They spoke only Swedish.'

Once the tensions of the internal ball and clamp joints of their skeletons were set right, the Clangers were a pleasure to animate. To support them when they were out of balance I spiked their toes into the moon rock, which had been specially made for that purpose from a mixture of plaster and polystyrene balls. Spiking in the inch-long tintacks did tend to make my thumbs sore but in general the Clangers were easy to work and their movements quite exact. The thing which really took the time was the flying.

On the Clangers' moon objects were continually landing or taking off. This wasn't too difficult to film if they were coming straight down or going straight up, you just pulled them up or let them down on a thread. That was no problem, except when the firework rockets on the human-type space module set fire to the scenery.

The difficult flyers were the ones that were supposed to come in or take off at an angle, like aeroplanes. I remember I came to the point of filming the first of these and realised that I hadn't actually worked out how to do it. This was a problem that would have to be solved because the Iron Chicken, the Sky-moos, the music boat, a flock of tin teapots and lots of other denizens of deep space were going to arrive and depart like that, not to mention the Cloud, which hovered and wandered idly about overhead.

The basic crane was not too difficult to assemble. I had a strong tripod with a 'screw-pan', which meant that, by turning a handle, the head of it could be moved around a tiny distance at a time. I bolted a long piece of wood to this and hung the music-boat on the end of it by a length of fine fishing-trace. With the tripod-head slightly tilted I found I could screw it slowly round and so bring the boat in to land in a wide arc. That was all right, but what I hadn't borne in mind was that things hanging on threads swing about, not only from side to side and back to front but also round and round. I tried various ways of steadying the motion so that I could film it in single frames, ending up with a wooden cross-piece clipped to the end of the wooden jib from which I attached up to eight different threads to various parts of the object to be flown, each of which had to be delicately adjusted and then painted with photographers' matt-black paint to render it invisible. This method of suspension succeeded in stopping the wilder swings but still allowed the object to vibrate slightly. The only way to deal with that was simply to wait. After each tiny movement I had to allow the vibration to die away before pressing the button on the camera. It was only a matter of seconds but it meant that a shot of, say, eight seconds' duration, which was two hundred frames, could take the best part of a day to film.

Filming *The Clangers* was the most challenging, absorbing and difficult work I had ever undertaken. I found it immensely satisfying, probably because it took all my concentration. By then I had, more or less, come to understand how to do single-frame filming, so that although I was working in tiny increments, moving the characters according to frame numbers marked on the script, I could mentally translate this into live motion and in my mind's eye see pretty exactly what the final film was going to look like.

By that time I had also learned a lot more about manufacturing sound effects and, using two tape-recorders and a collection of noise-makers, including bells, scrapers, whistles, crashers and a tin violin, I had found out how to build up some very creditable echoes and eerie resonances, effects that really helped to evoke the infinite vastness of space – in Peter's barn.

The *Clangers* films were duly shown and seemed, in general, to go down well. One or two commentators hated them quite fiercely but Owen Reed, the Head of Children's Television, enjoyed them enormously and said he thought the Clangers' moon was the most complete and convincing imaginary world he had ever seen. Coming from a man the main part of whose job was looking at films of imaginary worlds, that was a real compliment. Praise came from further afield as well. An engineer from NASA is reputed to have described *The Clangers* as 'a valiant attempt to bring a note of realism to the fantasy of the Space Programme'.

I shall always remember, with a certain dread, a note of realism that turned up in one episode. In it a human astronaut arrives in a space module and attempts to collect rocks from the Clangers' moon. The Clangers try to help but he is alarmed. Many mishaps befall him. He slips into a soup-well, is rescued, runs away so fast that he goes into low orbit and has to be captured with a fishing-magnet, and is finally stuffed back into his module. There is nothing unusual about any of that. What was unusual was the fact that it was scheduled to be transmitted on the same day as one of the Apollo missions was due to land on the moon. I pleaded with the BBC to show something else, but in vain. I am still haunted by the thought that if the mission had failed and the astronauts had perished (as well they might have done), that *Clangers* transmission would have been one of the blackest jokes in television history.

II. Realities.

One evening in 1970 our old Quaker friends John and Nora Starke came to dinner. At the time Prue had had a basin-full of committee meetings, school functions, housekeeping, and coping with my touchy relatives, and was feeling thoroughly fed up.

John and Nora recognized this condition and said: 'You should be in Wales.' We asked what they meant and they told us about a crummy cottage which they leased for a tiny rent from a farmer in mid-Wales. Whenever they had had enough of civilization they would drive down there and vanish. That part of Wales was a foreign country where the hills were very large and the natives didn't speak English unless they had to. John and Nora were quite certain it would do us good to go there and they offered to lend us the cottage at any time.

Prue and I took up the invitation. The cottage was crummy, primitive and damp but the air was exhilarating, clean and shining, and the isolation complete. Prue found it very peaceful. She said she was deeply envious of the Starkes' good fortune, though she added that if the cottage was hers she would do something about the pervasive damp and the unknown creatures in the roof. I reminded her that the cottage didn't really belong to the Starkes, they rented it for something like ten shillings a week from a Mr Jones.

'I wish it was ours,' said Prue.

One of Prue's most endearing qualities, one which was most precious to me, was her certainty about her own feelings. She knew, fully and wholeheartedly, exactly how she felt about anything she saw or heard. I, by contrast, was always uncertain, inconsistent and plagued by doubts and reservations.

The German TV station which had bought the rights to *Pogles' Wood II* had paid us slightly more than the BBC had originally paid. So, with money burning my pockets, I spent the best part of a week with John and Nora Starke, driving along narrow lanes and hill tracks looking at cottages. We had collected sheaves of estate agents' leaflets but, as so often seems to happen, there was something unsatisfactory about all the properties on offer.

Then, as we drove up one of the mountain roads, I spotted a solid-looking cottage on the side of the hill immediately below the road. It seemed to be empty so we stopped to have a look. The garden, or rather the patch of field that dropped away below the front door, was crowded with nettles and spotted with curls of rusty corrugated iron, barbed wire and broken things, including a squashed kettle and a rusty milk-churn. Peering through the dirty windows we could see that the inside was a tip. On top of a few bits of broken mouldy furniture a 1930s tin kitchen unit was lying on its side with a hole in it. There was a big fireplace into whose chimney generations of jackdaws had dropped so many twigs, bits and dry dead things that the pile had filled it to the top and spread out in a fan-shape across the rotting floorboards. In the field, buried deep among the nettles, we found a fallen estate agent's 'For Sale' board.

Could this be the place we were looking for?

Two days later I was waiting at the same cottage while John fetched Prue from the station. She got out of his car a few yards down the road and as she walked up towards the cottage she threw her arms wide and shouted: 'Yes! Yes! This is it!'

Then, as if for the first time, I was able to see the view – down the valley towards Ffarmers, up the valley towards where the tiny River Twrch rose in the folding hills. I saw the stately beech trees that sheltered the cottage and appreciated the way it was set, comfortably, with its back to the hill, looking down on its world of shaped fields marked out with stone walls, of bunched copses and reedy meadows where here and there the wandering river flashed as the sun caught it. Below us we saw the backs of a pair of buzzards, wheeling in the air above the meadow, their cries punctuating the distant bleating of the sheep.

'The silence!' cried Prue. 'Just listen to the silence!'

It was certainly one of the noisiest silences I had ever heard. Jackdaws were clunking, cows were lowing, and somewhere not far away a woodpecker was firing its machine-gun beak, but even so I knew what Prue meant; silence, like beauty, is in the ear of the beholder.

We sat on stones against the warm front wall and ate bread and cheese and bara brith, which is Welsh currant bread, with butter. No food was ever so delicious.

Then Prue looked in through the window, saw the debris and laughed.

'Are you sure?' I asked.

'Don't be ridiculous!' she replied, and her eyes were so full of excitement and happiness that I knew the question was ridiculous. This was her place.

After that there was nothing to be done except buy it. We drove down to Evans the Estate Agents in Lampeter, who succeeded in finding a file for the cottage, we put down a deposit and went home, buzzing inside like bees.

'It sounds quite lovely,' said Daisy, 'really beautiful, and I think your buying it is a marvellous idea. I hope you'll enjoy it as much as we all enjoyed the cottage in Essex.'

'I hope you and Ray will enjoy it as well,' I said.

Daisy laughed: 'Don't be daft. We shan't see it.'

I had to admit to myself that this could be true, if only because the journey would be too long and bumpy for her painful frame and it was going to be many months before the cottage would be able to provide the sort of comforts that Daisy now found essential to life. It also turned out to be true for another more serious reason, a reason that put all other thoughts from our minds.

Ray had been suffering from headaches. These were becoming more frequent and severe and to them were added occasional bouts of giddiness and loss of balance. Other more disturbing symptoms began to appear. We, that is Daisy, Prue and I, had a strong suspicion these were recurrences of his cancer. So perhaps had Ray, but that was a closed subject. After several weeks of deterioration our GP was at last able to bring himself to admit that this might be the case, but he said nothing to Ray.

Ray, aware that he needed nursing, insisted on being put in a local nursing-home but, after a few days, he was admitted to the Kent and Canterbury Hospital where, in a quiet private room, he very gently went out of his mind. His discourses remained as closely reasoned and perceptive as ever but what he was perceiving was not always reality.

Daisy rallied her powers. She commanded the services of Jack, a particular taxi driver working for a local firm, and he took her each morning to the hospital. There she sat with Ray, fed him, tended him and, as she later told me, they repaired their love.

Daisy mentioned to me that even though Ray's faculties were failing fast, he was still alert enough to express strong reservations about being fed the pink hospital blancmange. That day Prue and I were taking Ray's sister Margaret to lunch at Giovanni's Restaurant in Whitstable. Giovanni asked kindly after Ray and I told him about the blancmange. As we left he presented us with a basket containing six pots of freshly made crème caramel.

'Such a great man must not have to eat blancmange,' he said. 'These he will enjoy.'

Giovanni was right. When Daisy fed them to him Ray sat up and took notice. His appreciation of crème caramel was unimpaired.

Another of Ray's faculties that seemed very durable was his scholarship. He had the good luck to be attended by one of the senior consultants of the hospital, who was himself a classical scholar. Daisy told me that whenever Dr John came in to examine Ray they would deal lightly with medical matters and then launch themselves into a serious discussion about the metres of Aeschylus or some similarly abstruse classical subject, about which Ray still seemed to have complete understanding.

Even that understanding soon passed. His eyes became blank and, on the twenty-ninth of March 1971, Ray died.

'Nobody is to be nice to me,' said Daisy as she climbed slowly out of the taxi and paid off Jack for the last time. 'Nobody is to be kind,' she ordered as she marched up the steps of Red Lion Cottage and closed the door.

Prue and I understood and respected her resolution, but there were matters to attend to. After a while I went into Daisy's house through the French windows and we faced each other across the table and talked woodenly about sending notices and arranging the funeral.

While she had been looking after Ray I think Daisy's own ailments had been in abeyance. Now they were back and I could see that she was in considerable distress, particularly from the virtually permanent condition of shingles that afflicted the lower half of her body. Nevertheless she was determined to stay in charge and deal with whatever had to be dealt with herself. She did not speak about the future.

The funeral passed and the family came back to Red Lion Cottage to drink the Tokay. This was a special bottle of Tokay Essenz (1866), a legendary wine which Ray had kept because it was reputed to revive persons near to death. It hadn't done so and consequently, as instructed, the family finished the bottle.

After the funeral Daisy kept busy, writing and receiving letters and dealing with Ray's estate. I could see that these tasks would soon be done but she still refused to speak of the future and when I, rather tentatively, suggested that she and I might go away for a few days to a hotel in Brighton which she was fond of, she fended the suggestion off quite briskly.

She said: 'Don't be daft. I've got much too much to do. But listen, why don't you and Prue go away to your blessed cottage for a few days and let me get used to all this in my own way? You could leave the twins and Dan with John and Mary. They would be happy to have them. I shall be all right here.'

Prue and I appreciated that Daisy could do with some time without us under her feet and that her suggestion was practically a command. So it was arranged and we went to Wales.

Prue and I had a fairly rough few days. It was raining heavily and early April is not a good time to camp in a near-derelict cottage on a mountain, so we didn't try. We slept in a local hotel.

As we returned and I drove in through the gate of Red Lion House at about 2.30 in the morning, I saw that the light was on in Daisy's bedroom in the cottage.

I walked up the steps to Daisy's front door knowing, or perhaps fearing, what I was going to find. Her tear-stained note was in the typewriter. She was in her bed, still breathing, but very heavily. For a few moments I paced up and down, not knowing what to do. Then, as the law required, I rang the doctor. After a while he turned up and immediately summoned an ambulance. I went with the ambulance and spoke to the young doctor in the hospital casualty ward.

I said: 'Whatever else you do, please don't bring her back to life. She would be so angry!'

He looked at me as if I was mad.

I said: 'She made her decision. Let her go.'

As if I had uttered an obscenity he turned on his heel and walked away.

Late the next day a ward sister rang me and gently broke the news that Daisy had died without regaining consciousness.

'I am glad to hear that,' I said.

'Yes,' she replied, and her voice told me that she knew exactly what I meant.

'What do I do now?' I asked.

'Nothing for your mother,' said the sister. 'You could choose an undertaker tomorrow and ask them to ring the hospital. They will look after everything.'

'Thanks,' I said.

The next day I got up very early and went out into the field behind the house. It was a glorious morning. The first of the sun was lighting up the dew on the young green leaves. The air was new and bright, every bird in Kent was singing its part in the dawn chorus, and I asked: 'Is it true? Did you really want no more of this?' Her answer came back into my head as clearly as if she had been standing beside me: 'Yes, yes. I wanted no more of it. I had had enough and it was time to go. That's all. It doesn't matter. Don't mind.'

Then the tears came, washing through me in a flood. These were plain tears of ordinary grief, tears for the sorrow of how things are, where there is nothing to be done except weep and weep and wish it were not so.

III. Afterwards.

Ray's passing had been, on the whole, fairly well organized. He had acquiesced to fate and, in its time, fate had taken him fairly gently. There had been deep sadness at his funeral but it had all been, as I have heard Quakers say, 'in right ordering'.

Daisy's gesture was of a different order. Her defiance of fate, her rejection of her own decay, her taking charge of her own destiny, were typical of her and, in their way, glorious. But the effect was like a hammer-blow. I was numb and dazed, but in this I was luckier than Prue, who was shattered. During her last few months Daisy had become, to put it mildly, a bit 'difficult'. Prue had borne the brunt of this and had kept her temper, but in herself she had been feeling hostile towards the interfering old bat. She was actually very fond of Daisy and could have done with a chance to make her peace with her, but now it was too late. We both wept, but Prue's tears were full of a pain that was near to anger.

Kay Starr, now infirm and in her late eighties, wrote from her nursing home: '. . . I wish I'd had the guts to do it years ago . . . So dry your eyes my darlings, salute true courage when you see it and get on with your lives while you can.'

So we did as she said, turned back to our lives. Then I came to see how important it is to allow oneself to mourn, how necessary and proper it is, in spirit if not in apparel, to wear black. I walked on through my life, doing whatever came next, comforting Prue as best I could, loving our children, but without exuberance. I found I didn't want to do anything that I would ordinarily have enjoyed because to do it without enjoying it would be to waste it, and that would have been disrespectful. I wasn't miserable about this, it was appropriate, and I was thankful that our friends were able to see that this was so.

In June 1971 Prue and I attended a delightful party given as a wake for Ray and Daisy by Margaret and Bill Lacy at their restaurant in London. This was a tremendously happy and loving occasion which they would both have enjoyed enormously. In fact, as I mingled with the guests, I kept half expecting to come across Ray smiling expansively or Daisy recounting some exciting, if difficult to follow, reminiscence. The only speech was made by their old and dear friend, Gip Wells. He gave a brief, but beautiful, evocation of their lives, and we said goodbye.

It was time for me to go back to work. I still had *Clanger* films to finish but I wasn't exactly full of enthusiasm or ideas for the future, in fact my head was completely numb. So I confess I was relieved when I heard from the Rural District Council in Wales that, having been alerted to the existence of the cottage by my solicitor's enquiries, it had inspected the property and condemned it as unfit for human habitation. This meant that I would have to drive down to Wales immediately to try and negotiate a reprieve.

I saw the council people, who were quite friendly and willing to allow us time to carry out the required improvements, which we were going to do anyway.

I spent a cold night on a camp bed among the debris in the clammy cottage, listening to the sheep coughing in the lee of the cottage wall.

But the next morning was glorious. I cooked bacon and eggs over a camping-stove and ate them out of the pan. Then my legs, which had been docile and well behaved for years, demanded an outing.

We took off straight up the hill behind the cottage, over springy nibbled turf to the long ridge known as Craig Twrch, where sensible prehistoric people had once made their round houses.

There, where the morning wind blew clean through my body and the morning sun warmed the back of my neck and my hands, I could feel the bones of the living world close under my feet. My legs commanded me to sing and we bounded up along the ridge to the knot of rocks at the top. I stood on the highest rock and held open my coat. The wind took it and filled it like a sail. I leaned into it and for a moment I knew that all I had to do was hop up on my toes and I would lift off like a bird. I would ride the wind, circling out over the valley, uttering the shrill cry of the buzzard. My toes, being part of my legs and sensible, did no such thing. They knew quite well that I would just fall on my face and probably roll off down the hill like a loosened boulder.

So I just stood there, breathing in the air of Wales, looking around at the rolling hills, half-lit by the morning sun, and seeing the dark woody valleys which were slotted into their crevices, each with its own swift stream and leaping waterfalls. Below me I saw the pattern of stone-walled fields filling the low land where the river looped its way along, and I knew that Prue had chosen well.

Then it was time to go. My legs switchbacked down the hill and slid me the last steep twenty feet or so down a slide of bracken to deliver me with a thump on to the lane behind the cottage.

Later that year we would have a family holiday with camping gear and Kerris's boyfriend, who was a PE instructor, would help me move tons of wall stones to make a fortified terrace in front of the cottage. Later still I would find a builder, Mr Evans, who called himself an agricultural mason and mixed his cement in the middle of the sitting-room floor. He would put in doors and windows and proper stairs. After that I would build all the upstairs rooms in T&G boarding and bring a pipe from a waterfall half a mile up the hill so that Mr Evans could install a sumptuous avocado-coloured bathroom. And I would, eventually, make a hydro-electric station out of a washing-up bowl and a potato-peeler, and this would give us glorious home-made light. But all these joys were yet to come.

On that day I was to drive back to Kent and really come to grips with the question of what we were going to do with the rest of our lives.

The first thing I had to do was finish filming the last of the *Clangers* films. It was soon done. I gave them back to Peter to put in his puppet-chest, dismounted the camera and turned off the lights. We would keep everything for a while in case it was needed again.

As I packed up the *Clangers* material I felt that another era was over. I realised that, far from overlapping the work, I had been giving no thought at all to what our next filming project might be, and also that I felt a strong disinclination to do so.

However, in the late summer, some work came looking for us.

The Birmingham Repertory Theatre Company had just received its brand new architect-designed theatre and for its first Christmas production it wanted to put on a Noggin pantomime. This was to be a huge, no-expense-spared extravaganza with songs and music, dancers and a proper orchestra (and, they promised, no men in evening dress doing card tricks, no grand-circlers and no Apache dancers clouting each other with steel trays). A bright young man called Michael, who was to produce the show, came down to see us. He described the marvellous new theatre and told us that it could provide *absolutely* any technical facilities – film back-projection, mixed multimedia and live action, reveals, transforma-tions, explosions, storms, magic carpets, flying machines. We had but to ask and whatever it was it would be provided, as if by magic.

This was a very exciting prospect and it triggered my imagin-ation to come up with a number of first-rate multimedia ideas which were promptly turned down as being too difficult. That cleared the air a bit and we were able to begin thinking, or at least I was, because I was going to have to write the play.

The play I eventually put together was called *The Rings of Nudrug* and it was unashamedly derivative of the Noggin sagas, which was exactly what the theatre was hoping for. As well as a wicked Emir with his cringing lackey and a most evil and plaintive Nogbad, it included a complete, working flying-machine, a magic carpet, an exploding barrel and some exploding dungeon-bars, a family of damp oppressed trolls who, like the Firecake giants, finally defeat Nogbad and save the day, thus gaining their freedom. It was all good standard Nogstuff.

Peter had never designed a stage set before but his friend, the distinguished theatre designer Brian Currah, came down to Blean to give him a crash course in theatre and costume design. The sets and costumes which Peter designed were magnificent, the play was cast and went into rehearsal. The technical department took the challenge and started to build the amazing devices.

Norman Dannatt, the composer, an old friend of Prue's from the Watergate Revue Days, came up with some marvellous songs to go with Vernon Elliott's Nog music and all in all the *Noggin Christmas Show* was loud, rumbustious, hilarious and astonishing. The children loved it all and joined in with gusto, especially when the anti-heroes, Paul Chapman as Nogbad and Paul Henry as the Emir, being villains, cursed and swore at the audience when they were applauded, but bowed and curtsied their appreciation when they were hissed.

I enjoyed it a lot, and by the time it was due to close I was ready to start thinking about our next lot of films, or I would have been if there hadn't been something more important to do.

IV. Cotobro.

1972 came in with Kerris emigrating to Australia and Prue taking to her bed with her worst ever bout of bronchitis.

After the grim reality of the recent past I was deeply anxious to take care of her and determined to do something to try and stave off the annual illness. A few years earlier she and I had taken a trip to Italy, a marvellous, magical trip to the Cinque Terre which could only be reached by mule or a railway tunnel that Mussolini had caused to be driven through the rocky shore. Prue had loved that trip and the warm Mediterranean air had made her bloom.

I suggested that as soon as she felt well enough to travel we should leave wet England and find the sun. Prue had always had a fondness for southern Spain. So, feeling devilish affluent, I went to a high-class agency and rented a villa on the Costa del Sol for a month.

Prue and I and our three boys left England on a really chilly night in early March. As I stepped out of the cramped charter flight on to Malaga airport at about one o'clock in the morning, I breathed the air and found it fresh, warm and welcoming, like an English night in June.

We collected the keys of a neat little car from a yawning man in a grey suit and, by the light of a silvery moon, set off for our forty-mile drive, eastwards along the coast road. We were the swinging holidaymakers of the seventies, heading into our dream-time of sun-drenched leisure in a rented villa on the Costa del Sol.

The drive was astonishing, especially so because, driving on the right, our car was on the seaward side of the road, overlooking the water. The road itself was not very wide, or very well kept, in fact recent rains had brought down small deltas of mud and stones, but the views, of bays and inlets, of rocky outcrops covered with pines, olive groves and tiny white houses, with every detail sharp and calm in the moonlight, were breathtakingly beautiful.

'Look down there!' I would say.

'Watch the bloody road!' Prue would cry, cringing away from the sheer drop beside her.

Our instructions from the travel agency had been very exact. Just before Almuñecar we turned right down a wide newly metalled road towards Cotobro. This road snaked and looped down the steep slope towards the sea, gradually becoming narrower and more gravelly until by the time it reached Cotobro, a small glittering bay with a line of houses beside the beach, it was the dry bed of a stream.

The instructions said there would be a steep lane on the left leading up to the villa. It was there all right, but it had a line of barbed wire stretched across it. I stopped and inspected the wire. It was firmly stapled in, not meant to be moved, but the air was soft and full of the scent of growing herbs, and the light was magical.

In the car the boys were asleep and Prue was exhausted. In front of me the handsome villas in their lush gardens stepped, one above the other, up the steep slope. I took the keys from Prue and set off like James Bond, climbing swiftly, hand over hand, up terraced walls, over lawns and paved patios, past sleeping chaises-longues and cold barbecues, softly creeping up to front doors and silently trying the keys. Either the villas were empty or I was a good burglar – not a bark was heard.

In one of them the key fitted. I pushed the door, it opened. Full of excitement I ran down a side-path to the road and woke Prue. We took a bag each and I led her, yawning, up to the villa.

'Here it is!' I whispered and pushed the door open. We stepped into our villa.

'Bloody hell, what's this?' cried Prue.

'Water, I think.' I flapped my foot in it. Yes, the floor was two inches deep in water.

'Where's the light?' she asked.

'No,' I said. 'Don't touch the light. You could be electrocuted.'

'Oh, sod it!'

The villa was neat and clean, the beds had been made up ready for us with large Spanish candlewick bedspreads over them. These were eagerly wicking up the water into the beds. We grabbed them and pulled them off at once.

'Can't you stop the water?'

There was a faint hissing noise. I traced it to a plywood box in the garden. I kicked off the lid and turned off the tap. The hissing stopped.

Luckily the villa had been built a bit crooked so the beds in one of the rooms were still dry. We went down to the car and fetched the sleepy boys. Before they had time to wake up completely and enjoy the disaster we had tucked them into bed.

The water was seeping away. We found some dry bedding and got some sleep ourselves. In the morning I rang the agent's representative who sent a plumber. The plumber wept when he saw the mess and then took a big hammer and smashed the marble floor that he had laid with such care a year or two earlier.

After a couple of days Prue and I were sitting on the terrace drinking coffee. The boys had vanished.

I said: 'How's your bronchitis?'

She said: 'What bronchitis?' So that was something done.

After a few days we hardly saw the boys at all except at mealtimes. They had teamed up with the sons of a Belgian couple who lived in a small block of apartments built in the crook of the valley. The Belgian boys spoke good English and, being resident, knew all the local amenities. Prue and I made a convenient arrangement with Guido and Léa, their parents: at meal-times we would feed whatever crowd of boys happened to be about.

The apartments in the block where Guido and Léa lived were very cool and spacious, with deep covered balconies opening the whole width of the living rooms. I remember sitting with them one evening, admiring the way they had been planned.

I told them how Prue's bronchitis had vanished without trace and I wondered whether there were any more apartments as nice as theirs for sale and how much they would cost.

Léa said: 'You're sitting in one.'

Guido said: 'Four thousand pounds in used notes.'

So we bought it.

V. A Grievous Gift.

By now our ownership of property was getting a bit out of hand. Our newest acquisition, the *apartamento* in Cotobro, definitely put paid to Prue's annual bouts of bronchitis, so that was a good investment. Our friends Joyce and Alec Veitch and their family bought one of the other apartments in the block. Guido's building hadn't been too good and the electricity tended to go weak, which meant that the lights would dim. Spanish law was draconian and unpredictable and Guido turned out to be technically illegal and non-existent, as well as being something of a megalomaniac, but for several years we had marvellous family holidays there, times full of fun and easy living. We wouldn't have missed that for anything.

The cottage in Wales was also a great joy, even though it was constantly under attack from the insidious weather. My aunt Nell had decided not to live in Whitstable any more so, as a result, we still owned her now empty cottage and half of a flat in Hove which John and I had bought for her use. We still of course owned and lived in Red Lion House.

As well as all that it had gradually come home to me that Red Lion Cottage, the house that, a few years earlier, I had specifically designed for Ray and Daisy to live in, was now returned to me.

That grievous gift affected me more deeply than I had anticipated. Now that I stood in their place and it was empty, I knew that Ray and Daisy were really dead. And that with them many of the hopes that they had lived in, and the movement that they had lived for, had also passed away or become modified out of recognition.

The simple truths that George Lansbury had seen around him in the 1880s – the inherent injustice of the capitalist system, the insolence of privilege, the wickedness of exploitation, the wretchedness of poverty and the absolute wrongness of war – had long since ceased to be simple, and the clarion call to revolution that those realities had inspired had become muted. The bright vision that had lit the eyes of Ray and Daisy's friends at Bloomsbury-on-the-Marsh in the 1930s – the prospect of a just and loving social order based on the principles of true socialism – had not materialized.

Ray and Daisy had not been blind to these changes. They had lived through them and their grasp of political situations had always been clear and definite. I suppose, without knowing it, I had thought of Ray as being the referee of our safety in the world and had more or less left politics to him. I remember that whenever I wanted to know something about what was going on in the world I would usually start by asking him and, more often than not, I would simply accept his view. From now on, if I wanted to know what was happening, I was going to have to find out for myself.

It was too early for me to be sure what effect Daisy's absence had had on me because the echoes of the manner of her death were still too strong. That had brought home to me the simple fact that, like it or not, things are the way they are, and once you have checked them, tested them and can see for sure that there is no way they can be otherwise, then you've got to do what has to be done. It reminded me that I was now the keeper of several other people's safety and if, in my complacency, I should fail to act when action was needed, then whatever happened as a result would be, in some degree, my doing. These observations didn't come to me as a piece of rational argument, they came as a single cold shudder.

Ray and Daisy's death marked the end of an era in my own life. I was comfortably set in our home and family, and was running a successful and rewarding business. That could have continued peacefully for many years, and indeed it did continue for as long as fate was going to allow, but not quite so peacefully. I think some underlying assumption of stability must have been lost, because I became more aware of the world and of our situation in it and, perhaps as a result, my interests, anxieties and obsessions began to range more widely and this was going to lead me into other, less convenient, paths. But that was yet to come.

VI. The Cat.

Life went on. Peter and I had a *Pogles' Annual* to do and the BBC was waiting for us to complete some single-frame inserts for *Sam on Boff's Island* for its Education Department.

Then the BBC let us know what we wanted next, and thus we came at last to what was perhaps the largest, and certainly the most multifarious of our productions – the saggy old cloth cat.

Once again the chief character was not born (or created) for the part. We had to look for it. The BBC had told us that it wanted a colourful, all-singing, all-dancing, musical extravaganza for *Watch with Mother* but, as usual, had no suggestions to offer as to what should be in it.

As usual, Peter and I thought we had nothing in our heads. Also as usual, this turned out not to be quite true.

For a long time, in some far-flung corner of his mind, Peter had been harbouring an Indian Army cat. Retired, of course, and definitely pukka, this cat spent a lot of time at a children's hospital somewhere in the hills of the Raj. His visits were particularly popular because he told the children extraordinary stories. These were extraordinary because he could, if he so wished, cause his thoughts to appear, as if by magic, in a bubble above his head.

This was good news. A cat like that could be very useful to us, very useful indeed. But there were problems. Even though the cat could have been a glove-puppet like Basil Brush, and his thoughts could easily have been conjured with electronic magic, there was no way we could accommodate a hospital ward full of live argumentative children in Peter's barn. We were strictly a single-frame cartoon and puppet outfit.

Peter and I pushed ideas backwards and forwards for quite a long time. The cat, whose name, we concluded, was Bagpuss, was English, certainly retired, and sedentary, preferring to sleep on his own cushion. All cats, given the opportunity, will choose to sleep in a shop window, where it is warm and they can be admired without being disturbed.

Right then. A cat in a shop window. What sort of shop? What else was in it? What did it sell?

Once Bagpuss was firmly in place, the answers to the other questions came fairly quickly. Peter's youngest daughter, Emily, would own both cat and shop. There were various pieces of bric-à-brac in the shop window, some of which would, in certain circumstances, come to life. Like what, for instance? We scouted around and found a rag doll that Joan Firmin had made for a Pingwing film. Her name was surely Madeleine. Peter still had a felt toad that played a banjo. His name was Gabriel. By now we knew that Bagpuss had a set of 'familiars': mice, who lived on a mouse organ.

Mice? Cats and mice don't mix. Yes, but these mice were 'family' – Charliemouse who wore a check suit, Lizziemouse in a navy-blue dress, Eddiemouse, who had red trousers I think, and numerous others, whose names I made up as we went along. They acted as a disrespectful chorus, doing odd jobs, singing songs and setting up deceptions.

All right. So what was a mouse organ? It was a Marvellous Mechanical device, worked by a bellows – something between a pianola and a television set.

The place was filling up well, but we still felt the need for another, more serious, character. We thought of a dark, shadowy Professor Bogwood. We weren't sure we cared for him. Nor was the BBC, mainly because he was a human-type character. Also he had no sense of humour and wasn't a bit ridiculous. But all the same I still liked the idea of a distinguished academic personage who could claim to know everything; one who was dry and thin-voiced and would go '*Nerp, nerp, nerp*,' in a birdy way. I saw him as being a mixture of Professor Bertrand Russell and my uncle, G. D. H. Cole. That was it! A bookish bird, a bird bookend, a wooden woodpecker called, naturally, Professor Yaffle.

Good. That was the cast. What was the plot? Or rather, since this was to be a set of thirteen self-contained fifteen-minute programmes, what would be the pattern of activity into which the stories would fit?

Ordinary shops sold things. That was a bit too ordinary, and we couldn't cope with real live people coming in and out. So this shop didn't *sell* anything. All right, but what exactly would happen in Emily's shop?

Then the pattern began to emerge. Emily would bring things to the shop: broken, lost things. She would put them down in front of Bagpuss, say a poem to wake him up and leave them there. Then Bagpuss and his friends would wake up. They would look at whatever Emily had brought and decide how to mend it. They would do whatever was necessary to mend the article and then they would put it in the shop window so that whoever it belonged to could come in and collect it. That was all there was to it.

Fine. But what did they mend things with?

Well, certainly not pins and glue. The mice would clean whatever it was quite carefully, but the real mending would have to be done with songs and stories and pictures, with anything that the magic imagination could bring to bear upon its predicament.

That seemed like a reasonable scenario. The shop itself was

probably antique. In fact the whole scene would be set at the turn of the century, using some early sepia vignetted photographs as an introduction. I remember Emily Firmin wasn't all that keen about the idea of being photographed as a Victorian child and appearing, even in a set of still vignettes, at the start of each episode. She felt it would cause her embarrassment at school (which indeed it did, for a while), but she agreed to do it.

Now we had to find the people to play the characters. In this I was doubly fortunate. The introduction to *Sam on Boff's Island* had been a very bright piece of music. It had caught my ear, as one might say, and I made enquiries about its origin. It had been played by a couple of folk-musicians, Sandra Kerr and John Faulkner. Between them they could play every sort of instrument from a mountain dulcimer to an Irish fiddle. They knew and could sing every tune in the world and didn't bother with written music, except as a last resort. They were exactly suited to be Gabriel the Toad and Madeleine the Rag Doll and in those roles were happy to play whatever music and sing whatever songs would be needed.

Sandra and John took a very relaxed attitude to the composing and recording of the music. Once I had worked out a few episodes I would make a very rough list of the bits where I thought music might be appropriate. I would send it to them to think about. Then we would borrow a fairly silent room in a remote house and, taking the various articles that we intended to celebrate with us, would spend a happy day with the tape-recorder, thinking up and recording whatever songs and tunes came to mind. I had had a set of variable-speed spindles made for the tape machine, so we were able to record the accompaniment to the mouse songs at normal speed and then play it back at a slow speed while we all sang for the mice at the slow speed but in high voices. This, when played back at normal speed, finally produced the elegant fluting tones for which they became famous. (Incidentally, the mouse singing out-of-tune was me.)

I had to get started on the actual scripts. I put together the first story about a particularly intriguing article, a ship in a bottle. Bagpuss was extremely puzzled by this. 'A *ship*, in a *bottle*?' he muttered. 'Who could sail it? Where would it sail to?' We discussed this predicament, remembered a song about a duck, and a poem about some mermaids and recorded it.

We all listened to it and it seemed to be OK.

So then, while Peter was making the shop window set and jointing the characters, I started trying to think of other articles which would give scope for some interesting songs and stories. I couldn't possibly just *think* of such things. I had to find them, or rather, somebody had to find them or, better, make them. Joan Firmin, who made embroidered cushions, very kindly made one with an Athenian owl on it. She also embroidered the pictures for the story of the owls of Athens who were so proud of their beautiful singing that they demanded treasure and mocked the moon. So proud they were that the moon created nightingales to put them to shame. Joan also made the enamel pieces that were the jewels for the frog princess. She wasn't a frog to start with, just an ordinary bored princess, but when she was kissed by a frog she, naturally, turned into a frog princess, and, I believe, lived happily ever after.

The pattern worked surprisingly well. Once we had a suitable article, the ideas about it seemed to come by themselves. The Ballet Shoe was found in a cupboard. It was obviously old and worn. Also, as Professor Yaffle pointed out, *one* ballet shoe was not a lot of use except perhaps to a one-legged ballet-dancer. Madeleine suggested that shoes could be lived in – there was an old woman who lived in a shoe. That was the cue for the mice to pump up the Mouse Organ to show pictures of the old woman who lived in a shoe, while Madeleine sang the song. Professor Yaffle pointed out that a dirty old ballet shoe was much too small for anybody to live in. The mice contested this assertion and, being magically numerous, demonstrated that nearly twenty mice could comfortably occupy it. Yaffle was not amused, insisted that there was nothing you could do with one old shoe. Bagpuss wondered what could be done with it but Charliemouse knew exactly what to do. The mice would sail it. They would row, row, row it gently down the stream. That was the cue for another traditional song.

Gabriel played his banjo and sang the song, though the words he sang were not the traditional ones because they concerned the adventures of two mice in their quest for Stilton cheese.

Here is a snatch of it:

Tune: 'Row, Row, Row the Boat'

Verse:
> They rowed and they rowed without a care
>> and didn't look where they went.
> Well you might ask how you would fare,
>> travelling backwards without a care,
>> when you suddenly came to the top of the stair . . .
> Well over the stairs they went, they went,
>> over the stairs they went!

Mouse chorus:
> Bing, bang, bongo-bump, heavily down the stairs,
>> binglety, banglety, bongelty, bumpety.
> Down the apples and pears!

Verse:
> They picked them up from their dreadful fall
>> and dusted off their knees,
> And down the hall by the kitchen wall
>> they rowed and you could hear them call.
>> or you could if they hadn't been quite so small . . .
> 'Where is that loverly cheese, that cheese,
>> where is that loverly cheese?'

The song, which, as Yaffle agrees, is a lot of bosh, does nothing for the condition of the ballet shoe. Madeleine reproves the mice for singing silly songs when they should be cleaning and mending the shoe. The mice show solidarity and threaten to strike if they are not allowed to sing. Negotiations take place and they agree to work so long as they can sing at the same time. They sing as they wash and polish and fit new ribbons on to the shoe, until it is clean and beautiful and fit for a prima ballerina.

Professor Yaffle unexpectedly betrays his ignorance by admitting that he doesn't know what a prima ballerina is. So the mice have to bring in a clockwork dancing ballerina to show him. They wind it up and she dances for him. The Professor is enchanted. Besotted by her beauty he dances and falls head-over-heels in love with her, and head-over-heels into the ballet shoe where he gets wound up in the new ribbons. The mice untangle him and push the shoe into the window, so that if a one-legged ballerina should happen to come past she could come in and collect it.

That all fell into place quite neatly, as did the story of the Hamish, a tartan cloth frog-like object that had lain on our mantelpiece for years. His was a sad tale of Scottish solitude told to an eerie skirling of the bagpipes, played backwards. Professor Yaffle insisted that the thing was really a porcupine that had lost its spikes and was intended as a porcupin-cushion. That reminded us of a poem that Stephen Sylvester had written for us to go in a *Pogle Annual* about the adventures of a porcupine who was foolish enough to go up in a balloon, with a predictably unfortunate ending. Sandra and John set that to music and sang it for Madeleine and Gabriel. In the chords of that tune we found something that we had been looking for: the introductory music for the series, the opening theme that led through the antique vignettes to Emily's poem:

> Bagpuss, dear Bagpuss, old fat furry cat-puss,
>> Wake up and look at this thing that I bring.
> Wake up, be bright, be golden and light,
>> Bagpuss, oh hear what I sing . . .

And of course Bagpuss woke up, gave his celebrated yawn, and the story began.

But of course the essential key to unlock each episode was the article to be found. To locate these I would range about the place, picking things up and putting them down, scraping my brain for ideas about their history. This was quite hard work, but in fact far less daunting than sitting in front of a blank piece of paper with absolutely nothing in one's head. At least the things we found were tangible and their very existence stimulated speculation about their provenance.

We didn't always have to find or make real things, we could look into our memories. I remembered having once seen an ivory

Chinaman that rocked. I knew that would have a story, so Peter made me one, and a turtle to go with it. A raffia elephant that had been in our toy-box for ever and had lost its ears in some long-forgotten incident. In this case the most difficult task for Peter was to make a repaired replica of him for when he was mended. Peter couldn't mend the scrappy ear-less dirty one that Emily found in case I had to refilm it, so he had to make a completely shiny new one. Peter also made what is for me the *pièce de résistance* of the series, a beautiful folding Mouse Mill, which made chocolate biscuits out of breadcrumbs and butterbeans – a procedure which Professor Yaffle had great difficulty in coming to terms with.

The smallest giant of all was an imitation Staffordshire figurine. It had to be an imitation because it starts off broken and is magically mended, and nobody in their senses would deliberately break a real Staffordshire figure, even for a film. In the event I filmed the end of the story first, and when the film came back from the labs and we were sure it was all right, Peter and I ceremonially broke the figure in order to film the beginning of the story. The piece of Old Man's Beard simply came out of a hedge. We looked at that for a long time before we realised that it was the silvery royal beard of a king, a material that would make priceless carpets and do wonders for the weaving trade. The fiddle was an ordinary Irish leprechaun's fiddle which of course has better tone than most full-size fiddles even though it is as small as a finger. That was found in a bucket. Flying was just a trick with a basket and paper fans; the mice were responsible for that, but it did bring us the story of Uncle Henry and Auntie Ada, poor church mice, who flew up to scrape some of the gold off the sun with a teaspoon. Uncle Feedle was made for the song about the tailor and his mouse, 'Hi-diddle-unkum-feedle' (or words to that effect). That story didn't please the mice, so we had to think of a different one, so Peter's daughter Charlotte made Uncle Feedle a rag doll in a cloth country with an inside-out house.

The amount of material there was in those thirteen Bagpuss films was colossal. I'm not surprised it took me several months to get half of the programmes together. I remember I was filming number five, *The Hamish*, and I hadn't thought of anything for the last three – eleven, twelve and thirteen. Bagpuss himself did nothing to help. He was just a saggy old cloth cat, baggy and a bit loose at the seams – but Emily loved him.

And we loved making them. Giving them life was a splendid, if somewhat hectic, episode in our lives, and whenever I see the films again I feel very happy.

The BBC liked them too and for the next thirteen years – from 1974 to 1987 – they were shown regularly twice a year and became part of the world of a whole generation of children, who love them dearly to this day.

From a distance of the twenty-five years which have passed since we made the *Bagpuss* films, I have begun to be able to see how they earned that affection. They are simple, and they are well founded in a safe place. They are full of fun and, like a good meal, they are rich and satisfying. They also stretch the mind and flex the imagination. And the songs and the pictures are marvellous.

Looking back at that time, when I was busily making those safe gentle films in our make-believe world, it seems ironical to recall that even while I was doing it, I, personally, was feeling deeply disturbed and agitated about the safety and gentleness of the real world that I and my family were living in.

That was a very different sort of story.

13

LOOKING OUTWARDS

I. Non-politics.

In the early 1970s, along with, I suspect, quite a number of other people in the kingdom, I began to get frightened. I began to sense that something was going seriously wrong with the way our country was being run – if indeed it was being 'run' at all. I had an uneasy feeling that it was sliding slowly out of control.

I had a vague and probably rather simplistic picture of what was going on: some of the trade unions had grown large enough and powerful enough to take a proper capitalist market-type view of their role and screw the bosses for all they could get. The big employers and even the government, itself a very big employer, couldn't come to terms with that situation and, to all intents and purposes, seemed to have declared war on the unions.

Nowadays the relationship between the trade unions and industry seems to be fairly calm. Both sides have come to see that they are partners in the process of production, but in 1972 the doctrinaire enmities between Labour and Capital were too deeply entrenched for their relationship to be seen as anything but one of direct confrontation. The 'Captains of Industry' *knew* that the unions were led by 'Revolutionaries', whose sole purpose was to bring about, by fair means or foul, the destruction of capitalism, privilege and the very fabric of the nation. On the other hand the union leaders *knew* that their task was to bring about the end of the exploitation of the working classes and restore justice to their situation, which they saw as being one of near-slavery.

I remember Edward Heath's Conservative government, from June 1970 to March 1974, as a chronicle of disputes, deadlocks and crises. The states of emergency that were declared, the three-day week, the ninety-day wage freeze, and the mid-winter power cuts, were all symptoms of a system falling into what looked like terminal decline. I remember being surprised that society didn't collapse, surprised that there didn't come a day when nobody felt able to take the future for granted any more, a day when suddenly it would be 'every man for himself' with, perhaps, gangs of the dispossessed looting the new supermarkets, followed by a general breakdown of services, chaos and finally starvation. I don't know how near we came to that but in the dark times when it was cold and the electricity was off, the sense of impending disaster grew very strong. I dare say we came nowhere near that point but when I was in Germany in 1947 I had seen the *Kohlenklau*, seen the respectable people of Braunschweig scrabbling over the coal-wagons to fill their posh rucksacks with nutty slack, and I knew that civilized life *could* come apart at the seams.

As well as that sense of dread, what I felt most strongly in 1973 was a feeling of hopeless exasperation. Listening to the wrangles, the obviously vain assertions of authority, the obdurate declarations of solidarity and the emollient reassurances of politicians – which were perhaps the most frightening – I had the feeling that we, the public, were being treated as if we were stupid. I found myself becoming more and more dejected by the sheer irrelevance of what was going on in the House of Commons. It seemed to me that, at a time when the country most needed real government, Parliament had simply been hi-jacked by two parties of doctrinaire zealots, Labour and Conservative, whose sole interest was to defeat each other at any cost. That cost was already being borne by the country as a whole, in terms of lost markets, flat investment, rising unemployment and rampant inflation. Something had to be done about it, and quickly – but I had no clear idea what.

Life went on as usual, of course. Just thinking that something had to be done didn't make any difference to that, neither did talking about it, which I did rather a lot.

There followed an unusually muddled episode in my life, one in which I was alternately chilled with embarrassment at my own vehemence and at other times filled with a crusading zeal for some end which I couldn't really see clearly, let alone articulate. And underneath it all simmered an incongruous anger with party politics in general and party-political Members of Parliament in particular.

Prue disliked thinking about politics but she even more disliked my getting involved with it.

'It *irks* me,' she said, 'you going about haranguing people!'

'Why?'

'Because it's not *you*. It's not the sort of thing you do. You're not even a member of a Party, so nobody knows which side you're on.'

'You know quite well I'm not on either side.'

'There! You see what I mean!'

'Look, you know exactly what I think, and you know I've got to do something about it.'

'Oh all right, I suppose, but it you're going to play Winston Churchill and save the nation, why don't you just get on with it and stop talking about it all the time?'

Prue had a point there. I was being a bore.

So I wrote lots of letters to newspapers, some of which were published. Then, as the first General Election of 1974 was coming up, I wrote to Wyn Knowles, the editor of the radio programme

Woman's Hour, and asked her whether I might be permitted to make a Non-party Political Broadcast on behalf of the Poor Bloody Electors (or words to that effect). Somewhat to my surprise she invited me to come in and record it.

That called my bluff. But, 'in for a penny, in for a pound', I overruled embarrassment and put together a four-minute speech. In it I made an impassioned, if somewhat confused, appeal to the Members of Parliament who were about to take office to set aside the squabbles of party politics and do the job which they were being paid to do – work together to seek agreement on the best way to save the country from committing industrial suicide. The speech was well received and repeated.

After it had washed away and the election was over I felt calmer in spirit. I had actually done something, though nobody would ever know what effect, if any, it had had.

Nevertheless, the more I thought about it, the more clearly I saw that although political groupings were a natural phenomenon of the democratic process, they were not essential to it, and if their wrangling reached the point where it took over Parliament, so that its attention to its proper function, *the exercise of government*, was diverted and replaced with *an inter-party power struggle*, they became a betrayal of that function, a corruption that could destroy the credibility of the institution itself, bring government into disrepute and eventually make it impossible.

As the second General Election of 1974 was drawing near, I persuaded Monica Sims, the Head of Children's Programmes at BBC Television, to let me make a very short *Clangers* film which would expose some of the absurdities of political electioneering.

I made *Vote for Froglet* in record time – three days. I delivered it and it was shown, I believe, twice. It was all right, a pleasant little Morality Play, but not something that would bring the world to its senses.

Then, on September 7th 1974, the *Guardian* published an article by Professor S. E. Finer called 'In Defence of Deadlock'. When I read it I cheered, because here was the Gladstone Professor of Government and Public Administration, a fellow of All Souls, Oxford, saying, albeit in a more erudite and better-informed way, exactly the same sort of things as I had been thinking and muttering about! I can't tell you what a power of good that article did me. After reading it everything fell into place and I could at last see which side I was going to have to take in the coming election.

The burden of Professor Finer's argument was that the only way out of the aggressive stalemate in which we were stuck was going to be the election of a hung parliament, one in which neither of the massive doctrinaire parties had an overall majority. Consequently they would have no option but to compromise and negotiate a consensus. This would enable MPs to do their job, i.e., to get together and work for the common good. The key to this change would be to elect as many members as possible of the third party, the Liberals.

Polling day was drawing near. I broke with my family's socialist tradition and threw in my lot with the Liberal Party. I wrote and distributed a leaflet for the local Liberal candidate. I'm not sure she liked, or even understood, the message of it, which was that everybody should vote for the Liberal Party not because they supported its policies but because that was the only way to escape from the destructive wrestling of the two doctrinaire dinosaur parties – and bring back proper democracy.

The General Election came and went. Labour was returned again, this time with a tiny majority. The local Liberal candidate didn't get in.

For my own part, I was disappointed but not surprised.

The economy ground on. By the end of 1974 the spiral of prices and wage increases had pushed the cost of living up by 20 per cent, but civilization didn't come apart. The big unions went on using their muscle to get their way and so consolidated the climate of antagonism in which the Conservative Party would be moved to appoint a lady gladiator as its leader.

I came away with a firm conviction that government was too important and delicate a process to be left to politicians, especially those filled with a zeal to pursue doctrinaire ends. I could see that the only hope for civilization lay with the moderate, sensible people who, while longing for a quiet life, needed to realise that moderation and common sense must be a passion as real as any fanaticism, as it was the only light that would guide us through the dark rockery of economic decay.

II. Sun Worship.

When I look back at my life in the early 1970s I am astonished at the quantity and diversity of the projects and follies that I was engaged in. Where did I find the time?

The main project was, of course, work. During 1973 and 1974, while I was deep in non-politics, I wrote and made thirteen fifteen-minute *Bagpuss* films, wrote two *Pogle Annuals*, five *Bagpuss* books, two *Bagpuss Annuals*, two *Noggin* books and a stream of contributions to *TV LAND* weekly.

As if that wasn't enough, I had conceived and designed a handsome new studio which I proposed to build, myself, in the field beside Red Lion House. This was to have solar heating, a method which, in the wake of the great leap in the price of crude oil, was very much in the public interest.

Building the studio was a fairly long-term ambition, but during the preparations for it an incident occurred which was to take my attention and propel it like a rocket in a completely new direction.

I had thought out a very simple solar-heating system for the proposed studio, I made a small-scale model of a unit with a thermometer-recorder in it to measure the temperature of the air passing through, and propped it up in the corner of the garden, just to see if it would get warm. It did. It melted. I found it lying in the grass, a treacle-pie of congealed polystyrene and warped perspex. Although I was later to discover that this was not such a significant phenomenon as it had seemed, it was quite spectacular and I was tremendously excited. I was already persuaded that solar heating could be a really important and useful form of renewable energy, one which didn't use up fossil fuel, issue noxious hot vapours or breed quantities of eternally poisonous material, and it now seemed that I might have stumbled on a collecting system that could bring solar energy into service at a particularly reasonable cost.

But let me begin at the beginning. On a fairly dull afternoon in February I was sitting in a greenhouse. The greenhouse faced south and had been built as a lean-to against a solid brick wall. The temperature outside was cold, about seven degrees Celsius. The temperature inside the greenhouse was very pleasant, about sixteen degrees. In fact it had been much warmer in the greenhouse earlier on in the day, when the sun came out for about an hour. Then it had reached about twenty-five degrees, but that had dropped when the sun went in and now most of the warmth was radiating from the brick wall at the back, which had been heated by the sunlight.

Sitting there I felt very comfortable, especially so because there was nothing artificial about the warm atmosphere. It occurred to me that a greenhouse would be a very pleasant place to live in ... well, perhaps, providing certain obvious disadvantages could be overcome, like it wouldn't be advisable to throw stones, and there would be a certain lack of privacy. It would also become deucedly cold at night and, in sunlight, boiling hot.

Here was material for a really enjoyable think. Unlike non-politics, this subject did not involve people and prejudices, doctrines and destinies, only some generally benign facts. Just thinking about the sun's warmth warmed the spirit and I happily settled down to conjure different propositions from my imagination.

It was quite obvious to me that people wouldn't want to live like cucumbers, under glass, so I wondered about having a very thin greenhouse as part of the roof. How deep did a greenhouse need to be in order to collect solar energy? I imagined a fairly flat box about 4in (10 cm) deep with a glass top to let the sun shine in. It would be well insulated and inside it there would be a plate of some dark lightweight material that would heat up in the sun and give up its heat to air which was being passed through the box.

The warmed air would then be blown into the house by a ducted fan or, if the house was already warm enough, it would be blown through a heat-storage block like, for instance, a deep layer of pebbles under the floor. This would soak up the heat and slowly release it to the house during cooler times.

After some experimenting I chose concertina-pleated aluminium foil as the collecting material. This was so thin that it would heat up almost instantly when there was any solar radiation coming in, even from a cloudy sky – so full sunlight was not essential. I also found that it heated fresh air almost as well as recycled warm air. This meant that the house could have a plentiful supply of fresh air – a great blessing because so many state-of-the-art, energy-efficient, optimally insulated houses smelt of cooked cabbage.

In summer the system could provide hot water and also contribute to cooling the house. In full sunshine the air in the roof collectors would become very hot. It would pass over a water tank to heat the water in it and then be vented to the sky. This would remove much of the 'solar gain' received by the roof (a major cause of overheating), and also draw 'used' air out of the house, allowing fresh air to flow into it from outside, thus helping to keep it cool.

Even though by the end of 1974 my plan to build a new studio was defunct, I still wanted to go ahead with developing the system.

Solar heating had in fact been about for many years but mainly in places where there was plenty of sunshine and, because in such places there wasn't usually a need for house-heating, most of the systems were small and designed only to provide hot water. These worked really well in sunny climates and, perhaps as a consequence of this, it was generally assumed that 'water-transfer' systems were the best and therefore, in all circumstances, the most desirable.

The market responded to the current public interest in solar energy with a rash of new companies selling these standard water-heating units for installation in the UK. Unfortunately there is simply not enough bright sunshine in the UK to provide a worthwhile amount of really hot water except on particularly sunny days, so they turned out not to be a lot of use.

In the system I was proposing, any air temperature in the collector which was above room temperature – about twenty degrees Celsius – would make a welcome contribution. Even with cloudy skies that temperature would be reached quite often in the house-heating season and this meant that the air-transfer system would go on working for longer into the winter and start again earlier in the spring. It also had the extra advantage of warming up very swiftly, which would allow it to collect the heat from short bursts of sunshine. This was something the heavier water-filled units couldn't do. On top of that my system had no pipes and radiators, header-tanks, pumps, plumbing or water-plates, but only some pleated foil, a fan and a duct. This meant that the mechanical parts would cost less than one-third of the price of a water-filled system and the collector area could be the whole or a large part of the roof. This was very encouraging.

Eventually the moment of truth arrived. I took out patents and approached some of the big house-building companies. They had all heard of solar heating but the myth that water-transfer systems were inherently the best had become such an article of faith that they wouldn't even think about an air-transfer system.

However, I didn't give up. Although at that particular time a new lot of film work had turned up, I decided to go on with my research, and did so, in a quiet way, for several years.

Looking back over that period, during which I did succeed in making contact with some large companies, I can see that although solar heating was felt to be fashionable and virtuous, the final deciding factor was always going to be whether or not it would make money.

Nevertheless it was an interesting and enjoyable project. I made enough money from option licences and consultancy fees to build a half-size solar house in the field beside Red Lion House. This was made of wood and insulated with rock-wool but its thermal characteristics were much the same as those of an ordinary house. It had a large pebble-block under the floor to store the heat and a whole roof of aluminium-foil type collectors.

I received gifts of technical equipment and a great deal of much appreciated encouragement from various academics, including Dr Strange at the University of Kent and Professor Pat O'Sullivan at the University of Wales. I think they both quite enjoyed my rather ham-fisted approach to scientific research, as shown by my tendency to bypass all but the most essential mathematics and, having thought my way to a picture of how something might work, just try it out. I think they may have seen this as being a different style of philosophy rather than what it really was – sheer necessity.

The house worked very well indeed, keeping itself warm from early spring to late autumn and delivering hot water on request all through the summer.

Unfortunately this radiant demonstration of the efficiency of the system was not sufficient to convince the sponsor company that it would be profitable. The deciding factor, they told me, was that the artefact did not have a large enough 'maintenance component'. When asked what this was they explained that, to be worth marketing, a system needed to require regular maintenance, which the purchaser would regularly have to pay for.

In essence, what I was offering was a few boxes and a fan which, once installed, would probably work indefinitely. However wondrously efficient it might be, such a device could not command a high initial purchase price nor would it require much future attention. Thus its long-term profit potential was low. Also, as a high-profile company at the leading edge of technical innovation in the field of energy conservation, they had their reputation to consider and, however well it might perform, they really didn't think it would be appropriate for them to offer anything quite so primitive.

That was disappointing but, in a grisly way, understandable.

For a while I was discouraged but then, quite unexpectedly, I was approached by a big company that produced, among other things, canisters of household gas. Their research department had been impressed by the figures in one of my 'presentations', and they offered me a retainer of £2,000 a year to consult with them about their solar projects and help to develop new ones, using, where appropriate, my solar house as a test bed. I was very delighted about this and tried to join in with energy and gusto.

Quite soon I began to see that energy and gusto were inappropriate and that my attempts to carry the project forward were misplaced. They seemed slightly embarrassed by my eagerness to help and had some difficulty in finding work for me to do. After a while the penny dropped and I realised that they were really only interested in retaining the idea and reserving the patent in case they might want it later. Once I had grasped this life became much easier. I no longer felt I had to devote a lot of my time to earning the consultancy fee and was able to start on the essay that I had been intending to write for some years, a rather-less-than-learned paper outlining the general principles of the system I had designed.

In April 1979 I was slightly alarmed, as well as honoured, to be asked to deliver this paper at the International Solar Energy Society's conference at the Royal Institution. I became slightly less nervous when Julian Keable, who had instigated the invitation, told me he was hoping my lecture would serve to lighten the occasion. I think it may have done that, a bit. Certainly there were some good laughs.

That lecture was my swan-song for the solar project. The consultancy continued in a rather half-hearted way until 1981 and then, at a time when public interest in solar energy had almost completely evaporated, it was quietly dropped.

I was content to let it go. The ideas had been practical. I had made a solar house which had kept itself warm from early February to late November 1977. The concept – of using sunlight instead of burning up the fuel – was valid and, in real terms, globally important. It still is, but for now, in a world ruled by convenience and profit, it can only hope for praise, not action. Maybe one day, in the face of some yet-to-be-recognized imperatives, somebody will see the necessity and simply invent it over again – goodness knows it's simple enough!

I hope they will, and good luck to them.

14

LOOKING INWARDS

I. Prue.

Prue was not irked by my enthusiasm for solar energy. It's true she was a bit put out when, at the beginning of 1974, I made off with our only hot-water bottle and cut it up to make a measured-flow bellows to pump air through a plastic box in the garden, but the hot air duct in the solar house was marvellous for drying things and on the whole she felt it was a change for the better after my entanglement with non-politics. At least I wasn't getting into a lather and making an exhibition of myself.

That is not to say that Prue was particularly interested in what I was doing. She wasn't, but that was fine with me because she had plenty of interests and purposes of her own. She was an Elder and Overseer of the Society of Friends (Quakers). She also helped to run the International Club, the Cyrenians, the Council for the

Advancement of State Education, the Local Government Liberal Association and the house, as well as going to art, yoga and Spanish classes.

The house was rather empty. My stepchildren had flown. Kevan Myers, the eldest, was now in India, walking the hippie trail, Kerris was still in Australia, where she was to become a television producer, and Krispian was at university in Norwich reading American Studies.

In 1972, when they were thirteen years old, we had sent our twins, Simon and Stephen, to a Quaker boarding school. We had done this because they had ceased to be children and part of a pack, and had become leggy boys with quite distinct personalities, and we felt it was time for them to lead individual lives. The Quaker Headmaster had given us a solemn undertaking that Simon and Stephen would be recognized and treated respectfully as separate individuals, not indistinguishable identical twins as had so often happened in the past. So, with their approval, Prue and I decided to let them go there.

Now they had suddenly become ardently sartorial. With their hair bobbed, they wore shirts with very long pointed collars, tight jackets, strangely flared trousers and massive platform shoes that looked like leather buns. To our eyes the effect was more comical than elegant but, for the twins, conforming to the dernier cri of fashion was, apparently, utterly crucial to their social standing. We found it all a bit incongruous to the Quaker principle of simplicity and said so. The school found our comments meaningful, but did no more than join us in deploring the trend. It also found meaningful the fact that no serious attempts to distinguish between Simon and Stephen seemed to have been made. '*Mea culpa*,' sighed the Principal, smiling indulgently.

So all we had left of the tribe was Daniel, who was still at the local school contemplating the eleven-plus examinations, a black Labrador named Maud and a visiting cat called Woodie. Even so the house seemed to be quite busy, with people coming and going and things to do and plan all the time. Over the years we had co-opted part-time members into the family. Apart from Fiona, who had been a member for years, Prue and I were always happy to see

Dominique, who was French and had once been Kevan's girlfriend. From Australia, Kerris sent us a pair of star-crossed lovers who were fleeing from the oppressive conventionality of suburban Sydney.

Our lives just moved along, chaotically but contentedly, on quite a broad front.

And like that, I assumed, it would continue. And perhaps it would have done if Prue hadn't come to me one morning and said: 'None of it is any good.'

'None of what?' I asked.

'None of any of it. Nothing is any good.'

I looked at her eyes. They were different from usual but I couldn't say in what way. They looked heavy and dark, like dates.

'What has happened?' I asked.

'Nothing has happened. Everything is changed.'

'Changed?' I asked

'Yes ... no. Don't question me. I don't know. Something has fallen on me. On my head and neck, it's heavy and everything is going wrong and it's all my fault.'

'What fell on you? ... Was it some sort of worry?'

Prue took a long time to answer that. Then she said: 'That and blame and uselessness. I am useless. It has all been useless.'

'That's ridiculous.'

'I don't know what to do. Tell me what to do.'

'Well, you could put out the things for breakfast,' I said, rather crossly.

Very carefully, thinking very hard, Prue put out the mugs and plates, the marmalade and muesli.

'Is that all right?' she asked.

'I expect so,' I replied, looking the other way.

'No! Say!' she snapped.

'Yes, it's fine,' I said. But the penny had begun to drop. 'That's absolutely OK. Could you bring me an apple and an orange so I can cut them up?'

She brought them at once. 'Could I make the tea?' she asked.

'Yes. That's a good idea.'

She made the tea and we sat together to eat our ordinary breakfast.

'What are you doing today?' I asked.

'Oh God . . .' she muttered, and crouched down.

'Let's make a list,' I suggested.

We made a list and looked at it. We discussed it and agreed that everything seemed possible.

'Don't try to remember it all. Take the list and do the things one at a time.'

Without another word she left the table and went away. I sat there, forcing down my anger. Was it anger or violent impatience? Whatever it was I knew it was completely out of place, but even so it was scudding around inside me. I think it was probably fear. I didn't know what was going on. I didn't understand. This was not Prue.

Then I heard the Mini start up and I suddenly wondered whether she ought to be driving. Too late, she was out of the gate and heading into Whitstable.

When she returned several hours later Prue was still in darkness but slightly proud because she had done everything on the list and, better still, she had been cheerful at people.

'Nobody noticed,' she said. 'I can do things, but you must tell me.'

'OK,' I said.

So that became the pattern we followed.

Later, because Prue had refused to do so, I went to see our doctor, Dennis, about her condition.

'Depression,' he said. 'Probably endogenous.'

'So what do we do about it?'

'Just what you are doing – live through it.'

'Is that all?'

'Get her to come and see me.'

Prue still wouldn't agree to see the doctor, so we pottered on until, quite soon, it was time to go to Wales. There she found life much easier to cope with and we all had quite a peaceful holiday. I felt rather nervous about what her state of mind would be after we got back to Red Lion House, but I needn't have worried. By some miracle all her sadness and doubt had blown away and she sang continuously under her breath. She upbraided me roundly for being a sluggard and a kill-joy and immediately began to repaint the bedroom, starting in the bottom left-hand corner.

'Fetch me more paint,' she called.

'What colour?'

'This colour, you fool.'

'What sort of paint? Oil or emulsion? Undercoat or gloss?'

'Oh, paint! Just paint! Fetch it!'

On the way to the paint shop I called into the surgery. Dennis was there. I told him what was happening.

'Oh, she's just manic,' he said. 'Endogenous *manic*-depression. It's quite common. The mood tends to go down fairly slowly over a period of weeks and then suddenly it shoots up into mania.'

'What do I do?'

'Same as before. Live through it. Ask her to come and see me.'

'I'll ask her.'

Prue had no time to waste on seeing doctors. She had lots of more important things to do. She asked me what the hell I was doing shopping when I should be working on films. I reminded her that I hadn't any films to make at the moment and with great difficulty managed to stop her ringing the BBC in order to tell them to commission more films at once. Then I moved the furniture out of the bedroom so that she could get at the walls with her paintbrush.

After a few days the ebullience seemed to wane. I was relieved to see the wild flights of fancy being forgotten but I dreaded the thought of the depression coming back. In fact it didn't come back, or rather it did so slowly enough for us to adjust our way of life to it. We did this mainly by sharing jobs – so that when there was cooking to do one of us would cut up and the other cook. This was a very companionable activity, which I enjoyed a lot. It brought us close together and while we were doing it she was sometimes able to laugh. It didn't drive away the depression but it meant she could take part in life, and that would quieten her spirit.

Prue's confidence was at its lowest in January 1975, when she was due to fly to India. There she had arranged to stay, or rather walk, with Kevan for some weeks and then fly on to Western Australia to visit Kerris. This project, which she had earlier anticipated with great eagerness, had now become an impossible task, one so full of inevitable disasters that she couldn't even think of attempting it. I remember telling her that she was going to India even if I had to bring the Jumbo jet round to the front door, because I was sure that once she reached India she would be all right.

And so it was. The next day I received a telegram:

'ARRIVED SAFELY SANE LOVE PRUE'

Prue's time in India was glorious. I read about it when the letters began to arrive but in my bones I had felt it happening from the moment her telegram came. The marvels and pities of India touched her and greeted her with joy and as she rode in an ancient bus painted with brightly coloured gods and loaded with laughing people and their livestock, her heart sang.

By 1975 the hippie caste was well established in India and Kevan knew the rules and social observances – which side of the fire to sit and how to greet the Swami. He also knew the walks and was able to take Prue to see palaces with walls of air and palaces carved from the solid rock, and show her decorated elephants. They played Frisbee with a holy man and met a beggar who, being a holy beggar, gave them small bread rolls and honey, and recited the poem 'Twinkle twinkle little star' to them.

When they walked in the hills together, word had gone before and people came from their houses to smile at her, saying: 'Look! Here is the mother. Look! Here is the one who walks with his mother.' Perhaps this was notable because in those days most of the hippies were young, and older persons, especially parents, were rare. Prue, at fifty-three, was definitely old by Indian standards but she walked and laughed like a girl. It was a great wonder, and she loved it.

*

As I sensed Prue's happiness in India, a cloud was lifted from me and I became full of life. Daniel and I bought ourselves a colour TV and organized our time very agreeably.

That was all very well but in 1975, nearly a year after finishing the *Bagpuss* films, I still hadn't thought of any new ones. It was time to pay attention to earning our living.

I mentally summoned my creative Muse and had a few strong words with her, telling her in no uncertain terms to come up with a brand-new film series of astonishing novelty and genius.

Her reply was equally forthright: 'I have made you something like twelve complete worlds, all of them real and fully conceived down to the last nut and bolt, truck, shovel, sword, helmet and flipper. Barring miracles, mate, that is your lot.'

Monica Sims, the Head of Children's Television at the BBC, chose that moment to ring me and enquire lightly about the next film series we were going to offer her. I went to see her, rather shamefaced, to confess that as far as I could see there wasn't one. Slightly to my surprise she seemed almost pleased to hear it. She told me that what the BBC wanted, and had wanted for years, was *Ivor the Engine*. She didn't just want brand-new films. If I could make them again from scratch in colour, she would be delighted to have all the old black and white films, as well as any new ones I could think of.

This was an absolutely enormous relief – almost like a reprieve. The only problem was that I would have to locate and buy back the rights to the original *Ivor the Engine* films.

I managed to track down a firm called Rediffusion Holdings Ltd. which, I discovered, held these rights. They were delighted to hear that Ivor might one day be resurrected and insisted on giving me back all the rights, at once, for nothing.

I was very moved by this piece of unexpected generosity and, full of enthusiasm, set to and rewrote the films. Once again I asked Olwen Griffiths to join me in reading the voices. She introduced me to Tony Jackson for the other male voices and the three of us settled down to record the voice-tracks for the first batch of twenty films.

Tony is an absolutely first-rate actor, with a wide command

of voices. He had an immediate rapport with the inhabitants of Llaniog and brought them to life most accurately and hilariously. We spent some very happy days at the recording studios and I came away delighted with the results.

So, with the next couple of years' filming lined up and ready to go, I went to collect Prue from the airport.

II. Time Off.

Do you remember the summer of 1976? It was hot. It was so hot and dry that the top leaves of the trees shrivelled and the high branches began to droop.

On the afternoon of the first of September I was alone, driving back from Wales in my new 2CV motor car. In truth I was far from alone; several thousand other people were with me, sitting in their boiling vehicles on the arterial road at Chiswick, on the way into London. The whole traffic jam shimmered in the heat as the merciless sun beat down on it. This was not the heat of England, this was of the Sahara. There was no breath of wind. The air we had to breathe was so hot and dry and overused that I had really begun to wonder whether it was still serviceable. Certainly on that stretch of traffic jam this was a serious question because, for some reason, people were keeping their car engines running.

As I sat there sweating I dreamed of walking to a gate in a high brick wall, opening it and finding myself in some magic garden of deep shade, where the air was cool and the only sound to be heard would be birdsong and the gentle rippling of water.

So, not wasting any more time on idle conjecture, I drove my car up on to the grass verge, got out, locked it and walked over to an open gate in the high wall beside the road.

I went through the gate into a garden of deep shade, where the air was cool under a grove of immense trees overhanging a dark, formal pool on which birds were singing, or rather quacking. This garden could not be magic but it was, without doubt, mythical, for, on a grassy mound, amid the dark greenery surrounding a tiny perfect Greek temple, I caught glimpses of nymphs and satyrs, posing and capering on their plinths. That they were made of stone did not detract from their beauty any more than the sign beside me, warning that my dogs must be kept under control, did anything to diminish my delight at this extraordinary escape from reality.

I walked across to a gravel path and saw, down an avenue of statues, a perfect Palladian villa, where a man in a peaked cap was slowly issuing tickets to people sitting in deck chairs. To the right of the villa I saw a long ornamental lake, like a reach of some great imaginary river, spreading across the green. In fact it *was* the reach of some great river because these were the gardens of Chiswick House, where the ornamental lake is fed with water through a conduit from the River Thames. And the water was indeed spreading coolly across the green because on that day the Thames' tide was exceptionally high and its water was flooding back into the lake.

The gravel on which I was standing was scorching hot, blazing the sun's heat back up at me like a fire. My shirt was sticking to my back and through its thatch of hair the top of my head was beginning to cook. There was only one thing to do, only one place to be.

I took off my shoes and socks, rolled up my trousers and picked up a deckchair. Then, like a stout heron, I stepped delicately into the water and, feeling the blades of grass with my wet toes, walked across the deliciously flooded lawn until I came to a place where the water lay about four inches deep and the trees overhead arched their branches like the nave of a green cathedral. There I set up my chair, sat myself carefully down, looked around and saw that it was good.

It was more than good, it was cheap. The man in the peaked cap had been watching me balefully as he pondered his duty, which was of course to walk on the water to my side and claim twenty pence for the use of the chair. Then he must have come to a decision, because he waved a hand to me and turned away. I was excused the fee. Not that I would have grudged it, because it was clear to me that I had come to the chosen place. It was for this day that the gardens had been laid out. It was for this day that the great trees had grown and spread their leaves. It was to cool my ankles on this God-given day that the long lake had been dug with such labour, that the River Thames had chosen its tides. To have the honour to take part in its culmination was a privilege I did not deserve but of which I was deeply appreciative. I joined my hands behind my head and settled down for a long cool think.

This was a time out of life so I could let my mind wander away from immediate concerns. I decided it would be a good moment to take stock of my life, so I called up the memory of my parents' friend, the artist Stella Bowen, delivering her stern injunction as I sat in her studio holding the rabbit, in ... when would it have been? ... about 1942. She had said: 'You'd better make up your mind what you're going to *be*. If you fritter away your life on fancies you'll end up being a player at all trades and master of none!'

Now, thirty-four years later, I could see that I had indeed done quite a lot of frittering. To that extent her prophecy had come to pass, and I certainly hadn't managed to *be* anything. I had often been able to say that I was *doing* something – display-making, fabric-dyeing, photographing, solar-consulting, stage-managing, etc., etc. – you name it, I had had a go at it. But as for *being* something ... that was different. If I had taken up a career and had made myself a place in society, it might have given me more confidence. I could then have said: 'Speaking as a bookmaker (or a barrister, or a bishop) ...' The identification would have given my utterances substance and respectability, even perhaps dignity. All I could say was: 'Speaking as a person ...' or at bad times: 'Speaking as a nobody ...'

Did I mind that?

Well, no. Come to think of it I was happy with it, partly because it was simply true, and partly because if I had had the trappings of an image to carry about, my imagination would have been confined to its boundaries. I mightn't have been able to slope off into unseemly projects, mightn't have been able to travel light and fast, mightn't have been able to take my heart with me.

As for 'being master of a trade ...'? I had mastered a few procedures. During what I had thought of as the wasted years of frittering I had picked up experience and skills. I had learned to think from, and then to work from, first principles. I had learned to see a situation as it was and how to look closely and persistently for ways to do things that needed to be done. I had learned not to expect things and, above all, I had found the courage to get off my butt and have a go. That had been a rigorous apprenticeship.

So when, quite by chance, I had seen, as the solution to a problem with magnets, the idea of making small films, I was able to work it out and have a go at it. But I know I wouldn't have carried it off, indeed I wouldn't have dared to try, if I hadn't already had that training, if I hadn't worked for and earned an MA in both Pig-headed Self-reliance and Applied Improvisation.

So that injunction which had been haunting me through the years had been a nonsense. I was certainly not a master of the Art of Animation. Lots of people, from Walt Disney down, produced better animation than I did, but none of them could match my speed and economy. What I was master of was the Art of making small films at a price that would give us a good life – and, dammit, that would do.

My mind slipped away from wrangling with the long-dead artist. Life had been good, the day was cooler now and there were more recent, happier memories to enjoy.

I stretched out and thought of some.

There was this railway engine in Wales which Dan and I went to name. We wished luck to all who sailed in her and then Dan swung the bottle of brown ale to smash on her bows. It didn't smash, it dented the engine, so he had to do it again. The second time the bottle exploded like a hand-grenade but luckily Dan was at the far end of the rope. Later I had a chance to drive the engine. Have you ever driven a locomotive . . .?

'Excuse us,' said my ankles.

'What?' I sat up. I must have been asleep because the sun was low in the sky and the tide had ebbed away, leaving wet grass through which a cold draught was sneaking.

'We are cold,' they said.

'We are late,' I replied, and we hurried back to the car.

The arterial road was fairly busy but no longer jammed. When I got into the car I found the air inside stiflingly stale and hot, a legacy of the afternoon that we had dodged.

'Take us home,' I said.

III. Procedures.

As I drove home the mood of self-satisfaction that I had felt in the park began to evaporate. I was a fool and my folly was dangerous. I was also fanciful and self-indulgent, not paying attention to the real problem in our lives, which was Prue's predicament. Her depression would fall in front of her like a black mirror. At its worst this would take her whole attention, reflecting only her guilt for what she saw as her wilful inadequacy, and blocking or colouring her view of everything else in life.

On the other hand, although they took away the despair, I found her sudden excursions into manic exuberance far more disturbing and difficult to deal with. Then a mirror was still there, still blocking her view of reality, but the reflection it showed her was mighty and full of driving confidence.

The first sign of this would be the singing under her breath. This would continue all day, through every moment when she wasn't actually speaking. For me it was sharply reminiscent of the imaginary guitar which my brother John used to play when he wanted it to be known that he wasn't interested in what I was saying to him. With Prue it was different, of course, because she didn't know she was doing it, but even so I found the sound unnerving, as it was almost always the precursor of some exciting but impossible project – about which I was going to have to be beastly and try to get her to see that it wasn't on. This was a Catch-22 situation in that when she was exuberant, Prue would have no truck with critical comment, brushing it aside either without attention or with anger. When she was depressed, any word of criticism would reduce her to complete despair and that, in love, I could not face. So it seemed there was no middle ground except, we found, in time. I gradually discovered that our salvation lay in forgetting, in my capacity not to hold on to or force issues, but to let time take things clear away, so that when the moment came to do so we could put our arms around each other and still be there.

The rest of 1976 and the beginning of 1977 turned out to be pretty ordinary, as ordinary went in our lives – we bought another house! Prue had been very fond of the tall house we had once had on the seafront at Whitstable, so she decided to sell the shares which her father had left her and buy another one two doors away in the same block. Her idea was to make a small income from letting the rooms to students. She also hoped that having some independent interest and responsibility might prove to be an antidote to her bouts of depression. In this she was mistaken. Letting lodgings turned out to be a commitment to on-going aggravation which, far from giving her satisfaction, left her either in limp cowering misery or fierce avenging wrath, according to her underlying state of mind.

In 1977 Prue decided to take up the promise of university education which the war had postponed thirty-eight years earlier. She enrolled at the new University of Kent at Canterbury as a mature student, to study Theology.

For some reason I found this move profoundly frightening. I can't say why. Indeed I had very little idea what Theology was likely to be about but, none the less, the prospect of her studying it filled me with dread. I could find no rational explanation for this feeling so I minded my own business.

Having finished the remakes of *Ivor the Engine*, I once again found myself sitting in front of a blank piece of paper. Once again I was rescued by a piece of good luck. Frank Muir, who, with his colleague Dennis Norden, had written many of the funniest and most original radio scripts in the last two or three decades, asked me to prepare a set of films based on his stories about a small Afghan hound called What-a-Mess – a very pleasant prospect!

Another pleasant prospect came a little later – *Ivor the Engine* was nominated for a BAFTA award. The award ceremony was to take place at a glittering banquet at the Wembley Conference Centre. I invited everybody connected with the films but unfortunately Prue wasn't well enough to come. She suggested that I should invite our old friend Margaret Polmear in her place.

In the event *Ivor the Engine* didn't win an award, but we all had a good party. After the banquet was over Margaret and I noticed a 'pop-disco' going on in one of the side-halls. We wandered into this darkened place and saw psychedelic spotlights roving across a mass of writhing, jigging dancers and felt the bass beat behind the agonized vocal thumping into our heads like a soft hammer.

We stood and watched, I an overweight boy and Margaret a tall beautiful woman, regal and full of fun – but both of us well into our fifties.

'This stuff makes me feel really old,' I said. 'I can't dance to that sort of music.'

'Nonsense,' said Margaret firmly. 'They just don't know what sort of dance it is . . . listen!'

I listened. To me the music seemed quite formless.

'That's a veleta!' cried Margaret. 'An old-fashioned waltz. Can't you pick up the beat – *TUM TUM-ti, tum* . . . ?'

'Yes, but it's a bit fast, isn't it?'

'That's all right! Come on!'

Margaret took my arm and we swung swiftly into the dance. Chanting '*TUM, TUM-ti, tum* . . *TUM, TUM-ti, tum* . . .' in time to the music, we sailed and swirled across the floor. The other dancers moved smartly aside to clear a path for us. Twice around the ballroom we made our majestic progress and the floor was ours alone.

'That'll do!' panted Margaret. 'We must stop before we drop.'

So we twirled, bowed and, laughing happily, left. Margaret Polmear was a truly glorious lady. Prue and I loved her most dearly.

But that was to be the end of fun for quite a time.

Early in 1978 Prue went to see the top Harley Street consultant for endogenous depression. He put her on to a new medication which, he said, would deal with all her symptoms. It dealt with some of them but its main effect was to exacerbate the almost constant slight diarrhoea that she had been suffering for two or three years as what was called a hysterical side-effect of her depression.

Then, at the beginning of March, she came to me after visiting the doctor.

She said: 'I'm sorry. I've got cancer.'

The surgeon, a Mr C., interviewed Prue and was quite light-hearted about her situation. He said there was a small tumour in her colon, but it was very treatable. The procedure would be routine. Taking out a section of bowel was a fairly major operation but quite run-of-the-mill.

Prue was called into hospital on the eleventh of March and the operation was carried out on the fifteenth. Prue came through it well and was in good spirits, though very weak.

My turn came while Prue was still in hospital. On the instructions of our GP I had to go for an inspection of my interior by barium X-ray. This revealed a small object about the size of a pea, swinging on what looked like a sort of thread attached to the wall of my colon. Mr C. told me it was a polyp. He said it wasn't, yet, malignant but all the same he would 'deal with it surgically'. It would be a minor procedure. The hospital would call me in when a bed became available.

On the twenty-sixth of March Prue came out of hospital. Mr C. told us that the operation had been very successful and it was now simply a matter of recuperation.

I would have liked to have taken Prue to Spain for a while to soak up the sun, but she wouldn't let me because I was liable to be called into hospital myself at any moment and, the NHS being what it was, one couldn't afford to miss one's place in the queue. If we had known how long we were going to have to wait, we could have gone to Australia!

15

THE WINDOW

I. Operations.

In 1978 the local hospital had a very sensible system for accommodating patients coming in for operations. They would ring up on the Thursday to tell you to be ready to go in on the Saturday, but they would also advise you to telephone the ward on Saturday morning just to make sure the bed was available. It usually wasn't and after half a dozen of these near-misses I was in a right state of nerves, and by the time, late in October, I heard that I really was going to be admitted, I was a jelly of apprehension.

Prue and I came trooping into the rather impersonal-looking ward. There were several other men there, in beds, but we avoided each other's eyes. The nurse suggested that I should take off my clothes, put on my pyjamas and get into bed. This seemed to be an odd thing to do in the middle of the afternoon, but I complied.

Prue went home. I sat up in bed and read a book, or tried to.

It was only a small non-malignant polyp in the colon, hardly larger than a pea. I had seen it on the X-ray fluoroscope. Mind you, as Mr C. the surgeon had explained, they would have to get to it, and that would entail what he called a laporotomy – but he hadn't seemed a bit worried about that.

I couldn't read, so I fished my briefcase out of the locker and tried to do some of the bits of work I had brought with me. There was absolutely nothing in there that wouldn't keep. Everybody had been alerted about the operation. All the deadlines had been open-ended. There was money in the bank ... etc. Everything could perfectly well wait until the larger anxiety had been dealt with and that anxiety was, for once, something that definitely did not call for any action on my part. With a certain feeling of relief I closed the briefcase and shoved it back into the locker.

I sat up and looked around. It occurred to me that being in hospital could become a bit boring. Perhaps I was in for a dull time. I had no idea that my time there would turn out to be absolutely extraordinary.

The chap in the bed opposite had had his operation and was due to leave in a day or two. He was looking well so I put on my dressing-gown and slippers and ambled over to have a chat with him. His name was Reg and by trade he was a master-baker. I had always wanted to know how to make bread, and once he sensed this he was happy to tell me all about his early apprenticeship. For my part, having nothing on my mind except the impending operation, I enjoyed this enormously.

Apart for the fact that I was given nothing to eat, the days passed very peacefully but I remember that, when the day of the operation came, my legs insisted on my getting out of bed and pacing up and down in the corridor outside the ward, in order to use up the nervous energy. The sister came out and laughed at me. She held me still by the arms and told me that she had had dozens of patients far worse than me in her charge and they were all well and away. So there was nothing to worry about. I agreed ... and added: 'But even so, if it's all the same to you, I'd like to go on pacing up and down for a bit.'

Time passed. Eventually I was ordered back to bed and given

an injection to sedate me. It didn't do that. I was wheeled into the operating theatre, feeling quite drunk. Mr C. and his team were there, very jolly and full of fun. Then ... time telescopes. There must have been darkness, I could sense that. Now there was pain and raging thirst. I was back in the ward with my belly wrapped up in sticking-plaster. Time telescopes again.

The surgeon's second-in-command, Mr H., appeared at the foot of the bed, surrounded by a group of young persons in white coats, student surgeons perhaps. He told me proudly that the operation had been very successful. They had found nothing there. There was no polyp. Wasn't that good news?

Well, no. It wasn't. 'Wait a minute,' I said. 'Does that mean it was all unnecessary?'

'There ... was ... no ... polyp,' he repeated, as if to a child.

I was confused. 'But I saw it! I saw it on the fluoroscope. The radiologist saw it too.'

'Oh, that was just photography – technical stuff. You wouldn't understand that.'

'I've been a photographer for twenty-five years.'

The surgeon waved airily. 'Very well, if you're the expert I'm sure you know best,' he said, and turned away.

'But I saw it,' I said, to his departing back. He waved again and went on walking away.

Then, apparently, something must have gone wrong. I was aware that people in white coats kept coming with stethoscopes to listen to my belly. I don't remember a lot but Mr C. himself appeared and light-heartedly told me that the gut system hadn't started up again. He told me he was going to, as he put it, unzip me and do it all again ... which I believe he did, that afternoon.

The next is darkness, pain and thirst, dreadful thirst and wild panicky anger. In a steel-barred cot-cage, tilted so that lights shone straight into my eyes, I fought a desperate battle with two nurse-like ogresses for the possession of a wet sponge. I lost and felt a sharp jab, then more darkness.

Then, suddenly, I opened my eyes and saw daylight. I was back in the ward. That was a blessed relief but I seemed to keep dipping out of consciousness, not into dream but into darkness.

A mixture of utter panic, made hopeless by total physical weakness occupied me. I was spread-eagled on some wet steep roof with my hands splayed out flat on the wet slates to try and stop myself slipping down and falling. The slightest movement and I would start to slip, so all the time my attention was racing from corner to corner of my body, checking and checking again.

Two nice child-nurses looked down on me and smiled. Then they fiddled with the drip that was piped into my neck. Apparently it wasn't dripping properly. 'Could I help them?' 'Certainly.' It seemed that the drip would only drip properly if I kept my head turned away to the left. 'Could I please do that?' 'Yes, yes of course.' They turned to go. One of them added: 'But keep an eye on it, would you? Let us know if it stops again.'

'Very dicey, these drips,' they said as they walked away.

The problem lay upon me. To see whether or not the drip was working I would have to turn my head away from the left. If I did that it would stop working. But I had to do so because if it didn't drip I wouldn't stay on the roof. I had to tell them, but I mustn't turn.

Looking back it seems such a trivial problem. I could have called out or something, but I was weak and all my energy was using itself in panic-racing.

I had finally failed. I couldn't do one simple thing to help, the one easy task I had said I would do. I was no use. It was my fault for pretending, for showing off. I had pretended to have a polyp. I had defied and contradicted the surgeon. I had made them operate all over again, I had fought the nurses and now ... the last bloody straw! I couldn't even perform the one simple task that would save my life. 'Typical! Once again Bloody Oliver has bitten off more than he can chew, only this time it's for real, and final!'

Blame and electric panic, black shame and despair kept swinging across and thudding into my limp body as if it was a punching bag. How long it went on I don't know, but eventually it was night-time and the rest of the ward was dim and settled. I knew at last that with my own hands I had hauled the stone across my own grave and that I was underneath it. My own voice sneered silently:

'You put it there. You lift it off.' There was no lifting it off. I was done for.

The light was bright. Sister stood in the middle of the ward looking slowly around at her patients. Then she was holding me in her arms like a baby. I was weeping and incoherent with confusion and shameful apology for something ... being a nuisance. A nuisance about something ... the drip, yes. She held me and heard me. I had her whole attention and knew that I could have it for as long as I needed it. The drip was not important and it had been working. It had been regularly checked. 'There is nothing,' she said, holding me very tight, 'there is nothing, nothing, nothing, that *you* have to do about anything, except just be there and let us look after you. That is not being a nuisance because looking after you is what we are here for, and we like doing it.' Then she laid me gently on to the pillow and went on with her rounds. Nurses came and washed me, smoothed me, tidied me up. Perhaps, if I kept very still, I would not slip off the roof.

Two tall young men in white coats, New Zealanders I think, came to tell me that at the second operation they had found the polyp and had taken it away. They had used a new, highly technical device, rather like a snake with a television-camera in its nose. Amazing! I was pleased for them but I rather hoped they would go away soon. I couldn't hold my attention to them.

Time telescopes again. Was it the same day or the next? I had lain there while my eyes walked the landscapes of the mouldings on the ceiling and I had kept very still, my mind still clinging to the slippery roof, hoping against hope that I would not slip into oblivion.

It was early morning. From my bed I could see a small triangular section of glass at the top corner of the main window. It was lit by the pale purplish light of dawn. I had seen the light of dawn many times but there was something about it today, as if I was seeing it for the first time. I turned my head towards to the ward and there, implicit, was the silent roar of pain, panic and terror.

I turned my head back to the light. What was there about that light? I saw it as it was, part of the chilly November morning outside, just light, but it reminded me ... no, I recognized in it, a beauty. Cold it was, like an icicle, but all beauty, a single clear essence, untouched by detail. I can feel it now, as I write, cold as the frost on heather where the morning sun, creeping down the hillside, touches it with sunlight and turns it into dew.

I turned my head back to the ward again. Panic surged in.

I turned to the window. There it was, strong as ever, cold, clear, breathtakingly calm and beautiful. It was no passing glimpse, it was steady as a lamp post. All time stood still there. I could lie for ever and for ever I would be still.

I asked: 'Is this death?'

I could ask the question so it seemed it wasn't.

Day came. People were busy. Prue turned up with clean pyjamas. She saw me and said: 'Oh, you are upset, my darling.'

'Oh yes, I am upset! Please, please, let me be upset. Put your silly head close to mine and hear what I have to say. It is important. Listen!'

Words came: gibberish almost, dragged from under scraps of sobs ... 'A terrible beauty ... somewhere north of that dreadful hotel near Ross ... we will find it. There is a tree, sort of cone-shaped. We are there ... bare feet on cold grass but you are there, one day ... soon!'

These were the words of dreams through which I was groping for the feeling, trying to tell the huge future, the wide, rolling, clear-singing delight inherent in that cold simple light.

'Don't be upset!'

'Oh, yes! Please let me be upset at last!'

Close to her cheek my tears rolled down and made us damp. I was empty. Something was done.

Later still, maybe several days later, Mr C. himself came to see me. He looked puzzled. My charts, it seemed, were impeccable. 'Take out the pipes and feed him,' he commanded.

So, bit by bit, over the next few hours, the various pipes were taken out. I was allowed to drink. I was able to move about. I was almost whole, almost myself. I ate food. I tried standing up – and sat down again fast. I was very weak but all the time inside me I felt an excitement, not a taut violin-string excitement but an easy-going, calm looking-forwardness.

Iron-fingered physiotherapists pincered my chest and com-manded me to cough. I stood up and was able to take steps. I was full of something, expectancy perhaps, or was it just that I was looking forward to being better?

No, not just that. Something more ... something was new.

I walked very carefully to the big window at the end of the ward. Although the ward was full of people, I knew they were my friends. I knew I was with them but I was also alone, with a low growling of anticipation inside me.

As I reached the window and looked out, a vast wave of joy met me and bowled into me. It came, not through the usual channels of eye, brain, mind etc., but welled up in every part of me as a fountain-burst of delight ... hands, feet, ears and sewn-up belly!

It felt as if every cell in my body ran out into the streets of my blood and chased singing through my veins: 'Come on, fellows! The old bugger has let us out at last!'

And that was just my body.

My eyes?

They saw an ordinary windy day in November. The wind was scudding dead chestnut leaves across the roof of the maternity ward and slapping them on to the wet trunks of the trees. A few seagulls swooped and turned, fingering the wind. Heavy clouds were jostling in the sky. This was not a day one would take much notice of in the ordinary way, but I think I was seeing it all for the first time in my life. No more than that did I see, but what I saw there was so clear and complete, with a beauty so simple and essential, that I was poleaxed with amazement.

Now, hang on! This was not in the book. This was not anything I had ever experienced or expected. In my life beauty had lurked in the corner of the eye. Look straight at it and it is not there. Only the memory can hold it. (Let me go slowly now. Pray for my words because I am groping.) ... I was there for, maybe, five minutes, but those five minutes held eternity in every direction.

First there was this beauty. Everything I saw was no more than what it was, but, as it was, it possessed, was part of, a single clear essence of itself, and of everything else. (Oh dear, words!)

I felt a single flavour, I saw a single beauty which was the essence of what was there ... the seagullness of the seagulls, the flatness of the leaves, the shine of wet on the tree trunks ... these were among the multitude of joys that made up a whole joy that encompassed not only what I saw, but me and everything beyond it ... on, on and out of sight!

What hit me then was a realisation that this joy in life that drives through all things *is* the life that drives all things. I felt the huge engine, the driving, rolling river of life and death, of happiness and sadness, a river of which my dark fumbling life was only a tiny part, a leaf on the rapids, yet, in my realisation of it, I was part of the river itself, both a part of it and it a part of me.

Though I saw only what was there, that was what I saw in it, and I knew beyond doubt that this was not any sort of illusion. On the contrary, I knew that I was seeing clearly for the first time in my life ... seeing how things are.

And that was just my eyes!

My body was already singing, but my mind, the Head Office where nosy clerks add up doubts and consider reservations, was still trying to sort out what the blazes was going on. For a few seconds they held on to who I was and where I was, but the beauty was so clear, so complete and safe, and the relief so profound, that with an almost physical release I let go and gave myself entirely to the enjoyment, to the sheer delight of seeing.

The realisation that filled my mind and heart was not exactly a new revelation. It was more as if I had remembered something forgotten, or was finding something that had been lost, something I had known all along but in some fear or confusion had mislaid ... 'Of course! Yes. That is how things are. Oh that! Yes.'

I knew I had found the central truth that, without knowing it, my life had been spent seeking. I knew that in that realisation all happiness lies, all confirmation and all safety is found. That it had no words, that it was without a worked-out rationale was, in that huge beauty, quite irrelevant. But still, almost as a parting gift, the nosy clerks ran up a pattern of the glories. It went:

First there is this beauty which by some accident of fate you can now see. That beauty is the seeing of it. The seeing of it fills you with delight. That delight is love for it.

That which you are looking at you are loving with all your heart and yet that loving is not separate from what you are. You are the seeing and all you are doing is paying attention to what is in front of you now. The more carefully, the more clearly, the more fully you lay your mind and heart open to what you are seeing, the more you will appreciate, the more you are appreciating, the nature of what you see ... for that is what love is, just allowing yourself, or perhaps being allowed, to see. Love is a part of seeing and it is all happiness.

'And that!' laughed the nosy clerks, 'is your lot!' And, tossing aside their biros, they threw their arms around each other and ran out into the streets of my happiness.

Is that picture too far-fetched? Perhaps, but I know that there did come a moment when everything fell into place and the anxious, needling, self-conscious, wary 'self' that I carry about, stopped marking up, judging, evaluating, categorizing, and just switched off. It wasn't there. I wasn't there.

Well, no. I was there. I hadn't vanished. I had just stopped paying attention to myself. My self was there but I sensed that it had become complete. I had the feeling that it had always been trying to reach around to form a ring. Now that ring had clicked in. Now I was ready for use. Thin as paper, yet strong as steel, I was a fine ring through which all life roared like a blowlamp.

Of course I was there! I rejoiced in my own existence as I rejoiced in everything else I saw, but this self-awareness was something quite different from the self-consciousness of my ordinary times. This did not take my attention away from what I was seeing. This *was* the attention.

Then what happened?
Nothing, really. Something astonishing had happened inside my head, but there was absolutely no need to *do* anything about it. I remember flopping on to my bed, hoisting my happy legs up on to

the flat and lying there on the half-shell, still as sleep but marvellously awake in a wide golden lake of pure peace that stretched away in every direction.

That lake was time. Something had happened to time. It had stopped gibbering and jabbing at me. I was no longer tied to its tail like a tin can. It lay still and receptive all around me. Because the last vestige of the feeling that I should be anywhere other than exactly where I was had gone, I was able to enjoy and pay attention to what was here, now, without any hurry or sense of urgency. I had all the time in the world.

It would be some hours before anybody came visiting and I knew I was going to enjoy every moment of that time to the full. I had time for everything, time for everybody, time to walk through the garden of my mind, just enjoying it.

I remember turning to Jim in the next bed. I was lucky to have him for a companion. He was a quiet, worried man. We knew we were old friends the moment we met and we treated each other with the elaborate discourtesy that is the mark of true respect and affection.

I commanded him to tell me the story of his life, but slowly.

This, after some formal diffidence, he did. It was a saga that unfolded layer upon layer of amazing adventure and infamy in the far corners of the Empire.

How a Warrant Officer (Regular) came to be running two casinos and a cinema, while being blackmailed ever so politely by the High Commissioner of a central African state, is a tale that Kipling would have enjoyed. I enjoyed it. I lay in my lake and soaked it all up, occasionally darting in the odd question to get something clear.

The next few days were new to my life. Although the scene was always the same impersonal ward, every day had its own particular flavour. Even now, as I write, I have to keep reminding myself that each day, which feels so different in my memory, happened in exactly the same place. They each have a realness that is so individual and clear that it is almost a colour ... blue days, greenish days, golden days.

Everything I saw or did was a joy. Even pain, though painful, didn't matter. The sun shining on the chairs at the window end of the ward made a fairyland. I hoisted myself over there and sat in the sun. It seemed to bless me with a warmth that was love itself, something miraculous, the first sunlight I had ever really felt.

I remember thinking that it would be good to be old and be so peaceful. Friends might come and apologize for having left me for so long, and I would say: 'No, no. Time is my friend. We enjoy each other's company now. I am here and this is now. As here is here now and now is now here, I don't have to go running after either of them and they can't be left behind. We drift along together and among us time is still.'

The state of mind did not fade away. I did not fall back into my usual dubious self. I thought of the possibility but it seemed to be quite laughable. I saw myself as one sees a friend: warts and all. I remembered some of the legion of dreadful, shameful faux-pas that I had committed in my life. Usually these would wake me rigid with embarrassment . . . '*Eeeek!* Did I really say that!' . . . but now I laughed at them and at myself, not derisively but affectionately . . . 'The fool!' I had been forgiven.

Prue would come swinging in wearing her steel-worker's shirt and trousers, strong and sure as a thoroughbred racing camel. 'Style!' I said to myself. 'She has style!' and I held out my arms.

I mended miraculously fast. Incidentally, just to make sure, I asked Sister if there was anything in the drugs I was taking to bring about such a happiness. She laughed and said there wasn't. I was on one Valium a day just to stop me floating out through the window, but that was all . . . and why didn't I just enjoy being happy while I had the chance? Good advice!

Friends came, to bring me sympathy in my hours of suffering, and were assaulted by my friendliness. Lots of them came, far more than I expected or deserved, but never for a second was I anything but delighted to see them. Never once did I have to wonder what we were going to talk about. All I remember is the pleasure of seeing them. I seemed to have a stillness in my seeing which allowed me to look into people without intruding or disturbing, and then I seemed able to see out again, but through their eyes. It was as if I had no substance. I was a seeing, but my seeing lit them.

One of the effects of this single-mindedness was what seemed to be a marked improvement in the quality of my thinking, and also a very basic change in the *way* I was doing it. Certainly, at that time, and for quite a while afterwards, my mind was unexpectedly calm and confident. It was accurate, unbiased, unhurried and, quite simply, more efficient. I knew that while thinking I could set up literally any number of different qualifying considerations as side-circuits and be completely certain that, without my having to think about them again, if they became relevant they would punch themselves up.

I remember noticing how different that was from the way I usually thought. Usually I had to waste time dashing around on my mental scooter, checking and rechecking that everything I might be going to need was still there.

My mind also seemed to be capable of a different sort of thinking. This seems to have been more like a pondering, not a directed thought-process whose end is a conclusion, but a general contemplation of whole situations with the purpose of clarifying and relating observations. I was thinking in immensely broad terms whose forms were not words, categories or even conceived entities, but what seemed to be the essential defining flavours, the '*therenesses*' of the propositions and ideas that I was looking at – and both the thoughts and the thinking were parts of the same delight, a process for which I can only find one word: beauty!

Or, to put it simply, I was minding. I could appreciate the exact nature of whatever I was looking at with an emotional commitment that was very far from my usual grudging response. My personal views and opinions were just not entering into the perception, and yet, as a sort of side-effect, I had a far stronger sense of being alive and of belonging to life than I had ever had before.

II. Coming Home.

A word of advice: if ever you have a major abdominal operation, go home in an ambulance or hire a Rolls-Royce.

I had mended surprisingly fast and was soon well enough to leave hospital. Corseted like a duchess, dewy-eyed at parting from my friends, I was helped to the Mini and Prue drove me home. That five-mile journey from the local hospital to Red Lion House was excruciatingly painful. It felt as if I and my battered belly were being dragged over a rockery in a cardboard box.

We arrived home. The house was much as usual. The boys had slid the furniture about so that it blocked the way across the room. They were draped about on the chairs watching the television while the room slowly filled with smoke. Prue said she thought I should go straight on up to bed, but the smoke was really my responsibility. I had made the counterbalanced cowl over the fire-basket. The boys just hadn't adjusted it right. I reset it quite easily and then staggered up to bed. That incident may seem trivial but I think that was the moment I met myself again.

As I grew stronger I noticed that I was making a point of telling people about what had happened. I had been telling them about it all along, because I had been so full of happiness that anybody could have a slice. Now I noticed a subtle shift of purpose. Now I was talking about it in order to make sure it was still there. It was, but my old self was edging back. Like rats returning to a ship that didn't sink after all, the anxieties and urgencies of my ordinary life crept on board and began to gnaw.

Times were patchy. I could still lie flat on my bed, breathe out, smile and float away into clear certainty and calm. Kevan, who had been in India and had spent time in an *ashram*, came to see me. He was deeply delighted and glad for me, telling me that I had inadvertently fallen into the state of non-being that is the goal of spiritual development. We had a very happy time together, a time for which I was particularly grateful because I was beginning to need some reassurance. Prue had let it be known, in the nicest possible way, that she had heard quite enough about ecstasy – I had every sympathy with that. Other people were also reacting with less enthusiasm to my discourses, and I saw that I was becoming a bore. This thought chilled me and I began to feel guilty, as if I had lost, or let slip, something infinitely precious.

The doctor came and looked at me. He said how glad he was to see that I was beginning to be depressed at last. He informed me that a state of mild elation is quite usual after a serious operation, but if it persists it may require treatment. No doubt I would soon be normal again.

Thank you. Thank you very much. That was a shattering grief.

I duly fell in upon myself, into a standard depression, into self-obsession, self-pity, unconfidence, withdrawal, panic – all the usual stuff, just what the doctor had ordered.

And yet, somewhere inside me – and if anything it made me more angry with myself – I knew that none of this turmoil had anything to do with what I had seen. I knew that I had seen *how things are* and I knew that that is how they would still be if and when I would be able to see clearly again.

The doctor had been right. I did recover from the depression. I did become normal again. I was once again the old maverick, alone with his outlandish fancies but at the same time quite friendly and serviceable, busy doing whatever needed to be done.

For Prue, the lodging house at 8 Wavecrest continued to be a soap opera of disasters, but at least she was in good health and not too depressed. In fact she was full of fun and excitement because Kerris had come back from Australia in August to tell her that she was pregnant and that her baby was due in late March 1979. So Prue had already booked her flight for 5 March and was ticking off the days before she could take off.

Then the day came. We took her to the airport and launched her towards Australia and grandmotherhood.

As I watched Prue walk away I remember feeling deeply affectionate towards her. We had walked together through so much: through difficulties, disappointments, misunderstandings, incomprehensions, through poverty and plenty, through peevishness, boredom, exasperation, despair, laughter and long slabs of pure unremembered contentment, and underneath it all had lain the bedrock of our friendship, the shared foothold that took no account of passing change.

More recently, we had both been close to death. That would, in its time, bring change. But meanwhile I knew she would be safe and happy with Kerris and her friends in Australia, and I turned away, contented, to attend to my thoughts.

There was thinking to be done. I was still profoundly astonished by what had happened to me at the hospital window and I needed to think it through. For a time I had lived in a state of mind that was altogether unlike what I had hitherto regarded as being normal and ordinary. The experience had been astonishingly joyous and it seemed to me that if that sort of thing could happen as part of ordinary life, then ordinary life could well be something very different from what I had thought it was.

Some of the friends I spoke to about this were impatient with my desire to understand what had happened. They were adamant that it had not been part of 'ordinary' life, that what I had had was a *religious* experience, that by God's grace I had been granted a Revelation of His love. So why did I not just accept it and leave it at that?

Why not indeed? The joy that I had experienced was so overwhelming and so obviously a part of love that I had to open my heart to the possibility that it could in some degree have been divine.

I could also see that it had dealt very effectively with two human concerns that are usually thought of as being in the province of religion.

I had experienced forgiveness. This hadn't been so much a forgiveness of my sins as a realisation that the faults which I had felt to be sins were not in reality sins at all, but follies, often misplaced eagernesses. Also I knew that the forgiveness had not been given by some outside agency, it was I who had done the realising.

The other concern was immortality, the hope of the Life to Come. I had always held to an intellectual rationale about death; I could see that it was perfectly possible that I might not be anywhere at all after the end of my life. But, all the same, life would go on, other people would have the discourtesy to go on living after I was dead and I would be missing the fun.

Such thoughts are deeply uncomfortable, but all my life I had felt even more uncomfortable with the alternative that was being offered by the Church when I was young – that if I was very good, obedient and worshipful throughout my life I might, at some unspecified time after I was dead, be resurrected and allowed into Heaven. That had seemed, on the whole, to be so far-fetched as to be discountable.

Then this happened. I looked out of the window and felt the river of life. Everything, all the love that I had ever loved, all the love that had ever been loved, was there, flowing on in that river, and I knew that I was part of that river and that it was a part of me. And from that simple perception came a safety in which all joy and all knowledge were one and there was no more seeking to be done. I was a leaf on that river and there was no way I could ever wish it to stop on my account and there would be no death in my not being there. Others would feel the same joys in life that I had felt and in their feeling their lives would be just as real as mine had been. Nothing would have been changed, nothing lost.

The rationale that I had so glumly held to was not altered. It was just realised – made real. And, not to put too fine a point on it, that disposed of any ambitions for immortality that I might have been harbouring. I would quite like to have another glimpse of that moment before I die, that would make dying a part of the joy but, if not, it doesn't matter, it will always be there, a part of how things are, not of who I am.

During the weeks that followed I made a number of clumsy forays into religious-type conjecture, but I began to notice that the picture of a vision having been granted to me, personally, by a divine parental deity, was becoming incongruous. I think this was happening because the experience itself had radically changed my own internal situation. In the same way that a starving person, who has been dreaming longingly of food, once he is fed suddenly finds that he has no more hunger and therefore dreams no more, so I, who had lived in a shadow of anxiety in which the presence of God's continuing love might have been a source of comfort and reassurance, had suddenly come into a light in which all personal anxiety had dissolved, and with it had gone the separateness of my 'self'. So, ungracious as it may seem, I no longer felt the need of anything, even God's love, for myself, simply because at that moment there was no self there to need anything.

Let me say at once that I (being strictly agnostic) could never reject the possibility that my experience could have been divinely instigated. God may well move in mysterious and unexpected ways, possibly by exerting influence on the secretions of this chemical computer I call my mind – who can say?

But there was one thing I could say for sure, if only because it had been staring me in the face all along. This was that what came to me at the window was not a vision of something 'other', not part of a separate 'spiritual dimension'. Nothing extra had been added to what I was seeing. Quite the opposite – something had gone. Something had been wiped away, my window had been cleaned and I had seen no more than the glory of what had been there all the time.

III. Flights.

Prue returned, tanned and fit, full of happy stories of her time in Australia, of the good friends she had made there, and of the joys of having a granddaughter.

The photos of the infant Catherine were duly adored and in no time at all we were back into our ordinary lives, with Prue buzzing about in her Mini and me getting on with films and projects.

In due course Prue went for a check-up at Mr C.'s clinic. When she came back she said: 'I'm sorry. I've still got cancer.'

That which we had both feared, but had not spoken of for some months, had come to pass. Mr C. had told her that there was a recurrence on the suture-line and had announced that he was going to operate again immediately. This time, he said, she would end up with something called a colostomy, which, he added lightheartedly, would be no trouble. We both knew what a colostomy was – a plastic bag attached to her belly – and we weren't stupid enough to imagine it would be no trouble. However, we could cope with it.

Prue and I sat together and looked at the situation. Prue had the option of refusing another operation. This option had not been mentioned by the surgeon but, in theory at least, the decision was for her to make. She could either go along with the set medical procedure or stand against it, defy the doctors, and be allowed to die.

In the end Prue decided to let the procedure go ahead as announced. We waited, but Mr C.'s idea of 'operating immediately' turned out to be a bit slack. We had to wait several weeks.

Immediately after the operation Prue was very weak, but she was soon well enough for the specialist nurses to be able to teach her how to deal with the colostomy. Then, after about another week, she was well enough to walk along the corridor on my arm.

In the corridor we met a bright young man with a beard, one of Mr C.'s registrars. He had assisted at the operation and was delighted to see her looking so well.

'Excellent operation!' he said, beaming. 'Absolutely first-class.'

Thus reassured and light of heart, we returned to the ward. Prue went to her bed and I went to the sister's office to ask about something. The duty doctor was there and I told him how happy Prue and I were to hear that the operation had been such a success.

'Oh, yes,' he said. 'We only wish we could have got it all out.'

'You mean she still has cancer?'

'Oh, yes.'

'And she's going to bloody die!'

The doctor looked shocked. 'Well, if you must put it like that . . . yes.'

'So what was that bog-brush-faced tit doing telling us what an excellent operation it was?'

'It was an excellent operation, as operations go. It just wasn't completely successful, that's all.'

'So now, five minutes after that grinning oaf has allowed us to believe that everything is marvellous, I'm going to have to go and tell Prue that she is, after all, going to die.'

'It's just a bit of misunderstanding,' said the doctor, a shade impatiently.

I fell into a chair, my head reeling. The doctor left the room. One of the nurses, sensing an emergency, ran to fetch me a cup of tea.

I sat there, gripping the seat of the chair and glaring at the wall. Grief and rage were boiling inside me. After a while the doctor looked in again. 'Oh, you're still here,' he said.

'How can I?' I growled.

'Oh, I'll tell her if you don't want to,' he said, and trotted away.

When I had pulled myself together, I went to see Prue. She was sitting up in bed, weeping quietly. She took my hand and smiled.

'That was rotten for you,' she said. Then tears came and my anger blew away. There was no point in being angry.

A day or two later Prue was discharged. She had wanted to talk to Mr C. about her situation but she was told that Dr O'C. was now in charge of her treatment. He would be prescribing whatever was necessary and she could have a proper talk with him when she came in to see him the next day. In the event that didn't work out because Dr O'C. had a long queue of patients and only had time to mark crosses on her belly for radiotherapy. Prue asked him if they could have a talk about the future and he replied that an appointment had been made for her to have radiotherapy but if she decided she didn't want radiotherapy she didn't have to turn up. That was the talk.

Prue went for the radiotherapy the next day and it made her alarmingly sick, with agonizing pains which lasted for hours. She said she couldn't live with that.

That evening, it was the second of July 1979, Kerris phoned from Australia. She told Prue that there was a Dr Holt in Perth who had a new treatment for cancer tumours called 'Tronado'. She had spoken to him and he had said he thought he could treat her, but only if she came to Perth immediately, bringing the surgeon's notes.

I found Dr O'C.'s telephone number and told him about this. His reply was brief: 'If you can get to see Dr Holt in Perth, do so at once.'

The next forty-eight hours was a stampede. I bought flights for us, leaving at 9.30 a.m. on the fifth of July from Heathrow, wrote a letter to Mr C. asking for copies of his notes, rushed up to London to negotiate visas and renew my passport, wept when I discovered that the Passport Office couldn't do it in time and was reprieved when they discovered I was Noggin the Nog.

That was the good news. The bad news came the next evening when, after a day of rushing wildly about, packing, organizing, leaving messages and apologies – all the preparation for summary flight – a second-class letter came from Mr C.'s secretary, informing me that he had decided against Prue's travelling to Australia. I managed to find Mr C.'s telephone number and more or less ordered him to provide the notes. With little grace he authorized me to collect them from the hospital, which we did on our way to Wimbledon to stay the night with Prue's twin brother Cay and his wife Jeanne. Then, apart from leaving all our travel documents behind in their flat – luckily Jeanne had the presence of mind to come after us to Heathrow in a taxi – everything went fairly smoothly.

Once on the Jumbo jet and in the air, I crumpled up completely. But Prue, who had sprung into a full manic phase a day or two earlier, was full of energy, singing to herself and buttonholing the cabin staff for serious chats. I had never thought I would be glad to see her in that state, but I think she rode through those panic days on a bow-wave of indomitable exuberance, and for that mercy I shall always be profoundly grateful.

When Kerris and some of her friends met us at Perth airport and drove us out to her house in the suburb of Subiaco, Prue was in fine fettle, ready for a party, but I wasn't. I think Kerris must have noticed this because I found myself being politely led away by her friends Faith and Alan. Apparently I was to stay with them for a day or two. I didn't argue, I literally didn't know what time of day it was.

Faith was a very distinguished and successful Australian actress.

Alan, who was an academic at the University of Western Australia, was still very English after living in Western Australia for many years. I shall never forget their gentle unintrusive kindness and the sheer relief of being able to let go of my charge.

The next morning I walked out into a soft misty drizzle. Faith thought I was mad because July is their mid-winter, but by English standards the drizzle felt warm and welcoming, and I wandered, feeling very relaxed, along the wide suburban streets, marvelling at the amazing, strange flowers that grow in Australian gardens and the way the eucalyptus trees wear their smooth bark – hanging loosely about their trunks, like old socks.

When Alan came back that afternoon we went for a walk along the rocky edge of the Swan River estuary. Alan was a psychologist – not a practising psychotherapist but an academic. I mentioned to him my experience in hospital and, slightly to my surprise, he became intensely interested. This was due to the fact that 'the mind' was his subject, and he took a close professional interest in any reports or observations about its behaviour and capacities. He suggested, quite seriously, that as soon as possible I should try to find the time to write it all down.

This was very exciting but, happy though I was, and grateful to Faith and Alan for their hospitality and the much-needed respite that it had given me, this was not a time for writing. I had other, more urgent matters to attend to

The next day I went with Prue for her first interview with Dr Holt. He told us about the Tronado. This was essentially a very special sort of low-temperature microwave oven which fits around the patient and gently induces an exact amount of heat, enough to kill cancer cells but leave healthy cells unharmed.

Dr Holt didn't promise that the Tronado would *cure* Prue of cancer but he did say he thought it would take away the remaining growths and restore her to good health.

The Tronado treatment was not unpleasant but at first it didn't seem to be having any effect. Then, after a few weeks, her health began to improve. She became stronger by the day and quite soon the scans and X-rays showed no signs of any tumours at all. The treatment seemed to be working.

The course of treatment ended but Dr Holt suggested that Prue should stay on in Perth for a few weeks so that he could monitor her progress. Dan had flown out to join us. Stephen was already there, deeply involved in the fringe theatres. Kerris was now a television producer at the ABC, with a wide circle of friends and acquaintances, most of whom were actors and actresses who looked to her for work.

Time passed. Prue's emergency seemed to be over and she was feeling well, but I suddenly realised that I had run out of money. Although I had so far been able to do very little work on the films I was to make for him, I wired Frank Muir to ask for an advance. Frank instantly sent me £1,000, so we were solvent again, but even so I could see that it was time for me to go home and get on with some work.

So in the autumn of 1979 Daniel and I flew back to England, he to school and impending exams, I to make films and see to the future, whatever that was to be.

I brought with me some tapes of conversations with Dr Holt and details of the Tronado system. I had in mind to try and interest the UK medical establishment in the system, so I put together a presentation and took it to the top cancer research units.

My approaches were received with complete courtesy but no success. As far as the Tronado was concerned I was knocking at closed doors. That was furiously disappointing.

However, for me and Prue at least, the campaign did have one worthwhile side-effect. When Professor Peckham, of the Royal Marsden Hospital, heard about Prue's treatment he asked if she would consent to become his patient – almost as if she would be doing him a favour!

We were highly delighted and relieved, not only because we were both dreading the prospect of returning to our local hospital and the mercies of Mr C. and Dr O'C., but also because the Royal Marsden was the top cancer hospital in this part of the country and Professor Peckham was the top man in it. Whatever the final outcome would be, we could now feel sure that Prue would be receiving the best possible attention. We could do no better.

The Royal Marsden did a series of tests which indicated that as far as they could detect there was no sign of cancer in her body. However, just to be on the safe side, we were asked to come back every couple of months for a check-up.

Apart from these visits, each one of which was a journey into fear, Prue and I went on with our lives as usual. On top of all her other activities, Prue was now involved with looking after a hostel for Vietnamese boat-people near Maidstone, while I was mainly busy catching up with my film work. In her spare time Prue wrote essays on comparative religion for her University course, while I, in mine, tried to do as Alan had suggested, write down what had been happening to me.

IV. Agapé.

When Alan and I talked beside the Swan River in Australia, he had recognized my episode at the hospital window as being character-istic of phenomena known to psychologists as 'peak experiences'. He told me that research into these had revealed that such events were far more common than had been anticipated. Apparently something like thirty per cent of the population had similar experiences in their lives, but most of them were acutely diffident about talking or writing about something that was not only very precious to them but also completely out of the ordinary, and therefore very difficult to describe in words. As a result, he said, there was a shortage of first-hand evidence and consequently anything I could offer in that line would be welcome.

So I set to and started to try and put something together. I immediately found out that Alan had been quite right about how difficult it would be to find the right words to describe, in the linear mode of language, something that was not only completely unlike anything that had happened before but had also occurred as a single explosion of realisation.

I also came to understand the diffidence that people had felt about talking of something so precious and incongruous. Some of the perceptions I was coming to, although they were true and illuminating to myself, were so radical as to appear absurd, if not outrageous.

The first of these was that I don't exist.

That does sound a bit radical, I admit, but what I had realized was that the person I think I am, the self I am self-conscious of, has no actual, continuous existence. I live in this self-image, I work for it, serve it, have ambitions for it and, above all, eagerly seek approval and acceptance of it in the world and the seeking eyes of others. But it is, none the less, an illusion, an artefact of my anxiety which is being created and recreated from moment to moment as it sends up pictures of my potential inadequacy according to the degree of danger that it senses.

I'm sure this is perfectly ordinary, but self-consciousness also (by definition) diverts one's attention away from one's surroundings and in towards oneself. In so doing it acts like a sort of censor to the perceptions. At its worst, self-consciousness can make one idiotically embarrassed and overwrought or, in my case, grimly self-obsessed, miserable and oblivious to anything around me. At its best, in periods of intense concentration, I can become so unaware of myself that self-conscious is suspended. Then I am fully alive and my creative muse, or whatever it is, can just get on with its job. But that suspension is temporary. As soon as I look up worry clicks back. I think this happens because there is always a silting of anxiety lurking in one's mind, not enough to cause trouble but enough to cause some of one's appreciation to be reserved and one's attention to remain wary. I don't think there is anything wrong with that. It is the way thinking beings live and it encompasses a great range of happiness and delight as well as times of ordinary contentment.

I suspect that it is only in very exceptional circumstances, times when, perhaps by some brutality of fate, one's heart has been swept entirely clean of anxiety, that one may stumble inadvertently into a world which, although it is actually still the same one, seems, to one's eyes, to be utterly changed; a world in which one is both fully aware of oneself but at the same time completely given away to, and identified with, everything that one is seeing. That's what I meant when I said 'I don't exist'. Our language seems to have no way to express the perception that one might be a verb rather than a noun. What I am, what I exist *as*, is the attention. I am the process proceeding, the seeing and hearing of a time-river of perceptions which my mind-body is taking in as they pass and is being minutely changed from moment to moment by the seeing that is love. In that becoming is my life and the confirmation of my existence.

I finished the essays, showed them to a few friends, one of whom, an established scientist and a strict and particular atheist, said he thought they should be burned. I sent copies to Alan and asked him a crucial question – whether he thought that what had happened to me was peculiar to this particular eccentric person or was in some degree applicable to most people. He replied that he thought the latter was true. So I decided to offer the essays for publication as a book.

This was not a completely ridiculous idea. The 1970s was a great decade for those seeking fresh insights and new lifestyles. Zen Buddhism was very much in vogue and plenty of books on what might be called 'alternative philosophies' were being published. Most of these, it's true, originated in America but none the less I hoped there might be publishers in England who would find what I had written worthwhile bringing out.

I was wrong about that. They turned it down.

Publishers are not usually willing to give their reasons for rejecting work, but one was kind enough to tell me that because the book was difficult to categorize by way of subject, it would 'present marketing problems'.

A more robust rejection came from a fringe publisher specializing in books on 'self-fulfilment'. He just said the essays didn't deliver the goods. They lacked what he called 'spiritual inspirationality'. They did not provide, as he put it, a 'Do-it-Yourself Nirvana kit' – which was what he said the souls of his readers were seeking.

I couldn't argue with any of that. My essays were never intended to provide a recipe for bliss, salvation or self-fulfilment and they were definitely not a work of academic scholarship. They had simply reported a fortuitous change that had taken place in the way

I see things, and had discussed some of the implications that had arisen as a result. I had hoped that they might provide some food for thought. I was disappointed to find that none of the publishers shared that hope.

I shoved the manuscripts into a drawer.

To put away the essays was a disappointment, but probably a useful one. Not before time it reminded me of a truth which, in my exuberance, I had persistently overlooked. It is that you can tell people about a marvellous experience until the cows come home, but, unless they themselves happen to be in a state of mind which will allow them to empathize with it, they simply can't be expected to get the hand of it. At best, they might take an academic interest in the phenomenon. At worst they, quite understandably, could become thoroughly bored and irritated.

However, for myself, the situation was relatively simple. The episode had made a permanent difference to the way I saw myself, for which, in the years to come, I was to be grateful. And they had also brought some important and long-lasting changes in my feelings towards other people and my picture of the pattern of human life.

In the past I had gone along with the conventional view that people's actions and attitudes could be 'good' or 'bad', according to a balance between two separate opposing qualities or forces: *good* and *evil*.

I had now come to see that – in the same way that in physics there are not two opposing forces, *hot* and *cold*, but only one force, *heat*, and the absence of it (which we call *cold*) – there was, as a general rule, only one scale in human attitudes: *fear*, which is the blinder that closes our eyes to hurt and unleashes aggression, and the absence of it, *safety*, which can open our eyes to love, life and the possibility of change.

This meant that some of the actions and attitudes that I had thought of as morally 'bad' could well have been no more than a side-effect of fear, perhaps not of physical fear but of a more subtle fear of personal isolation – anxiety. So I was reminded, not for the first time, that the key to the clearing of perceptions and the consequent elimination of potential conflict lies in the giving and taking of the safety that mutual acceptance can bring.

Jesus Christ, for whose philosophy I have the greatest respect, put it more succinctly. He said: 'Love thy neighbour as thyself.'

I had always seen the truth of that injunction, but it had left me with a problem: where do I find, in myself, the *love* that I am to feel for the ugly sod? I can command myself to love him but, unfortunately, the only genuine emotion I feel is a sort of guilty inadequacy born of a muted exasperation with him (or her) for being so persistently and wilfully unlovable.

So love is not to be commanded. It is essentially an effect, the result of some prior reassurance. Consequently I can't expect myself to be able to feel genuine love until *after* I have received some confirmation of my own acceptedness, in fact until after I myself have received love and been made welcome by it.

That seemed like a ring with no starting-point and yet I was sure there must be some way into it, sure there was a simple possibility that I had missed.

The answer came to me in a slightly extraordinary manner, which I would like to tell you about.

It was early in 1979, Prue was still in Australia and I was staying in London. Sensing that the clarity I had felt was ebbing away, I had become frantically overwrought and impatient with myself, and was also having such frightening dreams that I was almost afraid to go to bed and be alone inside my head.

Then, one night, I dreamed that I had made a boat. I launched it and, somewhat unexpectedly, it floated. Still floating in it, I woke up clear-headed, single-minded and bursting with life and understanding. I ran to our friend Dommi and commanded her coffee and her attention.

My discourse was probably as confused as it was excited, I don't remember the words, but the gist of it was that somewhere inside myself I had been grappling with a problem that appeared to have no solution, but now at last I had managed to turn round and look at what I had been trying to solve it *with*!

I had been using the conventional idea of 'love' as the only possible starting-point and had been trying to engender it in myself.

That had been a nonsense! There was no need for me to *love* anybody! Indeed there was no need for me even to like them, no need to admire, condemn, compare or make any judgement of them at all! All I needed to do was see them, recognize their presence and make room for them.

Was that really all that was necessary?

Almost certainly not *all*, but it was a starting-point, and I had just seen, as clear as daylight, how it worked.

I knew, from myself, that most of the anxieties I feel are caused by a hunger for something – a simple *acceptance* of me as a person.

That acceptance may be something which I need. But it is also something which I can give, and give quite easily, because giving it only calls on me to *do* something. It doesn't call on me to *be* anything more than I am or to feel any emotions I don't feel. All I have to do is see you and greet the simple fact of your existence, acknowledging that it is the same as my existence, saluting the 'thereness' of you.

I can, by this expression of a perception that is so obvious to me, but which may be far from obvious to you, make room for you in the world, room enough for you to stand up and see how things are.

But then, if you accept my acceptance of you, I receive a greater gift because that is, in its turn, an acceptance of me, a confirmation of the reality of *my* existence. Then, as fear and hostility evaporate, one's attention turns away from oneself, life is good and one can do anything that needs to be done. 'Who one is' becomes irrelevant.

But isn't that what *love* is about?

Yes, of course, but, unlike what we call 'love', *acceptance* is not necessarily special, precious or particularly personal. It is just a part of ordinary seeing!

Later I came to see that the confusion probably arose from an old crudeness in our language. We tend to use one word, *love*, for a group of feelings for which the Greeks used at least three different words: *philos* – a particular devotion to something or somebody, *eros* – sexual attraction, and another word, *agapé*, which I would use in its oldest sense (*agapaō*: to treat with affection) for the attitude that I was trying to describe – friendly acceptance.

I see *agapé* as being simpler, more profound and much less disturbing than the emotion which we think of as 'love'. But I am sure it is the seed-bed in which love grows.

In my exuberance I wrote a poem about it. Here it is:

Agapé

I will not lumber you with love
nor climb on you to measure you for sins
nor wipe you over with forgivenesses
nor kick your shins.

I know your eyes do not see out of mine
nor are your tears the tears I shed
but I don't care,
for I will take your hand and make a place for you,
because you're there.

Not for some complicated ploy
of pity, piety or private greeds
but for an older, simpler joy that,
nothing wanting, nothing needs,
except to live.

For, as I see you feel the rain
and breathe the air,
so just to know the sun that shines on you
shines on me too
confirms the sunlight,
makes it sure,
tells us we live, are there,
that now will do,
that here is here,

and asks no more.

16

AFRICA AND AFTER

I. Elephant.

It's easy to find an elephant in England. You just go to the zoo, where, in London at least, they have their own ziggurat-type house and are, apparently, quite well disposed towards visitors. Elephants had always held a special place in Prue's heart and imagination, but the ones in the zoo did not quite fill it. She wanted to see a real one.

Finding an elephant in Africa was obviously going to be a more complicated project, but luck was on our side. Our dear friends Joyce and Alec had been posted to Nairobi where he held the position of Vice-president in charge of Africa for a multinational company. They made us a very generous offer: 'You find your way to our house and we'll set up the safari!' That sort of offer only comes once in a lifetime, so we didn't hesitate. We flew to Nairobi, taking Daniel and their son, James, with us.

In the event we had a marvellous holiday. We saw multitudes

of strange animals, passed lakes rimmed with millions of pink flamingos and travelled immense distances through magnificent countryside, but although we saw recently broken trees and dinner-plate footprints, both of which told of the passing of elephants, it was nearly a fortnight before, after much stalking, we were able to stop our Range-Rover silently in the middle of a dark wood.

The elephant was directly ahead, standing beside the track, looking at us with dark noncommittal eyes. As it stood it idly lifted pieces of the chocolate-coloured earth with its trunk and flicked them, with studied nonchalance, over its back.

There was no doubt in my mind that the elephant was waiting for us. We had badgered it and pestered it from all directions and now it had had enough. Alec stopped the car about thirty yards away and we sat and stared.

Apart from feeling seriously nervous I felt embarrassed and intrusive. This was the elephant's place, not mine. I had no business to be there. If it wanted to it could walk across and tip the Range-Rover over like a dinner table but, fortunately for us, at that moment, it was choosing not to do so.

I felt the presence of a thinking mind – not a set of reflex responses but a large intelligence, capable of slow, powerful elephant-type feelings, appreciations that were quite different from ours and perhaps more subtle, which its breed had developed during the millions and millions of years of complex evolution that had brought it to its present peculiar grandeur. I took out my camera and took a shaky picture of it through the windscreen.

'Right,' said Prue, 'that'll do.'

Alec slipped the car into reverse and, without revving the engine, backed quietly off and headed away. This time, as we slithered along the tracks, we kept catching sight of elephants.

At one point, as we turned a corner, a massive head appeared right beside the car and blasted a trumpet-call through the side window. That put the wind up us. And later, two or three times, we noticed elephants moving alongside us through clearings beside our track, almost as if they were escorting us out of their wood. I was happy to be obliging them.

Later I said to Prue: 'Have you seen your elephant?'

'Oh yes,' she replied, smiling. 'Yes, I have!' And she added: 'I can die now.'

'No, not yet,' I said, and turned aside. Tears were never far away.

II. Other Places.

After the warmth and brightness of Africa, England felt chill and sombre. Prue and I returned to Red Lion Cottage, which we had moved into, and took up the threads of our ordinary lives, I to finish the films for Frank Muir and start some *Noggin* films in colour which the BBC had asked for, and Prue to her various Quaker activities.

The year moved on. I had finished my films for Frank and was well into the *Noggin* films. Prue continued with her studies at university. At my sister-in-law Mary's request a kind policeman had climbed through the window of my aunt Nell's little flat in Hove and found her in her bed, quite dead, holding a cup of tea. Mary was very shaken indeed, but perhaps more by the suddenness of the discovery than the sad fact. If asked, I am sure Nell would have chosen just such a death.

Then, in the spring of 1981, I suddenly received an invitation to return to Australia in August to be Artist-in-Residence for six months at the Western Australian Institute of Technology, a large campus just outside Perth. This had come through Peter Efford, who worked there for the School of Art and Design. Prue and I had met him and his wife Georgia when we were in Perth in 1979, and had formed a happy friendship with them.

I was very flattered by the invitation but I felt a bit confused because I had no clear idea what being an Artist-in-Residence would entail. I also didn't feel that I should put such a distance between myself and Prue at this stage of her illness. So I was for turning the job down. Prue said she thought I should take it. In the end we decided to ask the advice of her consultant at the Royal Marsden.

The consultant was in no doubt about what was best to do.

'Go to Australia,' she said. 'Take Prue with you and let her have another course of the Tronado treatment with Dr Holt.'

'Oh, right-ho,' we said, and I took the job.

As I drove Kerris's old Datsun through the sunny, spacious suburbs of Perth and headed west towards the Western Australian Institute of Technology, the anxieties I had felt about taking up the post of Artist-in Residence came flooding back. I had written and asked, politely but persistently, what exactly I was coming there to do and had been answered, courteously and enthusiastically, with the assurance that I was exactly the sort of person they would want for the post.

As I turned into the hundred acre car park I met the same uncertainty as I had felt as I rode down to Dartington Hall School in 1939. And my reception turned out to be much the same as on that occasion – nobody noticed.

I walked in through what must have been one of the main gates and saw before me a broad, gently rising grassy hill, on the landscaped slopes of which were stacked a number of quite colossal buildings, reminiscent of the massive bunkers which the Germans built as municipal air-raid shelters during the war. Lots of brightly dressed people were there, walking, talking, going about their business. I consulted signposts and in due course found my way to the School of Art and Design, which was my destination.

There I met Peter Efford running along the corridor. He was obviously busy but he insisted on taking me for a cup of coffee and told me to make myself at home. 'You'll soon get into the swing of things,' he said.

I didn't seem to get into the swing of anything that day. I spent it walking about the campus, smiling at people and doing my best to look at ease.

The next morning Peter introduced me to the diploma students, half a dozen pleasant young people who, he said, were engaged in individual projects. He told them that I was Artist-in-Residence and they seemed pleased to hear it. I stood about for a while but, as they didn't seem to have any further use for me, I made my excuses and did some more walking about.

After a couple of days of this I cornered Peter and said I was sure there must be more to life than walking about and smiling. 'Of course!' he cried. 'You must have an office!' He found me an office, or rather half an office because I shared it with a chap who was in charge of the plumbing, but, Peter said, it would do as a base for operations.

I sat in the office and wondered what operations it might do as a base for. Suddenly Peter put his head round the door, his face wreathed in enthusiastic smiles, and said: 'Film would like you to come and see their presentation.' I jumped up. 'Lovely!' I said. 'What's it about?'

'They're very innovative,' said Peter, 'they do some really ground-breaking work. You may recognize the location. I believe it was filmed in London.'

Several people were sitting in the viewing-studio. We joined them, the lights went down and we watched the film, which was in black and white. Although the picture was lurching about because the camera was being hand-held, I could certainly recognize the first shot. It was taken from the end of a carriage in a moving tube train on, I think, the Piccadilly Line, with the camera pointing down the interior of the carriage, looking at the passengers. The shot was held for quite a long time, during which I noticed that the passengers were, understandably, becoming a bit embarrassed by the watching camera. I also noticed that the sound was completely out of synchronization, so that the noise of doors opening and the station announcements could be heard while the train was travelling, and while we were seeing the doors being opened, we heard the roaring of the train through the tunnel. I wondered what the next shot was going to be, in fact I was eagerly looking forward to it because I shared the embarrassment of the passengers. I really didn't want to go on staring at them in that intrusive way.

However, this was not to be. That shot continued for nearly half an hour and only ended when a grinning young man stepped into the carriage with a clapper-board and clapped it in front of the camera. The picture went black. The film was over.

There was some clapping from the audience and after a few

moments the same young man, still grinning, came over to us. I was so angry I could have hit him, but I didn't. I said: 'I think I must be a bit slow, but what was the film about?'

'Ah,' he said, conspiratorially, 'it was about *sound*.'

'Sound?'

'Yes! Sound has not received the recognition it deserves. Sound has always been regarded as the poor relation of the other components of film – pictures, lighting, production, etc. – those are the ones that take all the credit.'

'I see, but tell me something. This film, the film that you have made, is it intended to be watched by *people*?'

He looked at me blankly for a moment. Then he spoke quite sharply: 'It's like I said. We're trying to rectify an unfair situation. We are striking a blow on behalf of a neglected faculty. People have watched the film today. People will watch it again.' He turned on his heel and walked away.

'Terrific!' said Peter. 'The passion they have. It really gives one hope! Tell you what ... there's a show this afternoon by the Transcendental Realism group. They're a splinter from Film but they use projectors.'

'What? They use projectors instead of cameras?'

'Not exactly, I'm not sure. Shall we find out?'

'Yes, all right.'

'Exciting, isn't it!'

Transcendental Realism came about in four empty rooms in which four people carrying 8mm projectors on their shoulders were walking about projecting films of the interiors of other empty rooms on to the walls and into corners. As quite a number of people had come to the show, most of the images were being projected on to them rather than the walls so that they had to scuffle aside, doing their best to avoid tripping over the trailing cables. As this wasn't easy to do, the projected images tended to lurch about in a rather sea-sickly way and some bad feeling began to arise between the projectionists and their audience. I waited to see whether other transcendental aspects were going to be revealed, but when one of the projectionists fell over and pulled out his plug, so that the place was suddenly in blessed darkness, I slipped away, right away, out of the building, off the campus and back to the flat.

The next day I made an appointment to see Derek, the Director of the Centre for Communication and the Arts. He it was who had invited me. He could tell me what I was to do.

Derek told me how tremendously excited everybody was to know that I was there and what a privilege it was for the Institute to have me on the campus, but he brushed aside with polite laughter my idea that I should stoop to actually *doing* anything. It was enough for them that I should *be* Oliver Postgate. He was sure my very presence would prove to be an invaluable inspiration to the students.

I came away dazed with flattery but still none the wiser about my role. However, I think the penny must have dropped with Derek because members of the staff began to seek me out in order to ask intelligent questions in connection with my subject.

Some of these questions were quite baffling. I had no idea what I felt about the influence of Wladislaw Kotzk on the Trinka school of animation. Did I know where Smallfilms stood in the field of Animation? I didn't know where the field of Animation was, and I had no opinion about towards where the Art of Animation was progressing.

All this brought home to me with salutory force the fact that my sense of being a fraud was not just natural nervousness, it was well founded. There was another whole world out there, the world of study, a world in which people's reputations were being categorized in some hierarchy of comparison and esteem, a hierarchy administered by its priests, the critics and pundits, a hierarchy about which I knew absolutely nothing.

Nevertheless there was no doubt that this was the world into which I had been invited and which I was being paid to serve. But it was, as Derek had indicated, a world in which there was no call for any action – it was sufficient simply to *be*. Under my laurel wreath I could wear modesty as an ornament to my perfection and float about in a pool of veneration, just being *the* Oliver Postgate, the doyen of the Art of Animation. The idea was potty, particularly so because none of the students and very few of the staff had ever heard of me or seen my work. What the hell was I doing in this place?

A man in dungarees put his head round the door of my office. He said: 'Cup of tea in the basement.'

In the basement store-room, neatly cornered behind some folding screens and stacked equipment I found an old kitchen table covered with newspaper, four wooden chairs, and a gas ring. Frank came from Bristol and his colleague, Jan, was Dutch. They were the technicians.

Frank poured me a mug of tea.

'How're you feeling?' he asked.

'Totally buggered. Don't know whether I'm on my arse or my elbow!'

'Thought as much,' said Frank.

'Don't take it too seriously.' said Jan.

'Artist-in-Residence can be a dog's life,' said Frank. 'There was one who was a poet. Ended up standing by the door of the English Department shouting his poems at the people who came past.'

'How come?'

'Students didn't want to know.'

'The students? But didn't the School arrange lectures or anything?'

'That's not how it works here,' explained Jan. 'The curriculum is democratic. It's like a supermarket. The courses are named and their attractions are advertised and they're put up on the notice-boards along with the name of the lecturer who's taking them. Then the students can look them over and sign up for the ones they fancy. If you're a lecturer and not enough students sign up for your course, the course gets chopped and you get chopped with it.'

'So where do I fit into all this?'

Jan and Frank looked at each other.

'I don't think you do,' explained Jan. 'No Credits come from you because you're not a course. Your presence is an extra facility. I expect you'll find it advertised on the noticeboards and any student who wants to can come and make use of you.'

'Great! Perhaps they should wrap me in cling-film and set me out on a shelf.'

'I should say that's more or less what they have done.'

'That's nice.'

'I thought you'd like it,' said Frank.

'Thanks for the tea.'

'Any time. That's your mug.'

I was grateful for the company as well as the tea. I was at last beginning to get the hang of my situation and it made me feel slightly sick. I went back to my office.

Peter's smiling face came round the door. 'Coming to the pictures?' he asked, his eyes glowing.

Much as I loved Peter Efford, and he is one of the nicest men I have ever met, I couldn't quite manage to share his instant enthusiasms.

'Well . . . which pictures?' I asked, cautiously.

'Oh, a proper film – *Indiana Jones and the Temple of Doom*. It's on in town. I'm taking a group of second-year media students.'

'What? As part of their course?'

'Oh, yes. We have to keep up with the products of the commercial cinema, and Indiana Jones is a very significant work. It's got Harrison Ford in it.'

'Fine! I'm on.'

So we just went to the pictures. The students treated it as a hilarious outing and I found it a great relief to be able just to sit there and enjoy the film. Perhaps when it was over I would consider the question of whether and in what way Indiana Jones needed to be regarded as significant.

In the event that question came up sooner than expected. I felt a tap on my shoulder and one of the students leaned forward to whisper into my ear.

'Excuse me, can I ask you something?'

'Sure.'

'Is it good?'

'What?'

'The film . . . is it good?'

'Well . . . er, do you like it?'

'I don't know. I want to like it if it's good.'

'Then I expect it is good.'

'Right,' he said, and sat back, a satisfied customer.

Time passed. I did a lot more walking about and smiling but I didn't get to see the students' work until one day I was invited to attend a showing of one of the students' films.

This was a live film, not a cartoon, but it wasn't easy to follow because things didn't seem to have worked out very well for the producer. In fact the showing was accompanied by a detailed running-commentary describing the difficulties and failures which they had encountered.

I went to two other showings of students' films and was disturbed to find that each time the same thing happened. The films were muddled and the students gave running-commentaries of excuses.

Later I asked Jan: 'Do they really have such a terrible lot of difficulties?'

He said: 'They have difficulties, of course, but that's not what it's about. The disasters are a sort of insurance.'

'Insurance?'

'Yes.

'You mean they deliberately make the film badly?'

'Oh no, not deliberately. A disaster happens but I think the producer unconsciously welcomes it because it lets the film off the hook.'

'How do you mean?'

'It shows that the film itself doesn't really matter. It is just a sort of token of intent. What matters and is valuable is not what a thing *is*, but what it is *said to be*. Hours of conceptual discussion will have gone into that project and the student will have had to prepare a long and complicated spiel setting out its artistic purpose and significance. That is the work of art. And if the film itself can't be seen properly because the production didn't quite work out . . . well, that's a pity perhaps, but it can't be helped.'

'But that's absurd!'

'I thought you'd like it,' said Frank.

Perhaps, after a while, my lack of employment began to be noticed, because a couple of staff-members, people I had never met before, came by and invited me to join them at an informal seminar in one of the reception rooms. I was happy to accept the invitation and went along. Everybody helped themselves to canapés and glasses of wine – the Institute was always very generous in its hospitality – and we all sat down. In the silence I suddenly realised that everybody was looking at me.

'It *is* quite informal,' said one lady reassuringly.

'You mean you're waiting for *me* to say something.'

'Oh, yes. We're really looking forward to it.'

'But what do you want me to talk *about*?'

She waved her arms in wide, fulsome gestures: 'Oh, anything, anything, whatever you like!' she cried. 'That's up to *you*.'

'Oh.'

I should have done a runner but, perhaps because I felt myself to be under some sort of obligation, I didn't. I stood up and opened my mouth, but my mind was a complete blank.

To this day I remember nothing about that afternoon except a dreadful churning of confusion and panic.

Eventually I escaped and went back to my office. There I found a printed hand-bill on my desk. It advertised a film made by an Aboriginal group which was to be shown that evening. Pinned to it was a pencilled memo, apparently from the Director of the English Department.

'Oliver! Thought you might like to come to this. G.'

I remembered that when I had talked to Derek at the beginning of term he had told me how eager the English Department was to meet me and have the benefit of my attention. I had been vaguely waiting to hear from them but so far nothing had turned up. Perhaps this was it.

So that evening I drove back to the campus and made my way to the film and lecture theatre. The lights were on but the big auditorium was empty. I looked into the projection room and asked if this was right for the Aboriginal film.

'S'right!' said the projectionist.

I took a seat and, after a while, the lights went down and the show began. The film wasn't very comprehensible. It was a bit like a home movie that hadn't been cut. After about twenty minutes I got up and went round to the projection room.

'I think I've seen enough, thanks.'

'You the audience?'

'That's me.'

'Good on yer, sport,' he said and pulled a switch.

I drove home rather pensively. I decided that I could take a hint, but I wasn't quite sure what the hint was. Until then I had felt that the Institute's lack of attention had been fortuitous.

Now, however, the Institute had noticed my presence and had twice made use of me. Once it had assumed that I was available as an impromptu side-show, which was a bit crass, and once it had invited me to a film-show which absolutely nobody among the fourteen thousand inhabitants, including the person who had asked me to come, had had any intention of attending. That was contemptuous. I resolved that from that time forth I would be somewhat scanter of my presence.

I think I may have attended other happenings connected with the Institute, but I can't bring them to mind. The last clear memory I have is of attending a lecture on a subject rather intriguingly called Semiotics. The word meant something like 'the science of signalling', but the lecture wasn't about beacons or waving flags or traffic-lights, it was about the subtle way in which, the lecturer claimed, film directors deliberately choose and compose their shots and camera-movements in order to create particular atmospheres – sinisterness, impending danger, sexuality, and other less definable moods – and infiltrate them subliminally into the unconscious of the viewer. To illustrate this procedure he showed shots from Hollywood films. Each shot was examined and elaborate psychological motives imputed to its director.

The lecturer waxed eloquent about how essential it was to analyse the semiotics of any picture or film before one could hope to appreciate the motivation and purposes of the artist or director. He told us how vital it was for everybody to realise that not only a grasp of that discipline, but also the ability to put it into practice, was an absolutely essential prerequisite to any attempt to venture into visual communication technology, how ...

At this point I stood up.

The lecturer stopped. 'Yes?' he asked.

'May I please say something?'

'Er ... yes, I suppose so.'

I addressed my remarks to the audience. I was too angry to be sure exactly what I was saying but I think it went something like this: 'If there are any people here who have any ambition actually to make films or take part in the making of films, may I beg you, please, to be very wary indeed of the highly dubious procedures we have just been hearing about. I have been making films for over twenty years and I am quite certain that if I had allowed myself to become bogged down in the intellectual quagmire which our friend here has just been prescribing I would never have made anything worthwhile in my whole life, basically because it attempts to use the intellect to do something that is the business of the heart.

'I know how I choose the shots I take. I know how all the directors I have worked with chose their shots. They chose them because they *looked right*. What I am trying to say is that I am absolutely sure that to study and collect analyses and then attempt to fit them together and make them into a film would be the kiss of death. You can't reconstitute art from intellectual data. It is a part of love.'

My outburst was received in silence, which was finally broken by soft solo clapping from the lecturer.

'Spoken like a true Semiotist!' he said.

I went home. The outburst had surprised me as much as it had the audience. I realised that I hadn't so much been sounding off about semiotics – which is almost certainly a fairly harmless speculation, probably innocent of the charges I was making against it – as about the whole of my time at the Institute.

Up till then I had remained fairly docile. But, now that I had heard myself say it, I could see that '*trying to reconstitute art from intellectual data*' was a very fair description of what I had seen going on around me for the last four months.

However, I also had to accept the possibility that because I had never become fully involved with the Institute's work, my impressions might not have been typical. Consequently I felt it was part of my job to find out whether or not any of its members shared them. So I put together a carefully worded paper and sent a note to Derek asking if I might be allowed to deliver a short lecture one evening and perhaps follow it with an opportunity for questions and answers.

In reply I received a simple memo-slip to the effect that this was 'not thought to be appropriate'. So my period of engagement drew quietly to its close.

After term had ended and I had left the Institute I received a very appreciative and praiseful letter from Derek in which he said he thought I might not realise just how much I had contributed.

He could have been right about that.

III. Departures.

I don't think my impressions of life at the Institute were in any way false, but possibly my disenchantment with its unrealities was made more poignant by the realities that Prue and I were living with.

Perhaps the worst of these was the black jigsaw puzzle that presented itself each morning. First came the ordinary waking up. Then came the realisation of where I was. Close behind came the sense that something was dreadfully wrong. Numb with reluctance I would force myself to take up the black pieces and fit them together. Although nobody had yet said so, Prue and I both knew in our hearts that the Tronado treatment was not working. Scans and X-rays had indicated this. But could we be wrong about it? The final piece would click into place and be still. No. Prue is on her way to death. Then a small different thought would move in: this is another day. Perhaps it will be a good one, perhaps it won't, but either way it has to be lived.

Of course there were days that could only be bad. The treatment could make her feel weak and nauseous, and for that there was only bed, quiet and some pills. There were also days when a black desolation, quite different from her depression, would fill her heart. Then I could sense that she was out of my reach in some deep, old, not to be mentioned blame, for which she felt she was now paying the price. I can also remember one or two bursts of sudden rage. In one of these she threw her lunch at the wall because I was not her mother and what she wanted was her mother to be there and cook her a proper dinner, with brown gravy, and treacle pudding for afters. That shattered my composure and I fled to Peter Efford's office, where I sat, shaking uncontrollably, for what seemed like several hours. Peter took this in his stride, and so, in due course, did I. There was no issue to be settled, nothing to be explained. That evening I made a good dinner which Prue and I both enjoyed, even though there was no treacle pudding – which neither of us particularly liked anyway – and the incident was gone.

Prue and I rarely spoke of death, but I think our hearts must have understood that time was precious and needed to be enjoyed, because all our perceptions and appreciations seemed to be sharpened. The flavours were good and we were given many, so many, good days. Peter and Georgia Efford were unhesitatingly welcoming, so that when a good day came, Prue could simply announce that she would like to spend it in their rambling garden at Gooseberry Hill where Georgia grew twenty different sorts of mint. I would drive her over, plant her in a shady chaise-longue, and leave her, knowing that when I came back from my day at the Institute I would find her cool and content in their kindness, and we would spend a happy evening together, talking, drinking good wine and eating the most excellent food, Peter being a superb and dedicated cook.

For our wedding anniversary we bought a delicious, soft, light, blue and white dress with a belt of blue glass beads. Prue looked lovely as she twirled in front of the mirror, glowing with pleasure and laughing like a girl. Then, still laughing, she told me to be sure to give it to Carole after she was dead.

Later she fell into another bout of black despair, but this time she dealt with it by ceremoniously collecting up the papers of her Theology course and packing them away at the bottom of her suitcase. I think she put something else away with them. Perhaps it was something fairly simple, like her ambition to gain a BA from the University, or it may have been something more deep-rooted, like her lifelong association with the doctrine of original sin. I don't know but, whatever it was, her spirit became lighter and calmer and we sat together talking, quietly and easily, for several hours. We talked of the past and of my and our children's future, about her faith and my unfaith, about truth and hope, about our understandings and our misunderstandings, about our love, and we made between us a lasting peace.

Christmas came, a confusing time in which the thermometer rose to well over a hundred degrees Fahrenheit. I simply couldn't believe the heat, it seemed to blaze in from all directions. Nor could I believe in the tinselled snow or the plastic icicles in the shop windows. I saw Father Christmas, drunk and scarlet-faced, in full red gear with cotton-wool whiskers, come reeling down the street ringing his bell, his flip-flop sandals squelching into the melting tarmac of the road at each step.

After Christmas Prue spent a lot of time in bed. She was much weaker, and soon the doctors told us what we already suspected – that they could do no more for her than provide ever-stronger painkillers, and wait.

It was time to go home.

Once we were back in Red Lion Cottage and Prue was in her own bed, she rallied a lot. Mac, our GP, came to see her. She told him she was going to die soon and asked him for his best painkillers. Mac produced Fred, a new medical gadget which fed tiny amounts of morphia into her system. He looked me over and put me in charge of Fred. He also appointed me Keeper of the Medication Records.

For a while we put on a grand show. High on morphia, Prue held court from her bed while I ushered in a stream of friends, many of whom came soberly to bring her comfort in her darkest hour and left on a gale of laughter.

'I think you are ever so brave!' said one.

'Of course I am,' she replied, 'I've got no fucking alternative.'

At first Prue's energy had seemed inexhaustible but gradually it flagged until, on Mac's orders, I had to limit the flow of audiences. This I did, to a degree, but some of Prue's close friends, like Mary Hinshelwood, and Anne, the sister who had been in charge of the ward where I had had my operation some years earlier, continued to be welcome at any time because Prue didn't find their presence tiring, and their help and capacity to cope were invaluable.

Daniel and Simon were already with us and soon Stephen came back from his travels. They took the pandemonium in their stride. When the need arose they would look after Prue. They would clean and tidy her with fond affection and no sign of queasiness or melancholy, do what they could to make her comfortable and just get on with their lives. Their unobtrusive practicality was a great relief to us both.

The cancer followed its inevitable course and before long finding food that Prue could keep down became difficult. Then her exuberance could switch to anger. I recall that in the middle of one such outburst she suddenly stopped and looked at me.

'You're completely done for,' she said. 'Get in the professionals.'

So I engaged a regular supply of nurses who would come in and take over. We were glad of their help, which was very necessary, but they also jollied Prue along in a brisk, dismissive way that she found stifling and I found infuriating because, however ill she might have been, Prue was not stupid. So I was glad I was there, glad that I was able to hold her with my strong arms when the sickness tore at her as if to break her in pieces, that I was ready to take the anger and rejection as it welled up, to be winded by it of course, but still able to come back, so that when her arms reached out for me I would be there, to laugh or cry with her and give fate the Liverpool salute.

The rest of the family began to assemble. Kerris and her daughter Kitty flew in from Australia and Kevan turned up. By then Prue's energy was waning fast. A new nurse appeared. Her name was Pat and she was a specialist. Like the other nurses, she took charge, but she did so with a tender sureness that Prue and the rest of us found profoundly comforting. By now Prue was sleeping a lot of the time, but her waking time could easily turn into an ever-increasing frenzy from which the only escape would be sedation and more sleep.

Late on Thursday the twenty-fifth of March 1982 she suddenly sat up and said: 'Yes, but who is getting the lunch?'

I replied: 'I am, of course.'

'Oh, yes,' she said. 'Yes, of course, so you are, yes.'

She settled down on to her pillows and went back to sleep. At about ten o'clock the next morning, while we were all sitting around her bed, she stopped breathing.

'Whiskey,' said Pat. She went to the cupboard and poured out stiff doses. I sat with Prue for a few minutes longer. I had my eyes shut, I remember, as if I was trying to see into her darkness, but I soon began to feel *de trop*, like somebody who has stayed in a lift after it has reached its floor and the gates have been opened. So, rather gingerly, I undid my fingers, got up and walked out into the morning and the rest of my life.

And what a glorious spring morning it was, with clean new air and a perfect blue sky.

As we stood on the terrace in the sunshine Daniel noticed a commotion going on in the wood at the top of the field. A flock of small birds was harassing another, larger bird.

The bird rose from the trees and headed down across the field. As it passed over our heads the feathers of its face were shining in the sunshine, and we saw that it was a white owl. It circled the house once and then turned back towards the wood.

Seeing it reminded me that, many years before, Ray had told me the Greeks believed that the souls of the dead pass into the bodies of owls. 'Perhaps . . .?' I thought, but then I put the thought aside. I have always had every respect for the supernatural but never any wish to enquire into it.

IV. Rites.

My own first, overwhelming, reaction to Prue's death was a flood of blessed relief, relief that the unwinnable battle with so much bitter pain and hopelessness had ended, and had ended so gently.

I felt some pride too, in the knowledge that in the darkness of anger and despair, when blame, rejection, obstinacy and madness had been bashing between us, we had both held to the truth of our friendship and had known the other would not turn away – so there was no unfinished business, nothing left unsaid or unforgiven.

Now that time had ended for her, Prue was no longer trapped in the racked decrepitude of her last days. Now she was the whole of her time. She was the girl whose warmth, so many years ago, had been my passport to life, whose joy had been my joy and whose certainties had been my strength. She was the loving pivot at the centre of a rich rolling rumbustious family life, and she was the fighter who had defied the death sentence of the doctors and won from fate an extra three years of life. I was proud to have been with her.

We were all sad, in our fashions, but for me this was nothing like the raging regret that had torn through me – and Prue – when Daisy had committed suicide some years earlier. This sadness was quiet, and in it we were quiet together. In fact it felt as if Prue's love for us all had not gone but was still with us, like an affection in the air, lighting our feelings, dissolving antagonisms and drawing us together.

Prue had organized her funeral in great detail. There were to be no flowers and no ceremony, just a simple Quaker funeral – a Meeting for Worship. This can sometimes be completely silent, so, as many of those present would not be Quakers, she had chosen some short readings.

I'm afraid I disobeyed her in one respect. There was to be one flower, a single rose that I would place on the coffin before it was carried into the crematorium chapel.

We waited in the car park at the crematorium. The hearse

arrived, everybody was ushered in and I came forward and placed on the coffin, not the single rose but only its silver-paper wrapper – the rose must have fallen out somewhere.

The undertakers rose to the occasion. The bearers waited in the porch while I and their chief, in black tails and top hat, scuttled through the car park and found Prue's rose, damp and a bit crumpled.

I laid it in place and, chuckling decorously, the bearers carried her into the chapel.

The Meeting was quiet and full of thoughtful happiness. Kerris read a poem by Dylan Thomas: '... and death shall have no dominion', and Kevan read a piece from T. S. Eliot's *Four Quartets*, '... in the end is my beginning', which Prue had loved. As I was reading a piece that she had loved even more, Pat the nurse looked up and silently said: 'Prue, if you're watching, take a look at the undertaker's face!' The story I was reading was from *Winnie the Pooh* by A. A. Milne, 'Eeyore's Birthday', the one in which the donkey is given a 'useful pot' – and the undertaker had chosen that moment to put his head round the door in order to find out what was causing the unseemly mirth.

Once again my strongest memory is of the place. We trooped from the bleak impersonal chapel out on to a terrace, and there I saw a sweep of green lawn that led down to a broad vista of fields, woodlands and nesting farmhouses where a tracery of great trees was lit to glory by the hazy sun, and I was overwhelmed by the beauty of it; the peaceful grandeur of the English countryside that had been formed by centuries of summers and winters, of lives and deaths. That unleashed my tears, and, drunk with love and laughter, I put my arms around everybody and we all went home for a party.

A few days later, the children and I, still very much *en famille*, took Prue's ashes in a tin jar to the cottage in Wales and scattered them around her tree. This was a magnificent ash that stood by itself, looking down the valley which, ten years earlier, she had chosen, or perhaps recognized, as being the place where she would be happy.

There Kerris, rather diffidently I noticed, played Prue's last trump card – Easter eggs with small presents for us all. They had plotted this together a few days before she died. It was a lovely idea but, for some reason, I found it slightly unnerving.

We returned to Canterbury and went our ways – Kerris and Kitty to a round of visits before going back to Australia, Kevan to some excursion to do with the school where he was teaching, and Krispian back to Italy, I think. I can't remember exactly. Nor can I remember what the twins and Dan were doing. I know there were some films in the offing for me, but, before attending to them, I had to fly to Geneva.

17

DECADE OF DEMENTIA

I. The Unthinkable.

So why was I flying to Geneva so soon after Prue's death? The short answer was: because the Quakers in Geneva had invited me. But to explain why they had done this I have to go back to that morning in 1945 when Olga Wicks handed me the morning paper and said: 'We've dropped something nasty on Japan.'

I remember the thunderous mixture of emotions that came over me at that moment – horror mixed with an overwhelming pity, but tinged with something almost like relief: the thought that now at last the war which had taken so many millions of lives must end. And behind that came, more slowly, the seed of a deeper and longer-lasting dread. The realisation that the world was now a different place, that what had happened once could happen again, that Pandora's Box had been opened.

As I rode my rattletrap motorcycle along the quiet lanes of Essex, as I stooked the sheaves of wheat and led the strong brown horses in the harvest of that glowing summer, I couldn't tell myself that anything had changed. Life was going on as before, and it went on peacefully, from day to day, until gradually that dread faded into the back of my mind.

It stayed there, unnoticed, for many years, in fact through the main part of my life. I remember walking into Trafalgar Square on the fringes of a march to Ban the Bomb and later reading in the evening paper that an earl of my acquaintance, Bertrand Russell, had been arrested for sitting down and inciting a breach of the peace. But, although I applauded and admired his action, I wasn't really sure whether or not I agreed with him.

Many years later, in the 1970s, while I was working on solar energy, I had begun to feel uncomfortable about the government's nuclear power programme. It seemed to be unable, or unwilling, to entertain the well-established fact that its nuclear power-stations were producing quantities of eternally poisonous material which they, quite simply, didn't know what to do with. My confidence in the government's honesty was rattled and I found myself seriously wondering what other pieces of 'necessary' self-deception it might be engaged in.

As far as nuclear weapons were concerned, I had more or less gone along with the conventional view that the government's policy of 'deterrence' was probably the most sensible way to ensure that no nation would ever be tempted to use, or threaten to use, its atomic bombs for military conquest or blackmail. Deterrence was what made nuclear war unthinkable, and if the price the world had to pay for that security was the nuclear arms race, then it would have to be paid – or so I told myself.

I had been wrong about that. Not so much about the logic of the policy as about the assumption that the government was following it. There were, to put it mildly, some inconsistencies in the policy literature it was issuing.

For example: in paragraph 4 of one of the leaflets outlining its defence policy the government declared that:

... NATO's range of deterrents prevent the Soviet Union from even threatening to use the kind of force against the West which it has used against Eastern Europe ... The Soviet Union knows that any military conflict between East and West at whatever level could lead to devastating damage from which neither side could escape.

while in the next paragraph, 5, it stated:

... NATO's nuclear weapons exist for preventing wars – not for fighting them. Talk of fighting a nuclear war is dangerous nonsense, because there would be no winners in such a holocaust ...*

That sounded very plausible and a casual reader, or one anxious to be reassured, might have taken it on board without any further thought, but in essence what it was saying was that while on the one hand the government wanted the Russians to know that if they were to step out of line *'at whatever level'* we would not flinch from destroying both them and us in a nuclear exchange, on the other hand it wanted *us* to know that it didn't really mean it and wouldn't do it.

It was clear that the government was telling one thing to us and something different and essentially contradictory to the Russians. So the question was: 'Which of us are they lying to?'

That was an appalling question. Even to think about such a possibility was deeply unsettling. Nevertheless the evidence was there and the question had to be addressed.

Once again I found myself in a confrontation between complacency and concern, between my desire to ignore it (or find an easy comforting answer) and a chilling suspicion that something might have gone seriously wrong – that the unthinkable had begun to become thinkable.

The least I could do, I said to myself, was pay proper attention to the subject. I knew I was in favour of nuclear disarmament – that went almost without saying – but, using the clichés of the time, I told myself to decide whether I was a Unilateralist, one who

---

* *The Balanced View*, a C.O.I. leaflet issued in December 1981.

was in favour of immediate unconditional renunciation of all nuclear weapons, or a Multilateralist, in favour of making selected gestures of nuclear disarmament, but only through painstaking, protracted negotiations in order to ensure that these were equal and simultaneous on both sides, so as to maintain the balance of power.

Although I, personally, dearly wished the nasty things would go away, and would by nature be a Unilateralist, I could see that they could not be disinvented. So the government's contention that for us unilaterally to abandon our nuclear 'deterrent' would leave us open to nuclear blackmail did make some sense.

Multilateral nuclear disarmament also made sense, and the government maintained that it was pursuing an overall policy of multilateral nuclear disarmament but, it explained, it was doing so in the context of what it called 'necessary modernisation'. As this involved inviting in nuclear cruise missiles and spending billions of pounds on submarines filled with multi-headed nuclear missiles, this was not any sort of disarmament. It was a farce, like crawling slowly down an escalator that was moving swiftly upwards.

The difficulty was that the public arguments had become polarized between these two extreme views. My impression was that most people felt that if they chose which they would support, they could just pop it into a box labelled 'My Attitude to Nuclear Matters' and get on with ordinary life.

I tried to do that, but it didn't work. The box ticked.

I remember it ticked particularly loudly one evening when I was watching a discussion about defence strategy on the TV. I can't remember the details but they were discussing important consider- ations like 'nuclear parity', 'windows of opportunity', 'monitored tactical escalation' and 'acceptable collateral costs'.

I tried to follow the discussion but what gradually welled up inside me like a rage was the realisation that the discussion itself was an obscenity, that it could not, *should not*, be happening.

My reaction was partly an effect of the language, the sanitized language of nuclear carnage which was allowing them to evaluate nuances of unimaginable horror as if they were 'Best Buys' in some gruesome consumer magazine. I could see that this 'underspeak' was not just technical language, it had been invented to distance its true meaning from the very people who were using it. I suddenly realised that if the participants had seen and felt the reality behind the label-words they were thinking with, the words would have stuck in their throats. I also saw the clear and present possibility that this unwitting self-blinding could lead ordinary people and nations to commit acts of unbelievable inhumanity, simply because they hadn't fully understood what they were talking *about*. As I paced about the room, swearing, I also knew that, quite apart from the terrible language, something else had gone dangerously wrong and, furthermore, that I was going to have to get off my butt and do something about it. I didn't know what, but I was going to have to do something.

I looked again at the government's defence policy – that of threatening to 'use' nuclear weapons in the face of a conventional military attack, while at the same time maintaining that to even think of doing such a thing was 'dangerous nonsense' – and tried to see what it implied.

I had already seen that the policy was mendacious – deliberately ambiguous. But that was nothing new in international politics and if it deterred the Russians ...

Now wait a minute. Would it deter the Russians?

Then I realised what had been bugging me.

Seen as a deterrent that policy was completely unconvincing and, further, simply *because* it was unconvincing it was incredibly dangerous in that it set a booby-trap which could be tripped off at any moment and precipitate the world into self-destruction.

Today this may seem like dry history, but at that time it was likely to be our future and, believe me, if you couldn't block it out of your head, it was terrifying. Let me try to describe the situation:

If the government was 'misleading' the Russians and wouldn't really unleash Armageddon in the face of a conventional attack, then the Russians would read paragraph 5 and not feel any need to take any notice of the threat.

If the government was 'misleading' us, and really would unleash

Armageddon, then the Russians still couldn't be relied on to take any notice, because the threat to commit national suicide was so absolutely insane that it must be seen as a bluff.

Was the government bluffing? It wasn't likely to say, but the trouble with a bluff is that you have to pretend that you mean to carry it out. The means to do so must be fully installed and on instant automated readiness. Everybody must believe that whatever is threatened will if necessary be carried out.

In a celebrated speech, the Secretary of State for Defence, Mr Michael Heseltine, told us that we, the people of Britain, must show the world that we have nerves of steel, that we were ready to make any sacrifice in order to preserve our institutions and way of life. His view was that if we were resolute in our determination to combat any aggression with *all* the weapons at our command, then, at the nuclear brink, we could be certain that our enemies would pull back.

Meanwhile our 'enemies', being, one assumes, of similar mind, would also be approaching the nuclear brink with nerves of steel, resolutely certain that at the brink, we were going to pull back.

So, with both sides marching resolutely into suicide, what would have been likely to happen?

I don't think either nation would have failed to recognize the danger of such a situation. But, although it is just conceivable that one or the other *might* have pulled back, in the climate of that time it was by no means certain that they *would* have done so, or indeed that they would have had time to do so. It was far more likely that both sides would have activated the already threatened response and ordered a *retaliatory first strike pre-emption*. This would have been to launch a massive *first strike* of nuclear missiles targeted on their enemy's nuclear installations, not so much as a deliberate attack but as a necessary *retaliation* for the first strike which the enemy might not yet have launched – but, as they were certainly thinking of doing the same thing, it was obviously essential to *pre-empt* it and get our first strike in first. This would have been done in the hope (quite certainly vain) that our missiles would have managed to wipe theirs out before they could be launched – in a sort of mutual nuclear Pearl Harbor attack.

Of course neither side would ever have admitted to having any such intention, in fact NATO devised a policy called 'flexible response' in which it said it would only send relatively small nuclear missiles at first, saving the bigger ones till later, but it seemed obvious to me that that just wouldn't happen. The moment any nation felt that it was in imminent danger of receiving any sort of nuclear attack it would react with a scream of terror that would have had no rational component, and press all the buttons it had.

II. Into Gear.

Today, looking back at the 1980s with its strategies, threats and counterthreats of universal destruction, it all seems like a bad dream.

It is difficult to bring oneself to comprehend that we, the human race, have just lived through a period during which somebody might quite easily have slipped on a diplomatic banana skin, or perhaps just misread a radar signal, and thereby have unleashed an automated sequence of events which could have wiped all life from the face of the earth, that could have burned off the ozone layer, the fragile skin that protects it from the realities of space, and left it like most other stars, a dead rock, spinning unnumbered years in the void, a place where to all intents and purposes the human race never happened.

But that was how it was, and, however much we may tell ourselves that because it didn't happen it wouldn't have happened, the inescapable fact remains that it very easily could have, and we are very lucky to be alive. Bruce Kent, the Secretary of CND, called the 1980s 'the decade of dementia', and he was quite right.

In 1980 the government was not showing a lot of sanity, even in support of its own cause. After nuclear cruise missiles came to Britain it issued a well-meant pamphlet entitled *Protect and Survive*. This told us how to protect ourselves from the effects of a nuclear attack by reinforcing the stairs and hiding underneath them with a mattress, some sandwiches and a chamber-pot, for a fortnight. I think this absurdity must have triggered off an appropriate response in many people's minds, because CND, the Campaign for Nuclear Disarmament, which had almost faded away, was overnight besieged by new members.

I also remember hearing a government spokesman, speaking on television. On our behalf he was balancing the total devastation of a nuclear war against the possible injustices of a Russian occupation and in the end he decided for us '... Yes, better dead than Red.'

I think that famous utterance may have served to concentrate a lot of minds because small Peace Groups began to spring up all over the country.

My mind had also concentrated quite a lot. In particular I had come to see that my pacifism, my personal intention not to have anything to do with war or weapons, was completely irrelevant to the situation simply because the situation had absolutely nothing to do with either war or weapons.

I had also come to see that the feeling of obscenity which had hit me so forcibly earlier was both accurate and justified. Behind all the sanitized jargon lay the inescapable fact that mankind had made for itself instruments of such power and potential for mass destruction that they could not be 'used' for any purpose except to commit universal suicide.

What we and the world were faced with was not the prospect of *war* in any recognizable sense, but of mindless mutual extermination brought about by what would be no more than a failure of imagination on the part of the world's leaders. To see that this was so one did not have to embrace pacifism or renounce patriotism, or do anything out of the ordinary. One just had to be a person with enough sense and courage to grasp the folly of what was going on. Any old warmonger could do this if he or she was given the chance.

The key perception, the one that, for me, made everything fall into place, was the simple realisation that the things were not, and are not, *weapons*. It was also clear to me that, although the formal possession of one or two of the nasty things might be necessary (basically because, as they couldn't be disinvented, there had to be some safeguard against some power-mad despot making one and holding the world to ransom), the main bulk of the overkill arsenals held by the super-powers were not in any sense of the word *weapons*, and consequently the illusion that possessing them gave military power according to the quantities held was not only infinitely dangerous but also, quite simply, insane.

This showed that the *Uni*- versus *Multi*-lateral nuclear disarmament controversy was essentially bogus. It was not concerned with the nuclear dis-*arm*-ament but with nuclear dis-*junk*-ment, getting rid of material which was, in military terms, useless, dangerous junk. This process, if it could be seen clearly, would present no difficulties and could be effected quite easily in a way that would pose very little danger.

I talked to people, I put forward these perceptions and found that, in most cases, people either didn't understand them or found them unacceptable. I soon came to realize, with some dismay, that I had got into a position very like the one I was in in 1974. Once again I was 'Bloody Oliver' the isolated zealot, obsessed and driven by propositions that were often alien to the conventional wisdom of most of the parties involved and anathema to the comfortable assumptions on which most people's thinking was based.

As I had in 1974, I turned to *Woman's Hour* on BBC Radio and, to my relief and surprise, was once again made welcome. On 30 March 1981 I met Kay Evans at Broadcasting House, where we recorded a short but deeply felt speech to the nation. This, like the one seven years earlier, ended with me in a state of complete emotional exhaustion that called for the administration of comforting words and whiskey.

The broadcast caused quite a stir. One well-known broadcaster roundly condemned it as being subjective and naive, and its so-called 'political bias' was later balanced with a bland talk by a government spokesman (which, to my mind, tended to reinforce my message). It was included in *Pick of the Week* and, I believe, *Pick of the Year*.

For me the main effect of making the broadcast was that

having screwed my courage to the sticking-point, I was ready and able to cope with the numerous invitations to speak to Peace Groups that came to me as a result of it.

During June and July 1981 I addressed meetings in various parts of south-east England. What impressed me about the audiences, sometimes a dozen, sometimes a hundred or more, was that the people who had given up their evenings to come and listen were all different – bankers, bookies, housewives, hippies, teachers and tradesmen; ordinary people who had seen the same dangers as I had and had been sufficiently jolted to come out of their comfortable lives and get together to form these small Peace Groups. For a while I seemed to have become a one-man CND, and I would certainly have continued with this but for the fact that in August I had to return to Australia with Prue; she for treatment and I to start my stint with the Western Australian Institute of Technology.

While I was in Australia I found the time to put together a pamphlet. I called it *Thinking it Through: The Plain Man's Guide to the Bomb,* and offered it to the Menard Press. The publisher, Anthony Rudolf, accepted it and, at the beginning of 1982, just as I was bringing Prue home from Australia, it was published. That should have been an exciting event for me, and in a way it was, but of course at the time I had, to put it mildly, other things on my mind.

Shortly after returning from Australia I received a phone call from Peter Whittle, at the Quaker United Nations Office in Geneva. He asked me if I would gather up about fifty copies of my pamphlet and, when I felt able to, bring them to Geneva so that we could distribute them to the various delegates and diplomats who were there preparing for the United Nations' Second Special Session on Disarmament, which was due to take place in New York in June.

I eventually reached Geneva in early April. Peter Whittle and I scuttled through the halls and corridors of the Palace of the United Nations, delivering copies of the pamphlet to his many important acquaintances. We also arranged a couple of meetings at the Quaker House at which my words gave rise to anger (in an American diplomat), loud approval (from two Polish delegates), despair (in a Swedish diplomat) and, unexpectedly (from a glorious lady who was First Secretary to the UK Mission) – tears. She said: 'I may not come to agree with your conclusions in the end, but one thing I know is that you must walk through the world saying what you have to say, because only that way will we come to know what we are talking *about*.'

In Geneva I stayed with a Quaker couple, Ruth and Nicholas Gillett, who were working at the Quaker House. Nicholas came from a family of 'birthright' Quakers. His father, Roger Gillett, had known my father when he was a conscientious objector in 1916. My grandfather, George Lansbury, had had a lifelong friendship with the Quakers, so he and Ruth decided that I was a 'Birthright Attender'. This was a very Quakerly sort of joke.

Nico and Ruth drove a small clapped-out car, and I mean that *they* drove it, in that one would be at the wheel while the other offered constructive suggestions about whether or not it would be advisable in the circumstances to engage another gear, or mused aloud about the possibility that this might perhaps be a suitable occasion on which one could consider applying the brakes. Travelling with this 'Comité de Conduire', as I called it, was a hilarious as well as hair-raising experience, but we went to some marvellous places.

I remember, with startling clarity, driving up a narrow hairpin road hanging over precipices, to arrive, in the bright midday sunshine, at an ancient hamlet high in the Alps. The steep wooden houses and the wooden sledges, the barns, the cattle in the byres and the steaming stamping horses, were part of a nineteenth-century painting, as were the weatherbeaten people, wearing swaddled boots and dark bundled clothes. The winter snow was still standing there, more than a metre deep, but from narrow paths and tracks, from around the yards and even from some tiny pieces of garden, the snow had been carved away, so that one walked between cliffs of snow which stood all around, in high, flat-topped blocks. But what hit me, as I climbed out of the overheated car, was the air – the glorious new air that flowed icily into my lungs, filled my heart with delight and sent the blood tingling into my fingers. In that moment all things were clear and bright, lovely and filled with life and, as was regarded as being altogether proper in the circumstances, I laughed and wept for joy.

I arrived back from Geneva just in time to see the colour films of *Noggin and the Ice Dragon* and *Noggin and the Pie* on television. I had finished and delivered them – when was it? Only a few months earlier, but it seemed like a lifetime ago. Would I ever be able to think of and make films like that again? I had no idea.

Peter and I had also been asked to make a new set of films based on a classic book, *The Doll's House*, by the famous author Rumer Godden. The start of this was delayed because our contract was not to be with the BBC but with Goldcrest Ltd.., a large film company. They employed a firm of prestigious solicitors who acted very slowly and, I believe, at great expense. I was quite glad of the delay because it meant that I could get ready to go to New York to attend the United Nations' Second Special Session on Disarmament, which was to take place at the UN in New York at the beginning of June.

In New York I stayed in the apartment of a distant cousin, Peggy Postgate Sage, who had generously moved out and lent it to me while she stayed with friends.

As a holiday my stay in New York was delightful. Peggy took me around and showed me the sights, and New York itself was a wondrous place where it was exciting just to wander about the streets, watching the people and carrying very little money – in my socks in case I was mugged. But as a contribution to my campaign the outing was not a success. I had no access to the conference itself but I did manage to persuade a young man at the Quaker office to smuggle the five hundred pamphlets I had brought with me into the building. I also walked in the famous March of a Million to Central Park, but didn't reach it because there wasn't room.

I returned to Red Lion Cottage feeling rather despondent, to find a pile of letters from Peace Groups asking me to come and speak. So I got my act together and went out on the road.

During the next three years I spoke to over seventy meetings, wrote three more pamphlets, and issued a stream of leaflets. My contention, that nuclear 'weapons' were not really weapons at all, seemed to be fairly easy for ordinary people to get the hang of, and we had some excellent meetings, but it was still anathema to the proponents of the conventional view on both sides of the argument. I became very used to being called a traitor by Queen-and-Country patriots but it was less easy to accept being rejected by friends who, for want of a better word, I would call die-hard Pacifists. At one meeting, organized by the Quakers, the audience was made uncomfortable by my willingness even to entertain the concept of deterrence. In fact one of them, a man of about my own age, was outraged. He denounced my disloyalty and hypocrisy, and demanded to know how I, a pacifist, who had been to prison for his principles and had renounced all war and violence, could be so despicable as to be seen to condone any situation, any situation at all, in which even one of those filthy things would be allowed to continue to exist.

I replied that the filthy things were there, couldn't be dis-invented.

He told me I was a double-thinker and a turncoat, that I should be ashamed to mix with such vileness. Why could not I, like them, stand up and be counted as one whose life bears witness to the simple truth of love?

That riled me and I heard myself answer: 'Friend, you are whiter than white! Your purity puts me, and perhaps the world, to shame. But tell us just one thing – how dirty will you get to save the world?'

I was fairly angry myself but for a moment I feared I was to become the first Quaker martyr – I mean the first to be martyred *by* the Quakers – but his principles prevailed and he stormed out.

Although the government usually tended to honour pure paci-fists on the grounds that they were harmless, it was less indulgent towards those who opposed its nuclear policies on other grounds. One of its lines was to take every opportunity to allege (quite falsely) that the peace movement was political in purpose and was being funded by the Russians. In this it was greatly aided by members of some of the far-left political parties, known in general as the Trots. They saw the peace movement as having a political use and they joined in enthusiastically, using the meetings and marches as a platform for their own purpose, which was to proclaim that the capitalists were using the arms race for their own profit and that the only way to peace was to overturn the system.

This meant that each peace movement march, the body of which would consist of peaceful middle-class people just wanting to show their commitment to nuclear disarmament, would be led and accompanied by a fringe of prancing zealots chanting: 'Thatcher Out! Ban the Bomb! Thatcher Out!' That was usually enough to give the passers-by the opportunity they sought to conclude that the peace movement was part of the Loony Left and not worth bothering with – thus totally and tragically wasting the purpose of the march.

But, for me, the most difficult thing to cope with was the effect that what I was saying had on some of the pundits of the peace movement itself. Quite early on I had been taken aside and warned, fairly severely, that my 'emotional approach' and my tendency to dwell on unpleasant subjects like the realities of nuclear warfare was counter-productive because it disturbed people. The aim, my aim, should be to take a cool academic approach. In particular I should avoid coming out with radical observations like nuclear weapons not being weapons at all. I was told that people couldn't be expected to take any notice of notions like that because they undermined the established debate.

I was forcibly reminded of this at a forum about tactics which I attended. A leading member of one of the movements ('The Freeze', I think) was in the chair. He said: 'Yes, yes, Oliver, we all know you have some ideas of your own about the things not being weapons, but that's a sideline we haven't time for now. The main thrust of our campaign *must* be to find a way to persuade the military that it is time to put aside these terrible weapons.'

Sometimes it felt as if the whole world had gone mad.

III. Indian Summer?

And now, as Monty Python was wont to say, for something completely different.

When Prue and I had talked together that day in Australia, she had said: '. . . but do remember not to be old.'

'What do you mean?'

'Well . . . you've been kind and faithful and you've had a pretty thin time of it these last few years. Don't waste time being faithful to my memory.'

'Oh, shut up,' I said, and I meant it. Things were the way things were, we both had our work cut out getting from day to day. I had no time to bother with disturbing conjectures about something so irrelevant as my future.

'You're only fifty-six,' she said, 'just a boy!' And we laughed and said no more.

I never consciously followed, or even remembered, her injunction but I do know that my grieving for Prue took what some might think a rather unorthodox form. This was because we had, in our fashion, come to terms with her death and had shared our time of mourning while she was alive. So remembering her and weeping for her was a part of happiness, part of the tide of sharpened appreciation that had flowed into me after her death. That incongruous state of spirit brought with it a sharpened appreciation of, and susceptibility to, the attractiveness of women.

For some reason I had come to think that loving was lighthearted. What I didn't know, or more likely in my exuberance had forgotten, was that it could also be a key to jealous ownership, emotional manipulation, the imposition of unknown obligations and, in one case, revenge – in which I found I had been booked in to atone for all the hurt that men had inflicted on women through the ages. After one or two regrettable experiences I met a girl who seemed to be on the same wavelength.

Well no, she wasn't a girl but a woman in her mid-thirties, and I didn't meet her exactly. Prue and I had met her several times and we were already, in a sense, friends. But now we did, as they say, catch each other's eyes.

We had a marvellous, exciting, non-secret affair, of weekends at the cottage in Wales, at my house or in hotels. Obviously the affair was preposterous, but I enjoyed it absolutely, without reservation, and it lasted, well, three years or a bit less. When the time came for it to end I was seriously sad, but, as requested, I opened my hands and let go. She was warmly, lovingly grateful. It had been wonderful but it was over – and we went our ways.

But it wasn't over, not quite. A few days later she rang me and, coldly and carefully, rubbished the lot. The gist of her discourse was that our time together had all been a pretence, a pantomime of pity, that she had been lying to me all along, that anybody who was properly sensitive would have *known* that she had *had* to tell me lies.

I was profoundly confused, not so much because she had rubbished *me* – anybody could do that – as because she had rubbished so much glorious wholeheartedly-shared happiness. She had rubbished joy itself, and that I found deeply peculiar and creepy, so much so that, for some time, whenever incidents of amorous affection were shown on the television, I would instantly jump up and turn it off.

To this day I have no clear idea what inspired that apparently superfluous attack, but my friends told me it was nothing out of the ordinary, told me I was a fool to believe everything I was told – which indeed I was, and am – and anyway she might still have been lying. How could one tell?

What was abundantly clear to me was that I was woefully ignorant and ill equipped to take part in the battle of the sexes, whatever that may be, and had better stop being a fool and start being my age, which was, I suppose, sixty.

IV. Ends of Roads.

My dear friends Ruth and Nico Gillett had been on at me ever since Geneva to make a film for the peace movement. I had said that I hadn't got a film in my head, but I would think about the idea. At last, in the early part of 1984, I worked out a script for a film and told Nico that I would make it 'at cost' if anybody could find the money and, just as important, could provide an outlet for the film when it was made – because there was no point in making a film if it was just going to sit on a shelf in my studio.

Nico took the point and almost immediately came up with the United Nations Association, which would be willing to commission a film and, presumably, show it through the many local branches it had in the country, and the Rowntree Trust, which, Nico said, might be willing to fund it.

So, having finished the first series of *The Doll's House* and not yet having a contract for the second series, I cleared out my studio and started work on a rough film to be called *Life on Earth Perhaps*.

It turned out quite well, a brisk exposition of a situation and its implications, with some fairly positive suggestions about what could be done, including, implicitly, a message to the UNA itself about the role it could (and should) be playing in implementing the 1978 UN Resolution on Disarmament. I finished it early in 1985 and showed it at the UNA Annual General Meeting, where it and a speech I made were accorded an unexpectedly rapturous reception. Later I offered it to the television companies, but none of them would show it because it was thought to be 'political'. However, I believe it was seen fairly frequently at UNA branch meetings and I showed it several times at Peace Group meetings.

Meanwhile, ordinary life went on. Red Lion House had been sold, very happily, to a delightful couple, Doris and David, with whom we soon became close, respectful friends.

Dan and I continued to live at Red Lion Cottage. *Tottie II*, the sequel to the first series about *The Doll's House*, was ready to start filming and I began another year-long stint of concentrated work. This was interrupted when Peter and I were invited to take our films and ourselves as 'key-note' speakers for the BBC at a European Broadcasting Union conference on children's television programmes which was to take place at Tützing in Bavaria.

We had some good times there and gave a fairly rumbustious talk, throwing the unfortunate cloth cat, *Bagpuss*, from one to the other as a 'conch'. That was good fun.

Another welcome excursion was a holiday at a painting school in an old mill south of Bordeaux, which Mary Hinshelwood and I attended. I had always wanted to be Cézanne or, preferably, Alfred Sisley, who had painted Moret-sur-Loing so deliciously. So I set up my easel and slapped down about four paintings one after the other, in a frenzy of concentration which completely blotted out everything except what I was seeing.

I wasn't Cézanne, or Sisley. Looking at the paintings now that my delight in what I saw has faded, I can see that they probably have little connection with what might be called 'art'. What they do have, although the manner of their painting is rough and impressionistic, is a startling faithfulness to the feeling and look of the places. From the photographs I took from where I was standing I can see that I was successfully doing what I was intending to do, putting down on the canvas board, as clearly as I could, exactly what was in front of me – and loving every moment of it.

Then came the next film project, as usual in an unexpected way.

Having watched *Tottie II* on television, a lady in, I think, Cornwall, had sent Peter an absolutely minute Dutch doll, about 1in (25mm) long. It was broken but she expressed the hope that Peter would be able to repair it. While it was with him the doll fell on the floor and was swallowed by the vacuum-cleaner. Peter and Joan had to turn out the bag and sort through the dust and fluff to locate its tiny limbs. Peter duly mended it and made another one for himself. He also made a companion sailor-doll whose name was Victor, who lived in a tiny toy boat on the mantelpiece, while Pinny lived in a miniature china house next to it.

There was obviously a film series there, but I jibbed at the thought of trying to animate such tiny persons as single-frame puppets. So the films of *Pinny's House*, which Peter wrote for the BBC, were made, like *Ivor the Engine*, as cartoons. For thirteen episodes the unfortunate dolls faced every miniature disaster that their world brought, from being picked up by a thrush and fitted into her nest, to sheltering from the giant snow-flakes in an empty snail-shell.

I enjoyed the Pinny films but, even as I was making them, I knew in my heart that this was the end of the road for single-frame filming, the end of my having to sit in the shed for hours on end pushing pieces of card about with a pin. The ship of the family had come apart, the crew had taken to the boats. Keeping me afloat in my rubber dinghy didn't call for such a large income. Maybe the sales of showings of the films we had already made would suffice. For a while I wondered whether to sell Red Lion Cottage and buy myself a smaller, less demanding house, investing the profit to provide a small pension.

However, I made no decision and went on addressing meetings and writing pamphlets. I was honoured, and rather intimidated, by receiving an invitation to give a talk at the Yearly Meeting of the Society of Friends (Quakers) which, in 1986, was to take place at Exeter University. I took the precaution not only of writing out a special speech in full but also of writing and printing a leaflet to go with it. This was entitled, in true Quakerly tones, *Towards a New Peace Testimony*.

In it I set out the situation as I saw it – the threat of self-inflicted annihilation inherent in the nations' military strategies – and I ended with an extraordinary suggestion, that on this subject the Society should end its quietism and return to one of its own guiding principles, that of 'speaking truth to power', that it was time for the Society to get angry, time to 'answer to the wrath of love'.

It went down a treat, as my grandfather used to say. I think

Old George would have been proud of me, and, I hope, of what I had had to say.

In the robust and fairly hilarious informal session that followed, several Friends declared that I had laid a challenge before the Society, a challenge that it must not fail to take up and go forward with.

For various reasons, which I should have known about, the Society did not go forward with the challenge. My efforts to re-enliven its interest foundered and I was later reproved for suggesting unseemly behaviour.

The world went on being mad. After the Chernobyl nuclear disaster I heard the government's energy spokesman assure us that the inquiry had assessed the *unforeseen* risks that had caused it and that this had *proved* that our own nuclear power stations were perfectly safe! President Reagan's answer to the 'evil empire' of Communism – the Strategic Defence Initiative, known as Star Wars – grew and flowered. That was a far-fetched nonsense, but it was none the less frightening because for a while it almost seemed as if the American Dreamers were going to believe their own bullshit.

I soldiered on, talked to MPs, lobbied conferences, wrote letters to high-ranking military persons, even wrote another pamphlet, *The Emperor's New Clothes.* Also, at a conference, I met a number of Russian military scientists who seemed to feel much as I did, that the nuclear arms race was, and always had been, a nonsense.

Then, one day, a friend from one of the first peace groups rang me. She said: 'Have you noticed? Gorbachev has been reading your pamphlets!'

I don't suppose Mikhail Gorbachev had been doing anything of the sort, but what he was saying was certainly very like what I had been saying for years, and of course, coming from him the words carried weight.

By now the Iron Curtain was crumbling and, tacitly encouraged by Mikhail Gorbachev, the people of Eastern Europe were coming out on to the streets *en masse* to assert their independence, not, I felt, so much for doctrinaire political reasons as because, after years of sparseness, they were moved by a deep universal longing for

McDonald's Quarter-Pound Burgers and the Good Life which they symbolized.

The Western governments doggedly continued to claim that Russia had been *forced* to the conference table by the success of their policy of resolutely maintaining the 'power' of their deterrents, but I don't think anybody was listening any more. I turned away at last and accepted an invitation to visit the twelfth century.

18

CHANGING DIRECTION

I. The Cathedral.

One bright morning in the autumn of 1984, the Keeper of the Printed Books of Canterbury Cathedral came to call on me at Red Lion Cottage. She was golden-haired and smiling, far too small a lady for such a grand-sounding post but, as I later rather rudely put it, as bright as a marigold in a school play. Her name was Naomi and she had come to ask me to lend her my celebrated voice to record a tape-cassette guide for blind people to listen to as they walked through the cathedral.

I thought this was a grand idea so we sat at the table in the garden while I looked at the script she had prepared.

After a while I asked: 'Are you proud about your prose?'

'Not particularly. Why?

'Well, this stuff is ... er, unspeakable.'

I meant that literally; that it wasn't suitable for speaking, but the word was ill-chosen.

Naomi received the blow without flinching and replied with a smile. 'You can rewrite it yourself, then.'

'All right.'

I showed Naomi my holiday snaps – five large paintings of France – and we drove laughing back to the cathedral in my old 2CV rubbish-bin car. I don't think it occurred to either of us that this was the start of a long and happy collaboration.

I rewrote parts of the guide and we recorded it within a week or so, and it was done, or nearly done. The cathedral's expert blind man, Dennis Eldridge, tried it out and reported that if he had followed the instructions on the tape he would have gone head-over-heels down the stone steps into the crypt. So minor adjustments were made and it was delivered. As far as I know no casualties were reported.

The Printed Books which Naomi kept were glorious and included, among other treasures, a veritable zoo of huge tomes, many the size of paving-stones, full of splendid, if somewhat fanciful, hand-coloured engravings of birds and beasts. Some of these, like Gesner's *Animalium*, dated from the sixteenth century and had to be handled with great care as well as great strength.

The invitation to visit the twelfth century came in 1986 after Naomi had written, and I had recorded, a short sound-tape on the life and death of Thomas Becket, the 'holy blissful martyr' who was murdered in the cathedral in 1170.

The cathedral was pleased with the tape and suggested that we might find some pictures to go with it for an audio-visual show. Unfortunately we could find very few contemporary pictures.

It was observed, by both Naomi and my son Daniel, who was already becoming a professional cartoonist, that if we had been living in the twelfth century we would probably have settled down and spent the rest of our lives sewing a long tapestry, like the Bayeux Tapestry. It also occurred to us that if, in the twelfth century, they had had good quality paper and acrylic paint, they might well have done something a bit less laborious, something that might take no more than about a year.

As usual, the idea stuck in my mind, and soon I was sellotaping pieces of writing-paper into long strips and doing rough sketches.

It was obvious that painting a Bayeux Tapestry-type 'illumination' would require more funding than the cathedral was likely to offer, but fortunately my son Stephen's girlfriend, Sarah, was the daughter of Dan, who was Kingfisher Books, which published large illustrated young people's books of an entertaining and educational nature. So, in early 1987, I gathered up the sketches, the painted samples and a synopsis, and took them along to show him. I asked: 'Book?'

Dan said: 'Yes, we'll have it. There will be money. Go and do it.'

As I reeled out of Dan's office I felt a wave of emotion that was both familiar and alarming, a mixture of elation and panic, through which I heard an old warning voice mutter: 'Done it again, done it again!'

'Done what?'

'Taken on something you don't know how to do. Committed yourself to delivering inside a year the sort of thing that other people have taken a lifetime to complete, and which you may not be able to do at all because you don't know the first thing about it. That's what!'

'I can find out.'

'But you're not the right *sort* of person. You're not an *artist*. It isn't *your* sort of thing. People are supposed to go to college and do courses, learn about Composition, study the history of Art, get diplomas, before they even *think* about doing things like that.'

'So what's new?'

'Oh nothing, I suppose,' the voice muttered, and shut up.

The journey was marvellous. Naomi, being a historian, began sorting out original sources for the life-story of Thomas Becket while I read everything I could find. Together we lived slowly through that time, distilling from it in words and pictures a clear and awful impression not only of the lives of the people and their fervent concern for their future in the afterlife but also of the two pig-headed autocrats: the wilful priest Thomas Becket and Henry II, King of England (and quite a lot of France), loving friends and raging enemies by turns – who fought out their personal squabbles on the field of history and government, wrecking the day-to-day administration of the nation and making a thorough nuisance of themselves.

The story was long, complex, exciting, passionate and radiantly unnecessary. It was a struggle which Henry very nearly won, and he probably would have if Thomas hadn't chosen to play his final trump cards: violent martyrdom and a pair of hair-drawers infested with fleas and lice. These finally confirmed his absolute holiness, brought him to sainthood and gave the Church its victory over the state.

Doing the painting was a real pleasure, not only because it was a great relief to be back at work, proper commissioned work, but also because I could see a thin time coming up.

Our films were definitely going out of fashion.

The reasons for this were kindly explained to me by a member of the department at the BBC. Apparently an edict had been issued by the powers-that-be to the effect that the *viability* of programmes (i.e., their worth and chance of continuing), was henceforth to be *ratings-led* (i.e., judged by the number of people watching). As the purpose of television was to entertain (as opposed to instruct or educate), the basic policy was to give the children exactly the sort of thing that they were already known to enjoy and deliver it in a form and manner that was especially exciting.

I remember it occurred to me that if one was seriously determined to eliminate a whole culture and wipe out everything that had gone before, the way to set about it would be to rot it from the inside. This could best be done by ensuring that the next generation of our children, whose minds were new, empty and waiting for knowledge, were given nothing except what they *already* knew, or had been told, was what they liked – in effect force-feeding them with a diet of manic jelly-babies.

But, quite apart from that, it was explained to me that impeccable American educational sociologists had established that in order to prevent a child switching channels (and thus transferring the rating to another channel), a programme had to have a *hook* (i.e., an incident sufficiently violent to re-attract the attention) every three and a half seconds. Our programmes did not have this characteristic and consequently, whatever other qualities they may or may not have had, they were not to be considered suitable for television transmission.

So the new Head of BBC Children's TV 'had no plans' to show *Bagpuss* or any of our films, nor did they wish to commission any new ones.

Nevertheless, whatever the TV companies felt about them, our films were not quite dead.

Quite unexpectedly, the University of Kent at Canterbury invited Peter and me to receive honorary MA degrees. The Vice-Chancellor let it be known, in the most tactful way, that the degrees were being awarded to us *'in loco Bagpusis'*, because the true recipient, being a cloth cat and a fiction, was unable to receive it personally. However, it was intimated that Bagpuss would be welcome to attend the Degree Congregation at the cathedral if he were appropriately robed. Joan Firmin promptly made him a perfect mortar-board, hood and gown. Apparently one or two senior members of the University found the prospect of a cloth cat in academic dress taking part in the ceremony an affront to the dignity of the Foundation, but I understand that most of them entered into the absurdity with relish.

In the event the occasion passed off with perfect decorum. Naomi brought the cat into the cathedral in a covered basket and, once she had convinced the Head Verger that it was not a bomb, the basket was placed under the lectern and she took her place in the academic procession.

Bagpuss took no part in the ceremony until the time came for me to make a speech of acknowledgement on his and our behalf. Then, as I lifted him from his basket, there came from the assembled multitude a great roar of cheers and applause which continued for some moments.

Joking apart I was deeply moved, honoured and privileged by this piece of appreciation, not so much of myself personally, as of the work that Peter and I had for decades quietly churned out and fed to the voracious television. To see and feel, in that great cheer, a recognition that the pleasure which we had felt in bringing it into the world had in fact communicated itself to a whole generation, was an enormous, heart-warming joy. Over the years the surly old cloth cat had become the object of a great tide of affection. It made me very happy, and I returned to the twelfth century much refreshed in spirit.

October 1987 brought two disasters. One was for everybody – the hurricane. This came in the night, buffeting the house like a gigantic boxing glove, bringing down trees and tearing off roofs.

The other disaster, which came at midday on October 30th, was for Naomi alone. She turned to her colleagues and said: 'I feel terrible. I must go home.' She had been stricken with a heavy tiredness that would not go away. My bright, swift, glowing friend was still there but, like a car with a dud battery, her energy would fade, her face would turn grey and she would have to flop down.

Naomi tried to go on working but it was impossible. After many tests she was diagnosed as having myalgic encephalitis, known as ME. This was a relatively new illness which was not recognized, and was indeed resented and dismissed, by quite a number of GPs because the causes of it were not known. However there was absolutely no doubt in our minds that what Naomi had was a real illness, a genuine clinical condition that could not be overruled or written off as hysterical. Fortunately her GP was of the same mind. He supported the diagnosis and helped her to arrange her retirement. He did all he could for her, and we set about rearranging our lives around her condition.

Our working partnership had long since grown into a loving friendship. I set up a bed for her in my study next to the Becket easel so that she could rest while I worked. Her husband, Geoffrey, was a kind man but not as used to looking after people as I was. When Naomi was rotten he encouraged her to stay with me.

We discovered quite early, but alas not early enough, that trying to force oneself to soldier on through ME is the most damaging approach. Naomi had tried to do this and had become totally exhausted and shattered. Doing this is probably what set the illness firmly in place and has prevented her recovery.

Nevertheless, life was possible. Once she had managed to recognize and accept her limitations and allowed herself to have a ticket to be an invalid, we were able to arrange our lives quite well. She would spend part of her time with Geoffrey and Fred, their ancient and honourable black cat, and part of her time with me and Thomas.

We finished Becket, slew him, entombed him, surrounded him with pilgrims buying phials of his blood and even found a corner for Erasmus to stand and look at the gold and jewel-encrusted tomb nearly four hundred years later and ask a passing angel what was Christian about all those heaped-up riches.

'Search me,' replies the angel. 'Nothing to do with us.'

Naomi put the finishing touches to the text and we delivered the work to the publishers.

Sadly, when eventually it was published, the book was badly printed. Naomi's and my year's work appeared washed-out and fuzzy. That was deeply disappointing.

However, we now had the Illumination – fifty-four feet of handsome epic.

The first thing I did was set it up in the studio and make a film of it, a film which would later be made into videos. Then I had a set of portable stands and lights made to display the Illumination as an exhibition and looked forward to setting it up and showing it in some suitable setting, like the Chapter House of Canterbury Cathedral. Unfortunately the cathedral authorities declined to allow it to be shown, so that put an end, for the moment, to our ambitions.

Early in 1989 a small theatre company in the Midlands wanted to do a play about *Ivor the Engine*. I put together quite a good play but the company, which had engaged a pair of budding pop stars as leading actors, didn't really get the hang of it, so that apart from my friend Olwen Griffiths, and a young actor called Peter Robbins, who was a magnificent Dai Station and hilarious as Bani the elephant-keeper, the production was sad and ineffectual.

Although by then Naomi was not very mobile, often using crutches to walk any distance, she really enjoyed travelling by train. So in May, once we had discharged our responsibilities to the Ivor play, we left it to stew in its juice in the Midlands and took the train to Granada, a journey which took two whole days. My son

Simon, who with his Spanish girlfriend Dolors was living and working there, had found us a delightful apartment in a tiny narrow street. From this we made sorties into the centre of that intense city, where every day seemed to be a fiesta and, on platforms set up in the squares, fiery tiny tots in full costume were twirling and clicking among the stamping ferocious flamenco dancers.

Then, suddenly, in July 1989, came the break we had been waiting for: a suitable setting for the Becket Illumination – two months at the ancient Blackfriars Priory beside the river in the centre of Canterbury.

At first very few people came to see it. That was definitely depressing, but gradually things changed. More people, many of them local, began to come in. By the time our booking was up and we had to close, the visitors were queuing on the steps. We could have continued through the rest of the summer and probably made a bomb, but the Blackfriars had to return to its usual function as Art Room for the King's School.

Fortunately, during the exhibition, Naomi and I had received another invitation. This one was to the fifteenth century.

II. Triumphant Failure.

The fifteenth and early sixteenth centuries were an era of great explorations and discoveries in which the boundaries of the known world were much extended, and, as everybody knows, the greatest of these explorations took place in 1492 when Christopher Columbus sailed across the Western Ocean and located at last the direct sea-route to Japan, where the roofs were said to be made of gold. That was his opinion anyway. The fact that, before he was anywhere near halfway to Japan, America got in the way and so undoubtedly saved him and his crews from starvation, did not alter his view of the achievement. He knew he had, near enough, discovered Japan, and to his dying day he never recognized the now obvious fact that what he had stumbled on was a completely unknown continent.

Four hundred and ninety-seven years later the publishers of

Becket rang Naomi and me at the Blackfriars exhibition and asked us to do another book, in the same format, to depict the life of that enterprising mariner and his epic journey. This would be published in 1992 to celebrate the five hundredth anniversary of the event.

We readily agreed, but on condition that it would be properly printed, that we would make it our next job and start almost immediately. That was agreed and settled, except that the contract didn't come through for four more months, during which time I was out of work.

That was a nuisance, but there were other things to be done. Naomi's condition had deteriorated and she had at last consented occasionally to be pushed about in a wheelchair. Also she had already had enough of sharing a room with Thomas Becket and wasn't looking forward to sharing it with Columbus, so I cleared out the basement of Red Lion Cottage, removing several decades of stored treasures, and with hired help converted it into a rather pleasant flat with its own French doors to the garden.

One morning, some months after my last peace pamphlet, *The Emperor's New Clothes*, had been published and forgotten, the news came through that the Berlin Wall had been broken and was coming down.

I remember the feeling of relief and exultation that slowly grew inside me, bringing back the fire that had driven me in the 1980s. But this time the fire that filled my veins was not of dread but of gladness, the stone of fear-full misunderstanding that had lain across the world for so long had been rolled aside and the Cold War had been revealed as an absurdity. I rang Nico Gillett and laughed and wept over the telephone. Neither of us knew what the future would bring, nor could we foresee the spiteful worms of petty national strife that would crawl out from under that stone, but for us that day marked the end of the decade of dementia and, we dared to hope, the return of common sense to international affairs. I knew my work was done. It had not been done by me, that was for sure, but it was over. I could turn to Columbus with a lighter heart and a cleared conscience.

And what a marvellous idiot the old mariner must have been.

A man truly after my own heart, he pursued his vision through all adversity with an absolute persistence that was entirely oblivious to the intrusion of facts. In those days theological correctness was a far more decisive consideration than scientific accuracy or common sense, but even so the theological case he made for his project was far from sound. He was also shameless in his 'adaptation' of mathematics and unbridled in his indulgence in what amounted to pure wishful thinking. This was because he knew, as in his day Thomas had known, that his destiny had been given to him by God and that in following his Great Enterprise in faith and fortitude he was serving no other master.

Columbus, the Triumphant Failure was delivered in good time to be published for his quincentenary. This time the publishers had the plates made more professionally and the proofs looked really good. Unfortunately the books were printed in some far-flung colony and appeared with an all-over brownish tinge as if they had been flavoured with soy sauce. Once again I wondered why I had spent so much time and care on getting the colours just right. I resolved to make no more books like that.

There was more painting to be done. Shortly after the Becket Illumination closed, yet another invitation had arrived. This came from Dr Shirley Barlow, the Master of Eliot College at the University of Kent at Canterbury, who asked us whether, when we had finished paddling about in the Western Ocean, we would care to prepare and execute a mural for the college.

This, she suggested, could be a light-hearted depiction of the history of East Kent in general and Canterbury in particular, from the end of the last ice-age to the building of Sainsbury's new superstore.

I must say I was more than a little dubious about the project, partly because of the size – twenty feet wide and eight feet high – and partly because I knew absolutely nothing about the relevant history. However, as usual, the idea took root.

Naomi and I raided the library and consulted her expert friends. We uncovered a rich vein of pleasantly irreverent incidents and dramatic situations, including the fishmonger who was so irate with the insolence of the clergy that he 'smote a monk with an halybut'.

So, while I was finishing Columbus I put together a sketch for the mural with Moses in the top left-hand corner receiving tablets from a faceless Jehovah, and Karl Marx in the top right-hand one, hovering over the University, flourishing *Das Kapital*. With these deities in place I arranged a complex tableau of incidents, more or less historically consecutive, around a central group of pilgrims heading for the tomb of the Holy Blissful Martyr.

The University liked this and, at my request, commissioned a quarter-size colour cartoon. It also agreed, at my request, to be patient, because I was growing old and slow and less able to keep half a dozen projects in the air at the same time.

By this time Peter and I had more or less accepted the conclusion that our films had had their day, so we were quite surprised to hear from the Children's Channel, a satellite and cable company, that they wanted to buy showings of all our colour films. That was a marvellous piece of good luck and it did wonders for the bank account, but it also meant that I had to chase around to find the original films, check and assemble each one of them, have them cleaned and, eventually, transferred to master videotape. As well as working on Columbus, Naomi and I were giving talks on Becket and overseeing the Illumination exhibition as it travelled around the country. I was also writing eight books about *The Clangers* and, as if that wasn't enough, Naomi and I had started on a detective novel.

This was called *St Badwyne's Tower*, and it was set in a strictly fictitious cathedral city where there was financial skulduggery in the precincts. This was duly thwarted by the discovery of a corpse, but unfortunately the corpse was dry and about three hundred years old. It turned out that today's publishers were only in the market for fresh corpses with ample gore, and sex every fifty pages, which hadn't been our recipe and didn't fit with the plot. So that had to be abandoned.

I was also invited to give a couple of informal seminars to the Animation School at the Royal College of Art. These were so informal that they could hardly have been said to happen, but they taught me more than I really wanted to know about the way in which our simple direct craft had been inflated into a manic pretentious pseudo-art. This was probably more than the students learned about my work, ordinary story-telling, because that subject didn't seem to interest them at all.

They wanted me to see how visually stunning their work was and how well it fitted with the current state-of-the-art fashion, in fact how 'good' it was.

What they didn't want to know about and seemed quite unable to take on board was my perception, gently, perhaps too gently, put, that you can't really ask how 'good' a piece of work is by itself. You can only ask how well it does what it is setting out to do. A film is a communication and a communication has to communicate something. It doesn't matter how glossy, clever or avant-garde the pictures are, if they aren't *about* anything, they are about nothing, and consequently their success can't be judged.

That was what I had been trying to say ten years earlier in Australia: that there are, in every production, two components, *what* the work is about and *how* it is made. They are both necessary but the *how* is essentially the servant of the *what* – if only because a marvellously made film about nothing is still a nothing.

The *what* of our films were their simple, ordinary stories, simply, but beautifully pictured by Peter. The *how* was the animation, the simple, even crude, method by which they were made, a method which was essentially congruous in that it conducted the eyes and ears of the viewer through the story with the minimum of distraction. It is true that we couldn't have made them any other way because we couldn't have afforded to, but I don't think we would have wanted to. They were, and are, all-of-a-piece as they are. In fact, over the years, I have come to see that much of the enjoyment and affection that our films are held in came from the direct, unaffected direction. They tell their stories simply and do not bombard the viewer's attention with zappy distractions.

III. Winding Down.

Working on the mural, which was being painted on four huge plywood panels set up in Peter and Joan's barn, meant that I had to get up every morning and go out to work. Being back in harness again, doing visible, concentrated work in the place where I had made so many films, seemed to make my mind relax and I found I was able to stop panicking about my failing memory and take time over what I was doing.

Naomi, who had been so active and energetic before the onset of ME, was now dependent for most things on the services of either Geoffrey or myself. This she found frustrating, so she reorganized her finances and bought a small town-flat overlooking the sea at Broadstairs. From this she could potter round to the friendly corner shop on her wheeled walking-frame and, for a few days at a time, be independent. She still loved to travel by train, so every year we went in style, by autorail and wagon-lit to La Roche Canillac, a small steep village in the Corrèze, where we always took the same crummy gîte, owned by an aged but astute pair of country people. There we made good friends, first a warm and hospitable, if a shade formal, Parisian couple, Line and René, who had a most perfect little house and a garden full of roses. Later we met a German couple, Liza and Charlie, whose house was perched above a terraced garden as steep as a giant's staircase. In Charlie I found a great friend, a fellow madman, an Anglophile who loved original thought and ideas. We all got on famously together in a random mixture of French, German and English. I also discovered, by accident, signs of Le Tacot, a long-extinct railway, and spent many happy hours tracing its route.

As I approached the completion of *The Canterbury Chronicle*, as the mural was to be called, I knew that this was the last large-scale painting that I was going to attempt. The panels were occupied by over three hundred people, most of them up to no good, and I was weary.

The University Works Department made a complete pig's ear of setting the mural panels up. Roistering students flicked spoon-fuls of brandy butter on to it, which damaged the paint. I arranged to revarnish the painting. The offer was accepted but the Works Dept. didn't put up the staging for me to stand on. Eight years on I am still waiting for that, but I believe the people concerned have now retired. Theirs is another world, one in which people have salaries.

The fate of the Becket Illumination was slightly different. In association with the Victoria and Albert Museum, the Canterbury City Museums Department bought it to show in their grand new gallery. The grand new gallery didn't materialize, so the Illumination is now buried, possibly for ever, in the vaults.

I paused and asked myself why I needed to keep throwing myself into these large projects. Why couldn't I be quiet in my mind and enjoy my retirement? I was *the* Oliver Postgate. Could I not pin medals on my chest, put on dignity and rest on my laurels? For some reason I found this thought quite appalling, but at the same time I could see that the unquietness which drove me was both unnecessary and regrettable. I vowed that I would avoid committing myself to large projects and turn my attention to small things.

Naomi's hands had lost their strength and had become painful. I saw the need for two articles. One was a wrench or something for opening jars, turning taps and doorhandles. I tried out several contrivances but the one I finished up with was a simple strap-wrench with a shaped handle. This was so elegant and simple that for a moment I thought of manufacturing them. The other article was a plastic hook to open ring-pull cans of fish and roll off the lid without covering everything with oil. That was also quite elegant, being a simple shaped tool with no moving parts. Both of them were already patented, so I couldn't market them. This, I have to admit, came as something of a relief.

The next project was a bit larger. Our adopted village, La Roche, was built on a steep hillside around which the narrow roads writhed like serpents. Naomi was nervous of being pushed up and down the village, partly out of care for my still willing but gout-ridden knees but mainly for fear that I might accidentally let go of a handle or even that my dubious heart might pack up under the strain and she would be unleashed, like a loose roller coaster, to hurtle off down the hill.

So I turned my attention to designing a battery-driven outboard motor to fix on to her ordinary folding wheelchair. I set up a workshop in the garage and put together a fairly robust prototype made out of old plywood, luggage elastic and standard engineers' bits.

This one drove directly down on to the big wheels of the chair and, as the drive could be disengaged from each wheel separately, it had, in effect, power-steering. It worked really well and we took it to La Roche, where it proved to be a great wonder to the populace and a great blessing to us.

In 1995, my seventieth year, we lived quietly. I formally dismantled my much-loved, worn out, gimcrack filming equipment, cleared out my studio and divided it in half so that a neighbouring horse could live there. Simon and Daniel had both come back to live in small rented houses in Whitstable, Daniel with his new girlfriend, Rochelle. Now and then they came up to visit or for a meal, but they didn't take up residence.

Some time earlier, I had bought the flat below Naomi's in Broadstairs so that if I were to become old I might one day retire to the seaside. Although I had high blood-pressure, angina, dicey kidneys and various other boring old person's ailments, I was in fairly good nick and didn't intend to be old for quite a long time.

However, fate had other plans for me. In 1996 it set up something of a demolition campaign. This started with a small operation to remove a carbuncle from the middle of my back. That left a hole which had to be dressed every day by visiting nurses. That healed itself and in April we were able to take ourselves to a village called Fressin, near Hesdin in the Pas de Calais, where we stayed in a rather luxurious gîte owned by an English lady.

The country around there is dotted with small graveyards, tiny gardens of headstones marking the passing of groups of soldiers who died in the 1914–18 war. These were not unexpected but they were, none the less, a sharp reminder of that grey, bitter time.

In contrast we stumbled on the site of a single occasion of colourful carnage, the field of Agincourt. This was a long ploughed field set between two clumps of woodland, an entirely unremarkable piece of countryside on which one would not expect anything out of the ordinary ever to have happened. But in the village we found a small museum which recounted, in startlingly graphic terms, the details of the pageant of pure slaughter that had taken place on that dull ground over five hundred years before. It also told how, after it was over, the victorious English stripped the dead of their armour and weapons and left. Then the monks of a local monastery dug a great pit and without discrimination tipped the thousands of naked corpses, the flower of France's youth, into it. They filled in the pit, said a prayer, planted a cross and left it. A cross, perhaps the same one, is still there.

What came to both Naomi and me, that day and in the days that followed, was an overwhelming sense of the folly of it all. Agincourt had been the ultimate cock-up, in which wave after wave of the proud unthinking valorous French trampled their own dead and dying into the mud on their way to commit suicide against the new armour-piercing arrows of the English archers.

What came to us too was an inescapable perception of something which we seem to have lost – an appreciation of the simple, absolute, God-awful painfulness of pain. That appreciation is gently honoured in those small gardens of headstones for the soldiers of World War I, but otherwise it seems to be almost completely missing from much of our lives.

Then, in May, as I was driving back from Wales in a hired car, I was involved in the first major car accident of my life – head-on with a lorry. I was lucky to escape with my life and eventually returned home like a refugee, shaky and hung about with my possessions in plastic bags.

A few days later, by appointment, I presented myself at the Day Surgery Ward of the Kent and Canterbury Hospital to have my ancient gall-stones removed by a procedure called laporoscopy. This was a very modern, simple operation done by remote control which, I was told, would only require one day's stay in hospital.

They were wrong about that.

IV. The End of the Operation.

I regained consciousness and immediately regretted it. My belly was vastly distended and was filled with a pain so violent and absolute that I had to concentrate with all my might on the task of living from one moment to the next. My body was incessantly crying: 'This is not possible. This pain is not bearable.' My mind was replying: 'This is pain. You have no option.' People loomed over and spoke to me but I couldn't take in what they said or cause my mouth to make words. The surgeon came to tell me things but I couldn't find the attention to hear, holding the pain and nausea at bay was taking every moment of my consciousness. In the end a nurse gave me a huge injection which released my attention. The surgeon then told me that for some unknown reason my blood-pressure had dropped drastically during the operation and they had had to abandon it. But there was nothing to worry about. There was a slight swelling, a haematoma, in my side, but everything would be normal in a few days.

They were wrong about that too. It was a massive abscess and I had acute peritonitis. For this I was treated with cocktails of antibiotics for six weeks, during which time I was shunted in and out of hospital, had another major operation and ended up being sent to a terrible and, it turned out, terribly expensive nursing-home.

As had happened in 1978, the experience of moving close to death and coming back again caused in me an emotional upheaval which overturned my habits of thought and for a while allowed me to see again with the eyes of my childhood.

Small, as if through the wrong end of a telescope, I looked back at myself, or rather at my selves. I saw the affectionate, anxious-to-please infant becoming the smart-arsed show-off who, having been definitively labelled as contemptible, strove to show himself to be cleverer of funnier than he was, in the hope of just being allowed to be there. And in the same skin was a boy who had been born with a clear eye and an eager, impetuous, uncompromising imagination which, if anything, made him even more of a pest. He merges into the schoolboy, a facetious, posturing prat who simply wouldn't be *told* anything but would, persistently, keep questioning the questions.

That was all old stuff and, I suspect, very ordinary, but those children are still within me, muttering even as I write.

I saw the young man, a sheep, uneasy in ill-fitting wolf's clothing, stumbling confused through a life in which the only positive actions seemed to be blind leaps in the dark, gestures of solitary bravado in which I had held to my own perception of an idea or project and just shoved it through. Sometimes I got away with it, more often it had foundered. Once I got away with it beyond my wildest dreams and found I had set myself up to receive the greatest gift I could ever have hoped for, that of becoming an agent of delight, the means by which a river of fun and sheer enjoyment would be unleashed.

I meant it when I say I was the *means*. The twelve or so worlds which Peter Firmin and I put together, peopled and gave life to, are other places, with an existence of their own. I am always delighted when people come and tell me how much they enjoyed them, and I love their joy, but I am not just being modest when I say that I did not *create* that joy. I was just the cook. I also know, beyond a shadow of doubt, that if my primal purpose in making the films had been 'me-based', i.e., to enhance my personal glory, I would have produced crud, formula crud perhaps, but without integrity or life.

Not all my perceptions were simple and full of fun. Sometimes what I saw was so clear and dreadful that I had had to do the unthinkable – break faith with complacency – make a public exhibition of myself and, as one kind friend put it: 'become a member of the ranting class'.

But I could also see that I hadn't broken a faith. I had held to one: not to faith in God or ultimate goodness, but to faith in reality, nasty reality, the reality of danger. I had made the connections and held to them.

Now, as I clambered out of the valley of the shadow and the fear of death began to fall away, another feeling, something far more powerful, lifted me. This was an enormous elation, an overarching feeling of relief and delight in being alive, which was, and was expressed as, a profound love for all things and, in particular, for the long-suffering people nearest to me. It blew away all the baleful reserves and cautious inhibitions and bade me reach out my arms to them.

I came away from that episode several years older. Something, perhaps the antibiotics, had snarled up my nervous system so that I couldn't write properly. My pencil moved the opposite way and sometimes wrote wrong letters. Naomi was also recovering. For the first couple of weeks she had, with the occasional help of the District Nurse, tried to cope with me on her own. Because of the ME she had become so shredded with exhaustion that the Senior District Nurse, the grand and glorious Cynthia, had brought her Sister-boss to see her, not me, and had commanded her to rest. So she stayed with Geoffrey and Fred and was able to come and sit with me for long times of quiet in the busy hospital ward.

I recovered, perhaps even took back a year or two, but the violence of that year was not quite over. For my spirit at least, there was more to come.

A big new movie had been released. I didn't see it all but I saw excerpts from it and read parts of the script. The film was called *Crash* and it was about people getting their kicks from deliberately driving dangerously and deriving exquisite sexual pleasure from causing crashes and tangling with wrecked cars and torn bodies.

It may seem irrational to have been so affected by something so ephemeral, but I could not escape being overwhelmed by a crying rage of disgust and despair. Disgust because few human tragedies are so boring, pointless and totally regrettable as a road accident. To set aside the God-awful reality of such an incident, to glamorize it and imbue the blood and oil with sexy sleaze in order to provide a thrill seemed to me to show a peculiarly nauseous degradation of the imagination. Despair for the people, whose connection with reality and life had become so dulled and debased and . . .

'Cool it!' I said. 'It's only a film, for goodness' sake!'

'But the pain!'

'It's only make-believe. Just don't let it get to you. Don't make the connections. Nobody does!'

That was easily said, but I couldn't hold it off. Since then, I have to confess, gratuitous violence on television just turns me up. There is no entertainment there, only pain, and I switch off.

Am I right to do that? In a make-believe world should I not make an effort not to make the connections?

My mother Daisy had certainly 'made the connections', but hers was not a world of make-believe. She had been born into a time of hope, a time of great brightness for the human spirit. It was a fairly uncomfortable time perhaps for the human body, one in which poverty and oppression, hunger and disease, were for real and all around. But she saw them for what they were, saw the pity of them and with their own hands she and her comrades worked to make those evils a thing of the past. She had made the connections and knew that what needed to be done had to be done, if necessary by her.

Today many of the ideals that Daisy strove for have been realised, and we live in a time of great material ease. This 'Western' world which we have made for ourselves is a comfortable, well-regulated place in which almost everything is found. That, on the face of it, seems fine, but one of the effects of having made it seems to be that we now live in a world which no longer needs people, a world in which many people have no meaningful part to play in their own lives and have gradually become passengers, inert consumers, farmed, nurtured and given identity by supermarkets, spin-doctors and the bright, brittle media.

What I needed to remember was that in a world where very little is experienced first-hand, nothing needs to be taken for real. So we can choose as truth whatever we fancy, because it makes no difference, because we are just the audience. We take our pleasures and passions vicariously and, to keep us amused, our entertainers obviously have to keep pushing the boundaries of obscenity ever wider in order to bring us new and more extreme types of titillation. That is their job. That's how they make their money. It may not matter, much.

But there is perhaps a more dangerous side to this disconnection of the imagination. Nations and governments naturally have, as their priority, a duty to keep their people confident in them, and to keep their voters' complacency untroubled. So, led by the very real short-term imperatives of commercial advantage and electoral expediency, they have gone on doing apparently advantageous, but actually harmful, things – to the land and the sea, to the forests, the ice caps and the air, and to the animals and the people living on the rest of the planet – long, long after it has become obvious to anybody who cared to make the connection that they should have stopped.

Of course the most obvious of these dates back to Agincourt, where the new *bodkin-tipped* armour-piercing arrow gave the English archers a disproportionate killing-power and so brought King Henry his victory. Today the offspring of that development, modern armaments, give any Tom, Dick or madman the power to do disproportionate damage on a terrible scale, and give any tin-pot tyrant the potential ability to hold the world to ransom.

So, overall, what I have come to see is that most of the things which happen in the world today are not so much the results of policies which successive governments have adopted and carried through, as a slow invisible tide of come-uppances – the inadvertent effects of long-term mistakes, neglects and injustices, unnoticed by us perhaps but nevertheless done in our name – coming home to roost.

In Daisy's time the future was out in front. They could see it coming and they would build it themselves. Today, I suspect, the real future is what is slowly coming up behind us, but we can't see it clearly because somebody has stuck smiley faces over the wing-mirrors.

By the end of 1996 I had some come-uppances of my own to cope with. My energy and my powers of concentration had become, to put it kindly, somewhat limited.

So it was time for us to tidy up our lives. Red Lion Cottage was too remote for Naomi and it was large and expensive to run. I decided to sell it and move into the basement of the house in Broadstairs.

I have replaced the staircase that had been removed when the house was converted into flats, so Naomi's neat and comely flat is upstairs on the ground floor while my untidy badger's residence is below, though I have quarried out a tiny garden from some waste-ground at the back. Nothing much wants to grow in it except ivy and snails, but in the afternoon the sun touches the patch of grass. Perhaps one day I shall grow some Hendon horn-poppies there.

But in the morning the sun comes singing into Naomi's front room. There we sit in the bow window and have breakfast, watching the seagulls savaging the refuse bags and seeing strange craft sailing across the German Ocean (as an 1895 brochure described it).

Wendy and Richard, who keep the corner delicatessen, bake a French-bread roll and can put bacon and egg-mayonnaise in it.

With one of these, my lunch, in a paper bag, I walk down to the cliff-top promenade and sit on one of the park-benches (placed there in memory of past loved ones), watch the boats bobbing in the harbour, feel the sun and the gentle breeze, and sink my teeth into the crisp blissful baguette. There, in the clear air, it begins to seem possible that the world will be able to get by without me. My legs, so long the arbiters of my conscience, agree without reserve – it has managed to do so for quite a long time.

Like a diminutive Boadicea, Naomi buzzes about the town and along the windy cliff-tops in her three-wheeled electric chariot. Alas, her ME diet cannot include baguettes, or several other staple items of ordinary fare. So I do most of the cooking, not wisely nor too well. In fact I tend to use the gas cooker rather impetuously and, as a result, sometimes burn the handles of saucepans.

I thought of something to deal with that – a two-inch length of aluminium tube off an old suction-cleaner pipe. I split it down the side and slid it on to the saucepan handle. It works a treat.

I said: 'That's good. You could easily manufacture those and sell them – make a fortune!' And I thought: 'No, not again. No.'

FURRY TAILPIECE

Still wearing his academic cap and gown, Bagpuss looks down from the high basket where he lives. His eyes are glass and have no truck with age or mortality. Perhaps he has always known that he was to be immortal, known that last year, 1999, after a decade of being spurned by the programmers as old-fashioned, bumbly and slow, his films would suddenly win the poll for THE MOST POPULAR BBC CHILDREN'S FILM EVER!

Peter and I got wind of this possibility when we took him with us to the Animation Festival at Cardiff in 1998. There he was fêted, hugged and cuddled, thrown from embrace to embrace by joyful young executives who shed nostalgic tears for that long-lost haven of warmth, safety and sense – Emily's shop.

Suddenly new showings of the films are being booked, new videos produced. His image has been stabilized and digitized for the new century and he, with his friends at the shop, as well as *Ivor the Engine* and *The Clangers*, are poised at the brink of a new life.

I may invent no more saucepan-handle-savers, but I'm sure it will be my pleasure (and I hope profit) to spend my declining years attending upon His Feline Excellency.